VIOLENCE AGAINST LESBIANS AND GAY MEN

Between Men ~ Between Women
Lesbian and Gay Studies

Richard D. Mohr, General Editor

BETWEEN MEN ~ BETWEEN WOMEN
LESBIAN AND GAY STUDIES

Richard D. Mohr, General Editor

Lillian Faderman, *Odd Girls and Twilight Lovers: A History of Lesbian Life in Twentieth-Century America*

Richard D. Mohr, *Gays/Justice: A Study of Ethics, Society, and Law*

Kath Weston, *Families We Choose: Lesbians, Gays, and Kinship*

Violence Against
Lesbians and Gay Men

GARY DAVID COMSTOCK

Columbia University Press   New York

COLUMBIA UNIVERSITY PRESS
New York   Oxford

Copyright © 1991 Columbia University Press

Library of Congress Cataloging-in-Publication Data
Comstock, Gary David
Violence against lesbians and gay men / Gary David Comstock.
p.   cm.—(Between men—between women)
Includes bibliographical references and index.
ISBN 0-231-07330-5
ISBN 0-231-07331-3 (pbk.)
1. Gays—United States—Crimes against.   I. Title.   II. Series.
HV6250.4.H66C66   1991
362.88—dc20   90-47126
                                                         CIP

∞

Casebound editions of Columbia Universrity Press books are Smyth-
sewn and printed on permanent and durable acid-free paper

Printed in the United States of America
c 10 9 8 7 6 5 4 3 2 1
p 10 9 8 7 6 5 4 3 2 1

Book design by Ken Venezio

*Dedicated to my lover, Ted; my mother, Evelyn R. Libby;
also to those victims of anti-gay/lesbian violence who did not survive.*

*May our memory of them encourage us to work against this social
problem. May our insistence to live and flourish continue to build a
community whose contributions to this society are important and necessary.*

Contents

Acknowledgments

Theodore J. Stein, Professor of Social Welfare at the State University of New York at Albany, advised my collection and analysis of data and was the mainstay throughout my work.

I was very fortunate to be able to work on this project with Roger L. Shinn as chairperson of my doctoral dissertation committee at Union Theological Seminary. I am also grateful to my other committee members, ethicists Beverly Wildung Harrison and Larry L. Rasmussen and biblical scholar Robin Scroggs.

The following people were generous in providing access to archives and records: Harold Averill, Bet Birdfish, Deborah Edel, Joseph P. Gregg, James Lenahan, Morty Manford, and Carmen Vasquez. As the liaison from the Manhattan District Attorney's Office to the lesbian/gay community, Jacqueline Schafer was helpful in providing information about cases involving gay and lesbian crime victims; and I wish to thank that office for allowing me to cite the unpublished 80 Case Memo.

I gratefully acknowledge Toni Morrison's permission to quote passages from *Sula* (New York: Knopf, 1973), copyright © 1973 by Toni Morrison.

A portion of chapter 2 appeared in the March 1989 issue of *Journal of Interpersonal Violence* as "Victims of Anti-Gay/Lesbian Violence" (copyright © 1989 by Sage Publications, Inc.).

Many lesbian/gay organizations and publications throughout the United States and Canada provided data and distributed questionnaires for my survey. Without the help of Debra Ratterman, Lidell Jackson, and Aurelio Montemayor, the sample for my survey would not have been gender-balanced and racially representative.

I am especially grateful for the cooperation of lesbians and gay men who responded to my inquiries and realized that while anti-gay/lesbian violence is not an easy subject, it may be spoken about and brought into public discussion.

VIOLENCE AGAINST LESBIANS AND GAY MEN

Introduction

Violence against lesbians and gay men is becoming recognized as a social problem and is taking its place among such societal concerns as violence against women, children, and ethnic and racial groups. In October 1986 the U.S. House of Representatives Subcommittee on Criminal Justice, Committee on the Judiciary, convened a public hearing on anti-gay/lesbian violence. In his opening remarks, committee chairperson Representative John Conyers, Jr. states:

Antigay[/lesbian] violence has become a national issue since 1979, with the murders of San Francisco Mayor George Moscone and City Supervisor Harvey Milk.

Their deaths symbolized the growing political strength of the gay[/lesbian] community, as well as the hostility directed toward them, which became more prominent as a result of political empowerment.

Since that time, we have witnessed a rising tide of anti-gay[/lesbian] violence.[1]

Noting, also, that the response of local law enforcement agencies "has been terrible" and that "Federal law enforcement efforts have been virtually nonexistent," Conyers says the subcommittee finds that an inquiry into the violence directed toward "this group of citizens" and a determination of "what needs to be done about it" are "very important." In 1989 the House of Representatives passed legislation requiring that the federal government collect statistics on crimes motivated by bias based on sexual orientation, race, ethnicity, or religion. It was subsequently passed by the Senate and signed into law by the President in 1990.[2] My work focuses on the current situation of lesbian/gay people and is concerned with making a contribution toward overcoming violence directed against us. The study aims to describe and to understand anti-gay/lesbian violence and, by examining the conditions associated with such violence, to enhance our ability to predict its occurrence.

For the purposes of this study, anti-gay/lesbian violence is defined as physical violence perpetrated by non–lesbian/gay people against lesbians and gay men because of their sexual orientation. The study is limited to North America and emphasizes the United States, not only because this is my "neighborhood," but because the problem has been most extensively identified and studied here. A study of anti-gay/lesbian violence in other countries would likely offer opportunities for deeper insight and analysis, but because data have not been gathered systematically elsewhere, an empirical basis for cross-cultural or cross-national comparisons does not exist. Even in North America, documentation is in the initial stages; the task of gathering data, therefore, occupies a necessary and large part of my study. The descriptive dimension of the study, especially as regards the extent and organization of data, is, to my knowledge, unprecedented.

Because the data show that perpetrators are predominantly average young men whose behavior is socially sanctioned rather than intrapsychically determined, they lend themselves to a search for sociological rather than psychological explanations. Moreover, I avoid either a specifically "functional" or "structural" sociological theory in favor of a theoretical framework based on "social roles" because the data describe perpetrators' behavior as social role playing that is distinctively age and gender specific. A discussion of the function or overall structure of the roles is subsequent to identifying and describing the characteristics and behavior of perpetrators. Instead of approaching the data with a particular theory that assumes function and structure, I attempt to work toward a theory that embraces and respects the distinctive features of the data.

Chapters 1, 2, and 3 describe the experience of lesbians and gay men in post–World War II North America. Chapter 1 is a historical overview of the period from World War II to the assassination of San Francisco's gay supervisor Harvey Milk in 1978. Comparisons with earlier periods in Western history are made. Chapters 2 and 3 report and organize the findings from a survey of lesbians and gay men that I conducted in 1986. Chapter 2 contains the data on victims of anti-gay/lesbian violence, whereas 3 contains data on perpetrators as reported by victims. The findings in chapter 2 are compared with those of other surveys, most of which have been conducted in the 1980s. Added to the findings in chapter 3 is information from newsmedia reports about perpetrators and interviews with perpetrators.

The data from chapters 1, 2, and 3 are interpreted and analyzed in chapter 4 in terms of the Western patriarchal tradition. Sheila Collins' essay "The Familial Economy of God" is the primary resource for the history of patriarchy and provides the theoretical framework for analysis.[3] Collins understands the current social order in terms of roles that have been transferred from the historical patriarchal familial unit to the industrial workplace. These roles—Father, Wife, Brother, Daughter, Alien—are hierarchical and comprise the model she uses to explain socioeconomic dynamics in the United States. On the basis of their statistically typical behaviors, characteristics, and social locations, I apply victims and perpetrators of anti-gay/lesbian violence to roles within her model in an effort to understand the motive for and cause of such violence.

Although Collins does maintain that Western Christianity has been the "ideological glue" that has held together and served patriarchy and that the structures of and arrangement of power within dominant Christian denominations are patriarchal, her analysis focuses on the confluence of patriarchy and industrial capitalism more than on patriarchy and religion. Accordingly, in using her model to interpret the data, chapter 4 refers infrequently to Christian institutions, and its analysis is socioeconomic.

Chapter 5, however, does turn directly to the Judeo-Christian tradition, specifically in terms of biblical passages that condemn and/or punish homosexual practice. Their legacy and implementation into public policy and practice are outlined. A historical-critical exegesis of these passages follows, as does a discussion of the patriarchal basis of the document, the Book of Leviticus, in which the passages appear. Finally, the appropriateness of these passages as ethically normative for social and individual responses to anti-gay/lesbian violence is challenged in terms of an overarching theme or norm of Judeo-Christian scripture; that is, the transforming of pain and suffering in the Exodus event. This theme is found to be consistent with the documented response of lesbians and gay men to the violence that is and has been perpetrated against them: since the 1950s, organized responses by lesbians and gay men to the violence directed against them have been responsible for expanding, solidifying, and making more visible an emerging lesbian/gay community in North America.

The weight of this study falls more on documenting experience than on proposing ethical norms. An important task of the social ethicist, and one that is necessary for this study, is to identify, uncover, and take seriously those issues and people that are hidden, neglected, and/or marginal. Gathering, organizing, and analyzing data on anti-gay/lesbian violence are necessary. Research on the subject is limited and social recognition of such violence as a problem in need of solving is slow to come. A descriptive study, therefore, is essential, especially insofar as it is necessary to "prove" that the problem does exist. The breadth and depth of this task may seem to eclipse the other important tasks of proposing solutions and ethical norms. Without the data that the study reports, the latter discussion cannot occur. Thus, I seek to provide a starting point for subsequent studies by creating a necessary data base.

But this study is not without its own proposal of an ethical norm; that is, of that which needs to be done in response to anti-gay/lesbian violence. That my proposed norm is found in the experience of lesbian/gay people, rather than applied to that experience, is significant. The value of the study's descriptive emphasis is not only in producing "evidence" but as the resource in which the ethical norm is recognized and takes form. Such moral reasoning (i.e., looking for the "answers" to social problems in the experience of the oppressed and formulating moral responses in reflection on such experience) is consistent with recent developments in liberation theologies that recognize the epistemological advantage of the oppressed.[4] By taking seriously the experience of lesbian/gay people, I not only identify and describe a social problem in need of attention, but also discover and propose that which should be the social response to the problem.

That the response of lesbians and gay men to violence directed against them embodies the primary, and often neglected, biblical–ethical norm of the Judeo-Christian tradition is noteworthy. The experience of the lesbian/gay community challenges mainstream religions within this country to be accountable to this norm. Lesbians and gay men have typically understood that the support, care, and empowerment they need must be created in their own communities rather than in religious denominations. The communities they have created, in addition to providing what is denied them in various religious denominations, offer Jews and Christians an opportunity to reflect on their own lapses and to alter their practice. This discussion does not aim to ignore non-Jews and non-Christians as much as it seeks to come to terms with the dominant religious practice and influence in North America.

CHAPTER ONE

A Historical Overview

Until the 1970s and 1980s, information about violence against lesbians and gay men in the post–World War II period remained scattered throughout personal diaries, newsletters, and articles in mainstream newspapers reporting sensational murders.[1] The topic had been mentioned occasionally but was neither discussed in depth nor analyzed systematically in scholarly journals and treatises.[2] Only as gay and lesbian scholars, film makers, journalists, and activists began to collect and organize the stories of those who had lived during the earlier time did a past that was marked and shaped by beatings, robbery, and murder become recognized and preserved.[3]

This chapter provides a historical overview of the social situation for lesbians and gay men in North America from World War II to the late 1970s. Lesbian/gay experience during and after the war is compared with prewar experience and discussed in the context of economic changes in the twentieth century. The emergence in the 1950s and 1960s of the lesbian/gay bar as the focus of community organizing efforts is explained in terms of its being both the most frequent target of police raids and civilian violence as well as the primary social institution for lesbian/gay people. The technically extralegal, but socially sanctioned, nature of such violence is noted and compared with earlier examples of anti-gay/lesbian violence in Western history. Information about the Stonewall Rebellion of 1969 and the subsequent shift in lesbian/gay consciousness then precedes a discussion of new forms of violence and changes in public policy. The chapter concludes with observation about the assassination of San Francisco's gay supervisor Harvey Milk and the legacy of responding to violence in the lesbian/gay community.

THE GAY/LESBIAN EXPERIENCE DURING WORLD WAR II

In *Sexual Politics, Sexual Communities: The Making of a Homosexual Community, 1940–1970,* John D'Emilio credits World War II with having "created something of a nationwide coming out experience" for many gay and lesbian Americans, "not so much by permanently encouraging more homosexual behavior . . . but by shifting its location and changing its context." The U.S. military's preference for men and women who were young and single or with few dependents, a population group likely to include a disproportionate number of lesbians and gay men, inadvertently facilitated the forming of same-gender erotic relationships. Released from familiar homes and neighborhoods and placed in gender-segregated environments, self-identified lesbians and gay men were better able to meet each other. Those who had felt, but not acted upon, attractions to people of their own gender were suddenly presented with opportunities to do so.[4]

The men's military used psychiatric screening to keep gay men out, but the screening process, consisting of a few questions based on the most superficial signs of homosexuality, was ineffective. Gay men could easily slip by the psychiatrists. The women's military actually welcomed and accommodated lesbians. Wishing to avoid unwanted pregnancies and a reputation for being a sexual outlet for servicemen, the women's military deliberately created a women-only environment within which lesbians were treated with respect. Training manuals instructed women officers to praise "comradeship" among women, not to engage in "witchhunting or speculating," to ignore "hearsay," to approach problems with an "attitude of fairness and tolerance," to discourage stereotypes, and to minimize the difference between heterosexuals and lesbians. Lesbians in civilian life were also exposed to protected all-female environments. Women entered the out-of-home labor force in unprecedented numbers. They often moved away from hometown areas to cities where they worked among women and lived in make-shift all-women residences. D'Emilio notes that the "war opened possibilities for lesbians to meet at the same time that it protected all-female environments from the taint of deviance."[5]

THE GAY/LESBIAN EXPERIENCE AFTER WORLD WAR II

Post–World War II demobilization would strip away such opportunities and protection as efficiently as the war effort had arranged for and granted them. Traditional gender roles in employment, for example, were reestablished. Even though opinion polls indicated that most women in heavy industry wanted to maintain their jobs, employers routinely dismissed them. A propaganda drive by business and government was directed at women to tell them to give up their jobs for the returning soldiers. Stable heterosexual marriage and motherhood were reaffirmed as normative. Aggressive postwar searches for and purges of lesbians and gay men by the military contrasted sharply with the superficial measures used to detect gay men and the accommodation of lesbians during the war. Such "tolerance" had quite obviously been intended to satisfy the needs of the war effort and not those of lesbians and gay men.[6]

But demobilization and peacetime could neither undo nor halt completely the experiences that lesbians and gay men had had during the war years. Choosing to remain in the cities through which they had passed going to and from wartime assignments or to which they had moved for wartime employment, many did not return to their hometowns. Those cities that had served as ports and centers of war industry—Los Angeles, New York, San Francisco, New Orleans, and Boston—would in time emerge as the major centers of the lesbian/gay community. Later, lesbians and gay men from throughout the country would be attracted and gravitate to the visibility and presence being established in these cities. As the purges from the military were stepped up after the war, many felt that with a less-than-honorable discharge they had no choice but to live away from their hometowns with other lesbians and gay men. Lesbians and gay men began to create their own institutions and friendship networks within these cities.[7]

The Kinsey Report and Government Policy. The publication of the Kinsey reports on male and female sexual behavior in 1948 and 1953 served to strengthen these efforts and to challenge the assumptions and intentions of a heterosexually identified population. The reports were based on empirical findings from interviews with a cross section of white Americans and concluded that persons with homosexual histories are ubiquitous. Kinsey's findings led him to dismiss views that homosexaul behavior is abnormal, unnatural, or neurotic.[8] That lesbians and gay men could be everywhere and anywhere threatened many Americans who were settling into the renewed American dream of heterosexual marriage and child-rearing. Public leaders such as Henry Van Dusen, president of Union Theological Seminary in New York City, viewed the reports as evidence of a "degradation in American morality approximating the worst decadence of the Roman era."[9] Verbal assaults directed at the lesbian/gay population were reported in the press and quickly escalated into official public policy and law enforcement practice.[10]

Those choosing to launch verbal attacks could readily find their targets because of the concentration and visibility of lesbians and gay men in urban areas facilitated by the war and demobilization. The political agenda of the times—a drive to establish the concept and practice of the nuclear family and a concurrent effort to drive out communism—provided the rationale for a massive assault. D'Emilio notes that the "Cold War and its attendant domestic anticommunism provided the setting in which such a sustained attack was made. . . . Homosexuality became an epidemic infecting the nation, actively spread by communists to sap the strength of the next generation."[11] President Eisenhower issued Executive Order 10450 listing "sexual perversion" as grounds for exclusion from federal jobs; subsequently, screening procedures in hiring and evaluating workers were expanded. The House Un-American Activities Committee, chaired by Senator Joseph McCarthy, conducted hearings in which the term *homosexual* was synonymous with *traitor*. The military intensified its search for lesbians and gay men within its ranks. The government's labeling of homosexuals as moral perverts and national security risks provided local police forces with blanket permission to invade homes and public and private meeting places to harass and arrest lesbians and gay men on a range of inappropriately levied charges. To deal with the problem of detecting a population whose members could easily and effectively hide their identities, the FBI established liaisons with police departments across the country in 1950. Arrest records were routinely supplied by local vice-squad officers, even though convictions usually did not follow arrests.[12]

Although most states had abolished the death penalty for sodomy in the early nineteenth century, all but two still classified it as a felony in 1950, with only murder, kidnapping, and rape commanding heavier sentences. Even though full punishment was rarely prescribed, the presence of sodomy laws served to stigmatize homosexuality as criminal. Harassment of lesbians and gay men was facilitated by statutes proscribing disorderly conduct, vagrancy, public lewdness, assault, and solicitation. Although not designed to target and prevent homosexuality, the laws were used by local police to harass and increase the rate of arrest of lesbians and gay men. Furthermore, after World War II state legislatures turned increasingly to psychiatrists to solve the problems of sex crimes and passed sexual psychopath laws that officially recognized homosexuality as a socially threatening disease. Doctors were legally sanctioned to experiment with a wide range of procedures that included psychotherapy, hypnosis, castration, hysterectomy, lobotomy, electroshock, aversion therapy, and untested drugs on lesbians and gay men who were sentenced or committed to their practices and wards.[13]

Comparison with Post–War War I Period. The increased visibility of the lesbian/gay population and the unprecedented verbal attacks by officials and the media after World War II can be more clearly understood if the experiences of lesbians and gay men before and after the war are compared. Unlike the post–World War II era, the 1920s and 1930s were not a time when homosexuality was frequently or publicly discussed,[14] nor were lesbians and gay men a visible population. The topic maintained a centuries-old "not-to-be-mentioned" status except in the professional circles of medicine and psychology, and most lesbians and gay men themselves "did not even have the words to describe the longings they felt, much less any awareness that others like them existed."[15] Thus, a Senate investigating committee looking into allegations of homosexuality at the naval station in Newport, Rhode Island, in 1920, expressed more outrage over the corrupt methods used to detect "social perverts" than over the "sexual perverts" themselves.[16]

Although World War I may have afforded some opportunities for lesbians and gay men to meet and interact with each other, the shift of people to gender-segregated environments in World War II involved a far larger number and lasted longer. Lesbians and gay men did gravitate to cities after World War I, but in much smaller numbers and without the normalizing influence and confidence-building encouragement of a document like the Kinsey report. However, a new position on homosexuality did develop in the medical community in the 1920s. The "medical model," as it was known, viewed homosexuality as a congenital condition or defect, not as a vice. Although it did not approximate or anticipate Kinsey's conclusions about the normality and prevalence of homosexuality, the perception that "homosexuality [was] not a deed that one avoided but a condition that described who one was" diminished the tremendous burdens of guilt traditionally borne by most lesbians and gay men and occasioned feelings of greater acceptance.[17] A few in New York, Chicago, and San Francisco even felt encouraged to seek out each other and to form private groups in which to discuss this new perspective on their sexuality. Group life on a small scale was forming.[18] The beginnings of underground networking in the 1920s and 1930s foreshadowed the subculture and community building that was to come after World War II.

In the Context of Twentieth-Century Economic Changes. Neither the post–World War I situation nor World War II together or separtely can explain the unprecedented opportunities for lesbians and gay men to meet in the 1940s and 1950s. This development must be seen in the context of social and economic changes occurring in the twentieth cen-

tury. The emergence of large industrial cities, which provided the anonymity necessary to fashion a social life among lesbian and gay men,
had its beginning with the shift to industrial capitalism during the second
half of the nineteenth century. When the free-labor system replaced the
preindustrial household economy, families lost the functions they once
had as economic units. Without the need for families and relationships
to be organized primarily for the purpose of producing goods, "affection, intimate relationships, and sexuality moved increasingly into the
realm of individual choice." Large cities, which replaced rural centers of
business and production, "created a social context in which an autonomous personal life could develop." Although changing conditions had
their most apparent impact on relationships within heterosexual marriage and families, they also favored the formation of personal identities
and a way of life by lesbians and gay men. Even though approval of
homosexuality would not be immediately forthcoming, lesbians and gay
men no longer felt as compelled to stay within family units out of
economic necessity. Taking advantage of the general shift of the population to urban areas, they could move to and live within a setting that
afforded them an unprecedented degree of anonymity and freedom.
World War II, in occasioning a noticeable and abrupt increase in the
process of urbanization and industrialization, also facilitated a surfacing
of lesbian and gay neighborhoods and social networks that had begun in
the 1920s and 1930s but reached unprecedented proportions in the
1940s and 1950s.[19]

COMMUNITY ORGANIZING IN RESPONSE TO HOSTILITY

As mentioned earlier, the greater visibility of lesbians and gay men after
World War II not only allowed them to self-identify and interact publicly
to some degree, but also provided easy targets for arrest and verbal
attacks from disapproving quarters. Similarly, the publication of the
Kinsey reports occasioned a more supportive acknowledgement and
discussion of homosexuality as well as virulent opposition to those who
practiced it. But if the Kinsey reports and the increased visibility of
lesbian/gay people had the double-edged effect of attracting lesbians and
gay men to live more confidently and openly as well as setting in motion
attacks that left careers apparently ruined, the McCarthy investigations,
military purges, and campaigns by local police also had contradictory
influences.

By taking an aggressive stance, antihomosexual forces identified the
subject as one of serious concern. As attacks became more frequent in
the media, discussion moved from academic circles to the popular do-

main. A subject that had traditionally been too terrible to mention was more commonly read about, discussed, and pondered. "In repeatedly condemning the phenomenon, antigay[/lesbian] polemicists broke the silence that surrounded the topic of homosexuality" and testified to the changes that had occurred in the lives of lesbians and gay men. Although the negative publicity did intimidate many lesbians and gay men, by focusing their attention on feelings that they had hidden or expressed furtively, it also motivated them to explain and understand those feelings better and to find others with whom to experience them. "The attacks on gay men and women hastened the articulation of a homosexual identity and spread the knowledge that they existed in large numbers." The message garnered from reports of such hostility by a significant number of those who felt erotically attracted to people of their own gender was not that these feelings were bad as much as it was that there were others like themselves who lived in places to which they themselves could move. "Ironically, the effort to root out the homosexuals in American society made it easier for them to find one another." [20]

Such irony is captured in the following pattern of response and counterresponse that emerged after World War II and that has remained dominant in shaping lesbian/gay communities to the present day: (1) increased visibility of lesbians and gay men, (2) hostility, (3) insistence on greater visibility by lesbians and gay men, (4) hostility. Three factors —the role modeling or example provided by self-identified lesbians and gay men, opportunities to experience same-gender relationships in urban areas that afforded anonymity, and publication of supportive evidence of the normality of homosexuality [21]—facilitated greater visibility, and hostile reactions tended to bring these factors into clearer focus. The historical interplay of this pattern and these factors may be traced as follows: the visibility of lesbians and gay men, made possible by World War II and encouraged by the Kinsey reports, subsequently prompted investigations and purges that created an "entire class of social outcasts who were public homosexuals." [22] These people, with no place to go and having experienced the pleasure of friendships, social support, and same-gender erotic practices, migrated to and became concentrated in certain urban neighborhoods within which they eventually developed their own social institutions. These institutions became in time sufficiently visible to be the targets of hostility, some of which was reported in the media. Isolated lesbians and gay men throughout the country, upon reading and hearing accounts of this hostility, learned that others like themselves lived in places to which they themselves could move. As the residents of gay and lesbian neighborhoods increased and grew accustomed to the community life they created and experienced, they became less willing to relinquish it. Many—because they had already been publicly labeled as homosexuals by investigations and firings and/or because they did not want to give up their networks of sexual contacts, friendships, and relationships—simply saw no alternative but to stay and fight or minimize the dangers. Further hostility against them tended to clarify their sexual and affectional identities and their needs for sexual and social satisfaction.[23]

The Lesbian and Gay Bar. The emergence and spread of the lesbian and gay bar illustrate this pattern of visibility, attack, and insistence on greater visibility. The gay bar grew as a community institution that met the needs of neighborhood residents, withstood attacks against it, and became in time the center from which efforts to resist such attacks were launched: "Of all the changes set in motion by the war, the spread of the gay bar contained the greatest potential for reshaping the consciousness of homosexuals and lesbians. Alone among the expressions of gay life, the bar fostered an identity that was both public and collective."[24]

The gay bar served conflicting purposes for opposing parties. It satisfied the personal and social needs of lesbians and gay men, while it, among all the other community institutions, was singled out by local police forces as the most frequent target.[25] However, "when trouble struck, as it often did in the form of a police raid, the crowd suffered as a group, enduring the penalties together."[26] Thirty-six women, for example, went to jail one night in September 1956 when police descended on a lesbian bar in San Francisco. Collective endurance in time would be accompanied sporadically and gradually by organized resistance. In 1952 for the first time a few gay men began soliciting and collecting stories from those who had been the victims of police harassment. Law enforcement practices became the primary focus of organizing efforts within the gay and lesbian communities, eventually provoking in the late 1960s in Los Angeles the largest gay demonstration of the decade and in New York the Stonewall rebellion, which sparked the gay/lesbian liberation movement.[27]

Police Raids. Not a small amount of the police harassment consisted of verbal and physical abuse. Raiding a bar and randomly arresting those in attendance, without specifying charges or providing information about legal rights, were often the framework within which police officers would insult, threaten physically, and beat bar patrons.[28] The Washington, D.C., chapter of the Mattachine Society collected the following information on a bar raid:

Taken to a local station, they were fingerprinted, charged with disorderly conduct, interrogated for details about their personal life, and subjected to verbal abuse. One man who asked what the charges were was told by an officer that he had been arrested for "winking at my friend." He was then vilified as a "queer" and a "cock sucker" and beaten badly enough to require hospitalization.[29]

Although a record of this incident exists and was used to lodge a complaint against the police department, the overwhelming majority of abuses, along with the customary notification of employers and publication of names in the local newspaper, was simply endured. Such treatment was so common and expected by lesbians and gay men and the law enforcement agencies and court systems were so hostile that an untold number of false arrests went unchallenged, just as injuries and verbal assaults were survived and nursed within the privacy of a close circle of friends.[30]

Unprovoked violence by police officers was and is prevented by law.[31] But attempts to register complaints in court were usually dismissed by judges who took the officer's word against the arrested person.[32] Most lesbians and gay men, realizing the futility of registering complaints and not wanting to bring more public attention to themselves, quietly paid fines.

Violence by Civilians. Lesbians and gay men were also vulnerable to violent attacks by groups of teenage males and the "easy prey of petty criminals."[33] From diaries of and interviews with lesbians and gay men who lived through those times, the following summary of violent experience emerges:

Seedy characters haunted male homosexual cruising areas in order to beat and rob their victims. "Pickups" suddenly metamorphosed into thieves, seizing the valuables in one's home, secure in the knowledge that the incident would not be reported. Gangs of men stalked lesbian bars to attack women who rebuffed their sexual overtures. The police, if they intervened, were more likely to arrest the women than their male assailants.[34]

These assaults, like those perpetrated by police officers, were not legal. But those officials to whom complaints were made usually sided with the perpetrators. Incidents of violent assault were seldom reported by the victims. When they were, assailants were not often apprehended, punished, or criticized, whereas the victims were treated with indifference or hostility.[35] Without legal protection lesbians and gay men experienced increased amounts of violence as they gradually became more visible socially.

Those lesbians and gay men who still lived with their parents were often physically abused when their sexual orientation became known. Ruth Simpson, in *From the Closets to the Courts,* recalls the experiences of younger women during these times who were locked up at home "until they were able to go out with boys." From a group of similar stories, she cites one in which

a father stood at the top of the stairs in his home and threw large, heavy construction nuts and bolts from his workshop at his daughter, screaming "Freak!" at her. He beat her several times, not telling her why. It was only later that the girl found out that a "well-meaning friend" had told her father that she was a lesbian.

Locking lesbians in the home was a common reaction. Parents felt that as long as the girl could not get out, she would "come to her senses and change."[36]

Physical harm to body and property perpetrated by police officers, private citizens, and parents, therefore, added to the danger encountered by lesbians and gay men through screenings, investigations, purges, firings, false arrests, unfair convictions, and verbal attacks in the media. That one could without provocation be physically attacked on the street, at home, or in one's place of social gathering was in lesbian and gay neighborhoods an experience so recurrent that one lived with the hope of avoiding it while realizing that it could easily happen to oneself or to one's friends and acquaintances.

COMPARISON WITH ANTI-GAY/LESBIAN VIOLENCE IN WESTERN HISTORY

Extralegal Versus Legally Sanctioned Violence. Physical injury and death were not a new development in the history of lesbians and gay men. Accounts of beatings, burning, torture and assorted forms of execution have been compiled and provide ample evidence that within Western civilization the threat and/or practice of anti-gay/lesbian violence has been continuous.[37] Perhaps most noteworthy because of its comprehensive scheme and temporal proximity to the present is the Nazi extermination of homosexuals in Germany from 1935 to 1945.[38] However, the violence experienced by lesbians and gay men in post–World War II America differed from that reported from earlier years in Europe and America. Whereas the former occurred and occurs extralegally, the latter carried out laws decreed by ecclesiastical councils and monarchs.[39] The execution of a white man, William Plaine, by the Massachusetts Bay Colony in 1646; the choking to death and burning to ashes of a black man, Jan Creoli, in New Netherland Colony on Manhattan Island in the same year; the assignment of death "if any woman change the naturall use into that which is against nature" in the New Haven Colony sodomy statute of 1655; and Pennsylvania's abolition and subsequent reintroduction, under English pressure, of capital punishment for sodomy evidence the transfer and enforcement of such laws to colonial America.[40] With the advent of the Enlightenment, the French and American Revolutions, and the institution of representative governance, "there seemingly began a move away from capital punishment for such crimes as sodomy."[41] Thomas Jefferson's proposed revision of Virginia law to replace the death penalty for sodomy with castration; George Washington's court-martial and dismissal, instead of execution, of a lieutenant for attempted sodomy; the abolition of the death penalty for homosexual activity by Denmark in 1866; and a record of fifty-eight hangings for sodomy in England between 1804 and 1834 followed by the abolition of the death penalty for such offenses in 1861 signal the changes that were occurring in Western countries in the nineteenth century.[42] "After the [American] Revolution, Pennsylvania led the way in abolishing the death penalty in 1786 and other states began to follow its example in the next decade."[43] Laws against homosexuality did remain and prescribed long prison sentences, but punishment was no longer by death or physical harm.[44] The extermination of lesbians and gay men in Nazi Germany stands out as the exception.

Documentation of Extralegal Violence. Although the nineteenth century was the turning point for ending a tradition of legally prescribed violence against lesbians and gay men, the apparent increase of physical harassment, beatings, and murder reported after World War II in America would seem to signal either the beginning of a new tradition of extralegal violence or the continuation of such a tradition for which there is limited supporting evidence. Accounts as plentiful and reliable as those taken from official records describing executions and physical punishment carried out by church and state are not available for acts that might have been perpetrated by the public outside of the law.

There is some documentation for a short period of time at the beginning of the nineteenth century in England in which "attempted homosexuality [was] punished by the pillory and several years' imprisonment, the act itself by the gallows"; the former, however, was "almost as good as death," because "men placed in the pillory . . . were sometimes stoned to death by London street mobs."[45] Descriptions in newspaper accounts of such incidents and their existence over a quarter of a century suggest strongly that the practice was customary.

Shortly before 12 noon the "ammunition carts" started from the neighbouring market places. These were a number of carts drawn by butcher boys, who had previously filled them with offal and dung from the slaughter houses. Street vendors were also in readiness, carrying on their heads baskets filled with rotten apples, pears, cabbages and other vegetables and corpses of dogs and cats. All these articles were sold at high prices to the onlookers, who spared no expense in order to provide themselves with missiles. A group of fishwives were there, armed with stinking flounders and decaying guts. But these were not sold, as their zealous owners wished to keep them for their own use. . . .

Long before any of them [the prisoners] reached the places where the pillories awaited them, their faces were totally disfigured by blows, missiles and mud, and looked like living dung hills. About fifty women obtained permission to form a circle around them, and these incessantly bombarded them with rotten potatoes and eggs, and dead cats, offal, mud and dung from sloppails and buckets brought by some butchers of St. James Market. . . .

They were fettered and sealed in such a manner that they could not lie down and at the most could only protect their heads to a limited extent from the missiles by bending them. Some of them were badly injured by brick bats and their faces bled horribly. The streets through which they passed reverberated with the shouts and curses hurled at them by the mob.[46]

The openness with which the public planned and participated in this display of violence and its being granted "permission to form a circle . . . and bombard" the victims indicate that the behavior, although not legally prescribed, was within the bounds of official approval and expectations.

However, other newspaper articles about similar incidents suggest that such violence was restrained and discouraged by the police:

The Peace Officers, who resolutely defended their prisoners, behaved at the same time with great propriety. Their forbearance towards the outraged crowd, the majority of whom were females, was exemplary; for the showers of mud with which the carriage were assailed, rendered the officers who attended behind, and on the coach-boxes, anything but human in appearance.

Most of [the prisoners] who were [eventually] discharged, were very roughly handled; several of them were hunted about the neighbourhood, and with great difficulty escaped with their lives, although every exertion was used by the Bowstreet Officers to prevent such dangerous proceedings, and in doing which, many of them received severe blows from the missile weapons of the populace.[47]

Although the documentation is not clear about the legality of such violent activity, it shows that it was communally expressed and there was social approval and enthusiasm for it.

Because information about such public participation, either from other times or in other countries, is not available, a general claim cannot be made for a historical tradition of extralegal anti-gay/lesbian violence.

The most that can be said without speculation is that prior to the rescinding of laws prescribing death and physical injury for homosexual activity, only accounts of violence legally executed, with the exception of the preceding example, exist. After the abolition of such measures in the nineteenth century and up to World War II, extralegal violence is infrequently mentioned.

Extralegal Violence from Late Nineteenth Century to World War II. The paucity of reported accounts of extralegal violence from the late nineteenth century to World War II may simply reflect the scarcity of literature in general on homosexuality and by lesbians and gay men. Havelock Ellis, in the 1915 edition of his *Sexual Inversion,* quotes an informant who says that in American cities not only was homosexuality prevalent and its existence widely known, but the public and police did not react to it with extreme hostility or violence. Public attitudes, although reported as generally negative, were said to range from indifference to amusement and contempt. To be obviously gay or lesbian in public was "to invite remarks from newsboys and others"; for example, "when a group of street-boys caught sight of [a gay man] they sucked their fingers in imitation of *fellatio*." Beatings by the boys and robberies by small-time crooks, because they are not mentioned, may not have occurred. Police are depicted as familiar and cooperative with the gay and lesbian social scene: "the police know of these [bars] and endure their existence for a consideration; it is not unusual for the inquiring stranger to be directed there by a policeman." The public reception afforded the gay sexual underground depicted by Ellis seems to have hovered between benign neglect and hostility expressed without physical harm. Gay men seem to have been out and about, while the police and public were negative in opinion but not demonstrably or physically threatening. The extent to which this apparently uneasy but peaceful coexistence occurred may be more accurately reflected, however, in Ellis' other comment that "among my classmates, at the medical school, few ever had the courage to wear a red tie [which was the sign that one was gay]; those who did never repeated the experiment."[48]

In other sources, police raids and arrests are discussed: for example, in a paper read in 1892 at the professional meeting of a medical society in Virginia; in a journalist's memoirs of crime reporting in 1892; in a St. Louis medical journal in 1893 and 1907; in the report of an 1899 New York State legislative investigation of the government of New York City; and in a New York City newspaper in 1927.[49] In the New York State investigation, the documented questioning of police officers does show that illegal procedures and false charges to secure arrests were used to close down gay establishments. An eyewitness report of a police raid on the Lafayette Baths in New York City suggests that unnecessary violence often accompanied the carrying out of arrests and raids:

All at once there's a whistle, someone yells 'Hallo,' and everyone has to go to the front room. The bath is locked shut. Various people were struck down, kicked, in short, the brutality of these officials was simply indescribable. A Swede standing next to me was struck on the eye with a bunch of keys, and then he got hit in the back so that two of his ribs broke. . . . Everyone . . . was put in the paddywagon . . . , taken to the station, and jailed. By noon [the next day] we appeared before the magistrate's court . . . and were charged with things we hadn't done.[50]

Other informal recollections of pre–World War II experiences verify the use of violence by the police. Mabel Hampton, sharing personal stories about the 1930s at a meeting in New York City in 1980, recalled that lesbians were "often the object of severe police brutality." Using a rule of thumb that required women to wear at least three articles of women's clothing, policeman often beat and "obscenely manhandled" those "who preferred to dress in . . . 'drag.' "[51]

An article published by the *Journal of Criminal Psychopathology* in 1941 documents the participation of private citizens as perpetrators, also. By observing patterns in crime reporting in newspapers, F. A. McHenry found that the "presence of homosexuality as a factor in a reported crime or illegal act had long been discreetly presented by our newspapers . . . and serves to perpetuate the public fallacy that the aggressor is merely a head-strong boy who has let his temper get the better of him." McHenry's "reading between the lines" includes, for example, the observation that a report typically makes no mention of a crime's occurring in an area frequented almost exclusively by homosexuals. In addition to such incidents originating in the proximity of gay bars, other details corroborating the anti-gay nature of assaults are the young ages of perpetrators (sixteen to twenty-three years old), robbery as a secondary motive or afterthought, and the severe mutilation of the victim's body (i.e., beyond the goal of efficient murder). Also, that sexual overtures were used by the perpetrator to bait the victim is implied by the defenseless (i.e., partially dressed) position of the victim. McHenry finds that accounts fitting this description appear in "the press of any large city . . . [as] often as once a fortnight."[52]

That gay men were, also, the frequent victims of professional robbers is documented in a glossary in the 1941 edition of Dr. George Henry's *Sex Variants: A Study of Homosexual Patterns*. The following entry, listed among slang words, suggests common practice:

clip To rob a person, usually in connection with an intended or actual sexual act. *To make a clip* is to rob a homosexual or other client in this way, and is said of prostitutes male or female. A prostitute who is accustomed to robbing the homosexual client, usually before any sexual act occurs, is termed a *clip artist.*

The entry ends by stating that, although "clipping" is usually "surreptitious," against gay men "it is more often bare-faced and brutal."[53]

The following account by a former, young perpetrator leaves little doubt that the same patterns of anti-gay/lesbian violence experienced after World War II were customary before the war. In his April 7, 1978, column in the *San Francisco Chronicle,* Charles McCabe recalls his youthful days of "fag hunting" in New York City during the early 1930s as a "sport" commonly pursued by a number of gangs of high school-aged boys.

In retrospect he confesses the "cruel and decidedly inhuman" nature of the practice and provides a description of its pattern. The boys worked as a gang of six or seven, targeting a single individual. Their action was not defensive, but an offensive seeking out of targets in an area isolated by its location and the time of day and frequented only by gay men, "an area where hundreds of homosexuals cruised nightly." Their attacks were not spontaneous reactions to unexpected encounters; rather, they had a plan whereby they would "break up into pairs or singles though always keeping an eye on each other during the cruising" so that when one made a contact "the rest . . . followed along." They were sustained in their efforts by their conviction, based on their "religious training . . . and the whispered prejudices of [their] time," that they "were waging . . . a kind of holy war . . . [and] doing the world a favor." It was because the gay man "was so universally despised that aggression against him was viewed as a virtue." The boys feared no punitive consequences because the "homosexual had no weapon against [them] except his own guile or ability to buy [them] off." They knew that the "homosexual was totally vulnerable," that "all the cards were in [their] hands," including the cooperation of the "friendly cop."

McCabe says they operated with a sense of freedom, permission, and support to do whatever they wished to gay men: "Depending on the situation, we could either hoot and holler derisively, or we could beat up the guy, or we could take his watch and his money. In some cases we could, and did, do all three." The age and gender of the perpetrators; their belief in the virtue of their behavior; their confidence in the backing of traditional religious teachings; their pursuit and outnumbering of victims; the perceived vulnerability of their targets; the planning and manner of attacks; and the cooperation of participation by the police are the same features that would also dominate in the patterns of anti-gay/lesbian violence after the war.[54]

McCabe also inadvertently identifies the variable that signals the changes that would occur in anti-gay/lesbian violence before and after the war. The "whispered prejudices" of the time of his youth became in the 1940s and 1950s louder and more concretely expressed. Hostility toward lesbians and gay men would not be simply based on a general and quietly expressed disapproval of an underground and seldomly seen activity; rather, it would surface in response to the actual presence and concentration of lesbians and gay men in urban areas and to Kinsey's findings that homosexual activity was indeed practiced by a large number of Americans representing a cross section of the entire population.

The war produced different outcomes for those who were inclined or deciding to live as either homosexual or heterosexual people. Many of the former became more personally and publicly identified as homosexual, whereas the latter in response to a thriving postwar economy and a propaganda drive to marry and bear children became more staunchly heterosexually identified. The Kinsey reports were a potential threat to official efforts to make heterosexuality compulsory and lent support to the effort of lesbians and gays to interact with each other and form social networks. The McCarthy era, however, took advantage of the greater visibility of lesbians and gay men, Kinsey's finding that people with homosexual interests and histories were everywhere, and the heavy investment made by the overwhelming majority of Americans to settle down to the business of the nuclear family. Fabricating a connection between homosexuality and communism was a sure way to coerce these Americans to be fiercely anti-communist and more strongly devoted to the concept and practices of the nuclear family. Lesbians and gay men moved from being the seldom seen object of "whispered prejudices" in the first half of the twentieth century to being perceived as serious risks and dangers to the national security of the United States.

Homosexuals in post–World War II America were no longer simply gay men cruising for sex in isolated parks after dark. Lesbians and gay men became increasingly more noticeable and more active and organized socially. After World War II perpetrators of anti-gay/lesbian violence were able to add to their sense of virtue the heroism of protecting a population frightened by the publicity of a homosexual menace. Perpetrators also found available a greater number of targets in less isolated areas.

THE STONEWALL REBELLION AND CHANGE IN
LESBIAN/GAY CONSCIOUSNESS

The greater visibility of lesbians and gay men would in turn undergo a dramatic increase and transformation as a result of the Stonewall rebellion in New York City in 1969.[55]

On June 27, 1969 a seemingly insignificant disorder in a Greenwich Village bar symbolically ushered in [the] next stage of the [homosexual rights] movement. After the gay patrons of the Stonewall Inn were ejected from their bar by the local police, they erupted with unexpected outrage and rioted for at least four nights. The gay rioters utilized hit-and-run tactics reminiscent of guerilla warfare; the police responded with its special riot unit. This militancy proved contagious among growing numbers of young and dissatisfied members of the gay community who demanded personal respect and a thorough reorganization of society.[56]

Stonewall was both a continuation and rupture of the experiences of the 1940s, 1950s, and early 1960s.

Although a few individuals and groups had pressed for lesbians and gay men "to transform the shame of being gay into a pride in belonging to a minority with its own contribution to the human community," the earlier movement was dominated by accommodation to the prevailing medical views of homosexuality as a sickness and by a gradualist approach to making change by gaining the sympathy of influential non-lesbian/gay professionals to speak for them.[57] When activists like Barbara Gittings of New York City and Frank Kameny in Washington, D.C., argued that lesbians and gay men, not the professionals, were the experts about themselves, they met with strong disapproval from other movement leaders and aroused serious controversies in movement meetings:[58] "We owe apologies to no one—society and its official representatives owe us apologies for what they have done and are doing to us."[59] Their disclaimer, however, although representing a minority viewpoint among the earlier movement, would be the principle upon which the Stonewall rebellion launched the mass movement of the 1970s.[60]

Far from conforming their behavior to the expectations of professionals and to norms of heterosexual respectability, at Stonewall an assortment of fighting lesbians, street people, Puerto Rican drag queens, and effeminate gay men—marginal people even within their own marginal population—led charges against rows of uniformed police officers.[61] Their courage "proved infectious." Organizations that attracted "not only the politically disaffected," but lesbians and gay men who had little if any connection with the earlier movement and who had until this moment lived quietly and discreetly, proliferated. By June of the following year 5,000 to 10,000 marched to celebrate the first anniversary of the rebellion; by 1975 anniversary events were occurring in dozens of cities; within four years the number of organizations for lesbians and gay men had grown from fifty to more than 800; by the end of the 1970s the number of organizations was in the thousands. Not only was the number of visible lesbians and gay men increasing, their organizations spoke out and demanded recognition, respect, and equality in previously forbidden realms—at home, in school, with their biological families, and in the media.[62] Whereas World War II had inadvertently created a situation for lesbians and gay men, the Stonewall rebellion sparked the taking on of responsibility to create and shape their own situation.[63]

New Forms of Violence. If the increased visibility of lesbians and gay men and the growth of their social institutions after World War II made them the easy targets of extralegal violence by police officers and private citizens, what would be the response to the new, post-Stonewall, militant insistence on being heard and accepted everywhere? The apparent eclipse of the McCarthy era by the civil rights movements and elections of liberal politicians in the 1960s might suggest a more tolerant context in which lesbians and gay men could live and advocate their equal status in mainstream America. And, in part, acceptance and tolerance were demonstrated by such actions as the American Psychiatric Association's removal in 1973 of homosexuality from its list of mental disorders and by the proposal of U.S. Congresswoman Bella Abzug, along with twenty-four cosponsors, to amend the 1968 Civil Rights Act to prohibit discrimination based on affectional or sexual preference. But lesbians and gay men were to learn that the support of liberal politicians could diminish in the face of competing interests. In New York City, for example, events following the election of Mayor John Lindsay "shattered any illusions that [his] liberalism . . . automatically extended to homosexuals."

Motivated perhaps by a desire to mollify a police force hostile to his civilian review proposals, and also anxious to solidify his support within the business community, in late February 1966 Lindsay gave the green light to a massive crackdown in Times Square that aimed to rid the area of "honky tonks, promenading perverts . . . homosexuals and prostitutes." The next month, the police extended the cleanup campaign to "undesirables" in Greenwich Village. There they concentrated on Washington Square Park, whose western edge was a gay male cruising area dubbed the "meat rack" by those who frequented the park. Street arrests rose sharply, and chief inspector Sanford Garelik announced that these were merely a "first step in a broader city program."[64]

Subsequently, on the streets in Greenwich Village the presence of police increased, reports of beatings by police were reported in gay newsletters, and two unarmed gay men were the victims of a shooting and killing by an off-duty transit police officer, for whom a grand jury failed to issue an indictment.[65]

Although these incidents preceded the Stonewall event, police brutality under the Lindsay administration continued to be a serious problem to which post-Stonewall groups would have to devote their major organizing efforts.[66] Writing about the police harassment of the Daughters of Bilitis (D.O.B.) in New York City during her time as president of this lesbian organization in 1970, Ruth Simpsom remembers that the police often came to their social functions. On one occasion they came and pushed a woman "clear across the floor when she told them that unless they had a search warrant they could not come in." They left but came back another time in six police cars, "dumped large containers holding ice cubes, soft drinks, and beer all over the floor; generally messed up D.O.B.'s quarters, destroying property; and arrested two women, taking them into the precinct and holding them for about four hours." The charge, "selling beer without a license," was fraudulent. The police knew from discussions during their previous visits that as a nonprofit organization, D.O.B. was legally authorized to give beer to its members for a small donation.[67]

If violence by the police in the bars, baths, cruising areas, and social clubs seemed as though it was a continuation of that which had been customary since the 1940s, the venturing of lesbians and gay men into previously avoided public fora occasioned new kinds of attacks in unfamiliar settings and by a wider range of perpetrators. Whereas the meetings for groups in the 1940s, 1950s, and early 1960s occurred mostly in private homes and occasionally in public rooms that were rented by the evening, the growth of organizations after Stonewall necessitated and provided the funds for more permanently rented space for offices, meetings, and social functions. Occasionally, whole buildings were purchased, which was increasingly the practice of the Metropolitan Community Church. The acquisition and rental of property provided new targets that incurred attacks different from the usual assaults against body and life. Arson, burglary, and vandalism became new and frequent forms of violence with which lesbians and gay men now had to contend. For example, the headquarters for the Gay Activists Alliance were gutted by fire and its offices were ransacked and burglarized in 1972; and from 1973 to 1985 eighteen Metropolitan Community Churches were torched, with attacks on some, such as the one in Jacksonville, Florida, becoming so frequent as to require the installation of bullet-proof windows.[68]

As public demonstrations increased, so did clubbings by police at the demonstrations and in the precincts after arrests.[69] Other public officials also responded violently. In 1972 six members of the Gay Activist Alliance entered a formal press banquet at the New York Hilton Hotel and distributed leaflets that criticized "media oppression," particularly a recent editorial in the *New York Daily News* headlined "Fairies, nances, swishes, fags, lezzes—call 'em what you please." As they were leaving, several guests led by the president of the Uniformed Firemen's Association assaulted them, beat them, and threw them down an escalator. Despite the uncontested testimony of four New York City officials who were also guests at the banquet and had witnessed the beatings, only one perpetrator was charged, and he was acquitted.[70] Compared with the incidence of anti-gay/lesbian violence before Stonewall, this incident presents both differences and similarities.

Changes in Public Response and Policy. The assertive entrance of lesbians and gay men into a public event was different, as was the willingness of public officials to testify on their behalf. The coverage by the city media of the incident and subsequent litigation,[71] statements in support of the victims by newspaper columnists and liberal politicians,[72] and the insistence by the complainants on pressing a recalcitrant district attorney to proceed with the case[73] were unprecedented developments. Especially noteworthy, given the instances of anti-homosexual hearings and statements in the U.S. Congress in the previous decade, was the entry by Congressman Edward I. Koch in the *Congressional Record of the House of Representatives* condemning the "brutal, physical assault made upon members of . . . Gay Activist Alliance, who while seeking to publicly voice their opposition to . . . a revue which satirized homosexuals in a demanding way, were . . . unmercifully beaten to the ground." Warning against granting "special treatment" to one of the alleged attackers because he was a "high city official," Koch went on to criticize a "police officer who witnessed the attack . . . but failed to intervene"; the district attorney, for failing to cooperate with the complainants; and the court, for not using its power to intervene.[74] The performance of the police, district attorney, and the courts was consistent with previous experiences of lesbians and gay men.

The social position and occupation of the attacker, as well as his age of forty-one years, describe a perpetrator strikingly different from the teenage boys, small-time crooks, and police officers from whom lesbians and gay men had learned to expect violent treatment. That the ranks of perpetrators were beginning to include men of higher professional station is confirmed by a letter that Koch wrote to the Presiding Justice of the Appellate Division of the Supreme Court, Brooklyn, and attached to the remarks entered in the *Congressional Record*. In the letter he expresses "distress" over reading about the forming, with the alleged assistance of the police department, of a vigilante committee in the Borough of Queens "to take the law into their own hands and harass homosexuals"; he is particularly disturbed "that an attorney was a leader and spokesperson of this vigilante group."[75]

Previously, perpetrators sought out their victims. They went to areas and establishments frequented only by lesbians and gay men. Because they operated in out-of-the-way locations, usually after dark, their actions were seldom seen by the non-lesbian/gay public. Similarly, parents who abused their lesbian and gay children did so within the privacy of the home. Such activity continued into the 1970s, as is evident from Simpson's account, mentioned earlier, of the police brutality at private social functions sponsored by the Daughters of Bilitis. However, because the new, assertive political organizing and activity by lesbians and gay men moved many of them out of isolated night spots, private social gatherings, and unhappy homes into greater participation in the public domain, their encounters with violence were not only the result of being sought out or hunted in dark corners. Instead, they were seen as intruders who needed to be physically removed or prevented from entering. Unlike the violence that happened in out-of-the-way places, these newer incidents were often witnessed by non-lesbian/gay people, some of whom disapproved and protested. Although the only attacker to be arrested in the incident as the press banquet in New York City was a high city official, four other city officials came forward to testify against him. Although many of the same old patterns persisted in this case, lesbians and gay men had brought their lives more boldly into the public eye. Now there were witnesses; and although their responses were mixed, that there were witness at all and that some would oppose the acts of violence indicated change.[76]

RESPONDING TO VIOLENCE AS COMMUNALLY NORMATIVE

A pattern identified earlier in the discussion of post–World War II lesbian/gay experiences, therefore, is also apparent in the post-Stonewall experiences: increased visibility, followed by hostility and violence, followed by a greater insistence and effort to be more visible, followed by hostile attacks. Even the expressed support for and acceptance of lesbians and gay men by non-lesbian/gay people was fragile and vulnerable to hostile responses. The repeal in 1977 and 1978 of recently passed lesbian and gay rights legislation in Dade County Florida; St. Paul,

Minnesota; Eugene, Oregon; and Wichita, Kansas, testifies to the presence and power of an opposition that stood to match and defeat liberal support.[77]

The emergence of and participation by fundamentalist Christian organizations in these efforts took on the force of a crusade and the enthusiasm of a religious revival.[78] Paralleling the hysteria generated by McCarthy and replacing the fear for national security with the fear of pervasive and infectious moral degeneracy,[79] popular figures like Anita Bryant, a former Miss America runner-up, promoted effective repeal campaigns and received national publicity by generating the age-old and unsubstantiated theory that homosexuals recruit children to swell their ranks. Bryant's campaign, not unlike McCarthy's, provoked and inspired violence against lesbians and gay men.

Miami, which saw violence during the referendum battle, has had an increase in anti-homosexual crime. Several men have been shot at as they stood outside gay bars and Miami police are currently seeking 2 men who have been picking up guys in gay bars and then beating and robbing them once they leave the bar.[80]

Such violence reactions were not limited to her home state of Florida. Robert Hillsborough, a gay man, was murdered in San Francisco by two teenage boys, quoted by witnesses as having shouted, "Here's one for Anita," as one stabbed the body of the man fifteen times.[81] Other incidents, in which shouts of "Anita is right" accompanied gang rape and beatings, were noted in other periodicals following the successful vote for repeal in Dade County.[82]

Lesbians and gay men responded in a manner that reaffirmed the pattern. The murder of Hillsborough and the defeat of lesbian and gay rights ordinances across the country provoked lesbians and gay men in California to organize the defeat of the Briggs Initiative, a referendum coming up for a state-wide vote designed to deny lesbians, gay men, and their supporters the right to teach in public schools.[83] Randy Shilts, in *The Mayor of Castro Street: The Life and Times of Harvey Milk,* observes that the gay/lesbian movement in San Francisco at this time

experienced an explosion unprecedented since the first days of gay liberation fronts following Stonewall riots. Gays who had come to San Francisco just to disco amid the hot pectorals of humpy men became politicized and fell into new organizations with names like Save Our Human Rights and Coalition for Human Rights.[84]

Not unlike the men and women who had migrated to the Bay Area following the purges, investigations and firings, and demobilization after

World War II, these people too had come from less-than-accepting hometowns and families to which they did not or could not return. "These young gays might have taken their locker-room beatings at home, because they knew they could always go to San Francisco one day, but once in San Francisco, there was no place to turn".[85] They came to lesbian/gay neighborhoods under circumstances greatly modi-fied by the occurrence of the Stonewall rebellion and the gay/lesbian liberation movement that followed it, but like the earlier migrants they had found an alternative that they were not about to relinquish.

By this time in urban areas, other than those that had become known as gay and lesbian population centers after World War II, similar stands were being taken. For example, after the repeal of the gay/lesbian rights ordinance in Eugene, Oregon, a march was hastily organized. Partici-pants remember that

there was no one on that march who thought (as the bigots had hoped) that things would go back to the way they were before, or that lesbians and gay men would now abandon Eugene in defeat. Gay people had given too much during the past five months [in organizing against the repeal effort] *to go back into the closet after so publicly coming out of it.* Our work had made gay rights a serious, public concern, and that fact had to some degree changed the consciousness of the town [my emphasis].

Their assertiveness, insistence on visibility, and readiness to respond to violent reactions were demonstrated when a "drunk businessman who punched people and screamed at the march" was "forcibly restrained by a dozen angry lesbians."[86]

The experience and anticipation of violence by lesbians and gay men and the accompanying will to survive and increase their visibility were dramatically captured a year later by the assassination of Harvey Milk. Milk, the first openly gay man elected to city office in the country and the most prominent gay political leader, was assassinated by a man who had been a fellow city supervisor. In *The Mayor of Castro Street,* Shilts remarks that Milk lives "as a metaphor for the homosexual experience in America."[87] Milk achieved a pinnacle of gay visibility that reflected and magnified the coming out experiences of many lesbians and gay men during the 1970s. Milk's aggressive, populist politics embodied the new desire, need, and insistence to live more openly as lesbians and gay men. His election to public office, his outspokenness in the political arena, and his popularity among non-lesbian/gay people realized what had been a dream for many lesbians and gay men: that they should not only be recognized by but should be able to contribute to society. His assassination summarized the beatings, murders, and abuse that they had endured. It may have seemed like the sad ending of a dream, but lesbians and gay men identified immediately with the taped message Milk left behind in anticipation of assassination. It nourished a tradition of surviving yet another tragedy and continuing to live openly. His message—"If a bullet should enter my brain, let that bullet destroy every closet door"—rehearsed and updated a pattern that had been set in the late 1940s.

The gay man who made his way to the high offices of city government seemed no less vulnerable than the many gay men and lesbians who had been beaten in bars, in police precincts, in cruising areas, in their homes, and on dark streets. Physical violence seemed an inescapable reality. There were no signs of its diminishing as lesbians and gay men gained political footholds and a greater presence in the public domain. Milk's message to press further to live more openly continued a legacy. Lesbian/gay people expressed their continued commitment to increased visibility and participation with a candlelit march of 40,000 on the night of his assassination. Six months later, responding to the announced verdict of manslaughter for his assassin, Dan White, lesbians and gay men expressed their rage and disapproval in the "largest riot known in gay [/lesbian] history." Amidst a crowd of several thousand, "eleven police cars were destroyed by fire and sixteen were badly damaged." The focus of their protest shifted easily from the verdict to the police, to those "same police who claimed Dan White as one of their own, the police who had harried and hounded gays for years."[88]

None of the experienced police brass, who had spent so many years of their careers watching courteous homosexuals walking docilely into paddy wagons during the decades of bar raids, could have imagined a gay[/lesbian] crowd literally screaming for blood. . . .

Nearly three hours after the first rock had shattered the City Hall doors, a wide wedge of officers appeared, the flames of the burning police cars casting ominous shadows on their helmets. They marched sternly into the pandemonium, beating their batons on the pavement before them like a Roman legion out to make their final conquest. Minutes after walking into the crowd, small groups broke away from the wedge to take on knots of rioters. With the formation destroyed, Civic Center plaza became a melange of skirmishes between gays and police. Police were surprised and enraged at the depth of resistance they encountered. Gays beat back police with branches torn from trees, chrome ripped from city buses, and slabs of asphalt torn from the street.[89]

Ten years after the Stonewall Rebellion and on the opposite coast, lesbians and gay men continued to act and organize against, rather than retreat from, the violence directed at them. But Milk's assassination presaged a new development in the gay/lesbian liberation movement.

Within a year's time, Community United Against Violence (CUAV), the "first organization in the country to deal solely with . . . [and] to really address in a comprehensive and systematic way the issue of anti-gay[/lesbian] violence," was formed in San Francisco.[90] A similar "grass-roots, self-help" project began in the Chelsea neighborhood of Manhattan the following year and soon became the New York City Gay/Lesbian Anti-Violence Project serving the whole city.[91] Other projects in other cities were formed during this time,[92] and in 1982 a national anti-violence project was started by the National Gay and Lesbian Task Force (NGLTF).[93] At a time when lesbian and gay organizations and community activities were more numerous and widespread than ever before, community leaders saw a concurrent need to organize special projects "in response to a rising wave of anti-gay[/lesbian] violence."[94] Formed in the early 1980s, the Bias Incident Investigating Unit of the New York City Police Department would document in 1988 not only a 79 percent rise in reported anti-gay/lesbian crimes, but the largest increase of any type of bias crime (race, religion, ethnicity, or sexual orientation) for the past year.[95]

Can the violence ever be ended? Is the movement by lesbians and gay men a never-ending cycle of gain and defeat kept in place by the threat and practice of anti-gay/lesbian violence? Since the efforts by lesbians and gay men to gain equality within American society seem to have been consistently matched with and often repelled by physical violence, the question of whether or not their entry into society is possible at all needs to be asked. Do the attempts to gain various footholds at various times with various strategies overlook a possible larger fact, that the social structure and social order do not allow for the inclusion of lesbians and gay men except as marginal people? If the apparent progress from private social networking to public demonstrations and participation in the political process has been paralleled and adapted to by a widening range of perpetrators and by an expanding category of assaults, anti-gay/lesbian violence may not simply be the response of people who feel or think about homosexuality in a particularly disapproving manner as much as the institutionalized rejection of lesbians and gay men at whatever levels wherever they threaten to intrude. If the marginal status afforded lesbians and gay men has traditionally served to establish and define more clearly the social order, their attempted movement as equals into that order would certainly threaten those who base their own social position on the lower or marginal status of others. Although the movement for equality by lesbians and gay men may ignite age-old biases and assumptions, it also threatens the established arrangement of power and privilege. Whether the thrust of violence against lesbians and gay men comes more from prejudice and misinformation or from the relationships sustaining the social order is the question that needs to be answered, if the cause of such violence will ever be understood.

CHAPTER TWO

Empirical Data on Victims

Chapter 2 presents and discusses empirical data on the victims of anti-gay/lesbian violence. Following a review of the sources of information, the surveys that have been conducted, including my own, are discussed and their findings presented. Findings are organized according to a general violence category, subcategories of specific kinds of violence, and settings in which violence occurs. The data are analyzed according to such demographic variables as gender, race, and economic status of victims. A comparison with the rates of criminal violence experienced by the general population concludes the chapter.

AVAILABLE SOURCES OF INFORMATION

In the literature by gay men and lesbians of the 1970s and 1980s, anti-gay/lesbian violence is frequently mentioned and discussed. In their autobiographical and biographical statements[1]; political analyses and social commentaries[2]; novels, short stories, poetry and plays[3]; and articles in the social sciences,[4] it is a recurring concern and topic. In the 1970s, gay and lesbian newspapers began to provide regular coverage of incidents[5]; by the 1980s, many were staffed with one or two writers whose primary task was to report on physical assaults.[6] Two books, each by a gay newspaper journalist and documenting the murder of a gay man, were published in the late 1970s and early 1980s.[7] Some mainstream newspapers hired self-identified lesbian and gay reporters whose assignments included covering anti-gay/lesbian violence.[8] Other papers reported incidents more thoroughly than they had in the past[9] and presented messages by columnists and in editorials that disapproved of the leniency with which the criminal justice system tended to treat perpetrators.[10] Popular magazines and television news and talk shows have also attended to and expressed concern about violence against lesbians and gay men.[11] However, the information provided by the gay/ lesbian and mainstream media has been primarily anecdotal and descriptive; the political analyses and social commentaries written by lesbians and gay men and other writers have tended to discuss single incidents and to make general observations; and the social sciences have noticed anti-gay/lesbian violence as one of many problems faced by lesbians and gay men without giving it singular attention.[12] The task of comprehensively gathering data that reflect a wide range of experiences and analyzing them systematically has been undertaken by (1) lesbian and gay organizations and anti-violence projects, (2) lesbian and gay scholars and administrators in colleges and universities, or (3) lesbians and gay men working as liaisons to the lesbian/gay community for various municipal offices.

METHODOLOGICAL ISSUES FOR GATHERING DATA

Data have been gathered in two ways: by encouraging self-reporting by victims to a central monitoring agency and by surveying lesbians and gay men.[13] The surveys provide information about rates of victimization, specific types of physical assault, and the settings in which anti-gay/ lesbian violence occurs, and the self-reports help to clarify the surveys' findings by providing anecdotal data.

Because lesbians and gay men vary in their degree of visibility, they comprise a population that cannot be sampled representatively. Nonprobability or "opportunistic" sampling (i.e., sampling those who use lesbian/gay institutions) has been necessary but is not likely to reach lesbians and gay men who do not associate openly with other lesbians and gay men or black, hispanic, and other ethnic people who are marginalized even within lesbian/gay communities.[14] Of the thirty-four surveys conducted, responses are typically solicited through lesbian/gay organizations and bookstores ($N = 19$), friendship networks and word-of-mouth communication ($N = 12$), lesbian/gay media ($N = 12$), lesbian/gay bars ($N = 8$), lesbian/gay events ($N = 6$), college newspapers and events ($N = 3$), municipal agencies and offices ($N = 2$), women's groups ($N = 1$), and mainstream media ($N = 1$).[15] To preserve anonymity and to increase the likelihood of response, questionnaires are usually distributed with return-addressed, stamped envelopes.[16]

TABLE 2.1
Summary of Thirty-Two Surveys

Source/Year	Sample Size	Gender	Race	Econ. Status	Age
Discrimination-focused surveys					
Bell/Weinberg, San Francisco (1969)	977	x	x	x	
Cauthern, national (1978)	900	x	x		
Harry-1, Chicago (1982)	88	x	x	x	x
Boston (1983)	1340	x	x		x
Ames, IA (1983–84)	57	x		x	x
New Jersey (1983–84)	362	x			x
Richmond, VA (1983–84)	508	x	x	x	x
Yeskel-UMass (1984)	174	x	x		x
Des Moines, IA (1985)	238				
Louisville, KY (1985)	351	x	x	x	x
New York State (1985)	380				
Alaska (1985)	734	x	x	x	x
Cavin-Rutgers (1986)	213	x			
D'Augelli-PennState (1986)	132	x			x
Dallas (1986)	264	x	x	x	x
Vermont (1986–87)	133	x		x	x
Madell/Burke, Eugene, OR (1989)	35	x	x	x	x
Violence-focused surveys					
Miller/Humphreys, US-Canada (1973–77)	52	x			
Sepejak, Toronto (1977)	334	x	x	x	x
Harry-2, Chicago (1978)	1556	x	x		x
Minnesota (1978–79)	289				
McDonough, San Francisco (1981)	50	x			x
Wisconsin (1983–84)	213	x	x		x
NGLTF, national (1984)	2074	x	x		x
Philadelphia (1984)	167	x	x		x
Maine (1985)	323	x		x	x
Wichita, KS (1985)	96	x	x		x
Potter, Boston (1986)	110	x			x
Herek-Yale (1986)	215	x			
Comstock, national (1986)	294	x	x	x	x
NOW, Maryland (1987)	117	x	x	x	x
Morgen, Baltimore (1988)	542	x	x	x	x

The Surveys. Table 2.1 groups surveys as follows: those that asked one or a few violence-related questions among a majority of others about discrimination in general (listed as Discrimination-Focused Surveys in the table, including Bell/Weinberg, San Francisco[17]; Cauthern, national[18]; Harry-1, Chicago[19]; Boston[20]; Ames, IA[21]; New Jersey[22]; Richmond, VA[23]; Yeskel–UMass[24]; Des Moines, IA[25]; Louisville, KY[26]; New York State[27]; Alaska[28]; Cavin-Rutgers[29]; D'Augelli-PennState[30]; Dallas[31]; Vermont[32] and Madell/Burke, Eugene, OR[33]), and those that focus on violence (listed as Violence-Focused Surveys in the table, including Miller/Humphreys, US–Canada[34]; Sepejak, Toronto[35] Harry-2, Chicago[36]; Minnesota[37]; McDonough, San Francisco[38]; Wisconsin[39]; NGLTF, national[40]; Philadelphia[41]; Maine[42]; Wichita, KS[43]; Potter, Boston[44]; Herek-Yale[45]; Comstock, national; NOW, Maryland[46]; and Morgen, Baltimore[47]). Surveys are named according to the location of sample (if conducted by an organization) or by a person's name with the area surveyed (if conducted by an individual researcher). The survey by the National Gay and Lesbian Task Force has a national sample and is listed as NGLTF.[48] The year in which the survey was conducted and the size of its sample are listed. Surveys that provide information about gender, race, economic status, and age composition of their samples are indicated[49]; those that analyze their data according to any of these demographic characteristics are specified in endnotes and included in subsequent discussion.[50]

The surveys do not report on all violence encountered by lesbians and gay men, but on that which is directed at lesbian/gay people because of their sexual orientation by non-lesbian/gay people.

GENERAL VIOLENCE CATEGORY

Surveys vary in the amount and detail of information each provides. Some isolate and report on one aspect of anti-gay/lesbian violence—for example, reporting incidents to the police (Sepejak and Ames; see appendix C), murder (Miller/Humphreys), or victim recovery (Potter). Others record a wider range of experiences and serve as the primary resources for the following discussion. Most of the latter organize their data under a category of "general" anti-gay/lesbian violence. Surveys gathered information for this category either by asking a single question that generalizes all incidents (e.g., "Have you ever been assaulted because you are lesbian/gay?") or by summarizing the answers to several questions specifying various kinds of assault (e.g., "Have you ever been beaten, raped, robbed, etc.?"). Table 2.2 lists the surveys that designate a general anti-gay/lesbian category and provides the following information: percent-

TABLE 2.2

Summary of Findings from Twenty Surveys Using General Anti-Gay/Lesbian Violence Category

| Survey | Respondents (%) | Boundaries for Reporting Incidents | | Multi-question |
		Place	Time	
Wichita (N=96)	8	park	recent	
Dallas (N=264)	13	city	past year	
New Jersey (N=362)	17	state	7 years	
McDonough (N=50)	20			
New York State (N=380)	21	state		
Yeskel-UMass (N=174)	21	campus	as student	
Minnesota (N=289)	23	state		
Harry-2 (N=1556)	23			
Louisville (N=351)	24	county		
Boston (N=1340)	24	city		
Bell/Weinberg (N=977)	25			
Harry-1 (N=88)	26			
Richmond (N=475)	33	city		
Des Moines (N=238)	43			
Philadelphia-1 (N=167)	17	city	past year	x
Philadelphia-2 (N=167)	51			x
Maine-1 (N=323)	40	state		x
Maine-2 (N=323)	54			x
Comstock (N=291)	54			x
Madell/Burke (N=35)	57			x

ages of respondents who experienced violence, the restrictions placed on the time[51] or place[52] of reported incidents, and whether information was gathered by single or multiple questioning.[53] Lowest percentages are reported by those surveys that restrict incidents by time and/or place[54] and by those that ask respondents a single, general question about anti-gay/lesbian violence.[55] Highest percentages are reported by those surveys that ask respondents multiple questions about experiences of anti-gay/lesbian violence.[56] Because the surveys are not uniform in the restrictions placed on the reporting of incidents, in the definition and naming of the category itself, and in the detail and breadth of the questions asked of respondents, comparisons of survey results are limited.

Four surveys—Philadelphia-2, Maine-2, Comstock, and Madell/Burke—are of sufficient uniformity to permit comparative and conclusive statements. Each survey asked respondents to report lifetime incidents experienced everywhere; and each based its general violence category on a series of questions about various kinds of physical assault. Their samples are consistently gender-balanced and demographically diverse. Maine-2 sampled lesbians and gay men in eighty-nine different towns in the state of Maine; Philadelphia-2 sampled lesbians and gay men in the greater Philadelphia urban area; Madell/Burke sampled a small number of lesbian/gay youth in Eugene, Oregon, and its outlying areas; and Comstock sampled lesbians and gay men nationally with respondents from ninety-nine cities in thirty-one states and Washington, D.C. The Philadelphia sample is local, urban, affluent, and predominantly white. The Maine sample draws from a predominantly rural state with a barely visible black population; the majority of the sample is lower income. Comstock's sample, with respondents from rural, suburban, and urban settings, is predominantly upper income and racially balanced. In spite of its small size, Madell/Burke's sample represents the full range of class backgrounds and includes Asian, black, Native American, and Hispanic respondents; also, unlike the thirty- to thirty-five-year-old average age of respondents for the other three samples, its average is between nineteen and twenty years of age, with all respondents under twenty-three years of age. Using similar techniques and methods for gathering and organizing data from four diverse geographical areas, each of these surveys found that over 50 percent of their respondents had been victims of anti-gay/lesbians physical violence. Philadelphia-2 reports that 51 percent of its respondents had experienced some form of anti-gay/lesbian violence; Maine-2 and Comstock report 54 percent; and Madell/Burke reports 57 percent. That similar percentages are produced in spite of demographic differences indicates that anti-gay/lesbian violence occurs with common frequency throughout the United States. Additional support for the universal prevalence of incidents within this country is provided by the NGLTF survey, which found, among eight cities that "differ in size, geographic location, and public attitudes towards gay/lesbian people, [an] overall consistency in rates of victimization."[57] Although incidents may be more frequent in urban areas, anti-gay/lesbian violence occurs in suburban and rural areas also. The distribution of incidents reported in my survey is as follows: 79 percent urban, 12 percent suburban, and 9 percent rural.[58]

Some surveys break down the general violence category according to demographic data on respondents (see appendix tables B.1–B.5). They are consistent in showing that a smaller percentage of women than men report experiences of anti-gay/lesbian violence (appendix table B.1). Surveys by Bell/Weinberg and Richmond show that greater percentages of white people than people of color report violence (28 percent of white people compared to 15 percent of people of color [Bell/Weinberg]; 33

percent of white people compared to 31 percent of people of color [Richmond]), whereas data that I gathered shows a reversed picture, with 68 percent of people of color compared to 50 percent of white respondents reporting violence (appendix table B.2).

Among women (appendix table B.3), both Bell/Weinberg and Comstock find higher percentages for lesbians of color than for white lesbians.[59] Among men (appendix table B.3), Bell/Weinberg reports higher percentages for white men than for men of color (21 percent of men of color compared to 38 percent of white men), whereas I report a higher rate of victims among men of color (70 percent of men of color compared to 59 percent of white men). The wide differences between all the percentages reported by Bell/Weinberg and Comstock may be due to changes in life-style and willingness to report occurring in the nearly twenty years separating the surveys; also, my findings are calculated from answers to questions specifying eight kinds of physical assaults, whereas Bell/Weinberg asks respondents only about ever having been "rolled or robbed."

Comstock finds that, according to yearly income (appendix table B.4), the greatest and smallest percentages of victims are in the middle-income and upper-income groups, respectively, but with small percentage differences across groups (53 percent of the lower-income group compared to 61 percent of the middle-income and 49 percent of the upper-income groups). This pattern is the same for men and women.

Differences according to class backgrounds are small (appendix table B.5), with the highest percentage of victims coming from upper-class backgrounds and the lowest coming from middle-class backgrounds (56 percent of those from lower-class backgrounds compared to 52 percent from middle-class and 65 percent from upper-class backgrounds). Among women, however, more of those from lower-class backgrounds reported incidents of violence (50 percent from lower-class backgrounds compared to 36 percent from middle-class and 36 percent from upper-class backgrounds).[60]

Summary. The following tentative conclusions can be suggested on the basis of the preceding discussion of the general violence category as reported by the surveys: slightly more than half of socially active lesbians and gay men (i.e., those who frequent the institutions and organizations through which questionnaries are typically distributed) experience some form of anti-gay/lesbian violence. Comparable to data from the general population, which show higher rates of criminal violence against men than women,[61] the findings of surveys on anti-gay/lesbian violence show that men are more frequently victims than are women. Surveys vary in reporting whether victimization is greater among people of color or white people, but among women, a greater proportion of lesbians of color seem to experience violence. A higher percentage of middle-income people report violent experiences than do those with lower or upper incomes. More women from lower-class backgrounds and more men from upper-class backgrounds fall within the general anti-gay/lesbian violence category than do those from other class backgrounds. These conclusions can be tested and given a greater dimension by a discussion of the findings of those surveys that asked questions and organized responses according to particular subcategories or kinds of physical assaults.

SPECIFIC KINDS (OR SUBCATEGORIES) OF VIOLENCE

Eight surveys use standardized subcategories for physical violence: "objects thrown," "chased or followed," "spit at," "punched, hit, kicked, or beaten," "weapon assault," and "vandalism or arson." These subcategories were first used in the NGLTF survey and became normative for may subsequent surveys, including my own.[62] Table 2.3 lists the percentages of respondents in the eight surveys who were victims of various kinds of physical assault. (Maine refers to Maine-2 from here on, and Philadelphia refers to Philadelphia-2.)

With the exception of Yale, Rutgers, and PennState, which restricted incidents to the university's campus, the percentages for subcategories across surveys are similar. With the exception of Wisconsin, the largest percentages of respondents in each survey were chased or followed and had objects thrown at them. Being spit at and experiencing weapon assault were reported least. An averaging of subcategories across surveys suggests that 33 percent of all respondents were chased or followed; 23 percent had objects thrown at them; 17 percent were punched, hit, kicked, or beaten; another 17 percent reported vandalism or arson against their property; 11 percent were spit at; and 8 percent were assaulted with a weapon. Comparisons of general and college averages suggest that vandalism and arson occur more frequently, whereas beatings occur less frequently, on college and university campuses.

Subcategories According to Gender. Table 2.4 averages the findings of three surveys that provide percentages for the different subcategories according to the gender of respondents (see also appendix tables B.6 and B.7). A higher percentage of men than women reported experiences of violence in all subcategories, especially for being punched, hit, kicked, or beaten and for having objects thrown at them. However, the sizes of

TABLE 2.3

Percentage of Respondents Reporting Six Types of Anti-Gay/Lesbian Violence

Categories	Surveys (%)						Surveys (%)			
	NGLTF (N=2074)	Wisconsin (N=213)	Maine (N=323)	Philadelphia (N=167)	Comstock (N=291)	General Average	Yale (N=215)	Rutgers (N=213)	PennState (N=132)	College Average
Chased or followed	35	37	38	25	32	33	25	18	22	22
Objects thrown	27	21	26	22	21	23	19	12	13	15
Punched, hit, kicked, or beaten	19	23	16	10	18	17	5	4	4	4
Vandalism or arson	19	20	20	10	16	17	10	6	16	11
Spit at	14	13	11	11	7	11	3	1	6	3
Weapon assault	9	10	9	4	7	8	1	2	1	1

SOURCE: Summary of findings from eight surveys.

TABLE 2.4

Percentages of Female and Male Respondents Reporting Six Types of Anti-Gay/Lesbian Violence

Categories	Women (%)		Men (%)		Average (%)	
	chased	27	chased	34	chased	31
	object	13	object	31	object	23
	vandal	13	beaten	21	beaten	16
	beaten	8	vandal	15	vandal	15
	spit	8	spit	13	spit	11
	weapon	3	weapon	9	weapon	7

SOURCE: Average of findings from three surveys.
NOTE: Categories are in descending order of occurrence.

differences are consistently not great; they vary from a low of 2 percent ("vandalism or arson," with 13 percent for women subtracted from 15 percent for men) to a high of 18 percent (" objects thrown at," with 13 percent for women subtracted from 31 percent for men). The rank orders of subcategories for men and women are the same, except for "vandalism or arson," which is higher for women, and "punched, hit, kicked, or beaten," which is higher for men.

In addition to the subcategories used by the eight uniform surveys, Philadelphia and Comstock use "rape (sexual assault)." Six other surveys, not among these eight, also report information on rape. The findings of these surveys are summarized in table 2.5

Regardless of gender, between 3 percent and 16 percent of respondents report being raped because of their sexual orientation. From the four surveys providing gender-specific information, the range of reported rapes is from a low of 4 percent to a high of 18 percent for women and from a low of 4 percent to a high of 14 percent for men.[63]

Subcategories According to Race and Gender. My survey alone provides information about the subcategories of violence according to class backgrounds and the combined race and gender of respondents. The findings are presented in tables 2.6–2.11. The subcategories of "rape" and "robbery," which were not among the six standard subcategories of the uniform surveys but were used in my survey, will also be considered in these tables and subsequent discussion.

Table 2.6 shows that the percentages of lesbians and gay men of color experiencing violence in all subcategories, except for "spit at" and "vandalism or arson," are greater than those for white respondents. The greatest differences are between "chased or followed" (43 percent of

TABLE 2.5

Percentage of Respondents Reporting Rape (Sexual Assault)

				Surveys (%)				
Respondents	Phil. (N=167)	Comstock (N=291)	Alaska (N=734)	Morgen (N=542)	Boston (N=1340)	Minnesota (N=289)	Vermont (N=123)	Madell/Burke (N=35)
All	5	8	4	16	3	6	14	9/11 [a]
Women	4	5	5	18				
Men	5	10	4	14				

SOURCE: Summary of findings from eight surveys.

[a] In and out of school, respectively.

TABLE 2.6

Percentages of Respondents Reporting Eight Types of Anti-Gay/Lesbian Violence, by Racial Identities of Respondents

	Respondents		
Categories	Color (%) (N=68)	White (%) (N=223)	All (%) (N=291)
chased	43	29	32
object	31	18	21
beaten	21	17	18
vandal	16	16	16
robbed	13	11	12
raped	9	7	8
weapon	9	7	7
spit	7	7	7

SOURCE: Summary of findings from Comstock Survey.
NOTE: Categories are in descending order of occurrence.

people of color; 29 percent of white people) and "objects thrown" (31 percent compared to 18 percent for people of color and white people, respectively). Percentages differ slightly in the remaining subcategories. The rank orders of subcategories for people of color and white people are identical.

Tables 2.7–2.8 compare women of color with white women and men of color with white men. In comparisons among women (table 2.7) and among men (table 2.8), lesbians of color show higher rates of victimiza-

TABLE 2.7

Percentages of Female Respondents Reporting Eight Types of Anti-Gay/ Lesbian Violence, by Racial Identities

Categories	Women of Color (%) (N=12)		White Women (%) (N=113)		All Women (%) (N=125)	
	chased	45	chased	27	chased	28
	object	27	vandal	16	vandal	16
	vandal	18	object	12	object	14
	beaten	9	beaten	10	beaten	10
	spit	9	spit	4	raped	5
	raped	9	raped	4	spit	5
	weapon	9	weapon	2	weapon	2
	robbed	0	robbed	2	robbed	2

SOURCE: Summary of findings from Comstock Survey.
NOTE: Categories are in descending order of occurrence.

TABLE 2.8

Percentages of Male Respondents Reporting Eight Types of Anti-Gay/Lesbian Violence, by Racial Identities

Categories	Men of Color (%) (N = 56)		White Men (%) (N = 110)		All Men (%) (N = 166)	
	chased	41	chased	32	chased	36
	object	31	beaten	25	object	27
	beaten	22	object	24	beaten	24
	robbed	16	robbed	21	robbed	19
	vandal	16	vandal	16	vandal	16
	weapon	9	weapon	12	weapon	11
	raped	9	raped	10	raped	10
	spit	7	spit	9	spit	8

SOURCE: Summary of findings from Comstock Survey.
NOTE: Categories are in descending order of occurrence.

tion than white lesbians, and gay white men tend to report higher rates of victimization than gay men of color. However, the percentages for white women who have been "punched, hit, kicked, or beaten" and "robbed" are more than those of women of color; and the percentages for men of color who have been "chased or followed" and had "objects thrown" at them are greater than those for white men and are the same for "vandalism or arson." The rank order of subcategories shows "vandalism or arson" and "objects thrown" reversed for women of color and white women, with the former higher in the order for white women; however, the percentage of women of color who report "vandalism or arson" is greater than that for white women. In the men's order of subcategories, "objects thrown" and "punched, hit, kicked, or beaten" are reversed, with the former higher for men of color.

Among women and men of color (table 2.9), the percentages of respondents is very close or identical, with the exception of "punched, hit, kicked or beaten" (22 percent compared to 9 percent; men and women, respectively) and "robbed" (16 percent for men; none for women). The percentages of "chased or followed," "vandalism or arson," and "spit at" are slightly more for women. In the rank order of subcategories, "vandalism or arson" and "punched, hit, kicked, or beaten" are reversed, with the former higher for women. "Robbed" is higher for men.

Among white women and men, as shown in table 2.10, there are differences in percentages and in order of subcategories. Except for "vandalism or arson," the percentages for men are greater in all categories. The greatest differences are for these subcategories: "robbed" (19

TABLE 2.9

Percentage of People of Color Reporting Eight Types of Anti-Gay/Lesbian Violence, by Gender

	Women of Color (%) (N = 12)		Men of Color (%) (N = 56)		People of Color (%) (N = 68)	
Categories	chased	45	chased	41	chased	43
	object	27	object	31	object	31
	vandal	18	beaten	22	beaten	21
	beaten	9	vandal	16	vandal	16
	weapon	9	robbed	16	robbed	13
	raped	9	raped	9	raped	9
	spit	9	weapon	9	weapon	9
	robbed	0	spit	7	spit	7

SOURCE: Summary of findings from Comstock Survey.
NOTE: Categories are in descending order of occurrence.

TABLE 2.10

Percentages of White Respondents Reporting Eight Types of Anti-Gay/Lesbian Violence, by Gender

	White Women (%) (N = 113)		White Men (%) (N = 110)		White People (%) (N = 223)	
Categories	chased	27	chased	32	chased	29
	vandal	16	beaten	25	object	18
	object	12	object	24	beaten	17
	beaten	10	robbed	21	vandal	16
	spit	4	vandal	16	robbed	11
	raped	4	weapon	12	raped	7
	weapon	2	raped	10	weapon	7
	robbed	2	spit	9	spit	7

SOURCE: Summary of findings from Comstock Survey.
NOTE: Categories are in descending order of occurrence.

percent difference), "punched, hit, kicked, or beaten" (15 percent difference), and "weapon assault" (10 percent difference). Only "chased or followed" occupies the same place for men and women in the order of subcategories, after which "vandalism or arson" and "robbed" are the high and low, respectively, for women, and "punched, hit, kicked, or beaten" and "spit at" are the high and low for men. The same percentage of white women and white men experienced "vandalism or arson," but it is second in order for women and fifth for men.

TABLE 2.11

*Percentages of Respondents Reporting Eight Types of Anti-Gay/Lesbian
Violence, by Class Backgrounds*

Lower Class (%) (N=75)		Middle Class (%) (N=180)		Upper Class (%) (N=26)		All (%) (N=291)	
chased	33	chased	29	chased	54	chased	32
object	25	object	20	vandal	35	object	21
beaten	24	beaten	18	robbed	23	beaten	18
vandal	12	vandal	16	object	15	vandal	16
spit	12	robbed	12	weapon	12	robbed	12
robbed	8	raped	8	beaten	8	raped	8
weapon	8	weapon	6	spit	8	weapon	7
raped	7	spit	4	raped	8	spit	7

SOURCE: Summary of findings from Comstock Survey.
NOTE: Categories are in descending order of occurrence.

Subcategories According to Class Backgrounds. Table 2.11 considers the
subcategories of anti-gay/lesbian violence in terms of the respondents'
class backgrounds. The percentages for those who report having been
chased or followed, who have experienced vandalism or arson, who
have been robbed, or who have been assaulted with a weapon are
greatest in the group of respondents from upper-class backgrounds.
Greater percentages of respondents from lower-class backgrounds report
having had objects thrown at them; having been punched, hit, kicked,
or beaten; and having been spit at than do those from other groups.
Among the three class background groups, the percentages for respondents with middle-class backgrounds are never the highest in any subcategory. In the rank order of subcategories, "vandalism or arson," "robbed,"
and "weapon assault" are highest and "punched, hit, kicked, or beaten"
is lowest for respondents from upper-class backgrounds. "Robbed" rises
from a sixth place in the lower-class group to fifth place in the middle-
class group, and to third place in the upper-class group.

Summary. The findings of the three surveys reporting subcategories by
gender of respondents do not differ significantly. Their averaged findings
show higher percentages for men in all subcategories, but not by wide
margins. Rape follows this pattern in two of four surveys reporting this
subcategory. Comstock reports findings according to race, race and
gender, and class backgrounds of respondents. My comparison of subcategories by racial identities shows higher rates of victimization for

people of color, except in the subcategory of "vandalism or arson." Comparisons by race and gender show that among lesbians, women of color are more victimized; and among gay men, white respondents are. Within racial/gender groupings, the highest percentage for having been "chased or followed" is found among lesbians of color; the highest percentage of having "objects thrown" at them is found among gay men of color; the highest percentages of "punched, hit, kicked, or beaten," "raped," "weapon assault," and "robbed" are found among gay white men; and white lesbians do not have the highest percentage for any subcategory. Percentages for "vandalism or arson" vary least across racial and gender groupings; "robbery" and "objects thrown" vary most. "Vandalism or arson" is consistently higher for women in the order of subcategories, even though the percentages across gender groups are similar. "Punched, hit, kicked, or beaten" and "robbed" have significantly higher percentages for men and are consistently higher in the men's rank order of subcategories.

These findings do not measure the physical, emotional, and financial damage suffered by victims. At hearings conducted by the San Francisco Board of Supervisors on anti-gay/lesbian violence, Dr. Stewart Flemming described the medical treatment provided victims by the staff of the emergency department at the Ralph E. Davies Medical Center. Reminding the board that his staff represents "only one small emergency room which basically receives the so-called 'walking wounded,' as more serious injuries are transferred to San Francisco General Hospital's Trauma Center," he reported that the attacks on lesbians and gay men

are vicious in scope and the intent is to kill and maim. . . .Weapons include knives, guns, brass knuckles, tire irons, baseball bats, broken bottles, metal chains, and metal pipes. Injuries include severe lacerations requiring extensive plastic surgery; head injuries, at times requiring surgery; puncture wounds of the chest, requiring insertion of chest tubes; removal of the spleen for traumatic rupture; multiple fractures of the extremities, jaws, ribs, and facial bones; severe eye injuries, in two cases resulting in permanent loss of vision; as well as severe psychological trauma the level of which would be difficult to measure.[64]

Other sources concur. Melissa Mertz, coordinator of the Victims of Violent Assault Assistance Program of Bellevue Hospital in Manhattan, says that "attacks against gay men were the most heinous and brutal I encountered." She continues, "They frequently involved torture, cutting, mutilation, and beating, and showed the absolute intent to rub out the human being because of his [sexual] orientation."[65]

MURDER

Murder, of course, is a subcategory for which lesbians and gay men cannot be surveyed. Social science literature on the topic is limited[66]; and the anti-gay/lesbian nature of crimes is usually not recorded in uniform crime statistics. Police departments and district attorneys' offices occasionally make comments to the press about investigating a sensational murder or a "string of homosexual slayings"[67]; and lesbian/ gay anti-violence projects report periodically the numbers of murders that have been reported by friends of victims or solicited from law enforcement agencies.[68] Systematic procedures, however, for recording anti-gay/lesbian murders are nonexistent or in the initial stages of being developed.[69]

Finding that the "most valuable literature on homosexual murder victims and offenders has been provided by freelance writers and journalists,"[70] Miller/Humphreys gathered "information on homicides with homosexual victims over a five-year period from 1973 through 1977 . . . from six gay newspapers, 11 metropolitan newspapers, and from the files of the two cooperating police departments." Their sample of fifty-two victims included no women; but anti-lesbian murders have been reported in the commercial and gay/lesbian media.[71]

They found that in most cases victims were not simply killed but were "more apt to be stabbed a dozen or more times, mutilated, *and* strangled, [and] in a number of instances stabbed or mutilated after being fatally shot." Whereas knives were used in 18 percent of all reported homicides in the United States in 1976, in their sample they were used 54 percent of the time. The Miller/Humphreys findings show that "stabbing [was] the chief cause of death in 54% of the murders . . . 19% were shot, usually in conjunction with beating or stabbing, another 19% were beaten to death, 6% strangled or smothered, and one was thrown to his death from a roof."[72] Other sources concur with this evidence of overkill and excessive mutilation. In a study of autopsy findings by physicians, one psychiatrist stated that "multiple and extensive wounds are not uncommon in the fury of" anti-homosexual murder.[73] A homicide detective, Sergeant Mike Gonzalez, who has worked on the Miami, Florida, police force for twenty-eight years termed a nearly fatal beating of two gay men in 1984 the "worst beating I have ever seen."[74]

Miller/Humphreys also provide information about perpetrators that will be discussed in chapter 3. Next, however, the settings in which anti-gay/lesbian violence occurs will be discussed.

TABLE 2.12

Percentages of Victims of Anti-Gay/Lesbian Violence Reporting Settings in Which Incidents Were Experienced

Settings	All Victims (%) (N = 157)
outside lesbian and/or gay bar, disco, or baths	27
at one's own home	17
on a street in a predominantly straight neighborhood	15
in an area known for cruising (not adjacent to bar, disco, or baths)	12
on a street in a predominantly lesbian and/or gay neighborhood	12
in a public place for the general public (park, movies, restaurants, concert, market, etc.)	12
in college	10
in senior high school	10
at a lesbian and/or gay event (march, rally, dance, etc.)	8
at work	6
in junior high school	5
on public transportation	4
at one's parents' home	4
at other person's home	4
at other relative's home	2

SOURCE: Summary of findings from Comstock Survey.
NOTE: Settings are in descending order of occurrence.

SETTINGS OF ANTI-GAY/LESBIAN VIOLENCE

Table 2.12 lists in descending order of frequency the settings in which respondents to my survey reported experiences of anti-gay/lesbian violence. The highest rate of victimization is reported as occurring outside of lesbian/gay bars, discos, and bathhouses, followed by incidents that took place in the victims' homes (27 percent for the former; 17 percent for the latter).[75]

When settings are arranged according to the gender of the victims (table 2.13), the percentage of victims reporting violence in gay/lesbian-

TABLE 2.13

Percentages of Victims of Anti-Gay/Lesbian Violence Reporting Settings in Which Incidents Were Experienced, by Gender

Women (%) (N = 53)		Men (%) (N = 104)	
lesbian/gay bar	26	lesbian/gay bar	28
straight street	21	cruising area	18
own home	17	own home	16
public place	15	lesbian/gay street	14
college	15	senior high school	13
lesbian/gay event	9	straight street	12
other's home	8	public place	11
lesbian/gay street	8	junior high school	8
public transport	6	college	8
work	4	work	7
parent's home	4	lesbian/gay event	7
senior high school	2	parent's home	4
cruising area	2	public transport	4
relative's home	2	other's home	2
junior high school	0	relative's home	2

SOURCE: Summary of findings from Comstock Survey.
NOTE: Settings are in descending order of occurrence.

bar areas is the same for women and men. However, higher rates of victimization are reported by women for incidents occurring on streets in predominantly straight neighborhoods (21 percent for women; 12 percent for men), in college (15 percent for women; 8 percent for men), and in other persons' homes (8 percent for women; 2 percent for men). Men report incidents more frequently in cruising areas (18 percent for men; 2 percent for women),[76] in senior high school (13 percent for men; 2 percent for women), on streets in predominantly gay/lesbian neighborhoods (14 percent for men; 8 percent for women), and in junior high school (8 percent for men; none for women). These differences suggest that men experience violence more in lesbian/gay areas and in secondary school settings and and that women experience more in straight-identified, domestic, and higher-educational settings.[77] Except for incidents occurring outside lesbian/gay bars and in victims' homes, the rank order of settings for women and men differ considerably.

Table 2.14 lists and provides percentages for settings according to the racial identities of victims. People of color report significantly higher percentages of incidents experienced on streets in predominantly lesbian/ gay neighborhoods (20 percent for people of color; 9 percent for white

TABLE 2.14
Percentages of Victims of Anti-Gay/Lesbian Violence Reporting Settings in Which Incidents Were Experienced, by Racial Identity

People of Color (%) (N = 46)		White People (%) (N = 111)	
lesbian/gay bar	30	lesbian/gay bar	26
own home	24	straight street	15
lesbian/gay street	20	public place	15
straight street	13	own home	14
cruising area	13	cruising area	12
senior high school	13	college	11
junior high school	9	lesbian/gay street	9
college	9	lesbian/gay event	9
relative's home	4	senior high school	8
public place	4	work	7
lesbian/gay event	4	parent's home	5
public transport	2	public transport	5
other's home	2	other's home	5
work	2	junior high school	4
parent's home	0	relative's home	1

SOURCE: Summary of findings from Comstock Survey.
NOTE: Settings are in descending order of occurrence.

people) and in victims' homes (24 percent for people of color; 14 percent for white people). White victims report incidents occurring more frequently in places for the general public (15 percent for white people; 4 percent for people of color). People of color report no incidents of violence in their parents' homes. With the exception of cruising areas and areas adjacent to lesbian/gay bars, rank ordering of settings reveals differences between people of color and white people, but not as many as between men and women.

Summary. Regardless of gender and racial identity, victims in my survey report the highest rates of victimization in areas immediately adjacent to lesbian/gay bars, discos, and bathhouses. Other settings that are consistently high are streets in predominantly straight neighborhoods and victims' homes. Consistently low settings are parents' homes,[78] other relatives' homes, public transportation, and workplaces. Lesbians tend to report higher rates of victimization in non-lesbian/gay areas (e.g., on streets in predominantly straight neighborhoods and in places for the general public), whereas men report more in lesbian/gay areas (e.g., in cruising areas and on streets in predominantly lesbian/gay neighborhoods). People of color report a greater frequency of incidents in lesbian/ gay areas (e.g., on streets in predominantly lesbian/gay neighborhoods and in cruising areas), whereas white people report greater frequency in non-lesbian/gay areas (e.g., on streets in predominantly straight neighborhoods and in places for the general public). These findings can be supported and more conclusively stated when settings are placed in more general groupings.

GROUPS OF SETTINGS

Table 2.15 groups settings as follows: public lesbian/gay areas (outside lesbian/gay bar, lesbian/gay street, cruising area, lesbian/gay event), public non-lesbian/gay areas (straight street, public place, public transportation), home settings (own home, parents' home, other relative's home, other's home), and school settings (junior high school, senior high school,[79] college[80]). Workplaces are not included in any of the groups.

Among all victims, public lesbian/gay areas are reported most frequently, exceeding by 28 percent public non-lesbian/gay areas. Approximately equal percentages of respondents report experiencing violence in homes and at school.[81] Settings of violent crimes among the general population reveal a similar pattern: 52 percent in public settings; 32 percent, home; 9 percent, school; and 8 percent, other.[82] Lesbian and gay crime victims report greater frequency of incidents in school settings than do victims of crime in general (25 percent, lesbian/gay; 9 percent, general) and slightly less in home settings (26 percent, lesbian/gay; 32 percent, general). Although there is not an equivalent setting for public lesbian/gay areas among general crime settings, a comparison of my findings with national crime statistics shows that both anti-gay/lesbian violence and criminal violence in general occur most frequently in public areas.

TABLE 2.15

Percentages of Victims of Anti-Gay/Lesbian Violence Reporting Groups of Settings in Which Incidents Were Experienced

Groups of Settings	Victims (%) (N = 157)
public lesbian/gay area	59
public non-lesbian/gay area	31
homes	26
schools	25

SOURCE: Summary of findings from Comstock Survey.
NOTE: Settings are in descending order of occurrence.

TABLE 2.16
*Percentages of Victims of Anti-Gay/Lesbian Violence Reporting Groups of
Settings in Which Incidents Were Experienced, by Gender*

Women (%) (N = 53)		Men (%) (N = 104)	
public lesbian/gay area	45	public lesbian/gay area	66
public non-lesbian/gay area	42	schools	29
homes	30	public non-lesbian/gay area	26
schools	17	homes	24

SOURCE: Summary of findings from Comstock Survey.
NOTE: Settings are in descending order of occurrence.

Table 2.16 shows that for both lesbians and gay men, the highest
rates of victimization occur in public lesbian/gay areas. For women,
however, the percentage is almost equal to that which is reported for
public non-lesbian/gay areas where women experienced a higher percentage of incidents than men (42 percent for women; 26 percent for
men). Men experienced more violence in school settings than women (29
percent men; 17 percent women). Home settings rank slightly higher for
women than for men.

According to the racial identities of victims (as shown in table 2.17),
the percentages for public lesbian/gay areas are consistently highest.[83]
(See also appendix tables B.8 and B.9 in appendix B for comparisons of
men of color with white men and of white women with white men.)
People of color report similar rates of victimization in school and home
settings, both of which are higher than those for white victims (30
percent for each for people of color compared to 24 percent and 23
percent, respectively, for white people). White people report a greater
frequency of incidents in public non-lesbian/gay areas (36 percent for
white people; 20 percent for people of color).

Summary. These findings for groups of settings confirm the patterns for
the individual settings discussed earlier. Areas in which lesbians and gay
men are known to gather and live are the most frequent settings for
attack.[84] Women report more victimization than men in non-lesbian/gay
areas and in home settings; men report more in lesbian/gay areas and
school settings. People of color report slightly greater percentages for
public lesbian/gay areas than white people do and smaller percentages
for non-lesbian/gay areas.

TABLE 2.17

Percentages of Victims of Anti-Gay Lesbian Violence Reporting Groups of Settings in Which Incidents Were Experienced, by Racial Identity

People of Color (%) (N = 46)		*White People (%)* (N = 111)	
public lesbian/gay area	67	public lesbian gay area	60
schools	30	public non-lesbian/gay area	36
homes	30	homes	24
public non-lesbian/gay area	20	schools	23

SOURCE: Summary of findings from Comstock Survey.
NOTE: Settings are in descending order of occurrence.

TABLE 2.18

Percentages of Respondents Reporting Anti-Gay/Lesbian Violence in the Workplace According to Disclosure of Sexual Orientation in the Workplace

Disclosure of Sexual Orientation	*Respondents (%)* (N = 508)
Open to everyone	43
Open to employer/supervisor	40
Open to other lesbians/gay men	36
Open to a select few	34
Open to no one	21

SOURCE: Summary of findings from Richmond study.

Further Verification of Summary Findings. Two other surveys support the finding that lesbians and gay men are attacked more frequently in those places in which they are most identifiable and visible. Harry-2, for example, shows that, among the gay men he surveyed, the following variables affect the frequency of assaults: living in a gay as opposed to a nongay neighborhood (27 percent and 20 percent, respectively); having all or mostly gay friends as opposed to half, mostly, or all straight friends (28 percent and 20 percent, respectively); behaving in a feminine, masculine, or very masculine manner (39 percent, 22 percent, and 17 percent, respectively); and engaging in sex in public places occasionally or many times as opposed to never, once, or twice (27 percent and 21 percent, respectively).[85] Richmond's findings (table 2.18) show that among lesbians and gay men, frequency of assaults in the workplace varies according to the degree of disclosure of sexual orientation.[86] These surveys provide additional evidence that where lesbians and gay men gather and are most visible, they are subject to more frequent attack.[87]

Perhaps more important than noting the frequency of occurrence within particular settings is the general observation that in all areas of their lives, public and private, lesbians and gay men encounter violence directed at them because of their sexual orientation. Although percentages vary according to groups of settings in my survey, none is low. According to varying degrees of visibility, the percentages in Harry-2 do not differ greatly; and in the Richmond survey, even among those who are not open to anyone in their workplaces, 21 percent are still attacked or abused. An account by Barbara Smith in the introduction to *Home Girls: A Black Feminist Anthology* captures the pervasiveness of violence in the lives of lesbian and gay men.

In the past year, our apartment was broken into, ransacked, and robbed. The robber identified himself as a Black man by writing it on the just-painted walls. Having ascertained that I was Black and a Lesbian he also aimed the vilest obscenities at me. Incensed that a Black woman existed who was not a potential sexual partner for him, he said just that. For weeks after, we lived in terror. Since he knew where we lived, we were afraid that he might come back to rob us, attack us, even kill us. Or he could have gotten one of his friends to do the same. . . .

A few months later, I went out of town and, as was my usual practice, I let my friends in the neighborhood keep my car. My friends, who are also Lesbians, were experiencing constant Lesbian baiting from the Black teenagers on their street. When I returned from my trip I discovered that these boys had taken it upon themselves to burn my car up. . . . Although I was able to get another car, I have never parked it on my friends' street or even dropped them off in front of their door, for fear the boys will identify the car and do the same thing again. I am even reluctant to park nearby since they might be hanging out and see me leaving it. . . . Without provocation except the fact that we are physically here, these boys still harass my friends, my lover, myself, and other women who visit. From all appearances, we live in a "safe" neighborhood.

The robber and the car-burners are not people I've come out to. I'd love to have my privacy in relationship to them, but that is not how it works.[88]

Former executive director of NGLTF, Virginia Apuzzo, is right in her response to the findings of surveys on anti-gay/lesbian violence: "[They] confirm in plain numbers what many in our community have long understood. To be gay or lesbian in America is to live in the shadow of violence."[89]

CONCLUSION

When the rate of anti-gay/lesbian violence in the lives of lesbians and gay men is compared to the rate of criminal violence experienced by the general population, the former is disproportionately higher. Yeskel-UMass finds that 21 percent of lesbian and gay students, compared to 5 percent of the total student body, report having been physically attacked.[90] Philadelphia-1 compares its percentages (10 percent for lesbians and 24 percent for gay men reporting some form of criminal victimization because of their sexual orientation in the past year) with those for all residents in cities with populations of over 1 million in the 1980 edition of the U.S. Department of Justice's report, *Criminal Victimization in the United States* (4 percent for women and 6 percent for men[91]). The victimization reported in Philadelphia-1 is more than twice as great for lesbians and four times greater for gay men than that reported for women and men in the general urban population. Considering that its respondents were asked to report only that violence that was directed at them because of their sexual orientation by non-lesbian/gay people, the comparison is even more striking. With the addition of violent crimes unrelated to sexual orientation, the rate of victimization would presumably be even greater.[92] Also, federal statistics show that the Philadelphia sample, a "predominantly white, highly-educated group of individuals with a mean age of 35," represents those individuals who are least likely to be victimized.[93] Since the "poor, the less educated, the young (age 12 to 24), and members of racial minority groups have the highest rates of victimization,"[94] the actual rates of violence for a more representative sample of the gay/lesbian population in Philadelphia may be even higher than the survey results indicate. Results from my survey do, in fact, show that lesbians and gay men of color are more frequently the victims of anti-gay/lesbian violence than are white lesbians and gay men. In whichever way these findings are considered, that lesbians and gay men are the victims of violent attacks at a rate surpassing the general population emerges as a fact.

CHAPTER THREE

Empirical Data on Perpetrators

Based on information provided by victims in my survey, the characteristics and behaviors of perpetrators of anti-gay/lesbian violence will be
presented and discussed according to relationship to victim, gender, age,
racial identity, number per victim and per incident, advantages used to
overcome victims, and language used. Discussions about the reactive and
premeditative nature of attacks and about perpetrators who have killed
their victims follow. The data for these latter discussions are taken from
journalistic accounts of incidents that include statements by the perpetrators.

SOURCES OF INFORMATION

Perpetrators as a group have not been studied or surveyed, nor is the
rate of perpetrators in the general population known. Available sources
of information about perpetrators are victims' self-reports gathered by
anti-violence projects and human rights commissions[1]; media coverage
of incidents that occasionally describes or quotes perpetrators[2]; a few
brief interviews with former perpetrators in gay/lesbian media and social
commentaries[3]; in-depth journalistic accounts of murders[4]; occasional
references to and general observations about perpetrators in social science literature[5]; and public statements by officials and professionals,
such as school officials and teachers, police chiefs, and district attorneys
who have had experience with perpetrators.[6] Of these resources, only
anti-violence projects have organized information to yield a profile of
perpetrators by age, gender, racial identity, and behavior. This information is limited by the willingness and initiative of victims to report and is

not representative either of the general lesbian/gay population, victims of anti-gay/lesbian violence, or perpetrators.

Of the surveys discussed in chapter 2 that have attempted to sample the lesbian/gay population, only my own and those conducted by NGLTF and Potter[7] provide detailed information about perpetrators. The information that respondents to my survey provided about perpetrators is presented in the following discussion and tables. Findings from Potter, NGLTF, Morgen, Philadelphia, and Maine are used comparatively, mostly in notes.[8] Data collected by lesbian/gay community projects—Community United Against Violence (CUAV) in San Francisco; Project Understanding in Winnipeg, Manitoba; and Institute for the Protection of Lesbian and Gay Youth (IPLGY, now called the Hetrick-Martin Institute) in New York City—although not directly comparable to survey results, will supplement the discussion.[9]

IDENTIFYING PERPETRATORS

From a list of relatives, professionals, colleagues, associates, and contacts encountered in daily routines (see table 3.1), 66 percent of the

TABLE 3.1
Identifications of Perpetrators and Their Percentages of Participation in Incidents of Anti-Gay/Lesbian Violence, in Descending Order of Frequency *

% Assaulting Female Victims (N = 53)		% Assaulting Male Victims (N = 104)		% Assaulting All Victims (N = 157)	
unknown person	66	unknown person	65	unknown person	66
fellow student	13	fellow student	13	fellow student	13
police officer	6	police officer	9	police officer	8
friend	6	brother	9	brother	6
fellow employee	4	fellow employee	4	fellow employee	4
male relative	4	male parent	3	friend	4
ex-husband	4	friend	3	male relative	3
neighbor	4	neighbor	1	neighbor	2
brother	2	boss/supervisor	1	male parent	2
sister	2	doctor	1	boss/supervisor	1
church member	2	nurse	1	doctor	1
boss/supervisor	2	sister	0	nurse	1
doctor	2	male relative	0	church member	1
male parent	0	church member	0	sister	1
nurse	0				

NOTE: No responses by any victims for the following perpetrators: female parent; female relative; priest, minister, or pastor; psychiatrist, therapist, or counselor; and teacher.

victims of anti-gay/lesbian violence in my survey indicate that their perpetrators are "unknown people."[10] Fellow students are the next most frequently reported perpetrators, but at a significantly lower percentage than unknown persons (13 percent for students; 66 percent for unknown). Police officers follow at a slightly lower rate (13 percent students; 8 percent police).[11] (For more information about violence by police officers, see appendix C.) The finding that unknown persons, fellow students, and police officers are the most frequently reported perpetrators applies to both women and men. However, for women, friends are as likely as police to be perpetrators (6 percent of female respondents for each), and for men, brothers are as frequent as police (9 percent of male respondents for each). Given the opportunity to indicate perpetrators others than those listed on the survey instrument, lesbians report victimization by former husbands and male lovers (4 percent).[12]

No incidents with the following were reported in my survey: female parent; female relative (outside of immediate family); priest, minister, or pastor; psychiatrist, therapist, or counselor; and teacher. A small percentage of respondents to the NGLTF survey do report violence by all biological family members: father (by 4 percent of respondents), brother (3 percent), mother (2 percent), sister (1 percent), and other relatives (2 percent), with more lesbians than gay men reporting incidents with mothers (3 percent and 1 percent, respectively) and more gay men than lesbians reporting violence from fathers (4 percent and 3 percent, respectively).[13] Morgen finds that 8 percent of the respondents in his survey had experienced violence from all members of the immediate family, "with the women reporting almost twice as many assaults as the men."[14] Reports of anti-gay/lesbian violence by the full range of family members are, also, on file with various anti-violence projects. IPLGY, for example, reports that of their adolescent clients who have "suffered violence of some kind because of their sexual orientation . . . thirty percent of the violence came from family members, especially parents and step-parents, but sometimes brothers or sisters." Narratives describing specific incidents indicate that both male and female relatives are perpetrators. IPLGY has, also, documented physical assaults by priests and teachers.[15]

CHARACTERISTICS OF PERPETRATORS

Victims of violence were asked to remember the most serious incident of physical assault and to provide information about the genders, ages, racial identities, and behaviors of perpetrators. The following discussion is based on 117 reported incidents.[16]

TABLE 3.2

Percentages of Perpetrators by Gender and by Gender of Victims

Gender of Perpetrators	Incidents Involving:		
	Female (%) (N = 41)	Male (%) (N = 76)	All Victims (%) (N = 117)
male	85	99	94
female	15	1	6

TABLE 3.3

Percentages of Attacks According to Gender Composition of Attacks and Genders of Victims

Gender Composition of Attack	Incidents Involving:		
	Female (%) (N = 41)	Male (%) (N = 70)	All Victims (%) (N = 111)
male (alone or group)	83	99	93
female (alone or group)	7	0	3
male and female	10	1	5

Gender. Ninety-four percent of the perpetrators are male (table 3.2).[17] Women report a higher rate of victimization by female perpetrators than men do (15 percent and 1 percent, respectively).

Table 3.3 shows that females (alone or in groups) attack lesbians but not gay men (7 percent and none, respectively).[18] Female perpetrators attack gay men only when accompanied by male perpetrators.[19] The rate of attacks by mixed-gender groups of perpetrators is greater against lesbians than against gay men (10 percent and 1 percent, respectively).[20]

Age. Table 3.4 shows that nearly one half of all perpetrators are twenty-one years of age and younger, with the great majority less than twenty-eight years old.[21] These findings are similar to CUAV's reports about anti-gay/lesbian violence in San Francisco, which show that approximately 50 percent of perpetrators are under twenty years of age, 30 percent are between twenty and thirty years of age, and 20 percent are over thirty. CUAV, also, finds that these age characteristics hold for perpetrators of both anti-personal and anti-property violence.[22]

My survey finds that a greater percentage of women than men reports perpetrators in the three older age groups. Men report more in the three younger groups.

TABLE 3.4

Percentages of Perpetrators by Age and by Gender of Victims

Age of Perpetrators	Incidents Involving:		
	Female (%) (N = 41)	Male (%) (N = 76)	All Victims (%) (N = 117)
21 under	38	50	46
22 to 28	28	38	34
29 to 36	13	14	14
37 to 43	10	8	9
44 to 50	5	1	3
over 50	8	0	3

TABLE 3.5

Percentges of Perpetrators Assaulting Victims Younger, Same Age, or Older Than Themselves

Ages of Perpetrators Relative to Ages of Victims	Incidents Involving:		
	Female (%) (N = 39)	Male (%) (N = 69)	All Victims (%) (N = 108)
younger	18	36	30
same age	49	46	47
older	33	17	23

Table 3.5 shows that in nearly one half of reported incidents, regardless of the victims' gender, perpetrators attack people of their approximate age (see also appendix table B.10). In the remaining incidents perpetrators are more often older than the women they attack (33 percent who are older, compared to 18 percent who are younger) and younger than their male victims (36 percent who are younger, compared to 17 percent who are older).[23]

Race. The racial identities of perpetrators are reported in table 3.6. Regardless of the gender or race of the victim, perpetrators are more likely to be white than of color (67 percent and 27 percent, respectively). These percentages reflect national statistics for all crimes of violence (69 percent white, 26 percent black, 4 percent Hispanic).[24]

Anti-gay/lesbian perpetrators of color are less likely than white perpetrators to assault female victims (perpetrators of color, 10 percent female victims compared to 35 percent male; white perpetrators, 87 percent female victims compared to 56 percent male). However, this

TABLE 3.6

Percentages of Perpetrators According to Their Racial Identities and the Genders and Racial Identities of Victims

Racial Identities of Perpetrators	Incidents Involving:		
	Female (%) (N = 39)	Male (%) (N = 70)	All Victims (%) (N = 109)
of color (N = 29)	10	35	27
white (N = 73)	87	56	67
interracial group (N = 7)	3	9	6
	Racial Identity of Victims		
	Color (%) (N = 24)	White (%) (N = 85)	All Victims (%) (N = 109)
of color (N = 29)	42	22	27
white (N = 73)	54	71	67
interracial group (N = 7)	4	7	6

finding is mitigated by the small number of female victims of color in my sample, especially since the survey by Cauthern (see chapter 2) finds that 90 percent of surveyed black lesbians reported verbal harassment and/or physical assault by black men.[25] Perpetrators of color are more likely to assault victims of color than white victims (42 percent, victims of color; 22 percent, white victims), but the greater percentage of assaults on victims of color is by white perpetrators (42 percent by perpetrators of color; 54 percent by white perpetrators). When perpetrators from interracial groups are separated into specific racial identifications, the percentage of white perpetrators in all incidents increase to 73 percent, whereas that of perpetrators of color remains 27 percent (not shown in table 3.6).[26]

The frequency of violence by members of particular racial groups appears to be influenced (1) by the geographical proximity of racially specific neighborhoods to gay/lesbian neighborhoods and (2) by the public's identification and recognition of a neighborhood as lesbian/gay. As the Castro District in San Francisco became increasingly gay-identified and inhabited by lesbians and gay men in the 1970s, attacks by teenage males from the neighboring, predominantly Hispanic and black, Mission and Filmore districts became frequent. CUAV's first yearly statistics in 1979 show that of the reported assailants almost 60 percent were Hispanic, 33 percent black, and 14 percent were white. As the media publicized the rapid development of the Castro as a gay/lesbian neighborhood, reported attacks by perpetrators from more distant districts within the city and from the suburbs increased. Within a year the percentage of all reported perpetrators who were Hispanic decreased by one half, whereas that of white perpetrators more than doubled. Assailants from Asian neighborhoods began to be reported. Although the percentages for each racial group changed, the number of perpetrators in each racial group increased.[27] Residential proximity to lesbian/gay neighborhoods and public areas influences the participation by racial and ethnic groups in anti-gay/lesbian violence, but knowledgeability of these areas is also a contributing factor. Perpetrators are found in all racial groups[28] and travel the necessary distance to find victims.[29]

Of the respondents in my survey 7 percent (5 percent women, 9 percent men) have been physically assaulted because they were seen as part of a same-gender interracial couple. Two lesbian respondents, an interracial couple living in rural upstate New York, report that they have been the "victims of a KKK cross-burning."[30]

Reports of anti-gay/lesbian violence by members of organized neo-Nazi, religious far-right, and hate groups have been reported in the media, and some data have been collected by anti-violence projects.[31] A gay newspaper reports in 1978 that more than 100 teenaged men organized Ku Klux Klan chapters in two Oklahoma City high schools. One member claimed: "We are not just against blacks, like the old Klan. We are against gays and the clubs that support them and are going to try to shut them down because this activity is morally and socially wrong." Members are reported to have vandalized cars in the areas of gay bars and to have attacked bar patrons with baseball bats.[32] In 1988 the *New York Times* reported that neo-Nazi activity among U.S. youth is increasing and that lesbian/gay people are among the targets of their physical assaults.[33]

NUMBER OF PERPETRATORS PER INCIDENT AND PER VICTIM

In more than one half of the reported incidents in my survey, attacks were by lone perpetrators (see table 3.7).[34] Lesbians report greater frequency of attack by groups of three and four than gay men do (12 percent and 25 percent, respectively, for women; 10 and 18 percent, respectively, for men). Men report more attacks by pairs of perpetrators (20 percent for men; 12 percent for women).

Comparing the number of perpetrators to the number of victims per incident, table 3.8 shows that, whether alone, in pairs, or in groups of three or more, women are outnumbered by perpetrators approximately

TABLE 3.7
*Percentages of Incidents of Anti-Gay/Lesbian Violence According to the
Number of Perpetrators per Incident*

Number of Perpetrators per Incident	Incidents Involving:		
	Female (%) (N=41)	Male (%) (N=76)	All Victims (%) (N=117)
one	51	52	52
two	12	20	17
three	12	10	11
four or more	25	18	20

one third of the time and that men are out numbered between 40 and 50 percent of the time (sum of bottom three percentages in "one-victim" column; sum of bottom two percentages in "two-victim" column; and bottom percentage in "three-victim" column). Perpetrators outnumber victims in approximately 40 percent of all incidents.

Number of Perpetrators by Age. The tendency for younger perpetrators to outnumber their victims is shown by the data in table 3.9 (see also appendix tables B.11 and B.12 in appendix B). In 58 percent of attacks by perpetrators under twenty-one years of age assailants outnumber their victims. Women report no incidents of being outnumbered by assailants over twenty-nine years of age.

Number of Perpetrators by Racial Identity. Table 3.10 (see also appendix tables B.13–B.15 in appendix B) shows that perpetrators of color are more likely than white perpetrators to outnumber their victims (47 percent of perpetrators of color; 39 percent of white perpetrators). Perpetrators of color in groups are much more likely to attack male victims than female victims (52 percent male; 20 percent female). White perpetrators in groups are somewhat more likely to attack male victims than female victims (40 percent male, 38 percent female).

Table 3.11 (see also tables B.16–B.18 in appendix B) shows that both white and nonwhite perpetrators outnumber victims of color with greater frequency than they do white victims (64 percent of nonwhite victim incidents for both perpetrators, 44 percent of white victim incidents for nonwhite perpetrators, and 33 percent of white victim incidents for white perpetrators). Perpetrators of color are more likely than white perpetrators to outnumber white victims (44 percent, perpetrators of

TABLE 3.8

Percentages of Incidents of Anti-Gay/Lesbian Violence According to the Number of Perpetrators per Number of Victims

Number of Perpetrators per Incident	One-Victim Incidents			Two-Victims Incidents			Three+-Victim Incidents		
	Women (%) (N=13)	Men (%) (N=47)	All (%) (N=60)	Women (%) (N=17)	Men (%) (N=12)	All (%) (N=29)	Women (%) (N=11)	Men (%) (N=10)	All (%) (N=21)
one (N=55)	69	57	60	41	42	42	45	20	34
two (N=19)	0	23	19	24	8	17	9	20	14
three (N=14)	15	4	8	24	25	24	9	20	14
four+ (N=22)	15	15	13	12	25	17	37	40	38
% incidents outnumbered	bottom three %'s 30	42	40	bottom two %'s 36	50	41	bottom % 37	40	38

TABLE 3.9

Percentages of Perpetrators Who Outnumber Their Victims According to the
Ages of Perpetrators and Genders of Victims

Ages of Perpetrators	Incidents Involving:		
	Female (%) (N = 41)	Male (%) (N = 70)	All Victims (%) (N = 111)
21 under	58	58	58
22 to 28	50	35	39
29 to 36	0	25	12
over 36	0	20	7
all perpetrators	31	43	39

TABLE 3.10

Percentages of Incidents in Which Perpetrators Outnumber Their Victims
According to the Racial Identities of Perpetrators and Genders of Victims

Racial Identities of Perpetrators	Incidents Involving:		
	Female (%) (N = 41)	Male (%) (N = 76)	All Victims (%) (N = 117)
of color (N = 36)	20	52	47
white (N = 79)	38	40	39
all (N = 115)	36	45	42

color; 33 percent, white perpetrators) and victims in general (50 percent,
perpetrators of color; 38 percent, white perpetrators).

Number of Victims Most Frequently Attacked. In addition to data concerning the numbers in which perpetrators attack victims, victims in my
survey provided information concerning the number of victims per incident that perpetrators most frequently attack. Table 3.12 shows that in
over one half of the incidents perpetrators attack victims who are alone.
The frequency of attack diminishes by almost one half when victims are
with one other person (28 percent for pairs of victims; 53 percent for
lone victims) and by another 10 percent when they are with more than
one other person (18 percent for three or more; 28 percent for pairs).[35]
Among women and men, the pattern differs, however. Perpetrators
are more likely to attack gay men who are alone (66 percent of men's
incidents) and lesbians who are in pairs (44 percent of women's incidents). Perpetrators are least likely to attack lesbians and gay men when

TABLE 3.11

Percentages of Incidents in Which Perpetrators Outnumber Their Victims According to the Racial Identities of Perpetrators and Victims

Racial Identities of Perpetrators	Incidents Involving:		
	Victims of Color (%) (N=25)	*White Victims (%)* (N=91)	*All Victims (%)* (N=116)
of color (N=36)	64	44	50
white (N=80)	64	33	38
all (N=116)	64	36	41

TABLE 3.12

Percentages of Incidents in Which Perpetrators Attack Victims According to Who Are Alone and Who Are Accompanied

Female Victims (%) (N=41)		Male Victims (%) (N=76)		All Victims (%) (N=117)	
with a woman	44	alone	66	alone	53
alone	28	more than two	17	one other	28
more than two	21	with a man	14	more than two	18
with a man	8	with a woman	1		

they are with one person of the other gender (8 percent for women; 1 percent for men).[36]

Other Advantages. Perpetrators take advantage of victims in various ways (see table 3.13). The methods most commonly used are to *frighten* the victim with excessively violent threats (49 percent of incidents), to *surprise* or attack the victim from the rear (47 percent), to attack in a location in which *no help* can be summoned (47 percent), to be *larger* than the victim (45 percent), and to *outnumber* the victim (41 percent). Assailants frequently are *armed* (27 percent)[37] and attack lesbians and gay men who appear *out of place* (29 percent). Attacks have also been reported against physically disabled gay men and lesbians.[38]

Perpetrators use advantages differentially according to the gender of victims. Assailants of gay men more often frighten them (54 percent of incidents against men; 39 percent against women), are armed (32 percent, men; 17 percent, women), attack those who are intoxicated (17 percent, men; 2 percent, women), outnumber them (46 percent, men; 32 percent, women), and mislead them (16 percent, men; 7 percent, women).[39] Only men report incidents of having been drugged.[40] Women are more

TABLE 3.13

Percentages of Perpetrators Using Advantages Over Victims in Incidents of Anti-Gay/Lesbian Violence, in Descending Order of Frequency

Incidents Involving:					
Female Victims (%) (N = 41)		Male Victims (%) (N = 76)		All Victims (%) (N = 117)	
larger	54	frightened	54	frightened	49
no-help area	41	surprised	51	surprised	47
frightened	39	no-help area	50	no-help area	47
surprised	39	outnumbered	46	larger	45
outnumbered	32	larger	41	outnumbered	41
man vs. woman	30	out of place[a]	33	out of place[a]	29
out of place[a]	22	armed	32	armed	27
armed	17	victim drunk	17	misled	13
misled	7	misled	16	victim drunk	12
said armed	5	said armed	11	said armed	9
victim drunk	2	victim laden[b]	4	victim laden[b]	3
victim laden[b]	0	drugged victim	1	drugged victim	1
drugged victim	0				

NOTE: Percentages in each column total more than 100 because perpetrators often use multiple advantages per incident.

[a] Victim appeared out of place.

[b] With packages, for example.

frequently attacked by assailants who are larger than they (54 percent of incidents against women; 41 percent of those against men). Given the opportunity to indicate advantages used by perpetrators other than those listed on the questionnaire for my survey, lesbians report that in 30 percent of the incidents the assailant had the advantage of being a man directing violence against a woman.

The greater than 100 percentages per column in table 3.13 indicate that perpetrators favor the execution of their acts with several advantages. Combinations of advantages appear to be used more frequently against gay men.

LANGUAGE

Table 3.14 shows that language used by perpetrators typically disparages homosexuality and boasts about heterosexuality. Offensive language is used in a greater percentage of incidents involving women as victims than in incidents in which men are victims. Regardless of the victims' gender, language that disparages homosexuality is used most

TABLE 3.14

Percentages of Incidents in Which Perpetrators Use Various Kinds of Language, in Descending Order of Frequency

Female Victims (%) (N = 41)		Male Victims (%) (N = 76)		All Victims (%) (N = 117)	
disparaged homosexuality	43	disparaged homosexuality	21	disparaged homosexuality	29
was anti-woman, anti-feminist	36	boasted of heterosexuality	11	boasted of heterosexuality	15
boasted of heterosexuality	25	referred to God religion, Bible	2	was anti-woman, anti-feminist	13
referred to God, religion, Bible	8	was anti-woman, anti-feminist	1	referred to God, religion, Bible	4
was racially insulting	2	was racially insulting	1	was racially insulting	1
was ethnically insulting	0	was ethnically insulting	1	was ethnically insulting	1

NOTE: Kinds of language are in descending order of frequency.

frequently (43 percent of attacks against women; 21 percent of attacks against men). For women, language that is anti-feminist or anti-woman ranks second (36 percent of incidents), whereas for men, language that boasts of heterosexuality occupies second place (11 percent of incidents).[41] None of the victims in my survey reports incidents in which perpetrators referred to AIDS (acquired immune deficiency syndrome), but most anti-violence projects have logged such cases.[42] Morgen's survey of lesbians and gay men in the Baltimore area, conducted in 1988, two years after my survey, finds 16 percent of its respondents reporting harassment, threats, and assaults associated with AIDS; that 14 percent of these incidents occurred in the "past year," compared to 2 percent in "lifetime" experiences, suggests a marked increase in AIDS-related violence.[43] In its *Final Report* in 1988, the Reagan administration's Presidential Commission on the Human Immunodeficiency Virus Epidemic observes that "increasing violence against those perceived to carry HIV" is a serious problem: "The Commission has heard reports in which gay men in particular have been victims of random violent acts that are indicative of a society that is not reacting rationally to the epidemic."[44]

Reports in the newsmedia indicate that some physical assaults are preceded immediately by taunts and anti-gay/lesbian epithets. Such remarks may be used as "baiting" or as a prelude to violence. Other assaults are preceded by weeks or months of occasional verbal harassment. In Northampton, Massachusetts, for example, following public alert meetings prompted by the rapes of two lesbians, phone calls threatening arson, vandalism, bombings, and personal injury were made to lesbian businesses, meeting places, and individuals from October 1982 to October 1983, at which time a perpetrator was apprehended and sentenced.[45] In Lewiston, Maine, in 1985, after seven months of harassment, a 36-year-old gay man "knew his tormentors had come to get him in his home" when they attempted to break into his apartment. He shot and accidentally killed one of them. Claiming that he acted in self-defense, a grand jury refused to indict him.[46]

In some incidents perpetrators direct no language at their victims. In Winnipeg, Manitoba, Project Understanding's study of anti-gay/lesbian violence finds that in 40 percent of its reported cases, particularly those occurring in areas frequented by gay men who are cruising for sexual encounters, attacks are "sudden"[47] with "absolutely no verbal communication between the assailant and victim prior to the attack"; in some instances, no language was used during the attack either. Although language most commonly signals the anti-gay/lesbian orientation of attacks, the Winnipeg study finds that the location of incidents, such as parks used after dark almost exclusively by gay men; the apparent lack of another motive, such as robbery; and characteristics common to other attacks upon lesbians and gay men, such as the age of and advantages used by perpetrators, are reliable indicators too.[48]

In my survey also, only one third of the victims of anti-gay/lesbian violence reported language used by perpetrators (37 percent). When compared with incidents involving only anti-gay/lesbian verbal harassment (see appendix A), a greater percentage of language that refers to God, religion, or the Bible (39 percent, verbal harassment; 4 percent, physical assaults) and to AIDS (26 percent, verbal; 10 physical) is found.

REACTION VERSUS PREMEDITATION

Perpetrators' attacks can be either reactive or premeditated. Incidents of the former occur both in public and in the home. For example, *Newsweek,* in 1981, reports that in Portland, Oregon, a gay man "tried to enter what he mistook for a gay bar" and was promptly beaten to death by two teenage men[49]; and *Ms. Magazine,* in 1985, reports an incident at the University of Texas in Austin in which a father paid a surprise visit to his daughter, found her in bed with her lover, and beat the other woman.[50] Interviews with teenage perpetrators confirm the reactionary nature of many attacks:

We would never make a decision to go beat up fags. But if we were walking down the street and some guy passed that look "queer," we'd let him have it.[51]

What would happen is, the whole gang would be hanging around and some feminine guy would walk by and someone would say "let's get the fag!" We'd all surround the guy, scare him half to death, and rough him up a little.[52]

One of 'em [incidents] happened like in the evening, because I was with some other guys and we were drinking beer on the park bench, and we seen these two guys arguing, and we thought it was pretty funny, so we made fun of them and callin' 'em names and shit like that. I threw a bottle at 'em, and they got pretty mad and stuff, so they just left. . . .

No, I wasn't goin' out and lookin' to assault a gay person. I didn't have that plan in my head. It [seeing two gays together] came up and I didn't like it, and, you know . . . it bothered me.[53]

But no single set of circumstances or characteristics of perpetrators seems to predict reactive versus premeditated attacks.

Although the discovery or announcement of a lesbian or gay man's sexual orientation may spark an immediate violent reaction by family members, in other circumstances a family's response may be in the form of planned methods to remove, punish, or correct her or him. A man in Champaign, Illinois, in 1978, for example, was convicted and sentenced for shooting his ex-wife's girlfriend, whom he blamed for the break-up of his marriage. Evidence at the trial showed that because the defendant had purchased the weapon sometime prior to the shooting, his act was premeditated.[54] And in Ohio in 1981 a nineteen-year-old lesbian was kidnapped by her father and subjected to "deprogramming from lesbian mind control," a process that included rape and deprivation of food and sleep. The parents paid $8,000 for the "treatment" and were aware of the methods used.[55] And although groups of teenage males "hanging out on their own turf" may victimize the occasional passer-by who appears to be lesbian or gay, such groups are just as likely to penetrate lesbian/gay areas with plans to inflict physical injury on, destroy property of, or rob lesbians and gay men. To describe the premeditated violence by these latter groups of perpetrators the following discussion uses news-media reports that include statements by the perpetrators, their confessions upon being apprehended by enforcement officers, and court proceedings.

Premeditated Acts of Violence by Groups of Perpetrators. Newspaper accounts providing sufficient information to profile the characteristics and behaviors of such perpetrators have been used to construct table 3.15. As can be seen, this information confirms many of the findings of my survey. The following summary statements can be made from the data in table 3.15. In these five incidents occurring in five different cities from 1978 to 1986, perpetrators typically went to lesbian/gay areas in search of potential victims. Remarks and/or plans made before the attacks evidence premeditation. Using weapons ranging from fists to a gun and inflicting injuries with minor to nearly fatal consequences, perpetrators outnumbered their victims, often attacking a number of lone victims in quick succession. Robbery was a motive in only the Dallas incident.[56] Sexual overtures were used to mislead the victims in the Dallas and Washington[57] incidents. Remarks made after the attacks by the San Francisco[58] and New York[59] perpetrators indicate a lack of remorse. Perpetrators were from fifteen to twenty-one years old; the oldest was in the anti-lesbian incident in Portland.[60] Perpetrators were predominantly white, but also black and Hispanic, and from lower- to upper-middle-class backgrounds. A minority had police records. Reported sentences were not severe. Attacks occurred during nighttime hours in the summer and/or on weekends, times when teenagers typically socialize.[61]

Interviews with Perpetrators. Extensive, candid remarks by perpetrators, under circumstances other than those imposed by law enforcement officials and court personnel, are rarely, if ever, available. An exception is a set of interviews conducted by Eric Weissman and published in *Christopher Street* magazine in 1978.[62] Separate conversations are recorded with six perpetrators, four of whom had been involved in a single incident. Because the attack did not produce consequences severe enough to attract the media or police, these remarks provide insight into anti-gay/lesbian violence that is perhaps more ordinary, more frequent, and less likely to come to the public's attention than the incidents reported in table 3.15.

Weissman talked with six teenage boys, ages fourteen to eighteen, from middle- and working-class Irish and Italian families living in Greenwich Village in New York City. Two were Catholic high school students with low-B averages, one of whom planned to go to college. Two were A students in high school with plans to study business administration and business law in college. Two were college students, one in political science at an upstate university, the other at a business college in the city. On a summer night while "joy-riding" around Manhattan, four of

TABLE 3.15

Information from Newspaper and Magazine Articles About Groups of Perpetrators in Premeditated Attacks

	Location and Number of Victims				
	San Francisco (one man)	Dallas (five men)[a]	Portland ME (three women)[b]	New York (ten men)[a]	Washington (one man)
Setting	street in gay neighborhood	cruising in park	outside of women's bar	cruising in park	from gay bar to local park
Time	11/82 11pm	7/86 Wed 3am	9/86 Sun 1am	7/78 Wed 9pm	11/83 1am
Weapons	cane/fists	gun/fists	fists/feet	baseball bats	fists/feet/knife
Injuries	head gash, broken knee cap/wrist	lacerations/ fractures/ powder burn, robbed	broken teeth bruised ribs, arms, eyes; jaw fractured.	fractures, concussions (1 paralyzed)	hand cut, concussion, liver/kidney/ testicle damage
Number	five	four	three	six	two
Ages	15–17	18	21	15–20	17,18
Race	Hispanic	black	white	white	white
Class	middle	lower	working	lower-middle	upper-middle
Before attack	Drove to gay neighborhood after birthday	Robbed other gay men in park; asked for sex as	Drinking at nearby bar whose patrons known to	One later said, "We went out to get faggots be-	Faked i.d. to get into gay bar; sexually proposi-

	(A)	(B)	(C)	(D)	(E)
	tioned victim; invited him to party; drove him to local park.	cause we hate them."	harass patrons of women's bar; verbally harassed victims in parking lot.	prelude to beating and robbery.	party at restaurant in other part of city.
After attack	Took victim's clothes; arrested after victim called police.	Arrested one week later; bragged, joked to reporters.	Jumped into van driven by another, sped away; arrested soon after.	Arrested immediately by undercover decoy police.	Laughed, went home.
Record		assault (anti-gay)		robbery and purse snatch	
Sentence	probation, + 400 hrs community serv.	1,2–6 yrs; 2 dismissed	$100 fine; $250 restitution	1, 18 mos (+ restitution); 1, 90 days	

[a] A number of victims were robbed and/or attacked one after the other within a short period of time.
[b] One plus two drivers as accomplices.

the young men passed a delicatessen and noticed an after-hours delivery of a crate of oranges and a box of eggs on the sidewalk. Someone said, "Let's take them and throw them at the fags!" They stole the produce, drove to West Side Highway near Christopher Street, and parked the car. They walked to a spot from which they threw the eggs at a group of gay men. After running back to the car, they drove by the scene of the attack to inspect the damage and threw the oranges. They broke the window of a bar and sped away.

One of the perpetrators told Weissman that they had decided to attack "fags" out of boredom. They had nothing else to do. Another said, "It was a little game. We were trying to be tough to each other. It was like a game of chicken—someone dared you to do something and there was no backing down. . . . It was a symbol of prestige." Another agreed that "peer pressure does have a lot to do with it; sometimes you're forced into doing something to prove yourself to others." He thought the incident "was really just a joke" and that they "didn't want anybody to get hurt." The excitement and fun shared by these three is summarized in a statement by another who said:

Before, we were in a joking mood. It was Friday and we were feeling good, and this seemed like a practical joke. During, it seemed like a game—a little tense, but fun just the same. After, there were a lot of feelings. Relief. A kind of high. There was also a strong close feeling. That we were all in something together.

Only the youngest person interviewed by Weissman expressed outright hostility toward gay people. He said that he and other friends often went "fag-hunting" around the neighborhood because gays are a "disgrace to mankind" and "should all be killed." He was the only one who did not think that what they had done was wrong.

All but one said they had trouble accepting and understanding sexual activity and physical affection between men. For them it is "not right," "not natural," or "disgusting and immoral"; two said, "it goes against the Bible"; another that "all my life everyone told me it was wrong, and I guess that just sticks to you"; and another that "I don't see myself making it with a man, but I can't rule out the possibility." The dissenter said that he "would probably have a gay experience" someday and that "I'm kind of free and easy about sex, and I'd like to try it with another guy." Only the youngest felt compelled to correct or punish gay men for their sexual behavior; the others articulated a live-and-let-live tolerance, as reflected in these remarks by two of the young men:

"I guess gay people do what they want to do and I do what I want to do. . . . They have the same rights as I do and shouldn't be bothered."

"If they stay in the closet, I guess there's nothing much anyone can do about them. I really don't care one way or the other, as long as they don't bother me."

The sixth person in Weissman's interviews said he was able to excuse himself from participating in incidents.

"I've been there with my friends, but I've never participated. I would never do anything like that. Peer pressure doesn't really affect me that much. If my friends start to get down on me I just go home. People who do those things aren't really friends anyway."

Their apparently mild hostility or lack of hostility toward gay men and lesbians is confirmed by their responses to questions about a recent mayoral executive order banning discrimination in the police and fire departments. None definitely opposed the order. Four, feeling that being able to do the job mattered most, said they were in favor of or did not care about the order. One was more uncertain but thought that "their homosexuality would get in the way of their jobs." And the youngest said, "I couldn't care less if gays were in the fire department. It's the police that worry me. In the police department I don't like it because they can take advantage of the young kids in the neighborhood."

Concerning knowledge about homosexuality and acquaintance with lesbians and gay men, three of the young men had done reading and three had not; three knew lesbians and gay men, three did not. The one who had decided not to participate in the actual attack said he had a lesbian friend who was "a nice lady, a good woman." The youngest and most hostile said he knew some of his teachers were gay and that they treated him nicely. The apparent lack or unpredictability of the influence of knowledge, familiarity, and acquaintance is confirmed by two other sources.

The first is a simulated experiment with 156 male college students in which researchers had "expected that a cooperative and positive outcome experience with a person would attenuate aggression toward that individual at a later time following disclosure of his homosexuality." They find, instead, that "homosexuals were highly aggressed against regardless of type of prior interaction."[63] The second source is my own informal survey of first-year college students (see appendix E) in which I find that those who had been perpetrators were more likely than nonperpetrators to have talked with, tried to befriend, and known lesbians and gay men and to have read about homosexuality and listened to a speech by a lesbian or gay man.

The statement by one of the participants in Weissman's interviews—"We weren't trying to hurt anyone, we were just out for some fun"—

casts a benignity on their behavior that does not seriously consider the fear, discomfort, and injury of the victims. It, with their other remarks cited earlier, suggests that for some teenage males attacking gay men and lesbians is not an expression of hatred and disapproval as much as it is a recreational option.[64] Police officers familiar with teenage perpetrators point out that assailants consider these attacks a "kind of sport."[65] The coordinator of the Fenway Community Health Center in Boston places the practice of the "sport" in custom and tradition: "Beating up 'queers,' 'sissies,' or 'fags,' or 'homos' often begins at an early age. In some communities, it is seen as a rite of passage among males sanctioned, if not admired, by the community elders."[66] Because the "church is against [homosexuality], my parents are against it, [and] my friends are against it," the teenagers interviewed by Weissman saw gay men as marginal people whom they could attack for fun. Social disapproval of homosexuality was less their reason and more the permission for attacking their victims. It mitigated the responsibility for the damage and injury they might have caused. Apparently, they did not attack gay men because they hated and, therefore, wanted to punish or hurt them, as much as they attacked a socially vulnerable people to alleviate their own boredom (see also appendix F).[67]

If recreational enjoyment at the expense of an oppressed minority's safety and well-being appear more dominant here than do clearly expressed hatred and disapproval, the latter are foremost in other incidents reported elsewhere. Statements by perpetrators during attacks, such as, "I'll kill you because you're a faggot," "We don't like fags," and, "I have no use for homosexuals," are frequently reported by victims. And the testimony in court of a man who shot and killed his mother and her lover out of dislike for lesbians because "they are strong, powerful people" is not unlike the rationales offered by other assailants.[68]

But whether adventure and enjoyment or hatred and disapproval are more pronounced in a single incident, perpetrators are capable of and do inflict injury. While the tossing of eggs and oranges by the perpetrators interviewed above may seem quite harmless, other groups who have attacked with the same pursuit of adventure and fun have caused greater harm. A seventeen-year-old perpetrator in Bangor, Maine, describes an attack as follows:

We were just going to talk to him or scare him. I walked up to him and said, "Hi, how you doing, fag?" You could tell he was really scared. We did pick him up and brought him over to the rail [of the bridge over the stream]. . . . We threw him in. I didn't want to kill him—all I did was try to scare him. It was just stupid, very stupid.[69]

Two girls who accompanied him and the two other assailants said that afterward the three then "all shook hands with each other; they were all laughing, just laughing like when you tell a joke."[70] The adventure, comraderie, and enjoyment, as well as the proffered innocence of intention and feelings of regret,[71] mirror the substance of Weissman's conversations with the six perpetrators. Here, however, the victim died. That perpetrators can and do kill their victims is a dimension of anti-gay/ lesbian violence that is discussed next.

PERPETRATORS WHO HAVE KILLED THEIR VICTIMS

As the only study of anti-gay murder, the Miller/Humphreys survey (see chapter 2) is the single source of comprehensive and systematized information about perpetrators who have killed their victims. This study, however, examines and classifies perpetrators according to the characteristics and behaviors of victims, not of perpetrators. Victims are divided into two categories according to their lifestyles—those who live overtly as gay men and those who as "homosexual marginals" relate very little or not at all to the gay community and its institutions. Perpetrators are grouped according to the frequency with which they attack each category. The study finds that 64 percent of "homosexual marginals" compared to 37 percent of the more openly identified gay men "were murdered by pickups and hitchhikers, most of whom could be identified as hustlers," and 12 percent of the marginals compared to 42 percent of the overtly identified "were killed by 'gay-bashing' groups or groups of bikers." Miller/Humphreys reasons that because marginals tend to avoid gay institutions for fear of exposure, they "are more apt to spend leisure time in the company of runaways, derelicts, drug abusers, and hustlers encountered in bus terminals, all-night coffee shops, or on the streets"; anti-gay gangs, on the other hand, "seek victims in areas known to be frequented by gays . . . [and] are likely to find the more openly identified gay men in these locales."[72] Whereas the Miller/Humphreys study distinguishes perpetrators according to the behavioral patterns of victims, my research constructs a profile of perpetrators-who-murder according to the characteristics and behaviors of the perpetrators.

Using the data-gathering methods of the Miller/Humphreys study, I monitored and researched newsmedia coverage of anti-gay/lesbian murders from the mid-1970s to the present. Incidents were selected on the basis of the amount and detail of information provided about perpetrators.[73] The details for which I looked are listed in the left -hand columns of tables 3.16–3.18. The coverage of seventeen incidents was sufficiently thorough for their inclusion in the tables. These incidents are grouped according to the number of perpetrators per incident: table 3.16 consists of incidents involving groups of perpetrators; table 3.17 pairs of perpetrators; and table 3.18, lone perpetrators. These incidents do not represent the universe of anti-gay/lesbian murders. Because the media prefers socially prominent people[74] and/or unusual circumstances,[75] it is not a reliable source of information for routine violence in the lives of ordinary or marginalized people.[76] However, because the incidents have been gathered from mainstream, alternative, and gay/lesbian publications with monitoring by and research assistance from gay/lesbian individuals, archives, history projects, publishers, organizations, and violence projects throughout the United States and Canada, the sample is not without its comprehensive and representative qualities. At the very least, it is geographically diverse, spans a decade, and includes male and female victims and perpetrators.

Groups of Perpetrators. Table 3.16 details six incidents in which a victim or victims were killed by a group of three or more perpetrators. In five of the incidents the victims were white males; in the other, a white lesbian couple. Victims' ages range from twenty-one to forty-two years. Only victim Zeller was alone; in three incidents a second victim was able to escape; Heakin was among several other gay men; only in the Hyatt/Jackson incident were there two victims. The choices of settings by perpetrators reflect the findings reported in chapter 2—that is, public lesbian/gay areas—as most frequent, followed by victims' homes. Consistent with findings reported earlier in this chapter, the perpetrators are fifteen to twenty-two years of age; they are predominantly white; and their victims are older. They are from middle- and working-class backgrounds, and attack in groups of three to five. In the O'Connell,[77] Zeller,[78] Heakin,[79] and Howard[80] incidents, the perpetrators were accompanied by nonparticipating peers; young women were present in the attacks of Howard and O'Connell. Only in the Hyatt/Jackson[81] incident was a female an active perpetrator.

Prior to four of the attacks, perpetrators consumed alcohol or recreational drugs. Prior to all incidents, the perpetrators were with friends, either at a popular hang-out, on the way to a party, at a party, or gathered at the home of one of the perpetrators. The decision and/or plan to attack in each incident was made in a social-peer context. The attacks occurred during nighttime hours in the summer and/or on weekends, times when teenagers can and do typically socialize. All had access to automobiles for transportation to and from the settings in which attacks occurred. Discussion before and after the attacks indicate that adventure, enjoyment, boasting, and sharing stories about the experience were the perpetrators' apparent rewards.[82] Robbery was a motive only in the Zeller incident; but even here it was not primary.

Although perpetrators in the Howard incident said they were retaliating for a sexual comment made to them weeks earlier by the victim, this allegation remains without conclusive proof and with some support for its being unlikely. No sexual activity occurred between victim and perpetrators in any of the incidents. In the Zeller encounter, one perpetrator acted as a decoy to attract the victim sexually and to lure him into a position for attack by the others.[83]

In the Howard, O'Connell, Zeller, and Heakin incidents the assailants were not acquainted with the victims, went to an area they knew gay men frequented, and targeted a generic, not individually specific, gay man. Although Hillsborough's[84] assailants did not know him, they targeted and followed him and his lover home after a verbal altercation at a drive-in restaurant. Only in the Hyatt/Jackson incident were specific and known individuals (i.e., the female perpetrator's mother and the mother's lover) targeted.

In the courtroom trials for the Hillsborough and Hyatt/Jackson slayings, precautions to cover-up or remove evidence, extreme use of weapons other than fists and/or feet, and the targeting of specific individuals were cited to establish the perpetrators' intentions to kill and their knowledge of the victims' deaths at the time of the incidents. In the other incidents, such intent and knowledge could not be proved in court. Although a witness testified that Howard begged his assailants not to throw him into the stream because he could not swim, defendants denied having heard his plea. The perpetrators in the O'Connell, Zeller, and Heakin incidents claimed to have been frightened and surprised when they learned days later that the victims had died. Although their intentions may not have been, or were not able to be proved to be, to kill their victims, autopsies revealed a degree of physical trauma resulting logically in death.

Because incidents involved multiple perpetrators, legal defenses were typically based on technicalities concerning the cause of death (i.e., identifying which wound or blow inflicted by which assailant was fatal). A witness in the Hillsborough case was able to identify one defendant who had stabbed the victim fifteen times in the head and chest in quick succession. Each of the defendants in the Hyatt/Jackson case charged the other with having persuaded him or her with sex and drugs.

TABLE 3.16

Information from Newspaper and Magazine Articles About Groups of Perpetrators in Premeditated Attacks in Which the Victim Died

	Location, Victim's Name, and Victim's Age					
	San Francisco (O'Connell, 42)	Toronto (Zeller, 40)	Tucson (Heakin, 21)	Bangor, ME (Howard, 23)	San Francisco (Hillsborough, 33)	Belton, TX (Hyatt/Jackson, 38, 30)
Setting	street in gay neighborhood	cruising in park	outside of gay bar	city street frequented by gay men	in front of victim's house	in victims' home
Time	7/84 Sun 9pm	6/85 Sat 1am	6/76 Sun 1am	7/84 Sat 9pm	6/87 Wed 1am	1/30/79
Weapon	fists	fists/feet	feet	fists/feet	fist/feet/knife	gun
Cause of death	cranial-cerebral trauma	cranial-cerebral trauma	cranial-cerebral trauma	drowning	15 stab wounds in face/chest	1, gunshot wounds; 1, gunshot + drowning
Number	four	five	four	three	four	three
Ages	19–22	15–18	15–17	16–17	16–20	16–17
Gender	male	male	male	male	male	2 male, 1 female
Race	white	white	white	white	2 Hispanic, 2 white	
Class	working	working	middle	middle	working	

Intox.	yes	yes	yes	no	no	yes
Auto	yes	yes	yes	yes	yes	yes
Before attack	"Let's go to San Francisco to beat up some faggots."	"Let's get money from a queer; let's beat up a fag."	Decided to go to gay bars "to hassle some queers."	Said were seeking revenge for prior "sexual comment."	Followed victim home after verbal altercation at restaurant.	Boy testified girl persuaded him; girl testified boys frightened her into helping them. Attack was planned.
After attack	Laughed, bragged; more attacks same night; regrouped at drive-in restaurant.	Laughed, bragged; went home. Were afraid when they learned victim died.		Went to party; laughed, bragged. Ditched car; one gave up, two tried to leave town.	Had car repainted next day; resumed work schedule and recreational activities.	Drove to and left both bodies in reservoir.
Sentence	15 yrs-life; 1 acquitted	9 yrs each	probation til 21 yrs old	indeterminate til 21 yrs old	1, 10 yrs murder; 1, immunity; 1, convicted assault	1 2x15 yrs; 1, 2x40 yrs; 1,15 yrs
Record	1, juvenile record			1, underage drinking; 1, minor burglary	disturbing peace (anti-gay)	

In none of the cases were histories of psychological problems reported for defendants; and of the few who had arrest records, the offenses were considered minor and were dismissed as having no bearing on the cases by judges.

Typical of the defenses for middle-class perpetrators was the use of character witnesses to provide anecdotal evidence of "good family backgrounds," exemplary behavior in school, and participation in organized athletics. The purpose of such defenses, which proved to be successful in the Howard and Heakin cases, is to soften sentencing. In both cases, judges recognized the merit of such evidence. In addition to character references, the defense in the Zeller case produced testimony by psychological experts who said that social problems typically experienced by teenage males, such as alcohol abuse, peer pressure, and male bonding, but not hatred and/or disapproval of homosexuality, were causal.

In this and tables 3.17 and 3.18, sentencing for lower- and working-class youth appears more severe than for middle-class defendants. The working-class defendants in the Zeller case, for example, were less successful in using the character witness defense than were the middle-class defendants in the Heakin and Howard cases. Because the circumstances of the various cases, the presiding judges, and the laws and customs of the municipalities within which the incidents occurred vary, the observation that sentencing reflects class bias can only suggest and not accurately reflect general practices. However, news commentators have observed similar patterns of discrimination. After criticizing the apparently light sentences of probation in the Heakin case as "not even a tap on the wrist" and noting that "tougher sentences have been passed on other youngsters for acts of vandalism in which no one was physically injured," an editorial in the *Arizona Daily Star* recalled a similar case from the previous year in which two teenagers from a "poverty-ridden" area of the city were given prison sentences of sixty years to life and thirty to fifty years "for killing a man they said had made sexual advances toward them."[85]

Pairs of Perpetrators. Table 3.17 shows those incidents in which victims were killed by pairs of perpetrators.[86] The victim killed by Smith/Barr was lesbian[87]; victims in all other incidents were male. All victims were alone. With the exception of Chesher and Robinson, who were accomplices with Smith[88] and Johnson,[89] respectively, all perpetrators were male; all were white.

The following similarities with information from table 3.16 can be observed: range of perpetrators' ages, consumption of alcohol, and social-peer context preceding and/or following attacks; no reported histories of psychological or emotional problems, except Johnson, who had discipline and peer-acceptance difficulties in high school; few (only three of ten perpetrators had criminal records, but the criminal records that did exist were of a more serious nature than those in table 3.16. Differences are the following: more settings in victims' personal, private domains rather than in public lesbian/gay areas; more frequent use of weapons and more extreme mutilation of body; greater frequency of robbery, especially as primary motive; more perpetrators from lower class; and prior relationships with victims in all but the Kerr/Elben incident.[90] Also, unlike the perpetrators listed in table 3.16, Smith, Moore/Messmer,[91] and Johnson, although heterosexually identified and currently involved in affectional relationships with women, were self-employed hustlers.[92] Although their victims were former customers, sexual activity preceded only the murder by Chesher/Smith. (See appendix D for a discussion of the relationship of the occupation of hustling to anti-gay violence.)

Legal defenses did not rely on character witnesses; and sentencing was severe. Only the middle-class perpetrator was acquitted. Even though he admitted that he was the one to have wielded the sledgehammer in the incident and returned later to make sure the victim was dead, he was found not guilty by a jury on the basis of his testimony that he was defending himself from a sexual advance. In this latter case, as in those involving multiple perpetrators in table 3.16, the defense was built around the conflicting evidence and testimony showing which blow by which perpetrator was fatal.

Lone Perpetrators. Table 3.18 shows those incidents in which victims were killed by a single perpetrator. All perpetrators were male. In the Scott incident,[93] a lesbian was killed; the victims in the other incidents were male. In the White,[94] Kluke,[95] and Van Hook[96] incidents the victims were alone; Tyack[97] killed a gay couple; in the presence of his ex-wife, Scott murdered her current lover; and Crumpley,[98] shooting into groups of gay men, killed two and wounded six.

The following differences with tables 3.16 and 3.17 can be noted: time not restricted to weekends, summer, or night; gun as common choice of weapon; consistently older ages of perpetrators, with a range from twenty-two to forty-two; more middle-class backbgrounds; less consumption of alcohol; no reported criminal records; diverse settings, equally divided among public lesbian/gay areas, victims' home or car, and even a victim's workplace; decision and plan for attack not made in social-peer context immediately prior to incident; intention to kill and knowledge of death positively established in all, not some, of cases. The

TABLE 3.17

Information from Newspaper and Magazine Articles About Pairs of Perpetrators in Premeditated Attacks in Which the Victim Died

	Location and Perpetrators' Names				
	Cincinnati (Chesher/Smith)	Cincinnati (Moore/Messmer)	Winston-Salem (Johnson/Robinson)	Kalamazoo (Kerr/Elben)	Chicago (Smith/Barr)
Setting	victim's apartment	victim's car	victim's apartment	isolated area	alley
Time	9/84 Fri night	7/86 Sat 2am	1/84 night	5/85 Sat 1am	11/6/75 night
Weapons	rope	fists/crowbar/rock/tire-iron	rope/knife	fist/feet/sledge-hammer	fists
Cause of death	strangulation and robbery	bludgeoning of head, robbery	throat slashed and robbery	bludgeoning of body	bludgeoning of body
Ages		21, 22	19, 14	17, 19	over 21
Gender	male, female	male	male, female	male	male
Race	white	white	white	white	
Class	lower	lower	lower, working	middle	middle
Intox.	Yes	Yes	Yes	Yes	

Auto	Yes	No	Yes	No	
Before attack	Phoned victim; arranged to meet for drink; went to victim's apartment for sex.	Decided to "hustle a queer and get enough money for more dope."	Went to get liquor from victim; purpose changed; boy to girl, "I hope you've got nerve; I'm doing something that really counts."	Were at party, drinking alcohol; on way to another party when they encountered victim.	Previously verbally harassed, beat, and hospitalized victim who was former wife of one perpetrator.
After attack	Told friend they "messed up a queer;" returned to apartment to rob more.	Got more dope; "we told everybody who asked about blood on the car" that "we robbed a nigger, beat him up."	More attacks by Johnson in following months; Robinson confessed to police and blamed Johnson six months later.	Went to party; bragged; returned to make sure victim dead.	Arrested after attack near alley in which body was found.
Sentence	both, 5–15 yrs	1, 22–52 yrs; 1, life	1, life + 50 yrs; 1, immunity	1, acquitted	
Record	1, bad checks	1, auto theft	1, manslaughter		

TABLE 3.18

Information from Newspaper and Magazine Articles About Single Perpetrators in Premeditated Attacks in Which the Victim Died

			Location and Name of Perpetrator			
	San Francisco (White)	Bakersfield[a] (Tyack)	Champaign[b] (Scott)	Waterloo[c] (Kluke)	New York (Crumpley)	Cincinnati (Van Hook)
Setting	victim's office/city hall	rural road in car	victim's apartment	cruising in park	outside of gay bar	victim's apartment
Time	11/78 Mon 11am	8/3/81	1976	12/21/84 2am	11/80 Wed 10pm	2/85 Night
Weapons	gun	gun	gun	gun	gun	hands
Cause of Death	gunshot wounds	gunshot wounds	gunshot wounds	gunshot wounds	gunshot wounds	strangulation
Age	32	42	40	22	39	
Race	white	white	white	white	black	white
Class	middle	upper-middle		working	middle	working
Intox.	No	No		Yes	No	No

	Yes	Yes	No	No	Yes	No
Auto	Yes	Yes	No	No	Yes	No
Before attack	Told his aide he wanted to see both Mayor Moscone and Supervisor Milk; after killing Mayor, reloaded gun, went to Milk's office, asked to speak with him.	Speaking of his gay neighbors, said, "I don't like those people. If they give me any reason, I'll kill them."	Blamed ex-wife's lover for marriage break-up; bought gun; went to her apartment; shot her while ex-wife was present.	Reconned park; told police he went to park to "scare" homosexuals; "tired of them following and harassing me."	Stole gun. "I thought I'd go to Atlantic City, and if [I did] I thought I'd better get those homos now." Drove to gay neighborhood.	"My method was to lure a homosexual to a place where I could rob the person. I lured him to have sex with me." "I intended to break his neck."
After attack	Phoned wife; met her at church to pray; walked to police station.	Phoned police, "I killed the two gay guys next door."	Reported to police by ex-wife who witnessed shooting.	"Made it look like 2 queers had had a fight."	Drove to a church. At arrest, "How many homos did I get?"	Friend gave money; went south; continued to hustle gay men.
Sntnce	7 yrs, 8 mos	acquitted	14–25 yrs	life		death

[a] Bakersfield, California.
[b] Champaign, Illinois.
[c] Waterloo, Ontario.

following similarities with tables 3.16 and 3.17 can be noted: racial identities of perpetrators predominantly white; more severe sentences for working-class than for middle-class defendants, with acquittal for Tyack, who had actually confessed to the killings. As in table 3.16, the primary motive in these incidents is not robbery, with the exception of Van Hook; and as in table 3.17, perpetrators knew their victims personally in four of the five incidents. The reasons for the perpetrators' attacks overlap somewhat those provided in tables 3.16 and 3.17, but the adventure, enjoyment, and bragging characteristic of table 3.16 and the robbery motive prevalent in table 3.17 are, with the exception of Van Hook, replaced with a felt and expressed need to murder a particular lesbian or gay man or gay men generically because they were perceived by the perpetrators to threaten his social position or security. For three perpetrators this threat was perceived as posed by particular individuals. For example, White saw his failure as and obstacle to regaining his position as city supervisor directly related to the victim's political activities as a gay supervisor; Tyack disliked and sought to prevent the invasion of gays into his neighborhood; and Scott held his ex-wife's lover responsible for the dissolution of his marriage.[99] Crumpley and Kluke, on the other hand, expressed fear and disapproval of gay men generally and attempted to stop what they perceived as the intrusion into their lives of evil represented by gay men as a group. Unlike the perpetrators in tables 3.16 and 3.17, all of these assailants articulately justified and explained their activities to law enforcement and/or court personnel. White, Tyack, and Scott, making no attempt to conceal their activities, initiated contact and cooperated with the police. Kluke and Van Hook did plan and act to avoid arrest, but explained and detailed their activities when apprehended. Crumpley was easily found after the shootings and testified "eloquently and at length" on his own behalf in court.[100]

The defense attorneys for White, Tyack, and Crumpley presented their middle-class backgrounds, values, and occupations—White as a former fireman, policeman, and city supervisor; Tyack as a business owner and popular, respected community figure; and Crumpley as a former transit policeman, religious person, father, and the son of a minister. Although White killed both nongay Mayor Moscone and gay supervisor Harvey Milk, the defense chose to emphasize the gay identity of Milk in an effort to garner sympathy for the defendant from the nongay/lesbian jury. In its opening statement, after citing White's "good" record of civic responsibility, the defense presented the key to its case: "Good people, fine people, with fine backgrounds, simply don't kill people in cold blood. . . . Dan White came from a vastly different lifestyle than Harvey Milk. Harvey Milk was a homosexual leader. . . ."

Never refuting the fact that the defendant had killed both the mayor and supervisor, the defense portrayed White as an upright citizen, the "voice for the family," who protected himself, his family, and his city from forces that were changing the "traditional values of family and home."[101] Although the information about the defendants presented by their attorneys may be less than accurate, judges and juries are often sympathetic to the constructed image.[102]

Similar both to information gathered by Weissman in his interviews with teenage perpetrators and to reports about the perpetrators in the Zeller incident is the apparent lack of personal hatred for lesbians and gay men as a primary reason for the attacks by White and Crumpley. Prior to their assaults both perpetrators had demonstrated concern for and interest in the causes of lesbians and gay.[103] Crumpley's attack appears to have been provoked by confusion developed during his effort to understand gay men.[104] White's was predicated not specifically on his victim's having been gay or his hatred of this victim's gayness as much as on (1) Milk's having voted for a measure that affected White's electoral district and against which White wanted him to vote, and (2) Milk's successful opposition to the reappointment of White to the board of supervisors.[105] His shooting and killing Milk demonstrated not so much his adversity to or his hatred and disapproval of the individual's lifestyle or sexual/affectional orientation, but his loyalty to his source of strong support, downtown businessmen, and the police. They wanted him in office, pressured him to regain his seat, and would have, at the least, been disappointed and, more likely, have deserted him if he failed. Having been financed by downtown businessmen who needed his support as city supervisor for their development plans, having allied himself with the conservative policemen's association that needed his support to oppose pending legislation for affirmative action in the police department, having turned his attention from and lost the support of his electoral district, and having had his request for reappointment finally turned down by Mayor Moscone, White's killing of Milk can be more accurately understood as an action *for* his allies rather than as an action *against* an individual whom he hated because he was gay.[106] White killed Milk not because he was gay, but because he was the obstacle to his regaining his position. Milk was killed because he was a powerful, gay politician,[107] not because he was simply a gay politician. That Milk was gay or that his gay politics were unlike White's politics was not enough to merit White's murdering him; that Milk's politics were strong enough to prevent White's exercise of political power was reason to kill. Crumpley too did not kill gay men only because they were gay, but because he thought they had the power to intrude into and affect his life.

Although none of the perpetrators had reported histories of psychological or emotional problems, the defense for White claimed a history of manic depression and presented testimony from psychological experts supporting the defendant's mental illness. However, the psychiatrists who examined White when he entered state prison after sentencing decided against prescribing therapy because he had "no apparent signs of mental disorder."[108] Crumpley "successfully defended himself by saying that gay men who cruised him made him mad"[109] and was found not responsible by reason of mental defect or disease. In the Kluke case, as in the Howard case (table 3.16) and the Kerr/Elben case (table 3.17), the defendant argued that his attack of the victim was a violent response to and defense against a sexual advance by the victim. Such a defense has been used by several other perpetrators charged with murdering gay men. It is based on the legal principles of self-defense and/or temporary insanity, that is, the perpetrator defended himself from a sexual assault by the victim and/or he is absolved of responsibility because the sexual assault by the victim triggered a violent psychotic reaction by the perpetrator over which he had no control. Psychological defenses are most often used in an effort to explain the perpetrator's violent behavior as temporary and atypical, rather than as symptomatic of a psychological or personality disorder. Although defendants in other cases of anti-gay/lesbian violence do have reported histories of such disorders,[110] they are few and tend to be the exceptions. The same can be said for perpetrators with criminal records: although some have them,[111] they are not characteristic of perpetrators as a group (36 percent, or eight of twenty-two cases, in tables 3.15–3.18).

CONCLUSION

Tables 3.1–3.14; appendix tables B. 10–B.18: Findings from Comstock's Survey. Comparison of findings from my survey with national crime statistics for the general population show that the percentage of anti-gay/lesbian assailants who are strangers to their victims is 10 percent greater than the percentage of assailants who are strangers in all personal violent crimes (66 percent lesbian/gay, 56 percent general). Among male victims, the percentage is greater in incidents involving gay men by only 2 percent (65 percent, gay men; 63 percent, all men), but among female victims, it is greater by 23 percent in incidents involving lesbians (66 percent, lesbian victims; 43 percent, all women).[112]

Among the general population, 87 percent of the perpetrators of crimes of violence are male, compared to 94 percent for anti-gay/lesbian violence.[113]

Among the general population, 29 percent of the perpetrators are under twenty-two years of age, compared to 46 percent for anti-gay/lesbian violence.[114]

Percentages for the racial identities of perpetrators are similar (67 percent white for anti-gay/lesbian perpetrators, 69 percent white for all crimes of violence).[115] For both white lesbian/gay victims and white victims in general, the percentages of white perpetrators are similar (71 percent, lesbian/gay; 79 percent, all crimes). Among victims of color, however, lesbian/gay victims, compared to crime victims in general, are attacked by a greater percentage of white perpetrators than perpetrators of color (54 percent, lesbian/gay; 17 percent, all crimes).[116]

Perpetrators of all crimes of violence more frequently attack lone victims than do perpetrators of anti-gay/lesbian violence (87 percent, all crimes; 53 percent, lesbian/gay) and less frequently attack victims who are in pairs and in groups of three or more (10 percent pairs and 3 percent groups, for all crimes; 28 percent pairs and 18 percent groups, lesbian/gay).[117]

For all crimes of violence perpetrators are more frequently alone than are perpetrators of anti-gay/lesbian violence (73 percent, all; 52 percent, lesbian/gay). Also, anti-gay/lesbian perpetrators attack in groups of four or more with greater frequency than perpetrators of all crimes of violence (20 percent lesbian/gay; 5 percent, all).[118]

Perpetrators of violent crimes in general use weapons with slightly more frequency than do anti-gay/lesbian perpetrators (34 percent, all; 27 percent, lesbian/gay).[119]

Comparisons with national crime statistics about perpetrators of all violent crimes show, therefore, that perpetrators of anti-gay/lesbian violence tend to be younger. A greater percentage is male and unknown to their victims. Differences in racial identities can be detected only as regards victims of color; a greater percentage of lesbians and gay men of color experience victimization by white perpetrators than do victims of color in general. Perpetrators of anti-gay/lesbian violence are less likely than perpetrators in general to attack lone victims and are more likely to attack in groups. Perpetrators of violent crimes in general and perpetrators of anti-gay/lesbian violence use weapons with common frequency.

Tables 3.15–3.18, Findings from Reports in the Newsmedia. Perhaps even more striking than the paucity of criminal records and histories of psychological disorders among perpetrators are the observations by psychiatric and law enforcement professionals that assailants do not typically exhibit what are customarily thought of as criminal attitudes and behaviors. Many conform to or are models of middle-class respectability.[120] The exceptions in tables 3.15–3.18 are those who are both lower/ working class and primarily motivated by robbery; of the twenty-two incidents recorded in the tables, there are five such cases. Of the remaining seventeen incidents, ten, or over one half, involve perpetrators for whom the assault under discussion is their only serious involvement in criminal activity. The tendency of their defenses to minimize the danger done by the perpetrator and to blame the victim by discrediting him or her on the basis of the victims' sexual identity, and the tendency of judges and/or juries to recognize the merit of such defenses by acquitting or lightly sentencing the defendants, suggest that even this involvement is not regarded with the same seriousness as is criminal activity in general. In many of the trials evidence was produced to show that perpetrators are "noncriminal," "average" kinds of people and that their actions are neither serious nor unusual.

In the Howard case (table 3.16), the judge's decision to try the perpetrators as juveniles instead of adults and to release them into the custody of their parents during the legal proceedings was based on his determination that "they were ordinary kids from ordinary backgrounds." The boys' families were in the mainstream of the city's social life. The defenses for all three boys were based on "unsolicited character references from people who said the boys simply would not harm another human being." Staff members at the Main Youth Center, to which the boys were sentenced, considered them "lightweights" and "less hardened than most of their bunkmates." One counselor is quoted as saying, "These kids, as far as I can see, are atypical from our average kid [at the Center]. They're social beings. Most of the kids we see are anti-social." Unlike the other residents who had committed their crimes as a means of rebelling against society, the slayers of Charlie Howard committed theirs as a way of being accepted by it. The counselor suggested that "throwing a known homosexual off the bridge is something that would be a feather in their cap among kids at Bangor High [School]."[121]

In the Heakin case (table 3.16), the judge commended the parents for raising the defendants as "worthwhile citizens in the community." He noted that the boys were model athletes, good students, not dangerous to the safety of the community, active in organizations, living at home, and not drug users. In sentencing them to probation he claimed that the "four youths and their parents have been punished enough,"[122] apparently by the publicity and strain of the trial.

An editorial in the *Washington Post* criticized the judge in the Washington incident (table 3.15) for minimizing the seriousness of the assaults and thinking "it was nothing more than 'boys will be boys' and that they would naturally be provoked by a homosexual."[123]

That perpetrators are often "average boys exhibiting typical behavior" is illustrated perhaps most convincingly in the Zeller case (table 3.16).[124] The arresting officer's impression of the boys was: "If you went to [a shopping mall] and picked up any group of young males about the same age as these boys—that is what they were like. Average."[125] A mother, whose son knew the boys but was not with them the night of the assault, said, "I just thank God my son happened not to be there that night. . . . He is a good boy, but it could be him going to jail, too. It could be anyone's son."[126] Two factors seem to determine one's participation in many examples of anti-gay/lesbian violence: one of these is being an adolescent male; the other is being in the company of other adolescent males. In other words, expected or acceptable behavior for an adolescent male who socializes with other adolescent males is physically attacking lesbians and gay men. This is not a claim that all adolescent males in peer groups are perpetrators of anti-gay/lesbian violence; rather, it is an observation that the social behavior of a particular age-and-gender group, unlike that of any other group, includes attacking lesbians and gay men. A clinical psychiatrist testifying for the defense in the Zeller case stated that the young mens' "behavior was not uncharacteristic. The same action would have been perpetrated by any number of young men under similar conditions" (i.e., a group of boys socializing with each other and with nothing else to do).[127] To understand the reasons or causes for anti-gay/lesbian violence, therefore, requires not an analysis of individually specific behavior, but of group-specific behavior. Such analysis will occur in chapter 4.

Another subject for analysis in chapter 4 will be the role of perpetrators' attitudes and feelings. If language can be said to reflect feelings and attitudes, the findings in table 3.14 may reinforce data showing the absence of personally felt or expressed dislike and disapproval of lesbians and gay men. Not only do two thirds of the victims in my survey not report any language used by perpetrators in assaults against them, but the language that is reported lacks the edge of disapproval sharpened by references to God, religion, or the Bible that are common in incidents of verbal harassment not involving physical violence (39 percent, verbal harassment; 4 percent, physical violence). Furthermore, empirical studies show that those with personal prejudice against homosexuality tend to be older than the twenty-one-year-and-under group of perpetrators that emerges from my survey.[128] The significantly greater use of language in anti-lesbian violence correlates with the older age of anti-lesbian perpetrators and suggests that dislike and disapproval are more deeply felt and more commonly expressed toward lesbians than toward gay men.

Testimony by several people in the Zeller trial claims that the boys did not harbor feeling of dislike or disapproval of lesbians and gay men. In his interviews with former gay-bashers, Weissman also found that the unifying factor among the group of perpetrators was not a shared or similar attitude toward homosexuals, but a shared and similar interest in adventure, excitement, and relief of boredom. In an out-of-court interview the defense attorney in the Zeller trial observes that queer-bashing is common practice in the area not only for the defendants, but in general for teenage boys: "[They] go down to the park, roll the queers down the hill and have a good laugh and so on. It's a phenomenon." [129] The purpose would appear to be recreational rather than to express hatred. Among adult perpetrators, particularly White in table 3.18, evidence of personal hatred or feelings of dislike for their victims is also lacking; rather, their actions appear to conform to social sanctions against lesbians and gay men. Both the defense's arguments and the jury's verdict in White's trial recognized that the motive rested not in the defendant's personal feelings for the victim but in his adherence and loyalty to the police, traditional values, and the social order. Among robbers who prey on lesbians and gay men, also, the victims' vulnerability and lack of resource to police protection are the reasons for targeting their victims, not hatred for lesbians and gay men individually or in general. The marginal social position of the victims, not the perpetrators' personal feelings for them, is what makes lesbians and gay men the likely prey of robbers.

In summary, then, data about incidents reported in newspapers and magazines suggest that the primary reason for adolescent attacks on lesbians and gay men is recreational, and such activity is encouraged or permitted by social sanctions against homosexuality. The primary reason for adult perpetrators' attacks is to defend one's place in a social order that disapproves of homosexuality; and robbers attack lesbians and gay men because they are unprotected and considered unimportant in society. The analysis of perpetrators' reasons in chapter 4 will, therefore be sociological, and not focus on the perpetrators' personal, psychological characteristics.

CHAPTER FOUR

Understanding Anti-Gay/Lesbian Violence

In addition to showing that perpetrators represent the range of socioeconomic classes, data gathered from newsmedia coverage and interviews with assailants indicate that histories of psychological problems and criminal activity are scarce. Perpetrators appear to be, for the most part, quite ordinary or average young men within all classes and racial groups. The predominant characteristics, verified by findings from my survey and the newsmedia, are age and gender, under twenty-two years and male. I turn, therefore, to examine the role and position of adolescent males within the social order and choose a theoretical framework that is based on social roles rather than on psychodynamics or class structure. Sheila Collins' conceptualization of the social order in terms of the patriarchal family's assignment of power and status is used not only because it is based on the arrangement and interaction of social roles but also because it permits the formulation of hypotheses to predict relationships between social roles and violence. Collins' focus on patriarchy, a nearly universal organizing principle within social orders worldwide, has the additional appeal of providing an analysis of anti-gay/lesbian violence that may in time be applied to other findings.[1]

Although capitalism is discussed, it must at this time serve more as a case study than as the definitive example of the way in which patriarchy causes or contributes to anti-gay/lesbian violence. Although an interesting and worthwhile project would be to compare such violence as it may occur not only in various capitalistic countries but under various forms of patriarchal socialism, resources are not currently available to do so.

Data have not been gathered systematically elsewhere. Incidents in the Soviet Union, Cuba, South Africa, New Zealand, The Netherlands, Great Britain, and Iran have been reported, but these anecdotal accounts are insufficient in number and detail to provide a basis for comparison.[2]

PATRIARCHY

Patriarchy is the "manifestation and institutionalization of male dominance over women and children in the family and the extension of male dominance over women in society in general."[3] The patriarchal family that prevailed in Western European and Colonial American civilization was structured as follows: The oldest man or patriarch had legal authority over the other members. His wife was legally dependent on him and supervised the reproduction of his family and the development of the younger generation according to his guidelines. Boys grew up to inherit the patrimony, with the oldest inheriting the most. Holding the lowest rank within the family were the girls, who served their father and brothers until the father transferred each to the house of another patriarch, her husband. Slaves and servants were owned and controlled by the father/husband, but other family members were served by them and were delegated responsibility for their supervision.[4] In her essay "The Familial Economy of God," Sheila D. Collins calls these roles of the archetypical family Father, Wife, Brother, and Daughter. She avoids the usual couplings of brother/sister, son/daughter, mother/father, and husband/wife "to indicate the inequality in terms of power, status and rewards between members of the same generation."[5] She uses the term *Alien* for slave or servant to describe outsider status and absence of power in relation to any of the traditional familial roles.[6]

During the interfacing of patriarchy and industrial capitalism in the nineteenth century, the family unit underwent some significant changes itself but was also instrumental in shaping the emerging economy. Whereas individual family units had been the locus of economic activity before the rise of industrial capitalism, capitalism removed economic production from the household but retained the household's ordering of power. The internal dynamics or needs of industrial capitalism made for its convenient marriage with patriarchy. Capitalism is based on inequalities between people (i.e., those who produce and those who own the means of production).[7] The unequal status and power of members within the patriarchal family satisfied capitalism's requirement that all parties accept inequalities between people. To fuel competition, the driving dynamic of capitalism, the new economic system could rely on the patriarchal family's reverence for private property and suspicion of those outside the family. Capitalism was able to take people who had "internalized" or been socialized into patriarchal family roles and "move them into the workforce, out of the workforce and around inside it according to established patriarchal family role patterns."[8] No longer made up of many building blocks of productive family units, the economy was organized as one big patriarchal family.

Collins charts the transplant of family roles as follows: the Fathers became the "class of ruling men who own and [control] the resources and tools upon which all productivity is based." Those who manage and maintain the workforce are to this class of ruling men as Wife to Father. The patrimony that was formerly passed from Father to sons is trans-formed under capitalism "into access to the top of the hierarchy—access which is no longer inherited but must be competed for by the younger generation of men." These Brothers are "all those primarily white men who are employed in heavy industry, small business and management and who still dream of making it to the top of their particular ladder." The "illusion of access to the Father's prerogative" is sustained by the occasional example of outstanding success, achievement, or advance-ment and by programmatic pay increases, promotions, and other re-wards that accrue to "good" workers. Daughters are "those whose unpaid, underpaid or unrecognized labor" is managed by Wives and "serves the interest of the societal Fathers or is used to promote the Brothers' aspirations to the Father's role." They are primarily house-wives, immigrants, adolescents, poor people, and minorities employed as farmworkers, maintenance workers, waitresses, clerical help, and unskilled and temporary labor. These positions offer little status, chance for advancement, or job security; the benefits, if any, are few, and wages are low, frequently without built-in increases. Aliens are those whose sexual orientation, age, or racial, ethnic, or national identity bar them permanently or temporarily from full-time employment or competition within the familial economy. Daughters are compelled to accept and guard their limited job status because this waiting pool of unemployed people is used by the Wives to threaten and replace them should they complain or rebel.[9] (See table 4.1 for a schematic presentation of the transfer of patriarchal roles from the household to the capitalist econ-omy.)

The gender-specificity of some family roles was altered in the indus-trial economy. For example, the Wifely role fell to men. Capitalism required of this position an independence, mobility, and potential access to power that was inconsistent with a patriarchal view of women. Its successful operation, especially in advanced stages of capitalism, re-quired a variety, complexity, and geographical diversity of Wifely duties

TABLE 4.1

Schematic Rendering of Collins' Model Showing the Transfer of Patriarchal Roles from Household to Capitalist Economy

Role	Patriarchal Household			Patriarchal Capitalism		
	Age	Gender	Status/Role	Age	Gender	Status/Role
Father	older	male	Owns, rules, controls; manages older Brothers and some Aliens	older	male	Owns, rules, controls; manages Wives; pays Wives, Brothers, Daughters
Wife	older	female	Gives birth to and raises Brothers and Daughters for Fathers; manages some Aliens	older	male	Manages Brothers and Daughters for Fathers; uses Aliens as surplus labor and standard of deviance
Brother	younger	male	Obeys Father's Wife; works for Father; becomes a Father and takes own Wife	all ages	male	Managed by Wives; works for and paid by Fathers; few may become Wives or Fathers
Daughter	younger	female	Obeys Father's Wife; helps Wife and works for Father; becomes Wife to another Father	all ages	Mostly female; poor and nonwhite men	Managed by Wives; works for Fathers; serves/subordinate to Brother; few male Daughters may become Brothers
Alien	all ages	foreign, ethnic, or racial males and females	Obeys and works for Father and Wife; serves all family members	all ages	Mostly nonwhite females; lesbians and gay men; segregated racial and ethnic groups	Unemployed; temporary cheap, surplus pool of labor; may be used to replace recalcitrant Daughters; standard of deviance

and a greater number of Wives per Father relative to the in-house responsibilities of the housewife and the one-to-one marital arrangement of the family. In addition, a Wife had the possibility of becoming a Father, and a Brother had the possibility of becoming a Wife.[10] The gender exclusivity of the Brother and Father roles was preserved by filling the Wifely role with men. Consequently, in the capitalist economy the Daughter role expanded to include nearly all women. Marginalized or Alien men could be and were incorporated into the Daughter role, also; immigrants, for example, typically have taken low-paying, undesirable work, with the men sometimes able to move up the ladder into the role of the Brother.[11] When familial roles were adjusted to meet the requirements of the new economy, the adjustments favored the economic advantage of men. In other words, the patriarchal legacy of male dominance prevailed, even if the precise characteristics of the familial roles did not.

A person's role at home in her or his immediate family may be different from her or his role in the workplace; yet both roles are modeled, named, and assigned according to the ordering of roles within the traditional patriarchal family. A Father at home, for example, may be a Wife, Brother, or Daughter on the job. Or the Wife of a particular man at home may play the role of Daughter as a clerical worker in the out-of-home workplace. Furthermore, familial roles in the out-of-home workplace are not limited to individuals. Entire occupations can be understood as Wifely, Brotherly, or Daughterlike; the police, for example, may be seen as Wives who defend the status quo or keep order for the business interests of the Fathers.[12]

The exclusive and enduring power and privilege that adult men have, however, regardless of their socioeconomic status, is to own a wife.[13] In her novel *Sula,* Toni Morrison captures this patriarchal privilege or option that any man has.[14] Morrison writes of a young black man, Jude, who "wasn't really aiming to get married" but "had brought the subject up first on the day word got out that the town was building a new road" and would be hiring. Jude is described as one who "longed more than anybody else" to be hired, to move from his current job as a waiter to "real work."

He wanted to swing the pick or kneel down with the string or shovel gravel. His arms ached for something heavier than trays, for something dirtier than peelings; his feet wanted the heavy work shoes, not the thin-soled black shoes that the hotel required. More than anything he wanted the camaraderie of the road men: the lunch buckets, the hollering, the body movement that in the end produced something real, something he could point to. "I built that road," he could say.

"It was while he was full of such dreams" of manly work and accomplishment "that he spoke to Nel about getting married." It is only when he "got the message"—"after he stood in line for six days running and saw the gang boss pick out thin-armed white boys"—that "his determination to take on a man's role . . . made him press Nel about settling down." As chances for the job crumble and his dream explodes, marriage becomes "more attractive."

Whatever his fortune, whatever the cut of his garment, there would always be the hem—the tuck and fold that hid his raveling edges; a someone sweet, industrious and loyal to shore him up. . . . *Without that someone he was a waiter hanging around a kitchen like a woman. With her he was head of a household pinned to an unsatisfactory job out of necessity* [my emphasis].

"In return" for "his conquest," his taking Nel in marriage, Jude understood that he "would shelter her, love her, grow old with her." And Nel understood that she would be for him the solution to or replacement for his defeat in work: her "indifference to his hints about marriage disappeared altogether when she discovered his pain. . . . She actually wanted to help, to soothe," to let him be a Father by being his Wife.

Post–World War II Nuclear Family. More and more during the twentieth century, absent a rural, small-town economy based on household production, individuals no longer needed to remain within the family for economic reasons and were prepared and encouraged to leave for work in industry and to live in urban settings. Families no longer needed to be extended, coherent groups to work the farm or operate the household business. For the developing industrial economy the function of the household became the reproduction and socialization of succeeding generations of workers. And, in time, even the role of socialization and education was supplanted by the increased development, role, and influence of public education and the mass media. Industrial production could, in fact, as shown during World War II, operate efficiently and successfully when the family unit was not intact.[15]

Emerging from World War II as a dominant world power with unprecedented access to foreign natural resources, with controlling influence over international trade, and with a highly developed and developing industrial technology, U.S. business was well positioned not only to become a worldwide patriarchal organization, but to create an unparalleled market economy. The household unit, increasingly severed from its function of economic production and education, was revitalized for a new role—that of consumer in this market.[16]

Equipped with advanced media and information systems and with the cooperation of government agencies, public education, and mainstream religion, business reconstructed and celebrated the household family unit in the form of the postwar "nuclear family"[17] As part of the campaign to establish the supremacy of the patriarchal household, government committees and law enforcement agencies utilized the emergence and greater visibility of lesbian/gay neighborhoods and the publication of Kinsey's data to identify deviance and the cost one paid for it; investigations, exposures, arrests, and the ruining of individuals and their careers were fed to the media. That leaders in many and various realms of human endeavor complied to reaffirm and popularize an ideology of fatherly male rule in the familial household is not an exaggeration. For example, in his study of male gender-role socialization, Joseph H. Pleck reports that after World War II, in response to "general cultural concerns about the male role," the dominant school of thought to emerge within the discipline of psychology viewed traditional gender roles not only as desirable, but as necessary for good psychological development because of an inner psychological need for them. He asserts that the peaking of these concerns and the acceptance of this view was not a historical coincidence. In the 1950s, many men were rendered less than adequate providers after returning from World War II to find (1) women who had acquired skills in traditionally male jobs and independence from having to live with men, (2) a job market transformed by wartime technologies and demanding skills they did not have, and (3) postwar inflation. During this period of "crisis in the male role," the psychological discipline sought to rescue it with a school of thought that "rose to the zenith of its influence; . . . traditional roles, even if no longer required by social convention or law, came to be widely perceived as necessary for normal psychological development."[18]

Whereas the family unit in the early twentieth century served as a "protector" (as little islands of safety and security against the impersonal world of factory and city, i.e., as "the heart of a heartless world"[19]), the post–World War II family was cast in the role of "provider." The measure of an independent, self-sufficient family, therefore, was in the amount of goods it provided for its members; and the authority and responsibility for providing the financial means with which the household prospered was assigned to the male head. The traditional function of the household unit as biological reproducer was also encouraged; and in the form of the postwar "baby boom" consumers were produced for the market as workers had been for the factories in the late nineteenth and early twentieth centuries. Normative and compulsory heterosexuality was necessary to the enterprise.[20]

LOCATING ADOLESCENTS IN COLLINS' MODEL

The reshaping and changing of the household family from its function during the eighteenth and nineteenth centuries to that of the twentieth eventually removed teenagers from direct participation in economic production. The shift of teenagers from full participation in household production to parental dependence and preparation for adulthood has been consistent with economic and industrial developments. Teenagers were no longer considered useful to any great extent in industry. Several reasons are apparent:

1. In the shift from agrarian to industrial economy, the need to produce children to perform household duties was removed; and, subsequently, in the shift from child to adult labor in the factories children were no longer used or allowed to supplement family incomes.
2. Scientific and technical advances have enabled industry to increase production without engaging a significantly greater proportion of the population.
3. With the replacement of physical by indirect and mental labor, knowledge has become the key productive force.
4. Scientific advances that have increased life expectancy among the general population and the tendency toward increased production by a small, highly-trained labor force have resulted in reserving the older years as a desired and deserved goal of leisure-time activity and rest, and the younger years as a time of preparation and training for adulthood.[21]

Although these changes appear to be inevitable for advanced industry under any economic system, capitalism has relied on traditional patriarchal assignment of power and status according to age to create an age-designated group of people who would accept being told they are not ready for marriage and full employment.

Professor of human development and education Mihaly Csikszentmihalyi reminds us that the conception of "adolescence" itself is recent. Less than a century ago, at puberty teenagers customarily took on the role of "full-fledged human beings" as wives, husbands, parents, and workers. Adolescence has subsequently become inserted between childhood and adulthood as a "kind of temporal warehouse or greenhouse in which young people are parked until needed." "In terms of physical and mental vitality, teen-agers are at the top of the arch of life," but feel "that they have been put on hold . . . while their best years drift by." Csikszentmihalyi posits, and others concur, that the teenage years in our society are inherently problematic because "waiting for [social] maturity is often frustrating."[22]

A measure of this frustration is found in data collected through years of research at the University of Chicago by Csikszentmihalyi and associates. In addition to finding that teenagers spend little time with adults and a considerably greater amount with friends and peers, his study shows that they "report being significantly less strong, active, alert, and, especially, less motivated" than adults, including senior citizens. "Almost twice as often as adults they say, 'I wish to be doing something else. " Csikszentmihalyi concludes "that teenagers feel their position to be one of weakness and constraint" because they are not encouraged or allowed to "interact effectively with their environment" or to "use whatever skills or aptitudes they have to meet the opportunities for action in the environment."[23]

Adolescence, as a period during which people are expected to anticipate and look forward to becoming adults, contributes to the driving dynamics of capitalism, competition and upward mobility. Teenagers are taught to believe that by studying hard, getting good grades, and getting enough education they will be successful. Although tracking systems pigeonhole and stigmatize students from an early age and statistics show that educational opportunities are not equally available, education successfully conditions students to believe that they get what they deserve and work for and that they make their future.[24]

In addition, adolescents are a cheap source of labor for low-status, low-paying jobs. Socialized to believe that they do not yet warrant decent wages and challenging positions, high school and college students compete for a limited supply of part-time, temporary work, usually in food service and maintenance. They fill these Daughter-type jobs and expect to leave them for better, full-time, permanent positions upon graduation. This "brush" with boring work inspires wanting and striving for a more rewarding future.

Cast as helpers in the service occupations of the economy, at wages lower and unemployment rates higher than those of any other age group, adolescents are peripheral to the normative world of marriage and the workplace. Adolescence renders teenagers Daughters in the familial economy and near-Aliens to the familial household. Regardless of any hope and assurance that they will be husbands, wives, parents, and gainfully employed, daily reality includes few experiences of those roles and positions. Ready to develop primary and independent affective relationships and to take on occupational challenges, they remain their parents' children, dependents with minimal earning power.

With Csikszentmihalyi, scholars in the field of adolescent development agree that if adults do not recognize that young people need "powerful skills," "worthy challenges," and "adventures involving risks," and if we do not treat them "as fully formed persons who should be responsible for their lives, and who should have access to meaningful experiences," we should not be surprised that they will "learn to enjoy activities that cause harm to others" and themselves. A 300 percent increase in teenage suicides over the past three decades and the same pattern for juvenile "crime, homicide, illegitimate pregnancies, drug use, venereal disease, even psychosomatic complaints" evidence, in Csikszentmihalyi's words, "desperate attempts on the part of young men and women to find challenges suited to their limited skills."[25] One of the young people in his study

characterized most of his favorite activities as "rough sports." The foremost among these is football. . . . He says he likes "mauling people, and hurting 'em so they're afraid to come again." It is important, he says, because "I want others to know about me.". . . If you hurt someone, or shoot an animal in hunting, you know you are somebody. . . . The pain on the face of the adversary or the lifeless carcass are witness to your awful power.[26]

That "they cannot find suitable challenges in their communities" (i.e., that they are "bored") emerges as the most frequently given reason by teenagers for criminal and rebellious behavior.[27]

Most of the so-called crimes committed by teenagers, however, fall into the general category of disobedience, rather than burglary and assault. Kenneth Keniston and the Carnegie Council on Children, in *All Our Children: The American Family Under Pressure,* report:

Although state laws differ . . . offenses commonly cover seven categories of behavior: (1) disobedience of "reasonable" orders of parents or custodians; (2) running away from home; (3) truancy; (4) disobedience of the "reasonable" orders of school authorities; (5) acts which are permissible for adults but are offenses when children commit them, such as possessing alcohol or tobacco, or frequenting pool halls or taverns; (6) sexual immorality, sometimes called leading a "lewd and immoral life," or being a "wayward child"; and (7) acting in a manner injurious to oneself or others. Other forbidden acts include "being in a disreputable place," "associating with bad companions," "keeping late hours," "begging alms," "being found in or about a railroad yard or truck terminal," and "using profane language."[28]

Problem teenagers tend less to be hard criminals and much more to be those who demonstrate certain legal adult behaviors prematurely (e.g., sexual activity, getting pregnant, formulating their own time schedules and associating with certain friends, consuming alcohol). That which makes their behavior problematic is the conflicting rush of teenagers to be adults and the effort of adults to slow down or stop them. Whereas these behaviors are usually unacceptable by prevailing social standards, they nevertheless mirror those of adults.

This information about adolescents in America provides some insight into the activities of teenage perpetrators of anti-gay/lesbian violence. The adventure, recreation, and relief from boredom sought by perpetrators of anti-gay/lesbian violence describe also the interests and needs of adolescents in general. The thrill of scaring and hurting another person expressed by troubled or bored teenagers is likewise descriptive of anti-gay/lesbian perpetrators. The frequency with which anti-gay/lesbian attacks originate in peer group social situations and with which they are motivated by an effort to meet group expectations and participate in group activities is probably not unrelated to the overwhelmingly greater amount of time teenagers spend with peers than with parents and adults. Like rule-breaking teenagers who have been caught for drinking, truancy, premarital sex, or reckless driving, perpetrators of anti-gay/lesbian violence do not typically have criminal records, do not exhibit the traits of the criminal population, and are not anti-social.[29]

Similar to the usual rowdy or rule-breaking teenager in many respects, anti-gay/lesbian violence is noticeably different in two others: people are victimized and often seriously injured or killed; and perpetrators have been known to justify their actions by referring to parental expectations, religious teachers, and social standards. Although the consensus of parental, religious, educational, law enforcement, and justice system authorities is that typical problem behaviors are negative and should be curbed, the same disapproval historically has not been leveled at violent behavioral toward lesbians and gay men.[30] Fortified with a "boys will be boys" rational, permission for anti-gay/lesbian assaults has been granted in the form of: (1) familial, church, and community norms which exclude, disapprove of, and are hostile to lesbians and gay men[31]; (2) the failure or refusal of high school educators to protect lesbians and gay students[32] and/or to teach about the full range of human sexualities[33]; (3) the tendency of the police to respond slowly or not at all to incidents of anti-gay/lesbian violence and/or to release perpetrators and apprehend victims; and (4) the practice of judges and juries to acquit or sentence lightly those who are apprehended for physically harming or killing lesbians and gay men.[34] (See appendixes C, E, and F and discussion of tables 3.15–3.18 in chapter 3.)

Concluding, therefore, that such violence is merely compensation for the frustration, boredom, alienation, and inferiority associated with the social position of teenagers is not sufficient. Not only is there considerable social support for this kind of activity, but from such a conclusion it would follow that those adolescents who are poorest, most underprivileged, and most nonachieving would be the most likely assailants, which the data does not show. Teenage women, who would seem to have less status and power than teenage men, are conspicuously underrepresented among perpetrators, even more so than in statistics for criminal violence in general (see Conclusion, chapter 3). Perpetrators are not only predominantly male and white, but just as likely, or even more likely, to be middle class; doing well in their classes; involved in school and community activities, organizations, and athletics; popular, friendly, and sociable; enrolled in college-preparatory programs in high school or enrolled in college; and/or in the military (see discussion and tables 3.15–3.17).

The socially constructed powerlessness of adolescence is causally related to the perpetration of anti-gay/lesbian violence; but it is a partial cause. Stated otherwise, industrial capitalism's role in creating adolescence as we know it in America does not fully explain the reasons for anti-gay/lesbian violence. A full explanation, and the turning point within it, rests on an examination of the socialization of men.

GENDER-ROLE SOCIALIZATION

Studies of criminal and rebellious behavior by teenagers show that acts of physical violence are committed with greater frequency by young men than by young women.[35] Studies of gender-role socialization[36] show that males in our society are expected and taught to be socially and physically aggressive and sexually dominant,[37] whereas warmth, emotional expressiveness, and such qualities as being sensitive, supporting, nurturing, noncompetitive, and not dominant are considered positive traits for women.[38] Empirical studies also show that the socialization process begins at birth[39] and is firmly in place throughout early childhood.[40]

Considering teenagers' criminal rebellious behaviors in light of gender-role socialization, one should not be surprised to find that they tend to be different for young women and men. Although these activities are considered by adults and social standards to be inappropriate, antisocial, or illegal, they appear to be extensions, exaggerations, or socially premature demonstrations, rather than violations, of the gender-role behavior they have learned.

Teenage females, who are expected to have babies and manage a home someday, tend to limit their "acting-out" behaviors to the female-specific arenas of womb and home, but overstep the the expectations by fulfilling them too soon (i.e., before a certain age and/or without a husband).[41] Following from socialization that encourages aggressive behavior, sexual domination of women, and physically overpowering others in such socially accepted institutions as athletics, the military, and personal self-defense,[42] teenage males may overstep the boundaries of these expectations by destroying and stealing private property, physically attacking others on the street and at school, and/or premarital rape.[43] It is perhaps too obvious, but nonetheless ultimately clarifying, to note that the problem behaviors of females tend toward creating life and breaking household rules, whereas those of males tend toward harming bodies and destroying property. Furthermore, studies show that those behaviors commonly referred to as "rebellious" are more likely for young men to be truancy, reckless driving, speeding, substance abuse, and shoplifting, whereas for young women they are more likely to involve running away from home[44] Not only do males tend to act out more than females in the public arenas of school, market, and street, but they are physically aggressive and often violent. The location of rebellion for teenage women tends to be the home, and the offending action is not in attacking but leaving it.[45]

Teenagers do not vary significantly from other postchildhood age groups in their expressed desirability for gender-role stereotypes. But research shows that teenagers not only mirror the behaviors and follow the standards, but also enforce them. A study involving undergraduate college students finds that "perceived popularity (i.e., liking) [is] . . . indeed endangered when an individual behaves counter to a sex-role stereotype." In three diverse experimental scenarios women were punished "for violating the norm of feminine passive-dependency" and men were punished for violating the norm of "masculine aggression or self-assertion." Although college students are often a population that "tends to be critical of traditional social norms and conventions, [it] nonetheless believes that the existing sex-role stereotypes are desirable." Data from surveys of high school students reveal that, because they tend to be "more concerned than . . . college students with such matters as successful dating, popularity, and dress," they are even more homogeneous in evaluating and criticizing peers according to gender-role standards. Research with early-adolescent males shows that positive "feelings of adequacy" are much more significantly related to "high sex-role identification" than to "academic performance" or "home life." These and other studies suggest, also, that young "men may react more strongly than women to sex-role violations," that penalties for gender-role violations are "most strongly administered by men," and that recognizing and conforming to the cultural stereotype of masculinity is more important for high "self-esteem" in young men than is the counterpart for young women.[46]

That young men would be the most frequent perpetrators of anti-gay/ lesbian violence would seem to follow from these data. Not only are young men expected and encouraged to develop skills in dominance and violence, but they, more than young women, conform to gender-role expectations and are more likely to punish those who do not. Young men are expected to accept the inferiority attached to their age and the superior status assigned to their gender. Academics, athletics, and the military are the socially proffered arenas in which male behavior is to be developed, but adolescent males accurately perceive these activities to be preparatory to and removed from the competitive reality of adult Brothers. And to offset the lack of real control and participation in the social order, adolescent males do not have recourse to the patriarchal household privilege of household Fatherhood as do all adult Brothers.

One consequence or resolution of the contradictory message to be powerful while not having any real power is violence directed by adolescent males against children, women their own age, members of marginalized ethnic and racial groups, and lesbians and gay men. A study commissioned by the president of Rutgers University in New Jersey finds that "fraternities 'demean human dignity' and are hostile toward women, minority-group members and homosexuals."[47] Other studies show that among the adolescent male population, 5–16 percent are perpetrators of sexual assault; seventeen-year-olds have the highest rate. Victims are most often female and male children who are more than five years younger than the perpetrators; the majority are younger than eight years of age.[48] Women from their own age group, but slightly younger, are their next most frequent victims.[49] Concerning anti-black and anti-Semitic assaults, vandalism, and harassment, the New York City Police Department reports that approximately 78 percent of those arrested on bias charges in 1985 were nineteen years old and under, half of them younger than sixteen.[50] According to my survey of lesbians and gay men, nearly half of perpetrators of anti-gay/lesbian violence are twenty-one years of age and younger. Although rates of perpetrators of racial, ethnic, and anti-gay/lesbian violence among the adolescent male population have not been determined conclusively, in my informal survey of college freshmen 16 percent of the male respondents reported having attacked lesbians and gay men. This rate is similar to the one cited earlier for sexual assaults of women and children.

Adolescence, therefore—as a socially and culturally constructed stage of human development in which skills training, challenges, and opportunities do not meet the real potential, interest, and needs of teenagers— fosters power-seeking, adventurist recreational activities at the expense of others who also lack power within the social order. Engaging in these activities, for the most part, are those who have been socialized to be physically aggressive, to express themselves assertively in the public arena, and to resolve problems with violence. The simultaneity of this socialization and the denial of their having real social power and status are potentially explosive. These perpetrator–victim patterns reflect the patriarchal assignment of power and status according to gender, age, and race in the social order and the external and unprotected position of Aliens.

SOCIAL LOCATION OF LESBIANS AND GAY MEN

Lesbians and gay men, perhaps more than any marginalized population, are ineligible for and dismissed from the household unit and the workplace. For example:

1. Criminal statutes in more than one half of the states prohibit sexual relations between consenting lesbian/gay adults.
2. No state recognizes marriage between lesbians or gay men.
3. Lesbian and gay parents, who come out subsequent to marriage and then divorce, with few exceptions lose in child custody litigation. Lesbians and gay men who seek to adopt or foster-parent children also face restrictions.
4. Lesbian and gay men encounter problems in securing and maintaining housing without recourse to protective legislation.
5. Employers who dismiss or refuse to hire and promote lesbians and gay men are free from legal challenge or penalty in most municipalities.[51]

Occupational stereotypes and acceptance of gay men as dancers, interior decorators, and hairdressers help to define and maintain their marginal status. As such, in the social consciousness, they are excluded from the important and necessary realms of material production, managing technology, and basic survival. They do that without which society can maintain itself and prosper. Their work is seen as cosmetic, superficial, insignificant, entertaining, and unmanly. Its social value is minimized further because women are the principals who interact with it, appreciate it, and are served by it. Hairdressers, more than those in other occupations, are least valued because they "do little more than serve the vanity of women." Although data show that gay men are not statistically concentrated in these occupations more than in others, the stereotypes effectively control, diminish, and isolate their talents, skills, and participation in the workforce.[52]

Although the stereotypes misrepresent the range of occupations in which gay men are actually employed, empirical data do indicate other patterns of employability confirming their inferior and marginal positions. A study conducted by sociologists Maurice Leznoff and William A. Westley and published in 1956 found that the "overt [male] homosexual tends to fit into an occupation of low status; the secret homosexual into an occupation with a relatively high status rank."[53] Their findings were confirmed twenty years later in another study by Martin S. Weinberg and Colin J. Williams.[54] At the same time, sociologist Laud Humphreys also was finding that a "disproportionately high number of male homosexuals find employment as hospital orderlies and technicians, travelling salesmen, retail sales clerks, short order cooks, and waiters"; doubting that gay men are drawn to "these jobs because they enjoy changing bed linen, washing dishes, waiting tables, or stocking merchandise," he concludes that probably "these are the only positions open to discreditable individuals."[55] That gay men must be discreet to gain and hold higher-status occupations continues to be true today. In its survey of chief executive officers of Fortune-500-level companies, the *Wall Street Journal* finds that only 2 percent of the executives would hesitate to promote an employee to management-committee level because he is divorced; 1 percent because she is female; but 66 percent would if he is homosexual. This study concludes that the "real pariahs in business, the men who will find no less prejudice today than 20 years ago, are those who have never married."[56]

Because women in general are much less likely than men to be involved in high-status employment, the absence of lesbians in these positions is not irregular. Lesbians, also, do not appear to experience "occupational socialization" in the same way as gay men "who are tracked into sales and art, then stigmatized because of it"; female-specific occupations are themselves "so status-devalued to begin with that lesbianism is a subordinate issue."[57] The concentration of lesbians and gay men in low-status, Daughter-type jobs appears, therefore, to represent a comparatively greater loss of or fall from status for gay men than for lesbians. However, female-specific employment is precarious enough without the added danger of anti-lesbian discrimination. The combination of sexism and heterosexism in employment practices pushes lesbians closer to Alien status than acceptance as Daughters. That which is common to and oppressive for both lesbians and gay men is that, with few exceptions, they can be (and frequently are) dismissed from jobs without recourse to protective legislation.[58]

CONCLUSION

The social locations of adolescents and lesbian/gay people are similar. Neither would appear to have power or status in the institutional family or workplace. Physically, affectively, and cognitively, they are adults whose sexual activity is restricted or forbidden; whose familial status is marginal, unstable, or nonexistent; and whose employability and earning power are minimal or unrecognized. The position of adolescents, however, is temporary, whereas that of lesbians and gay men is static. Lesbians and gay men serve, in fact, as a negative, fixed standard against and away from which adolescents move. Those who have the farthest to move from the Alien role (i.e., male adolescents who are to become Brothers, Wives, and Fathers) are the most frequent perpetrators of anti-gay/lesbian violence.

The preparation of teenage males for adulthood anticipates their position within the Brother role. The closed ranks within which adult Brothers in the workplace compete and from which they exclude Aliens are reflected and foreshadowed in the patterns and behaviors of perpetrators of anti-gay/lesbian. Absent the universal, patriarchal privilege of owning a wife, teenage males are granted the permission to demonstrate physically their power over certain Aliens. Their attacks on these people have customarily been ignored, approved of, and/or rewarded by Brothers, Wives, and Fathers. It is the single domain in which they have special power and autonomy. It is a domain that for the most part is external to the household in which they were raised and to the economic sphere they will enter.

The Involvement of the Nuclear Family. Certainly, the nuclear family, as the normative household unit in which or in sight of which teenagers have been raised, prescribes appropriate behavior and proscribes deviance from it. Messages to adhere to it are both informal and formal. Children copy the values and behaviors of their parents, as well as receive instruction from them. In my informal survey of college freshmen, the majority of young men say they have been brought up to disapprove of homosexuality (77 percent), whereas the majority of young women (52 percent) say they were raised to accept it as natural or as a legitimate choice for some people. Of male respondents, a greater percentage of the perpetrators of anti-gay/lesbian violence than nonperpetrators (83 percent compared to 68) say they were raised to disapprove. The findings not only suggest that males are more likely to be raised to disapprove and to be perpetrators, but also show that those males who are perpetrators are more likely to have been raised to disapprove than those who have not been perpetrators.

When family members are cited as perpetrators by victims of anti-gay/lesbian violence, they are mostly brothers who attack their gay brothers, and less frequently their lesbian sisters; former husbands of lesbians are next; fathers are cited more often than mothers, the latter mostly by lesbian daughters; sisters are cited least (see table 3.1).[59] Although the incidence of domestic anti-gay/lesbian violence appears negligible compared to that in other settings and by other kinds of perpetrators (see tables 2.12–2.14), its pattern reflects traditional patriarchal roles and assignments of power (i.e., Fathers set standards, Wives coordinate their implementation, Brothers enforce them). Brothers, who themselves do not have a lot of power in the familial household but look forward to someday being household Fathers, exercise this small measure of power and control that Daughters do not. Wives become directly involved as perpetrators mostly when Daughters identify as lesbians, and Fathers become involved when Wives do.

That those in the more powerful positions within the household family (i.e., Fathers and Wives) are involved mostly when family women identify as lesbian may suggest that lesbians are perceived as a greater threat to the familial, and perhaps social, order than gay men. The absence of reports by gay men of violence by former wives may simply signal the nonviolent conditioning of women; it may also signify an important difference in the social locations of lesbians and gay men. Husbands who come out as gay men and forfeit ownership of a household Wife give up a patriarchal privilege. Household Wives who come out as lesbians, on the other hand, deny a household Father his privilege by refusing to serve, to be owned, to be subordinate to him, and to produce and raise children for him.[60] Although both gay men and lesbians violate social norms and are penalized, only the latter appear to be punished physically by high-ranking household members. (See table 2.16 for greater frequency of anti-lesbian violence in the home setting; also see tables 3.16–3.18.)

Older Perpetrators. The notion that lesbians pose a greater threat to the social order and more material damage to males within it is supported further by findings concerning anti-lesbian violence outside the family. First, although perpetrators of anti-gay/lesbian violence are statistically the approximate age of victims, they are more often older than lesbian victims and younger than gay victims (see tables 3.4 and 3.5). Second, other data show (see tables 3.16 and 3.17) that the older age of perpetrators correlates with the victims' achieved status, power, or wealth, that is, the challenges, threat, or invasion they pose to the perpetrator's social position (see appendix F). A lesbian—by her refusal to be a Wife for a household Father and/or a cooperative Daughter in the workplace— may undermine the authority, position, and material needs of adult men more than a gay man who relinquishes or can be easily dismissed from his position as Brother or Wife in the workplace.[61]

Because lesbians and gay men have not achieved social equality, opportunity, and positions, incidents by older perpetrators remain scarce; but should lesbians and gay men press into the mainstream, the response from the closed ranks of Brothers may add a dimension and degree to anti-gay/lesbian violence not heretofore commonly experienced. Two examples from the late nineteenth and early twentieth centuries support such speculation: the lynching of black people in the South[62] and the violent suppression of labor organizing.[63] In his 1944 study *An American Dilemma: The Negro Problem and Modern Democracy,* Gunnar Myrdal reports that organized extralegal violence against blacks by whites peaked at times of increased economic progress for blacks (e.g., during Reconstruction and immediately after World War I). Although low-income whites were the frequent perpetrators, local doctors, lawyers, businessmen, and police officers were instrumental in supporting, organizing, and participating in lynchings.[64] Labor organizing too, as the effort of the lower working class to gain better wages and working conditions, was opposed by a middle class of small businessmen, community leaders, newspapermen, floor supervisors, company foremen, and the better-paid employees. Fearing that their positions would be taken over and their wealth would have to be shared, these Brothers sided with the Wives, those responsible for operating mills, mines, and factories with a cheap labor force. Fathers relied on their business Wives to provide Brothers with sufficient favors, protection, and authority to guarantee their continued loyalty. Fathers also relied on their Wives in the state bureaucracy. They could call on the governor, state militia, federal troops, and deputy sheriffs to put down violently strike efforts by Daughters and "rioting by Negroes."[65]

Harvey Milk's ascent into San Francisco politics and his eventual death at the hands of a fellow supervisor serve as further evidence to support this hypothesis. White knew that Milk was key in convincing the mayor not to reinstate him to the post from which he had resigned and to which he subsequently sought reappointment. Milk had the power to prevent White's reclaiming status and position. White's exact motive was never established, and speculation continues; but Frances Fitzgerald's assessment and summary in the *New Yorker* (July 21, 1986), although not using Collins' terminology, explains White's action as his failure to close ranks with his other Brothers against an intruding Alien. She observes that, as the supervisor who had been for big business and real estate development and the voice of the Police Officers' Association, he was pressured first by real estate men and then by the police to ask for his job back. In Collins' terms, the Fathers and Wives spoke, and White, the Brother, obeyed. Fitzgerald also observes, correctly, that he had given as his original reason for resigning the need to provide better for his family (i.e., in Collins' terms, to be a better Father to his household Wife and family). She, more acutely than other journalists, however, locates his personal dilemma and reason for acting within what Collins calls the Brother role. She writes,

The developers meant nothing to him—that was politics. But the police—well, they were his buddies. He hung around with them even while he was on the board. And if you have been a policeman or a fireman, and if you had been a trooper on the line in Vietnam [and White had been all three], you know that your honor and your life depend on your not letting your buddies down. White (as someone may have reminded him) had let his buddies down—had let them down by quitting [as their voice on the board of supervisors].

For a time, White thought he could get his job back. "I've got a real surprise for the gay community," he told a reporter from a gay newspaper a day or so after he heard that Harvey Milk had opposed his reappointment. He had hope, but then he learned that the Mayor had decided against him. That evening . . . the realization hit: he sold out his buddies for his family life and a baked-potato stand [the business to which he planned to devote himself after resigning as supervisor]. He wrestled with his guilt all night long; then, in the morning, he made his plan. He carried it out, and afterward his conscience was clear; he had done the right thing; he had sacrificed himself for his buddies.[66]

That police remained his friends and expressed approval for his murdering Milk further supports Fitzgerald's analysis. That the critical factor in perpetrating violence against Aliens who threaten to enter the Brother role is Brotherhood (i.e., the closing of ranks) conforms to patterns observed in anti-labor and organized racial lynchings. For the most part, Brothers have not felt or experienced such a massive threat from lesbians and gay men; however, violent reactions have been documented at certain times when they have felt threatened.

The greater visibility of lesbian/gay people and their neighborhoods, the social activism of the lesbian/gay movement in most social institutions, and the attention of the media to both has been paralleled by a documented increase in anti-gay/lesbian violence.[67] More participation by older perpetrators has also been reported and is reflected in the frequency of perpetrators who are twenty-two to twenty-eight years old (see chapter 1,[68] and tables 3.4 and 3.18 in chapter 3) but does not alter in a statistically significant manner the average age of perpetrators.[69] If the increased rates of violence do indicate responses to greater lesbian/gay visibility and activism, they remain, for the most part, the responses of young men.[70] The continuing young age of perpetrators would seem to correlate with the continuing Alien status of lesbians and gay men.

Openly identified lesbians and gay men have not, for the most part, even achieved Daughter status in the economy, from which they could push into the Brother role. Although they have the numbers and concentrations in urban areas, lesbians and gay men have not utilized strikes and boycotts as social action[71]; their voting power has been felt only in a few municipalities[72]; those in high-status employment usually remain closeted or are screened out; and some have won election to political office, but these are few, local, and predominantly gay white men.[73] Any threat to Father-rule apparently continues to be held in check by Wives who have enacted restrictive legislation, block passage of protective legislation, restrict employment, establish moral and religious codes, and control the education of the young, and by Brothers who implement these laws, rules, policies, and programs. These measures effectively maintain the marginal status of lesbians and gay men. In addition, the police do play the Wifely role of imposing the threat and reality of violence against lesbians and gay men should they "misbehave" or become "too" visible. Coordinated, periodic raids, entrapment, surveillance, and "round-ups" are common enough to make lesbians and gay men weary and wary of police violence (see appendix C). Eight percent of the respondents in my survey of lesbians and gay men report experiences of anti-gay/lesbian violence by police officers; the police are identified as the third most likely perpetrators (see table 3.1).

The Special Province of Adolescent Males. But the two most commonly identified perpetrators are young male strangers and fellow male students. The great majority of anti-gay/lesbian violence neither occurs in areas that are socially central nor is perpetrated by socially powerful individuals. It is not a mainstream phenomenon. Those who perpetrate the great majority of violence are other Aliens who least want to be identified as such and have some meager, but not harmless, means of separating themselves from association with this role.

Added to these similarities of Alien status between adolescent males and lesbian/gay people is Kinsey's finding that in their late teens, nearly every other male has some homosexual contact; the rate is, in fact, greater among teenage males than among any other age group except single males between the ages of twenty-six and thirty.[74] Many teenage males, therefore, face a serious conflict of (1) their socially constructed and sexually felt similarity with a socially powerless, deviant, and feminized category of people and (2) the socially constructed expectation that they be powerful, masculine, and heterosexual. A dilemma for teenagers in general is the experience of heightened physical, sexual, emotional, and affective development and the simultaneous efforts of adults to postpone and control it. Homosexual activity as one manifestation of that development is typically least understood, discussed, and tolerated by adults. Many teenage males bear a horrible secret.

That both homosexual activity (with the exception of single men in their late twenties, as noted earlier) and anti-gay/lesbian violence are more prevalent among adolescent males than among any other age or gender group may not be coincidental. Whether those who engage in homosexual activity are more or less likely to be perpetrators is not known.[75] But some teenage males may attempt to resolve a conflict between their sexual experiences and the social expectations placed on them by attacking lesbians and gay men. Some of the findings reported in chapters 2 and 3 may be interpreted and understood in terms of such conflict: for example, the rage and extreme mutilation characteristic of some incidents may signal the seriousness of the conflict for some perpetrators; the attraction to and nonhatred for victims expressed by others may represent the extremes of personal feelings and social expectations; the sexual overtures often used by some perpetrators to bait and lure victims may evidence the skills and fantasies emergent from their sexual feelings and experiences; and the greater frequency of anti-gay over anti-lesbian violence (and perhaps especially of anti-gay rape) may reflect the preferred targeting of the gender more closely associated with the feelings and interests that are in conflict with the social norm. Given the prevalence of homosexual contact, the pervasiveness and rigidity of prohibitions against it, the tendency for teenagers to want to conform to social norms, compensating for one's own socially unacceptable behavior by physically attacking others who engage in it cannot be viewed as either unusual, anti-social, or the result of being psychologically disturbed.

As noted earlier, in their effort to demonstrate adult behaviors prematurely, adolescents are essentially conformist, and superficially rebellious. Because of the lack of attention to and provision for their need to behave as adults, teenagers often demonstrate adult behaviors on their own turf, on their own time, to and with each other, and in their own way. Behaviors often become an exaggeration of the adult model. Anti-gay/lesbian violence is no exception. Targets are those whom adults shun and denigrate, but adults do not typically use violence against them. Also, the violence is executed out of sight of adults and is shaped by factors specific to the realm of adolescents. For example: (1) teenagers like to think that their ideas about homosexuality are their own, even though they reflect those of their parents; (2) incidents occur most frequently during school and during those out-of-school hours in which teenagers typically socialize, especially on weekend and summer evenings; (3) incidents often precede or follow socializing with peers, such as partying or hanging out; (4) perpetrators often do not act alone, but with and because of peers; and (5) incidents are often spurred by those feelings that adolescents typically share (i.e., boredom and the need for action, adventure, risk, and thrill). However, compared to adult responses to most other teenage behaviors that involve violence and rowdy behavior, disapproval and punishment of apprehended perpetrators by parents and authorities is lacking. Understanding, approval, or rewards are not uncommon.

Fathers, Wives, Brothers, and Aliens. The perpetrator of anti-gay/lesbian violence acts under the institutional and historical aegis to abuse the outsider, the Alien. Although Fathers, Wives, and the most powerful Brothers in the economic and political spheres may not explicitly advocate, condone, or coordinate their acts, (1) the organization of their status relative to less powerful Brothers, Daughters, and Aliens models, predicts, rehearses, and normalizes the perpetrator—victim patterns; (2) their policies and programs that shape and determine socialization and education give perpetrators not only the informal permission to act, but the means and skills to do so (i.e., male dominance and male violence); and (3) their institutionalized marginalization of lesbians and gay men provides an apt target.

Anticipating their membership within the closed ranks of Brothers, young men will continue to prepare for adulthood with the option of perpetrating violence against lesbians and gay men (i.e., by banding together to dissociate themselves from Aliens). As pre-Brothers temporarily saddled with Daughter—Alien status they will continue to exercise their one privilege—the use of violence—to distance themselves from that role. They will begin to form those patterns of Brotherly behavior that exclude Aliens and demonstrate loyalty to Fathers and Wives. When they come of marriageable age and are eligible for gainful employment, they will have the patriarchal privilege and status that is granted to all heterosexual men. No longer bordering on Alien status, they will not need to use what was the single resource available to them to establish their male privilege.[76] Until then, however, attacking lesbians and gay men allows them to do what men "should" and "have the right to" do and what is lacking in their own lives. It allows them to be "masculine," to be physically aggressive, to be dominant over someone else, to do something exciting, to be in control.

Lesbians and gay men are unlike other marginalized groups whose service or purpose for the economy is as a source of cheap and needy laborers for the least desirable and lowest status (with the possible exception, as discussed in chapter 1, of World War II mobilization, in which the military was desperate for able bodies). They appear, in fact, to be systematically ineligible for any kind of employment. The lack of civil rights and affirmative action legislation for lesbians and gay men suggests that they are the least likely of Aliens to be integrated into the social order. That the "bottom line" requirement for any role *within* the social order is heterosexual marriageability underscores the unlikelihood of their eventual acceptance, short of changes within the order. They lack what racially and ethnically defined Aliens have had in common with those in the social order and that has facilitated their movement into the order. In its survey of 2,823 high school students in New York State, the findings of the Governor's Task Force on Bias-Related Violence are not surprising and confirm this conclusion:

> One of the most alarming findings in the youth survey is the openness with which the respondents expressed their aversion and hostility toward gays and lesbians. While racism and ethnocentrism were found to be very much alive among the youth of New York it was rarely openly advocated. The young people are aware that bias based on race and ethnicity can no longer be overtly condoned. There is no such awareness concerning the rights of gays and lesbians and the students were quite emphatic about their dislike for these groups and frequently made violent, threatening statements. Gays and lesbians, it seems, are perceived as legitimate targets which can be openly attacked. This is an attitude which draws strength from the example set by all the major social institutions which continue to deny homosexuals the status of equals.[77]

The patriarchal organization of household and workplace and of state and economy is defined not only in terms of inside relationships, but in terms of those who are not allowed to enter. Lesbians and gay men are the standard of that which is unacceptable, against which those who prepare for adult roles can measure and gauge their behavior. Perpetrators of anti-gay/lesbian violence recognize the vulnerability and unacceptability of those outcasts. They take advantage of the vulnerability to establish their own acceptability and power.

Four factors seem to be critical in the perpetration of anti-gay/lesbian violence. The first is the fixed Alien status of lesbians and gay men; the second is the temporary Alien status of adolescents and their preparation by Fathers and Wives for adulthood; the third is male adolescents' postponed access to and striving for household Fatherhood and Brotherhood in the workplace; and the fourth is the institutionalized permission granted by Fathers and Wives for Brothers to behave violently toward Aliens. Although the framework for these factors is the arrangement of roles within the traditional patriarchal family, their interaction especially as represented in mobility and striving, would appear to be informed by capitalism. However, absent data on anti-gay/lesbian violence in other systems (i.e., more or less competitive, hierarchical, communitarian, egalitarian), capitalism cannot be established as unique in contributing to or causing such violence in general.

The understanding of anti-gay/lesbian violence as determined by the political and economic situation in North America, therefore, may or may not be applicable elsewhere. However, the four factors cited earlier do comprise a social consequence and dynamic that is identifiable in this situation and that needs to be considered in formulating an ethical norm that will help to end anti-gay/lesbian violence as described in my study and present a challenge to patriarchy. Chapter 5 will attempt to develop and propose a moral response to anti-gay/lesbian violence.

CHAPTER FIVE

A Biblical Perspective
on Anti-Gay/Lesbian Violence

I turn to the book of Leviticus in Judeo-Christian scripture for two reasons: (1) it is explicit in condemning male homosexuality and prescribing death for those practicing it, and (2) it has influenced and continues to buttress social policy and legal practice concerning lesbians and gay men. An examination of the document shows that it is a resource as well for understanding the motive and cause of anti-gay/lesbian violence in our time and for predicting its future development.

The anti-homosexual passages in the Bible will be identified and their legacy and current impact outlined. After a discussion of the literary form, predominant theme, and historical context of the primary anti-homosexual document, parallels with current data are drawn and used to predict the future of anti-gay/lesbian violence and to suggest an ethical response to it.

DEFINITE BIBLICAL REFERENCES

There are eight possible references to and disapproval of homosexuality in Judeo-Christian scripture—Genesis 19; Leviticus 18:22, 20:13; Romans 1:18–32; 1 Corinthians 6:9; 1 Timothy 1:10; Revelations 21:8, 22:15.[1] Biblical scholars are far from agreeing on which refer definitely to homosexuality[2]; but consensus is that the two verses in Leviticus alone clearly indicate and prohibit homosexual relations.[3] And only one of these prescribes physical punishment.

You shall not lie with a male as with a woman; it is an abomination [Leviticus 18:22].

If a man lies with a male as with a woman, both of them have committed an abomination; they shall be put to death, their blood is upon them [Leviticus 20:13].[4]

But here too some scholars argue that because these verses are immediately proximate to prohibitions against the cultic practices of other nations (Leviticus 18:21), they condemn only certain kinds of homosexual activity, specifically that which involves male temple prostitution and idolatry.[5] The evidence against this interpretation is the proximity of the verses to an even greater number of prohibitions that are related not to cultic practices but to sexual behavior in daily life (e.g., adultery, incest, sex during menstruation, and bestiality [Leviticus 18:19, 20, 23; 20:10–12, 14–16]). Also, if the intention were to forbid male prostitution, specific mention of such would have been made as it is for female prostitution (Leviticus 19:29).[6] Furthermore, scholars have not been able to establish that the male temple prostitution practiced in biblical times was homosexual.[7]

Of the other six possible passages, Genesis 19 (the story of the destruction of Sodom) and Romans 1:18–32 (the Letter of Paul to the Romans) are the next most frequently discussed as definite references. Among the dissenting scholars is John Boswell, who reports that "many patristic authors concluded that the point of the [Sodom] story was to condemn inhospitality to stranger [and] rape," not homosexuality.[8] Boswell also argues that in his Letter to the Romans, Paul condemns not homosexually oriented persons, but heterosexuals who engage in homosexual activity, that is, who indulge themselves by engaging in "behavior which is unexpected, unusual, or different from what would occur in the normal orders of things."[9]

Because the meaning of "natural" and "unnatural" relations, "shameless acts," and "consumed with passion" in Paul's Letter is not clear, the passage is ambiguous; but the suggestion is strongly sexual and/or same-gender, and death is recognized as the appropriate due.

Their women exchanged natural relations for unnatural, and the men likewise gave up natural relations with women and were consumed with passion for one another, men committing shameless acts with men. . . . Though *they know God's decree that those who do such things deserve to die,* they not only do them but approve those who practice them [my italics; Romans 1:26b–27, 32].[10]

As one who was well versed in Jewish law, Paul's statement concerning "God's decree" would likely refer to Leviticus,[11] even though the phrasing is softened from "they shall be put to death" to "they know they deserve to die." This continuing recognition of Leviticus in the first century A.D. underscores its centrality and uniqueness as a fundamental prohibition against homosexuality. The inclusion of women in Paul's Letter may suggest that the traditional application of the prohibition, in spite of its reference to males only, was expanded in time to same-sex behavior for both women and men.[12]

LEGACY OF LEVITICUS

The legacy of the Levitical prohibitions is found in postbiblical Jewish literature and rabbinical thought and in post-Constantinian Christianity.[13] Examples of the former are (1) an explanation for the prohibition and severity of the punishment in the Talmud and (2) *Sifra*, a rabbinical commentary on Leviticus, which warns against female–female and male–male marriages.[14] Examples of the latter are (1) in 342 C.E., five years after Constantine's death, the first Roman imperial edict, reflecting the anti-homosexual policy of Paul by condemning male homosexuals to "exquisite punishment"; (2) in 1532, Holy Roman Emperor Charles V's order that "if a man commit unchastity with a . . . man, or a woman with a woman, they have forfeited their lives and shall be condemned to death"; and (3) in 1730 in Holland, with reference to Leviticus, a proclamation justifying a campaign of burning, hanging, beheading, garotting, and drowning homosexual men.[15]

In North America, a word-for-word translation of Leviticus 20:13 was adopted into legislation by the colonies of Massachusetts, New Hampshire, New York, New Jersey, and Pennsylvania, and expanded to include lesbianism in Connecticut.[16] After the Revolutionary War capital punishment for homosexuality was eventually repealed in all of what had been the original colonies; Pennsylvania was first, in 1786, and South Carolina last, in 1873.[17] However, the "religious and legal influence continues to be found in the wording of some legal proscriptions against homosexual behavior."[18]

Absent its direct application in legislation, Leviticus has continued to be used to shape and justify social policy and practice toward lesbians and gay men.[19] Most recently, two major institutions have invoked the prohibition. In 1986, in its "Letter to the Bishops of the Catholic Church on the Pastoral Care of Homosexual Persons," the Congregation for the Doctrine of the Faith, with the approval of Pope John Paul II, wrote:

In *Leviticus* 18:22 and 20:13, in the course of describing the conditions necessary for belonging to the Chosen people, the author excludes from the People of God those who behave in a homosexual fashion.

In *Romans* 1:18–32, still building on the moral traditions of his forbears, but in the new context of the confrontation between Christianity and the pagan society of his day, Paul uses homosexual behavior as an example of the blindness which has overcome humankind.[20]

Also, in 1986, the United States Supreme Court upheld the constitutionality of the state of Georgia's sodomy statute. The majority opinion stated that "proscriptions against [homosexual] conduct have ancient roots"; a concurring opinion held that "condemnation of those practices is firmly rooted in Judeo-Christian moral and ethical standards"; and a dissenting opinion objected to the "petitioner's invocation of Leviticus [and] Romans" and "assertion that 'traditional Judeo-Christian values proscribe' the conduct involved."[21]

Current Impact of Levitical Prohibitions. Although the prescription of death in the Levitical prohibitions currently serves less the purpose of advocating physical punishment of lesbian/gay people and more that of supporting disapproval of their sexual/affectional behavior, violence may be consequential and/or tolerated. Evidence of the former can be found in the reports from around the country of stepped-up police harassment and increased general harassment of gay/lesbian people that followed the Supreme Court's decision.[22] An example of the latter is the rationale provided in The Letter to the Bishops that finds "violent malice" against homosexual persons "deplorable" but sees the increase of such "irrational and violent reactions" as a not surprising response to social approval of homosexuality and the introduction of civil legislation "to protect behaviour to which no one has any conceivable right."[23]

Research has not attempted to measure the impact of the Levitical prohibitions specifically on social attitudes and behavior toward lesbians and gay men. Available studies show only that those who attend church regularly and are more "orthodox," "devout," or "fundamentalist" tend to be more disapproving.[24] Based on their 1948 study of sexual behavior in the human male, Kinsey, Pomeroy, and Martin conclude that even in the present day, when ecclesiastical courts do not have legal jurisdiction and the church's influence is more indirect, the "ancient religious codes are still the prime sources of the attitudes, the ideas, the ideals, and the rationalizations by which most individuals pattern their sexual lives."[25]

Opposition to homosexuality may typically be based less on knowledge and application of specific biblical passages and more on a general familiarity with "the Bible" through popular knowledge and assumptions about church tradition and teachings.[26] As noted in chapter 3, actual perpetrators of anti-gay/lesbian violence may assume generalized permission from "the Church" or "the Bible" but do not claim either as their primary reason for attacking lesbians and gay men. Few people in general seem to realize, for example, that the definite prohibitions against and prescription of death for male homosexuality consists of two verses, a number that is tiny compared to the entire volume of scripture and small even in the context of the book of Leviticus itself (859 verses). Even the lists of sexual offenses, to which these verses belong immediately, represent neither a large part nor a major theme in Leviticus. Nor is the prescription of death limited in Leviticus to homosexuality. Other such punishable behaviors are those for cursing father or mother; for committing adultery with neighbor's wife (both man and woman); for committing incest with father's wife (both man and woman); for committing incest with son's wife (both man and woman); for marrying a woman and her mother (all three); for committing bestiality (both man or woman and beast); for being a medium or wizard (man or woman); for being a harlot, if the daughter of priest; for working on the Sabbath; for cursing or blaspheming the name of Yahweh; and for killing a person (Leviticus 20:9–16, 27; 21:9; 23:13, 16, 30; 24:17, 21).[27]

Nonetheless, the gravity of capital punishment, even if mentioned only once and not limited to homosexuality, renders these verses not insignificant. It provokes important questions: What kind of document requires the inclusion of such proscriptions and punishment? What kind of social context influenced and shaped this document? For what reasons was it written and/or compiled?

LEVITICUS' PLACE IN THE CANON OF SCRIPTURE

Leviticus is the third book in the Pentateuch, the Five Books of Moses. It follows the book of Exodus and precedes the book of Numbers. The book of Genesis is concerned with the primeval history and history of the patriarchs; Exodus, with the crucial event in Israel's historical traditions, its deliverance from slavery by Yahweh; Leviticus, with instituting ritual worship, the organization of priests, and familial land tenure; Numbers, with the census and ordering of Israel's families; and Deuteronomy, with centralizing worship in one place. Although compiled and written at various times and places and by a variety of people, the whole Pentateuch is arranged as a narrative in which the books are historically and geographically progressive: the stories in Genesis occur throughout the Middle East but emphasize and conclude in Egypt; Exodus begins in Egypt and ends at Mount Sinai; Leviticus occurs at Sinai; Numbers begins at Sinai, endures the wanderings through the wilderness, and ends on the plains outside of Canaan, the land promised by Yahweh; and Deuteronomy, in the form of Moses' farewell and advice to Israel, takes place on the border of Canaan. The invasion and conquest of Canaan follow in the post-Pentateuchal books of Joshua and Judges.

The Literary Form of Leviticus. Leviticus itself is a compilation of statutes, ordinances, laws, and commandments within an "extremely simple" narrative framework: Israel is "envisaged throughout the book in the same situation, namely sojourning at Sinai." The narrative consists of "quite short stereotyped introductory and concluding formulae" that are repeated to link a number of different sets of instructions from Yahweh. The introductory formula is "And Yahweh said to Moses, 'Say to the people of Israel' "; the concluding formula is a variation of "This is the law . . . which Yahweh commanded Moses on Mount Sinai." The story is secondary to the major subject matter, the instructions themselves; the document is decidedly more legislative than narrative. The number of instructions is so "preponderantly" large, "varying in scope," and "simply linked" by the narrative that their arrangement "appears to have little coherence."[28]

The instructions are arranged in four major groupings of approximately equal size:

1. The first (chapters 1–10, 252 verses, 29 percent of the document) consists of instructions for sacrifices, followed by the institution of Moses' brother, Aaron, and his male descendants, as the official line of priests.
2. The second (chapters 11–16, 238 verses, 28 percent of document) consists of regulations concerning "cleanness" in matters of childbirth, leprosy, bodily discharges, and animals that may be eaten.
3. The third (chapters 17–22, 167 verses, 19 percent of document) is known as the Holiness Code, a collection of precepts covering sexual and social relations, sacrificial offerings, the eating of meat, and the "separateness" of priests and cultic gifts.
4. The fourth (chapters 23–27, 202 verses, 24 percent of document) is often considered as part of the Holiness Code but is distinguished by the uniqueness of its establishing the Year of Release (or the Jubilee Year), which is the occasion for the restoration of one's property and family.[29]

THE PREDOMINANT THEME OF LEVITICUS

In the third grouping of instructions—specifically, among chapters 18, 19, and 20—a contradiction seems apparent. In chapters 18 and 20, male homosexuality is condemned, and it is punishable by death in the latter; chapter 19, however, mandates love for one's neighbor and for the stranger who sojourns with you.

You shall not take vengeance or bear any grudge against the sons of your own people, but you shall love your neighbor as yourself: I am Yahweh [Leviticus 19:18].
The stranger who sojourns with you shall be to you as the native among you, and you shall love him as yourself; for you were strangers in the land of Egypt: I am Yahweh your God [Leviticus 19:34].[30]

For our times, prescribing both death for gay men as well as love for the stranger would seem to be contradictory. How can one both love and kill those who are other, marginal, outsiders, strangers?[31]

An exegesis of Leviticus shows that its "love of neighbor and stranger" is not the same as what some today may interpret to mean love of those who are outside of the familiar social circle. The Hebrew term for *sojourner* or *stranger (ger)* has little, if anything, to do with outcasts or marginal people. It is more accurately translated as "resident alien," one who was born elsewhere but has the economic and familial means to live and work as an accepted member and according to the standards of the community. There is to be "one law for the sojourner and for the native." The term for *neighbor (rea')*—immediately adjacent to and interchangeable with terms for *companion ('amit), brother ('ach)*, and *fellow countryman (ben-'am)*—reinforces homogeneity as the condition for communal love. To love neighbor and sojourner is to love those who are immediate to and most like oneself. To indicate foreign or outsider status, other terms are used (*zar* and *ben-neykar*); and their context is regulations that deny access to certain communal and cultic practices.[32]

One looks in vain for an example of inclusive community, egalitarian principles, or a theology of loving outreach and pluralistic justice in Leviticus. Leviticus is about defining a separate community that sets itself apart by virtue of its superior differences with others. The term *quadosh*, whose root means "set apart" and which is translated as "holy," occurs (with its cognate forms, e.g., *sanctify* and *holiness*) 152 times in Leviticus (20 percent of all occurrences in Hebrew scripture).[33] Yahweh's being holy and Israel's being set apart are emphasized by repetition throughout the document as well as by such summary statements as the following in chapter 20. Here the term *dbl*, meaning "to distinguish or separate," occurs four times as well.[34]

You shall therefore keep all my statutes and all my ordinances, and do them; that the land where I am bringing you to dwell may not vomit you out. And you shall not walk in the customs of the nation which I am casting out before you;

for they did all these [sexual, social, and cultic violations], and therefore I abhorred them. But I have said to you, "You shall inherit their land, and I will give it to you to possess, a land flowing with milk and honey." I am Yahweh your God, who have separated you from the peoples. You shall therefore make a distinction between the clean beast and the unclean, and between the unclean bird and the clean; you shall not make yourself abominable by beast or by bird or by anything with which the ground teems, which I have set apart for you to hold unclean. You shall be holy to me; for I Yahweh am holy, and have separated you from the peoples, that you should be mine [Leviticus 20:22–26].[35]

The passage is explicit in stating that the numerous cultic regulations throughout the document are for the purpose of distinguishing Israel from the other nations. They delineate precisely who may be inside and who will be put outside of the community, that is, who will be "cut off from their people."[36]

Because the preceding passage occurs at the end of the section in which the death penalty for homosexuality is prescribed (20:13) and because a similar introduction and summary (18:1–5, 24–30) frame the section containing the other prohibition of homosexuality (18:22), these regulations appear to have been part of the effort to establish and protect Israel's exclusivity.

Other regulations, specifically the social legislation, appear to facilitate even further this exclusivity by mandating mutual support among those who are insiders. The regulation to let the fields lie fallow (to rest) every seventh year in 25:1–7, when compared with the same in Exodus 23:10–11, is illustrative. The reason for the regulation expressed in the latter is so that the "poor of your people and . . . the wild beasts may eat," whereas in the former, the "sabbath [the rest] of the land shall provide food for you, for yourself and for your male and female slaves and for your hired servant and the sojourner who lives with you, for your cattle also and for the beasts that are in your land." Concern for the poor, widows, and orphans, a theme recurring throughout Judeo-Christian scripture, is conspicuously absent here, replaced by concern for oneself and for those within one's familial organization. Poverty is discussed in chapter 25, but in the context of the laws for the Year of Release, which concern not the outsider or lower class, but "your brother (blood relative, fellow-tribesman, fellow-countryman), if he should become poor"; and the responsibility for helping him falls to kin (25:25, 35, 45). The distinctive feature of the Year of Release is "property-restitution" and "bankruptcy law" for the land-owning class; it "is essentially an effort to hold the [patriarchal] family together."[37]

THE HISTORICAL CONTEXT
FOR THE COMPILATION OF LEVITICUS

Leviticus, as a document that seeks to establish Israel's separateness, should be understood in terms of the times in which and the reasons for which it was compiled and written. Of the three literary sources in Hebrew scripture—the Yahwist (J), the Elohist (E), and the Priestly (P) —J and E and are the oldest, and there is little, if any, trace of them in Leviticus. The P documents, though borrowing from and incorporating earlier material, were compiled and written after the fall of Israel's monarchy. The P source is notable for reframing, according to the needs of the present, the period before Israel's entry into Canaan.[38]

Leviticus is a P document whose description and interpretation of Israel's sojourn at Sinai is shaped by two current events—(1) the overthrow of Jerusalem by Nebuchadnezzar of Babylon in 586 (or 587) B.C.E., with its subsequent dispersion or exile, and (2) forty-nine years later, the decree by Cyrus, the Persian emperor who conquered Babylon, restoring Israel as an autonomous religious community.[39]

The Conditions of Exile and Restoration. Biblical scholars and historians tell us that the dispersion or exile to Babylon was a "forced removal of royalty, state officials, priests, army officers, and artisans who probably constituted no more than 5 percent of the total populace."[40] The edict of Cyrus allowed them to return. This was part of a wider policy of extending to certain subject people considerable autonomy and respect for their indigenous cultural and religious life when this was an advantage to the Persian empire. It was to Persia's advantage to prevent a weak point of defense in the west by stabilizing Jerusalem and the surrounding province of Judah. To avoid granting it *political* independence, Persian encouraged and backed the development of Jerusalem's *religious* autonomy and the codifying of existing religious laws as the basis for colonial law.[41]

For returning Babylonian exiles, a " 'declassed' elite who had once known excessive privilege" as the upper class of Jerusalem, the choices were limited but obvious.[42] With political independence and the restoration of the monarchy as the remotest of possibilities, these exiles returned committed to reviving, reforming, and restoring Israel's religious tradition, custom, cult, and history. Restoring Israel as an autonomous religious community "was a political act initiated and imposed upon the Jewish community by the collaboration of Persian imperial authorities and a Jewish colonial elite imported from the exile to Judah."[43]

Little is recorded of the situation in Judah during the exile. A reference in the second book of Kings (24:14; 25:12) to those who stayed as the "poor people of the land" and the despair expressed over the destruction of Jerusalem in the book of Lamentations indicate that conditions were unsettled and poverty common. Many towns and villages had been destroyed and Jerusalem was largely in ruins. Of special importance for the future was Babylon's not having transplanted a foreign upper class to Judah, as it had done in the other four provinces in the former kingdom of Israel. When the exiles were able to return, they did not have to compete with a ruling class established in their absence; but they did have the task of controlling a land that had been open to the influx of neighboring peoples and the tendency for native Judahites to adopt their social and religious customs. In Leviticus, the placing of the sojourner and the native under one law and the repeated warning against doing as the surrounding nations do were attempts to establish order and control with the authority of Yahweh's voice from the past.[44]

Leviticus' Interpretation of History. The book of Leviticus attempts to reinterpret the history of Israel in favor of these new developments. The postexilic formalization of cultic practices and of sexual and social regulations and the organization of priests are set and legitimated in the context of Yahweh's speaking to Moses at Sinai. Routine practices mentioned in the book of Exodus become elaborated and elevated in Leviticus to resolve Jerusalem's current socioeconomic problems in favor of the returning exiles. The attempt by the returning, former ruling class to establish, under the authority of the Persian ruler, a historical precedent for the consolidation and control of Israel's religious community is transparent.[45] The elevation of the Sabbath from a provision for weekly rest to a means for returning land and property to those who had left them is the prominent example.[46]

Neither the restoration of rights of ownership in the land nor the term *sabbatical* (or seventh) *year* (*shenat shabbatone,* multiplied by 7 to get the forty-nine years after which the Year of Release followed) is mentioned elsewhere in Hebrew scripture. The scriptural basis for the Year of Release is contained exclusively in Leviticus; the Bible contains no evidence of the historical observance of it.

The numerically ordered festival calendar—which builds on and progresses from the seventh day Sabbath to holiday observances in the seventh week, seventh month, seventh year, and finally 7 times seven years—is unique to Leviticus and replaces the older agrarian and seasonal ordering of holidays in Exodus.[47] But although biblical commentators tend to agree that the jubilee has little, if any, real historical precedence and that the Year of Release is a postexilic reformulation of ancient law ("the sabbath principle . . . carried to its extreme limit"[48]), none, to my knowledge, has suggested that its inspiration may have been the anticipation or occurrence of Cyrus' decree coming forty-nine years after the fall of Jerusalem.[49]

To have a provision for property restitution prescribed at Sinai, formulated according to ancient sabbath law and matching the time frame of the exile, would be to the advantage of returning exiles. It might provide for the immediate return of property and reestablishment of local political power as well as serve as the normative date from which future transactions were made (e.g., power may be maintained by those families whose lineage can be traced back to return in that year). Historical evidence shows that among families for control of the priestly organization rested on return dates from Babylon.[50]

Parallels Between Leviticus and Data on Anti-Gay/Lesbian Violence. The contradiction initially apparent in Leviticus' dual prescriptions of love for the stranger and death for homosexuals is illusory. It does not encourage discussion that might produce a corrective norm for the problem of anti-gay/lesbian violence. However, the overarching concern in this document—which is the establishment of a separate, exclusive community—does offer insight into the problem of such violence in our time because the motive and cause are similar for both.

In comparing data on perpetrators (as applied to Collins' model in chapter 4) with the preceding discussion of Leviticus, the parallels are apparent. For example:

1. An adolescent male in North America today is likely to demonstrate aggressive, dominant, violent behavior against those who are socially even less powerful because it is one of the few options open to him, especially if he wants to conform to appropriate gender-role behavior and maintain the gender-role privilege expected of and by men.

2. By comparison, a Babylonian exile returned to Jerusalem to establish a ruling religious elite because it was one of the few options open to him, especially if he wanted to demonstrate a measure of upper-class behavior and maintain the status expected of and by the upper class.

This favoring of a particular group—adolescent males or declassed exiles—was and is by design of and benefit to those who control the social order. To continue the parallel:

1. Those least likely to accept the boredom and lack of challenge in adolescence are males, because they are also socialized to be aggressive, adventuresome, and in control. Permission for "boys to be boys" (i.e., to victimize sissies, queers, deviants) suffices to hold them in check with "minor league" male status but also reinforces social standards. The high rates of and benign regard for date rape and homophobic violence among teenagers indicate the willingness with which male dominance and standards of deviance are enforced.

2. By comparison, those most likely to be restless and least likely to accept continued exile and powerlessness after Cyrus' decree are those who had been socialized as the ruling elite of Jerusalem. By permitting their return to establish a religiously autonomous, but politically dependent, community, Persia was able to use their eagerness to stabilize a weak spot on the western border of the empire. Like that of our adolescent males, this was "minor league" autonomy in service of the greater Persian social order.

An important question for my study is, "Does the establishing of special, but limited, privilege and power for a group within a social order mean that lesbians and gay men will be the likely or inevitable targets for physical attack, punishment, or exclusion by that group?" On the basis of the two examples here (young males in North America and the religious leadership in postexilic Jerusalem), the answer would appear to be "yes, if the social order that is maintained by and grants the group its limited privilege is patriarchal." The condition on which young men are permitted to behave as they do is the conformity of their behavior to standards of heterosexual male control and superiority. By comparison, on the condition that they support and conform to the imperial order, the exiles were allowed to return. We can be sure that if the practice of teenage males were the targeting of corporate executives or married men, the social response to their activities would be markedly different from that of their targeting lesbians and gay men. And we can be sure that the returning exiles would not have gotten far if their intention in returning to Israel had been to promote a gynocentric, egalitarian, open mode of worship and familial organization. In exchange for a measure of control and power, each group enthusiastically distinguishes itself from, punishes, or victimizes those whose freedom would violate the organizing principle of the social order that grants the group its limited but special privileges. The hierarchical priestly organization of "unblemished," married, heterosexual males that they establish to rule their separate community [51] reflects the organizing principles of the social order to which they owed allegiance (imperial Persia) and from which they had fallen (monarchical Israel); their prescribing capital punishment for gay men underscores the eagerness with which they would enforce those principles.

Leviticus as a Patriarchal Document. Support for and the practice of patriarchy are evident throughout Leviticus.[52] For the immediate purposes of this study, however, the lists of sexual regulations of which the homosexual prohibitions are a part deserve special attention.

The sexual regulations in chapter 18 are addressed to men and forbid sex with mother, aunt, step-mother, aunt by marriage, sister, half-sister, step-sister, step-daughter, sister-in-law, daughter-in-law, grand-daughter, step-grand-daughter, and neighbor's wife. Absent from the list are wife and daughter. Biblical commentators typically claim that the daughter is assumed as forbidden or omitted by accident.[53] However, feminist scholars point out that the sexual violations are phrased not as offenses against women but as offenses against men who violate rights of ownership, use, and exchange. A patriarch owned his wife, and he owned his daughter until he gave her away in marriage. The daughters of a man's kinsmen are, therefore, forbidden, but the "patriarchal God sees fit to pass over father–daughter incest in silence."[54] Also, by prescribing capital punishment for sex only with neighbor's wife, father's wife, and daughter-in-law, chapter 20 seems to show that ownership and not consanguinity, for example, is the serious issue in the sexual regulations. It is the sexual use of those women who belong to other male relatives or fellow-countrymen that is forbidden.[55]

Because the prohibitions against male homosexuality and the prescription of death for it follow immediately the preceding regulations in both chapters 18 and 20 it would seem that for a man not to possess a woman sexually, to possess a man as a woman, or to allow oneself to be possessed as a woman are also extremely serious violations of patriarchal behavior.

In Leviticus sexual violations are expanded and detailed as nowhere else in Hebrew scripture (cf. Exodus 20 and 21; Deuteronomy 27). Death is not prescribed for sexual violations, nor is homosexuality mentioned in other sets of laws. The introductory and concluding frameworks for each of the lists in Leviticus (18:1–5, 24–30; 20:7–9, 22–26) are unusually detailed and narrative compared to the brief formula used for the other sections of instructions within this same document. The authoritative qualifier "I am Yahweh" is borrowed from the older Elohist (or E) source, in which it appears sparingly, but is used here repeatedly.[56] The lists themselves are not unified, coherent, or integrated; for example, the variety of reasons (defilement, profanity, abomination, and perversion) for the offensiveness of each behavior, the mixture of singular and plural address (even within a single instruction), and the variously expressed punishments signal collection and accretion.[57] Each list is characterized by a large measure of bombast framing a loose collection of laws. Relative to other sets of laws in Hebrew scripture, these lists appear as desperate attempts to delineate, exaggerate, and apply patriarchal principles.

This desperation is related to and embodied in other concerns expressed in Leviticus; for example, the extensive attention to bodily discharges (chapters 12 and 15). Anthropologist Mary Douglas observes that "when rituals express anxiety about the body's orifices the sociological counterpart of this anxiety is a care to protect the political and cultural unity of a minority group."[58] Biblical scholar Norman Gottwald concludes also that the "passion to differentiate Israel as a distinct people with its own peculiar marks of circumcision, Sabbath, food laws, festivals, and sacrifices" was a *"stabilizing strategy . . .* to preserve Jewish community in the midst of disorienting exilic and restoration conditions." That these instructions and distinctions were compiled and made during the "profound shock that Israel underwent in the transition from political independence to colonial servitude" is not insignificant to the study of homophobic violence in our day.[59]

It is this characteristic of exaggerated patriarchy in the face of diminishing national power that allows for some prediction concerning anti-gay/lesbian violence in North America.

A SPECULATIVE SCENARIO TO PREDICT ANTI-GAY/LESBIAN VIOLENCE

The lesbian/gay movement has come of age during the post–World War II period of U.S. economic growth and international power. Without intending to undermine either the gains lesbians and gay men have made or the suffering we have endured, I suggest that we have been tolerated and become more visible in a country that has enjoyed stability and expansion for forty years. Its thrust has not been to exclude and define itself narrowly, because its position has not been threatened or uncertain. However, if predictions about its future loss of stature and economic stability are accurate, we might expect that it will seek new ways to exercise its authority, however reduced and limited. An early signal of efforts to prove itself powerful in the face of its diminishing standing may be the invasions of Grenada and Panama and the bombing of Libya. These efforts seem to "relate more to image than national interest, to public relations rather than political concerns."[60]

Economist Benjamin Friedman observes that the United States entered the 1980s with a government debt ratio (26 cents out of each income dollar to pay off the debt completely) equal to that of the 1870s and 1920s. The series of budget deficits that followed broke that record of steadiness with a debt ratio of 44 cents for each dollar of income by 1987. Friedman holds as responsible the abrupt change in fiscal policy initiated by the Reagan administration, which was based on the "supply-side" argument that the "incentive effects of across-the-board cuts in personal tax rates would so stimulate individual's work efforts and business initiatives that lower tax *rates* would deliver higher tax *revenues.*" However, "net business capital formation sagged instead of increased," because major tax cuts were not accompanied by significant limits on government spending. The promise of increased investment and productivity was stymied as a growing deficit absorbed the country's assets. "Seven years of our new fiscal policy—all years of peacetime— more than doubled federal indebtedness, while the size of the nation's economy increased by barely half."[61]

The shift in fiscal policy has been from one of tax and spend to one of spend and borrow. To continue spending without incoming tax revenues, the government has simply sold assets to and borrowed from foreign investors. As a result, the U.S. government owes nearly one half of the rapidly increasing debt to foreign lenders.[62] Until 1981 the United States had been a "net creditor country and increasingly so"; the new "policy has transformed us from a creditor to a debtor" nation. Friedman observes that "world power and influence have historically accrued to creditor countries"; Japan and West Germany have now emerged as the world's largest creditors.[63]

The United States is not in a position simply to regain lost power. Assets and position have already been transferred, or the momentum of the process is so great as to be irreversible. Foreign investors will not likely give them or sell them back to the U.S. simply out of kindness.[64] The changes will include not only a reduction in U.S. international influence and an increase of foreign control of business here, but a greatly reduced standard of living for individuals.

Domestic solutions—to spend less and tax more—will be neither easily implemented nor adjusted to without great alarm and hardship by American workers and consumers. In the past, such efforts to remedy much smaller deficits have created recessions, which will seem minuscule compared to one caused by trying to narrow today's enormous deficit. Typically in recessions, moreover, difficulties do not fall equally on all people. Friedman foresees inequalities multiplying "enormously." When the "reduction of American incomes required to restore international equilibrium" does occur, the effect will be harsher than ever before "because it will take place in the context of little real growth." In addition to "handing over our assets to foreigners to service our debt," the "new fiscal policy has left a lower stock of productive capital and therefore a lower level of productivity than we otherwise would have had." When standards of living plummet, especially unequally among groups, conflicts and boundaries between groups will sharpen.[65]

Friedman notes also that consonant with the new fiscal policy, and in contrast to the emerging creditor nations, has been the U.S.'s strengthening of its military position. Maintaining military superiority while the U.S. economy stagnates and the economies of other nations gain will offer no long-term or "practical prospect"; other nations will need the military protection and support of the United States less and less, and supporting the military establishment will become a greater burden for this country. Friedman concludes that the rewards of military primacy, which include the "confidence and responsibility that come from full control over its deployment," pale "when the costs become too great in relation to a nation's resources."[66]

I use Friedman's analysis not to predict a specific future, but simply to propose a scenario as a context for ethical analysis. Even if Friedman is mistaken,[67] there are sufficient sources of anxiety in our society—fear of war, terrorism, crime, the drug traffic, poverty, homelessness, and AIDS—to encourage the kind of scapegoating that can lead to anti-gay/lesbian violence.[68] Observable changes and developments in post–World War II public policy, however, tend to confirm and complete the Friedman scenario.

In the decade following World War II, the tightening of the patriarchal reins—as reflected in reestablishing the family as nuclear, returning women to housework and/or secondary-worker status, defining men as providers for the household, and formalizing the repression of political and sexual "deviance" in the form of the McCarthy hearings and the Cold War—was instrumental in gearing up the United States for dominance in world affairs. Once in power, the social order could tolerate resistance against these measures and soften them. The civil rights, peace, student, women's, and lesbian/gay movements evidence such protest; and civil rights and affirmative action legislation, greater access to and curricular reform within higher education, military and diplomatic withdrawal from Vietnam, the *Roe* v. *Wade* Supreme Court decision, and the repeal of sodomy laws in some states and the passage of gay/lesbian rights ordinances in some municipalities evidence their incorporation into public policy.

Signaling the retrenchment and eventual cancellation of these permissions for (using the terms from Collins' model; see chapter 4) lower-echelon Brothers, Daughters, and Aliens to gain acceptance are the following developments in the late 1970s and 1980s: the defeat of the Equal Rights Amendment[69]; the defeat of and difficulties in passing proposed gay/lesbian rights legislation[70]; the resurgence and popularity of a "return to classical pedagogy" in higher education[71]; the documented widening gap between rich and poor[72]; military adventurism (Libya, Grenada, and Panama)[73] and fantasy (Star Wars)[74]; renewed space exploration[75]; and the Supreme court's *Bowers* v. *Hardwick* decision, its unsolicited request to hear argument concerning one of the most fundamental pieces of civil rights legislation, its dismantling of affirmative action programs, and its reconsideration of *Roe* v. Wade.[76] Increases in reports of rape and racist harassment on college campuses and of anti-Semitic, racist, and anti-gay/lesbian incidents in the public sphere[77] may be reactions that support these policy statements, reflect in individual behavior the loss of and desperate attempt to regain power nationally, and/or express a perceived loss of control by those who feel socially entitled to it. The tendency toward the precise formulation of restrictions in matters of daily life and sexuality does not seem unlike that observed in Leviticus. The exaggerated and desperate grasp for power in the face of diminishing national standing may tie us to the situation in Leviticus and let us use that document for understanding what we can do during our times.

If we have begun to expect and rely on a progressive social agenda that assumes eventual equality, a reading of Leviticus should show that some abrupt turnabouts and challenges could easily disrupt and threaten expectations and practice. As a nation whose social order remains patriarchal, its desperate attempts to recount and redefine its authority along traditional lines would mean a renewed emphasis on heterosexual male superiority; and lesbians and gay men would be identified and targeted more emphatically and by more than male adolescents. The inequality of economic hardship imposed by a recession might engender anti-gay/lesbian action by more groups experiencing the loss of previously held power and security. Legislation restricting sexual choice could legalize or more pointedly sanction anti-gay/lesbian violence. If we have begun to expect and rely on the progressing liberation of lesbians and gay men as demonstrated during the past forty years, a study of anti-gay/lesbian violence from a biblical perspective suggests that we should seriously consider and prepare for a change of events.

History may support such speculation. The four periods of systematic and state-sanctioned violence against homosexuals that are documented in the post-Medieval West are (1) clusters of trials and executions in Geneva in the 1560s, 1590s, and the decade following 1610; (2) the campaign of killing homosexual men in Holland in 1730, as mentioned earlier; (3) a record of more than fifty hangings in England from 1806 to 1836, as recorded in parliamentary tables on criminal offenders; and (4) the extermination and work camps for homosexuals in Nazi Germany. Each nation in each period was experiencing extreme economic stagnation or hardship, foreign encroachment or competition, and/or a diminution of previously held international status.[78] One should also remember that it was not until its monarchy fell that Israel formalized anti-homosexual legislation; and it was as dependents of powerful nations—and vulnerable to intrusion, invasion, and competition from neighbors—that the American colonies enacted their legislation.[79] Such speculation is, of course, flawed by the apparent lack of systematic documentation of anti-gay/lesbian violence during other times, especially those marked by serious national and social insecurity, such as during the Revolutionary War, the War of 1812, and after the Civil War in the United States. But even here a pattern is suggested by reports of individual incidents of anti-homosexual punishment and violence that are not documented at other times.[80]

A SURVIVALIST, COMMUNAL NORM MEETS A BIBLICAL NORM

I remember the remarks of a gay man at a memorial service five years ago in New York City for those who had died of AIDS and anti-gay/lesbian violence. He had lived in Berlin before Hitler's rise and had managed to escape. He was direct in saying that he wanted to convey a particular message very clearly. He told us that if anyone had tried to tell him and his friends what was going to happen in Germany, none of them would have believed it. He said that to be a gay man in Berlin was to feel so free that he could not imagine then that it would ever end.[81] The experience of that day, especially as I have studied anti-gay/lesbian violence and attempted to work as a gay scholar and live as a gay person, remains normative for me today.

However, lesbians and gay men in North America in the 1980s have an advantage that appears unprecedented. The modern lesbian/gay movement gained its impetus and was sustained by organized resistance to anti-gay/lesbian violence and harassment. As discussed in chapter 1, organizing efforts in the lesbian/gay community in the 1950s focused on police brutality and raids of lesbian/gay bars, which also provoked in Los Angeles the largest public demonstration by lesbians and gay men of the 1960s and in New York City the turning point of the movement, the Stonewall Rebellion of 1969. In anticipation of possible assassination, San Francisco's gay supervisor, Harvey Milk, left this message in 1979:

"If a bullet should enter my brain, let that bullet destroy every closet door." Within a year of his being murdered, the first anti-gay/lesbian violence project was formed. Others on a national level and in most major cities followed and became in the 1980s one of the most prominent kinds of organization within the gay/lesbian community.

If a biblical perspective can serve as a resource for predicting the future of anti-gay/lesbian violence, the experience of lesbians and gay men can serve as a resource for surviving and perhaps altering it. If resistance to violence has indeed been the primary organizing principle for the postwar lesbian/gay community, increased violence may not necessarily take lesbians and gay men by surprise nor catch them unprepared for it. That which is most remarkable and historically unique about the postwar lesbian/gay movement may provide the perspective, experience, and principle that will determine the survival of lesbians and gay men. I cannot describe the shape that strategies may take as much as identify that which is a usable resource from the lesbian/gay community's experience in the past forty years. Although the scope and manner of violence that gay men and lesbians face in the future may be unlike what they can imagine, their common experience and recent history would suggest that their community has been shaped by their ability and willingness to respond to extreme physical oppression. It may be this practice that lesbians and gay men are best advised to develop even more consciously as normative for their survival and communal advancement.

A Biblical, Ethical Norm—The Transformation of Pain, Suffering, and Death. Although the brevity of the particular anti-homosexual passages in Leviticus has been noted, the tertiary role that its narrative theme, the "Sojourn at Sinai," plays in the Pentateuch has not.

Since the narratives of the sojourn in the wilderness treat a theme which is subordinate and dependent, because it needs to lean on major themes both before and after, the choice in ascertaining the original elements of the Pentateuchal tradition finally rests between the themes of "the exodus from Egypt" and "the taking possession of the arable land," both of which are in essence closely related, even though the former has the greater weight and thus the right to be accorded priority.[82]

Like the other major themes in the Pentateuch—"Promise to the Patriarchs" (Genesis), "Guidance in the Wilderness" (Numbers and Deuteronomy), and "Guidance to the Promised Land" (Deuteronomy)—the "Sojourn at Sinai" of Leviticus depends on and is comprehensible only in terms of the primary event of the Exodus.

Also, subsequent to the Pentateuch throughout Hebrew scripture, "one of the most fundamental and frequently repeated statements of faith . . . is that Yahweh . . . is the one who 'led Israel out of Egypt.' " Not only can the entire history of the Pentateuchal traditions be understood from the standpoint of the Exodus, but it is the event that was and is remembered, rehearsed, and held as central in communities of Jewish faith, as well as by the Christian church. "The belief in the deliverance from Egypt belonged to the oldest and most universal heritage of the Israelite tribes" and is manifest today in the continuing celebration of the Passover Feast for Jews and in liberation theologies for many Christians. Pilgrims fleeing to North America in 1620 and the movement to abolish slavery in the nineteenth century also found scriptural support and guidance in the story of the Exodus.[83]

Drawing on all three sources—the Yahwist (J), Elohist (E), and Priestly (P)—the book of Exodus tells the story of the deliverance from slavery in Egypt with repeated emphasis on the oppression, affliction, physical hardship, and suffering of the slaves.[84] Yahweh's well-known words to Moses are, "I have seen the affliction of my people who are in Egypt, and have heard their cry because of their taskmasters; I know their sufferings, and I have come down to deliver them out of the hand of the Egyptians" (Exodus 3:7–8a).[85] Central to the event is the unacceptability of pain and suffering inflicted upon one person or people by another. Pain or suffering is the human experience upon which this event turns; and it turns to alter it. The Exodus is an event or story about overcoming and transforming pain and oppression. The story of the Exodus is first and foremost a story of change from slavery to freedom.

The response of lesbians and gay men to anti-gay/lesbian violence may occasion the remembering of this event that is historically certain and supposedly immediate for Christians and Jews. The redirection of Christians and Jews to these events by those who are marginalized and not taken seriously in our society also seems to echo the original and normative location and generation of these transformative events (i.e., in the lives of slaves and outcasts). Christians and Jews today may be as surprised as were the Egyptians to find that those favored as models for freedom, salvation, and liberation are to be found among the least favored socially. The ethical norm of the Exodus overarches not only the narrative theme of Leviticus but its regulations as well. It compels one to reject the authority of such passages as Leviticus 20:13, because they prosper painful, static suffering. The Exodus is the occasion not for obedience and silence, but to transform the social conditions under which pain and suffering occur.

The reluctance of organized religion in the United States to participate in transforming the pain and suffering of lesbians and gay men suggests that the Exodus event is not always ethically normative. It may be a story or standard that is repeated and celebrated in worship and doctrine, but it does not always inform practice. The Exodus is perhaps more normative for those who suffer and work to transform their suffering outside of the churches and synagogues than for those who are within them and remain cut off from such suffering. The normative response of lesbians and gay men to violence directed against them and the reluctance of the organized religion to join them support the notion that ethical norms are formed more in the direct experience of and resistance to oppression than in the retelling of stories about oppression. Experience would seem to be more formative than either tradition or scripture. The ethical norms of lesbian/gay community building appear to renew and re-create the Exodus event without benefit of the formal organizations that preserve and ritualize those events; the formal organizations that preserve and ritualize those events, on the other hand, appear often to miss the opportunity to relive those events with those who suffer today.

APPENDIX A

Reported Experiences of
Anti-Gay/Lesbian Verbal Harassment
from Comstock Survey

Number of respondents in survey: 291 (women, 125; men, 166; people of color, 68; white, 223).

Percentage of all respondents who report having been the victim of anti-gay/lesbian verbal harassment, which includes anti-gay/lesbian names (e.g., *faggot, dyke, sissy, manhater, queer, pervert,* etc.), insults, or threats of violence, having been directed at them by heterosexual people because of their sexual orientation: 89%
   By gender of respondents:
   women, 86%
   men, 91%
   By racial identities of respondents:
   people of color, 94%
   white, 87%
   By race and gender of respondents:
   women of color, 92%; white women, 85%
   men of color, 95%; white men, 89%
   By class background (and gender) of respondents:
   lower, 89% (women, 89%; men, 89%)
   middle, 91% (women, 87%; men, 93%)
   upper, 85% (women, 81%; men, 90%)
   By yearly income of respondents:
   under $5,000, 85% (women, 81%; men, 89%)

$5,000–10,000, 90% (women, 88%; men, 92%)
$10,000–15,000, 85% (women, 90%; men, 82%)
$15,000–20,000, 86% (women, 77%; men, 95%)
$20,000–25,000, 91% (women, 90%; men, 92%)
Over $25,000, 83% (women, 77%; men, 87%)

Language used by perpetrators (percentage of respondents reporting verbal harassment); language that
disparaged homosexuality, 71%
referred to God, religion, or the bible, 39%
boasted of heterosexuality, 32%
referred to AIDS, 26%
was anti-feminist or anti-woman, 26%
was racially insulting, 13%
was ethnically insulting, 9%

Settings of incidents (percentage of respondents reporting verbal harassment):
outside lesbian/gay bar, disco, bathhouse, 41%
on street in predominantly straight neighborhood, 32%
in senior high school, 30%
at work, 29%
in a place for the general public, 29%
at lesbian/gay event, 29%
in college, 25%
on street in predominantly lesbian/gay neighborhood, 24%
on public transportation, 21%
in junior high school, 21%
in parents' home, 19%
in other person's home, 16%
in an area known for cruising, not adjacent to bar, 13%
in own home, 13%
in other relative's home, 9%
other, 7%

Perpetrator's identities (percentage of respondents reporting verbal harassment):
unknown (stranger), 62%
fellow student, 30%

fellow employee, 27%
neighbor, 14%
police, 14%
friend, 12%
female parent, 12%
brother, 12%
male parent, 11%
sister, 10%
boss, supervisor, manager, 8%
other male relative, 7%
priest, minister, pastor, 6%
teacher, 6%
nurse, 5%
psychiatrist, therapist, counselor, 4%
fellow churchmember, 4%
doctor, 3%
other female relative, 2%
other, 7%

Information about perpetrators taken from 243 reported single incidents (percentage of incidents of verbal harassment; totals equal more than 100 because incidents often involve more than one perpetrator):
Gender:
male, 89%
female, 15%
Race:
white, 75%
black, 16%
Hispanic, 8%
other, 2%
Asian, 1%
Age:
under 21, 51%
22–28, 32%
29–36, 15%
37–43, 6%
44–50, 6%
over 50, 3%

Number of harasser(s):
one, 39%
two, 19%
three, 14%
four, 14%
five, 5%
six, 6%
seven +, 2%
Number harassed:
alone, 35%
with one other, 35%
with more than one other, 30%

APPENDIX B

Further Tables

TABLE B.1

*Percentages of Respondents Reporting General Anti-Gay/Lesbian Violence,
by Gender of Respondents*

Survey	Women (%)	Men (%)	All (%)
Wichita (N = 96)	0	11	8
Bell/Weinberg (N = 977)	3	35	25
Philadelphia-1 (N = 167)	10	24	17
Richmond (N = 475)	28	35	33
Philadelphia-2 (N = 167)	39	63	51
Comstock (N = 291)	42	62	54
Alaska (N = 705)	59	65	61

SOURCE: Summary of findings from seven surveys.

TABLE B.2

*Percentages of Respondents Reporting General Anti-Gay/Lesbian Violence,
by Racial Identity of Respondents*

	Respondents		
Survey	Color (%)	White (%)	All (%)
Bell/Weinberg (N = 977)	15	28	25
Richmond (N = 475)	31	33	33
Comstock (N = 291)	68	50	54

SOURCE: Summary of findings from three surveys.

TABLE B.3

Percentages of Respondents Reporting General Anti-Gay/Lesbian Violence,
by Race and Gender of Respondents

	Women (%)		Men (%)	
Survey	Color	White	Color	White
Bell/Weinberg (N=977)	5	2	21	38
Comstock (N=291)	58	41	70	59

SOURCE: Summary of findings from two surveys.

TABLE B.4

Percentages of Respondents Reporting General Anti-Gay/Lesbian Violence,
by Yearly Financial Income and Gender of Respondents

	Income Groups (%)		
Respondents	*Lower* *(under $15,000)* N=87	*Middle* *($15 to 25,000)* N=88	*Upper* *(over $25,000)* N=93
All	53	61	49
Women	43	44	40
Men	63	76	55

SOURCE: Summary of findings from Comstock Survey.

TABLE B.5

Percentage of Respondents Reporting General Anti-Gay/Lesbian Violence,
by Class Backgrounds and Gender of Respondents

	Class-Background Groups (%)		
Respondents	*Lower* *(N=75)*	*Middle* *(N=180)*	*Upper* *(N=26)*
All	56	52	65
Women	50	36	36
Men	60	64	80

SOURCE: Summary of findings from Comstock Survey.

TABLE B.6

Percentages of Female Respondents Reporting Six Types of Anti-Gay/Lesbian Violence, in Descending Order of Occurrence

Philadelphia (%) (N=80)		NGLTF (%) (N=654)		Comstock (%) (N=125)		Average	
chased	21	chased	31	chased	28	chased	27
vandal	10	object	16	vandal	16	vandal	13
object	9	vandal	14	object	14	object	13
spit	6	spit	13	beaten	10	spit	8
beaten	4	beaten	9	spit	5	beaten	8
weapon	1	weapon	6	weapon	2	weapon	3

SOURCE: Summary of findings from three surveys.

TABLE B.7

Percentages of Male Respondents Reporting Six Types of Anti-Gay/Lesbian Violence, in Descending Order of Occurrence

Philadelphia (%) (N=87)		NGLTF (%) (N=1474)		Comstock (%) (N=166)		Average (%)	
object	34	chased	37	chased	36	chased	34
chased	28	object	33	object	27	object	31
beaten	16	beaten	24	beaten	24	beaten	21
spit	16	vandal	20	vandal	16	vandal	15
vandal	10	spit	14	weapon	11	spit	13
weapon	6	weapon	11	spit	8	weapon	9

SOURCE: Summary of findings from three surveys.

TABLE B.8

Percentages of Male Victims of Anti-Gay/Lesbian Violence Reporting Groups of Settings in Which Incidents Were Experienced, by Racial Identity

Men of Color (%) (N=39)		White Men (%) (N=65)	
Setting			
public lesbian/gay	67	public lesbian/gay	66
schools	36	public non-lesbian/gay	28
homes	23	homes	25
public non-lesbian/gay	23	schools	25

SOURCE: Summary of findings from Comstock Survey.
NOTE: Settings are in descending order of occurrence.

TABLE B.9

Percentages of White Victims of Anti-Gay/Lesbian Violence Reporting Groups of Settings in Which Incidents Were Experienced, by Gender

Women (%) (N=46)		Men (%) (N=65)	
Setting			
public non-lesbian/gay	48	public lesbian/gay	66
public lesbian/gay	41	public non-lesbian/gay	28
homes	24	homes	25
schools	20	schools	25

SOURCE: Summary of findings from Comstock Survey.
NOTE: Settings are in descending order of occurrence.

TABLE B.10

Average Ages of Victims and Perpetrators

	Incidents Involving:		
Ages of:	Female Victims (N=41)	Male Victims (N=76)	All Victims (N=117)
victims			
low	19	10	10
high	39	40	40
average	26	26	26
perpetrators			
low	14	13	13
high	55	45	55
average	29	24	27

SOURCE: Summary of findings from Comstock Survey.

TABLE B.11

Number of Perpetrators per Incident According to the Ages of Perpetrators and Genders of Victims

	Incidents Involving:		
Ages of Perpetrators	Female Victims (N=41)	Male Victims (N=70)	All Victims (N=111)
21 under	2.63	2.92	2.84
22 to 28	2.75	1.83	2.11
29 to 36	1.13	1.57	1.33
over 36	1.22	1.20	1.21
all perpetrators	2.27	2.41	2.36

SOURCE: Summary of findings from Comstock Survey.

TABLE B.12

Number of Perpetrators per Victim According to the Ages of Perpetrators and Genders of Victims

	Incidents Involving:		
Ages of Perpetrators	Female Victims (N = 41)	Male Victims (N = 70)	All Victims (N = 111)
21 under	1.08	1.93	1.61
22 to 28	1.83	1.31	1.48
29 to 36	0.60	1.57	0.91
over 36	0.71	0.75	0.73
all perpetrators	1.07	1.60	1.37

SOURCE: Summary of findings from Comstock Survey.

TABLE B.14

Number of Perpetrators per Incident According to the Racial Identities of Perpetrators and Genders of Victims

	Incidents Involving:		
Racial Identities of Perpetrators	Female Victims (N = 41)	Male Victims (N = 76)	All Victims (N = 117)
of color (N = 96)	2.20	2.73	2.65
white (N = 196)	2.44	2.51	2.48
all (N = 292)	2.38	2.60	2.53

SOURCE: Summary of findings from Comstock Survey.

TABLE B.15

Number of Perpetrators per Victim According to the Racial Identities of Perpetrators and Genders of Victims

	Incidents Involving:		
Racial Identities of Perpetrators	Female Victims (N = 79)	Male Victims (N = 117)	All Victims (N = 197)
of color (N = 96)	1.10	1.97	1.80
white (N = 196)	1.20	1.53	1.37
all (N = 292)	1.17	1.69	1.48

SOURCE: Summary of findings from Comstock Survey.

TABLE B.16

Percentages of Incidents in Which Perpetrators Were Alone When Attacking Their Victims, According to the Ages of Perpetrators and Genders of Victims

	Incidents Involving:		
Racial Identities of Perpetrators	Female (%) (N=41)	Male (%) (N=76)	All Victims (%) (N=117)
of color (N=36)	60	42	44
white (N=81)	47	49	48
all (N=117)	49	46	47

SOURCE: Summary of findings from Comstock Survey.

TABLE B.17

Number of Perpetrators per Incident According to the Racial Identities of Perpetrators and Victims

	Incidents Involving:		
Racial Identities of Perpetrators	Victims of Color (%) (N=25)	White (%) (N=91)	All Victims (%) (N=116)
of color (N=96)	2.55	2.70	2.65
white (N=196)	3.00	2.33	2.45
all (N=292)	2.80	2.43	2.51

SOURCE: Summary of findings from Comstock Survey.

TABLE B.18

Number of Perpetrators per Victim According to the Racial Identities of Perpetrators and Victims

	Racial Identities of Victims		
Racial Identities of Perpetrators	Victims of Color (N=39)	White (N=157)	All (N=196)
Victims of color (N=96)	1.65	1.88	1.80
white (N=196)	1.91	1.27	1.37
all (N=292)	1.79	1.41	1.49

SOURCE: Summary of findings from Comstock Survey.

TABLE B.19

Percentages of Incidents in Which Perpetrators Were Alone When Attacking Their Victims, According to the Racial Identities of Perpetrators and Victims

Racial Identities of Perpetrators	Incidents Involving:		
	Victims of Color (%) (N=25)	White (%) (N=91)	All Victims (%) (N=116)
of color (N=36)	36	48	45
white (N=80)	36	50	48
all (N=116)	36	49	47

SOURCE: Summary of findings from Comstock Survey.

APPENDIX C

The Police as Perpetrators
of Anti-Gay/Lesbian Violence

Data from other sources support the frequency of violence by the police found in my survey (see chapter 3). The quarterly reports of the Community United Against Violence (CUAV) in San Francisco from January 1984 to March 1986, for example, show that an average of 8 percent of reported incidents (with a low of 4 percent and a high of 17 percent per quarter) involved physical assault by law enforcement officers.[1] Incidents are also reported with noticeable frequency in the gay/lesbian, alternative, and mainstream media.[2]

Newspaper coverage shows that in addition to the targeting of individuals, police have been known to conduct authorized and unauthorized raids on bars and bathhouses during which unprovoked and unnecessary violence has been perpetrated.[3] Off-duty police have also been reported to assault lesbians and gay men and to be assisted and/or not arrested by uniformed police called to the scene of the crime.[4]

The study by Project Understanding in Winnipeg, Manitoba, finds that in response to calls for assistance by victims of anti-gay/lesbian violence the practice of on-duty police officers is frequently (1) to refuse to intervene, either to protect the victims or to apprehend the perpetrators; (2) to minimize the seriousness of reported incidents, because the victims are lesbian or gay; (3) to blame the victims; and (4) to harass verbally and/or to abuse physically the victims.[5] Reflecting on eight years of experience, a county attorney in Iowa recently observed that lesbians and gay men are often "physically assaulted on the streets, with the police looking the other way."[6]

Although violence by police officers that exceeds the "requirements of . . . arrest and the protection of themselves and the community"[7] is technically illegal or outside of the law, it is practiced. As the district attorney of New York County said in his statement for the October 1986 hearings on anti-gay/lesbian violence before the U.S. House of Representatives Committee on the Judiciary, Subcommittee on Criminal Justice, "at times, [lesbians and gay men] have been, and in many areas of the country continue to be, taunted, harassed, and even physically assaulted by the very people whose job it is to protect them."[8]

A 1951 case study of a municipal police force by sociologist William A. Westley[9] shows that the use of illegal violence is considered "morally acceptable and legitimate" by police officers "with respect to to the conviction of the felon and[10] . . . with respect to the control of sexual conduct."[11] The study cites the remarks of a patrolman who "misuses" his powers against "sexual deviants":

Now in my own cases when I catch a guy like that I just pick him up and take him into the woods and beat him until he can't crawl. I have had seventeen cases like that in the last couple of years. I tell that guy if I catch him doing that again I will take him out to the woods and I will shoot him. I tell him that I carry a second gun on me just in case I find guys like him and that I will plant it in his hand and say that he tried to kill me and that no jury will convict me.[12]

The following statement, made in 1976 by a former police officer in the Los Angeles Police Department, is further evidence that inappropriate arresting procedures and excessive violence are commonly used against lesbians and gay men:

The L.A.P.D. has always maniacally prosecuted vice and victimless crimes far beyond what they have to do. . . . Well, the police will beat up anybody. . . . Let me tell you about reality. . . . If a guy [arrested] hits you, being a human being . . . you hit him back, only you don't hit him back once, you hit him back three times or four or five however many it takes to get the rage out of your system, because you're a human being. . . . He knocks one tooth out, you knock all his teeth out. . . . Just life. So when a gay says: "Cops beat us up. The cop beat me up." Well, the fact of the matter is, I've nothing to brag about, but I was a vice cop and I probably arrested 300 to 400 gays in my life.[13]

The Council on Religion and the Homosexual, formed by church ministers in San Francisco, conducted a major study of local law enforcement practices in 1965 and found that "through deceit and inducement, lure and suggestion, both police and [Alcoholic Beverage Commission] undercover agents encourage solicitations for sexual acts," a manner of enforcement which "fosters oppression, blackmail, and discrimination."[14]

Westley finds that because "policemen cannot and do not employ sanctions against their colleagues for using violence"[15] (even those "who personally condemn the use of violence and avoid it whenever possible refuse openly to condemn acts of violence by other men on the force"[16]), a collective permission allows those inclined to use it to do so without fear.[17] A 1976 report on the Toronto Metropolitan Police Complaints Bureau by Justice Morand concurs. The *Morand Report*'s findings show that the "investigation [by police officers assigned to the Bureau] of serious allegations of excessive force, are incomplete, not impartial, and largely unsupervised"; and, furthermore, that the "police tend to support each other to defeat allegations against a fellow police officer."[18] Although Westley notes that it is the "emphasis on secrecy among the police [that] prevents them from using legal sanctions against their colleagues,"[19] other sources indicate that the disapproval of homosexuality shared by most police officers permits and encourages the use of illegal violence against lesbians and gay men.[20]

Another and later study of police behavior conducted in the mid-1960s by Arthur Niederhoffer, a criminologist, police academy instructor, former police officer, and university instructor in New York City,[21] shows that from a "randomly arranged list of the most disliked segments of the police clientele," a sample of 186 New York City policemen ranked "homosexuals" as the most disliked group, second only to "cop-fighters."[22] Both Westerly and Niederhoffer conclude that policemen do exhibit an exaggerated hatred of "sexual deviants" and that their intolerance "manifests itself in extremely rough treatment of the offender [sic], the 'take him out in the alley and beat him up' attitude."[23]

Although the commonly and publicly stated justification for the pursuit and arrest of homosexuals is to protect average citizens from sexual solicitation and exposure to lewd behavior by unsavory characters, an empirical study published in a 1966 issue of the *UCLA Law Review* presents evidence that such protection is not necessary.[24] In its examination of the enforcement and administration in Los Angeles County of the California Penal Code regulating adult homosexual behavior, the study finds the following:

Societal interests are infringed only when a solicitation to engage in a homosexual act creates a reasonable risk of offending public decency. The incidence of such solicitations is statistically insignificant. The majority of homosexual solicitations are made only if the other individual appears responsive and are ordinarily accomplished by quiet conversation and the use of gestures and signals having significance only to the other homosexuals. Such unobtrusive solicitations do not involve an element of public outrage.[25]

Not only do "interviews with police departments indicate that communications from citizens complaining about solicitation by homosexuals are rare,"[26] but court records also show that 51 percent of the homosexual misdemeanor arrests were made by police decoys initiating and making sexual propositions.[27] The study concludes that the "rare indiscriminate solicitations of the general public [by homosexuals] do not justify the commitment of police resources to suppress such behavior."[28]

Nor are claims by the police to be acting to prevent the sexual abuse and recruitment of children by lesbians and gay men based on documented evidence that such a problem exists.[29] Studies find that 90 percent of all reported child molestations are by adult males of female minors.[30] However, the police themselves have been known to jeopardize the welfare of children for their own interest in accomplishing arrests. The following example is illustrative. In his documentary treatment of a nationally publicized homosexual scandal in Boise, Idaho, in 1955, John Gerassi points out that the sheriff, who claimed to want to protect the youth from being led astray, settled on apprehending a young man who, by the time the episode had surfaced, was enrolled at West Point. The young man was implicated for an encounter that had happened when he was fourteen; he was now seventeen. Gerassi asks the sheriff, "Why get the kid who was now out of the whole mess mixed into it again?" The subsequent trial brought an end to his career in the Army. The sheriff was not willing to respond to the question. The boy's father claims that it was a "political witch hunt" to get at himself, a city councilman, through his son.[31] Another incident is reported by Laud Humphreys in his study of impersonal sex in public places.[32] Humphreys interviewed a young man who as a fourteen-year-old had been recruited, paid, and used by the police of a Louisiana city to engage in sex with older men for the purpose of subsequently signing a statement against them at the police station. The boy explained:

Well—like I got in trouble. I guess you'd say I did a little shoplifting and got caught. . . . Well, then, my folks were pretty stiff with me then, and I threw a big thing about not wanting them to know. So this one officer offered me a way out. He took me down to the vice squad—and they put me to work. . . . In that summer, I cleared about two hundred dollars from them. It was all cash and never listed in the police department or anything like this.[33]

Although studies show that children do not need police protection from lesbians and gay men, similar evidence does not exist to show that police officers are not above using children for their own purposes.

Nor, as regards the assertive arresting of lesbians and gay men, can the police claim simply to be enforcing indiscriminately one set of laws as they do all laws.[34] Kinsey shows in his 1948 study *Sexual Behavior in the Human Male* that a truly thorough "call for a clean-up of the sex offenders in a community" would mean apprehending 95 percent of the male population. That many men reported having engaged in premarital intercourse, mouth–genital contacts, relations with prostitutes, extramarital intercourse, homosexuality, and animal intercourse—all illicit activities at that time.[35] But laws are selectively enforced; and lesbians and gay men are frequently targeted for preferential arrest. Sherri Cavan's 1966 ethnography of bar behavior provides the following example:

While the court may rule that regardless of whether they are heterosexual or homosexual in nature, "any public display which manifests sexual desires . . . may be and historically has been suppressed and regulated in a moral society," in actual practice the legal suppression and regulation of such activity in public drinking places is typically encountered only in homosexual bars.[36]

Diana Sepejak's 1977 study "The Willingness of Homosexuals to Report Criminal Victimization to the Police" observes further that "selective surveillance" is based not on "realistic probabilities" but on prejudice. She states that "homosexual establishments are frequently surveyed, not for violations of any sex laws *per se,* but for such things as the possession and proper display of liquor licenses." Harassment is involved "if these establishments are surveyed more frequently than those establishments which cater to the majority." Sepejak adds that the "fact remains that homosexual establishments regularly have their liquor licenses checked, church socials rarely do."[37]

That the police tend not only to enforce laws selectively, but to favor and support the continuation of laws that can be used against lesbians and gay men is demonstrated by their organized attempts to prevent the repeal of such laws. For example, the Canadian Association of Police Chiefs, at their annual conference in 1968, voted against endorsing proposed legislation to decriminalize homosexuality. In 1967 and 1969 the Toronto police force also mounted organized opposition to such a change.[38] Concerning lesbians and gay men, the police appear to be interested not simply in enforcing legislation, but in influencing it.

Although some criminologists maintain that the "laws which are selected for enforcement are those which the power structure of the community want enforced,"[39] other evidence suggests that police as individuals and as a group act independently of social and political pressure to single out lesbians and gay men. For example, even though the Canadian Association of Police Chiefs based its opposition to changing legislation on the claim that the "life-style of homosexuals is abhorrent to most members of the society [the police] serve," the willingness of the legislature and the public to discuss and change former rules and attitudes suggests that the police are acting contrary instead of according to public opinion. Police resistance to regarding lesbians and gay men as anything other than sexual deviants and their organized stand against any official and/or community support that calls for such changed status for lesbians and gay men are no more sharply demonstrated than in the opposition of police to hiring lesbians and gay men as fellow workers. For example, the United States Commission on Civil Rights made the following recommendation in 1981:

Although homosexuals presently do not enjoy the protection of federal civil rights laws accorded to racial minorities and women, this does not prevent cities and police departments from taking steps to remove hiring barriers and to ensure that police services are provided in a fair and unbiased way and that all members of the community are treated with respect regardless of actual or perceived sexual orientation. One step that could be taken to minimize the confrontations that commonly take place between the police and the homosexual community is the hiring of [gay and lesbian] police officers.[40]

Yet the International Association of Chiefs of Police continued to endorse a "no hire policy for homosexuals in law enforcement."[41] The official publication of the Police Officers Association in San Francisco stated in 1979 that "insisting on recruiting a certain percentage of homosexuals into the field of law enforcement is as reasonable as insisting on the same representation of diabetics, epileptics, child molesters, rapists."[42]

Characteristics of individuals who serve as policemen provide a profile of lower-status males who desire to enter an occupation in which they are permitted to use violence. A policewoman observes:

Women come and stay in the police department to avoid dull jobs and get good pay. . . . But the men come for strange reasons. They're a bunch of egomaniacs; they're insecure and want to bolster themselves and prove their manhood. They try to be big shots and feel like men by bossing people around. . . . The men say the women aren't aggressive enough. . . . But that's 'cause women aren't searching for manhood; we don't need to bully people.[43]

Studies find that policemen tend (1) to come from working-class and lower-class backgrounds, (2) to have high school educations, and (3) to have been previously employed mostly as unskilled or semiskilled workers, or in clerical and sales positions.[44] One sample shows that less than half are married or parents.[45] A researcher reports that "police have profound doubts about their social status; unsure whether they belong to the working or middle class, they strongly desire acceptance in the latter."[46] And although the job is reputedly associated with risk, toughness, heroics, and excitement, " 'dangerous' activities represent less than 10 percent of police patrol time."[47]

The police cadet appears to be a low-ranking male who seeks higher status in a job that does not in reality offer it. National surveys asking the general population to rank the prestige of occupations give mediocre social status to policing: "Despite the fact that the officer has power over our highest social values (life and honor, liberty and justice) policing remains a tainted occupation, and the officer is regarded as someone who does society's dirty work."[48] The "feminized taint" of the occupation is "rescued" by the accompanying authority to be armed and to enforce the law with violence, if necessary. Policemen admit that homosexuals are high among those against whom they frequently use illegal or unnecessary violence.[49]

That lesbians and gay men do not typically seek out and rely on the police for protection does not come as a surprise, therefore. Seventy-eight percent of the respondents in the Richmond survey indicate that they "receive less than equal protection from Richmond city police."[50] The Winnipeg study finds that in 56 percent of the cases in which police assistance was sought the behavior of the responding officers was markedly unsatisfactory; it concludes that the "reluctance by gay people to call for assistance of the police has . . . arisen in part from unfortunate past experience with city police officers."[51] Considering such a history of neglect and abusive treatment by law enforcement personnel, New York County District Attorney Morgenthau says, "it is no wonder, then, that violence against gay men and lesbians . . . often goes unreported."[52]

Robert J. Johnston, Jr., chief of the New York City Police Department, agrees that "crimes against the gay/lesbian community are probably severely under-reported."[53] In my survey, of those respondents who had experienced some form of anti-gay/lesbian violence,[54] 73 percent said they had never reported an incident to the police. (See table C.1 for a breakdown of nonreporting according to the gender and race of victims.) Of those who had been the victims of very serious anti-gay/lesbian violence,[55] 58 percent said they had never reported an incident to the police. (See table C.2 for a breakdown of nonreporting figures according to the gender and race of victims.) Other surveys find percentages of nonreporting ranging from 67 percent to 91 percent.[56] A 1983 study by the mayor's office of San Francisco, *The Mayor's Survey of Victims of Personal Crimes,* "concluded that 82% of the victims of anti-gay violence did not report their assault to the police."[57] By contrast, among

TABLE C.1

Percentages of Victims of All Forms of Anti-Gay/Lesbian Violence Who Did Not Report Incidents to the Police

all victims	73% (114/157)
female victims	77% (41/53)
male victims	70% (73/104)
victims of color	82% (56/68)
white victims	72% (80/111)

SOURCE: Findings are from Comstock Survey.

NOTE: All forms of anti-gay/lesbian violence include: chased or followed; objects thrown at; spit at; arson or vandalism to property; punched, hit, kicked, or beaten; assaulted with weapon; robbed; and/or raped.

TABLE C.2

Percentages of Victims of Very Serious Anti-Gay/Lesbian Violence Who Did Not Report Incidents to the Police

all victims	58% (58/101)
female victims	60% (18/30)
male victims	56% (40/71)
victims of color	59% (15/27)
white victims	58% (43/74)

SOURCE: Findings are from Comstock Survey.

NOTE: Very serious anti-gay/lesbian violence includes arson or vandalism to property; punched, hit, kicked, or beaten; assaulted with weapon; robbed; and/or raped.

the general population, according to the 1984 U.S. Department of Justice statistics, 64 percent of crime victims do not report to the police.[58]

Of those victims in my survey who reported incidents to the police, 51 percent found the police helpful and courteous, 67 percent found them indifferent, 23 percent found them hostile, 5 percent found them physically abusive, and 19 percent found them competent. (See table C.3 for a breakdown of responses according to the gender and race of the victims who reported.[59]) Victims gave the following reasons for not reporting: 67 percent said they had previously experienced or perceived the police as anti-gay or anti-lesbian; 40 percent said they could not risk public disclosure of their sexual orientation; 14 percent feared that reporting would incur abuse from the police; another 14 percent said they did not have witnesses; and 9 percent said they did not think it would be worth the trouble.[60] Among the general population, 6 percent

TABLE C.3

Response of Police to Reported Incidents of Anti-Gay/Lesbian Violence
According to Victims Who Reported Incidents

Victims Reporting	Helpful, Courteous	Indifferent	Hostile	Physically Abusive	Competent
all (N = 43)	51%	67%	23%	5%	19%
female (N = 12)	50%	100%	25%	8%	17%
male (N = 31)	52%	55%	23%	3%	19%
of color (N = 12)	17%	67%	42%	8%	8%
white (N = 31)	65%	68%	16%	3%	23%

SOURCE: Findings are from Comstock Survey.

NOTE: Totals are greater than 100 percent because some respondents reported for more than one incident.

of crime victims do not report because they think the "police would not want to be bothered," and 3 percent do not report because the "police would be inefficient, ineffective, insensitive."[61] Police-related reasons for nonreporting are more frequent for victims of anti-gay/lesbian violence (67 percent and 14 percent) than for victims of crime in the general population (6 percent and 3 percent). There is also a qualitative, as well as a quantitative, difference in these reasons. For lesbians and gay men they tend to be based on fear of hostility and abuse by the police; for the general population they tend to be based on anticipation of indifference and annoyance by the police.

Some changes in relations between lesbian/gay communities and the police have been observed in recent years.[62] Kevin Berrill, director of the National Gay and Lesbian Task Force's Violence Project, notes that "where gay men and lesbians have acquired some degree of political power, reports of police harassment have decreased and cooperation between gay people and the police has increased."[63] For example:

In the Washington, D.C. mayoral race [of 1978], gay people played a key role in the election of Marion Barry, who promised to be more responsive to the concerns of their community.

Before Barry's election, police/gay relations in that city were poor: A 1978 white paper prepared by the local Gay Activists Alliance cited numerous instances of police harassment, verbal abuse, unequal enforcement of the law and lack of response/follow up to reports of crime by gay people. Since Barry's election and the appointment of Maurice Turner as Chief of Police, only one report of alleged anti-gay brutality by a police officer has been received by the Civilian Complaint Review Board. In addition, an official police liaison to the gay community has been appointed, and gay and lesbian awareness training is now mandatory for all new recruits.[64]

In other cities too lesbians and gay men have organized meetings with law enforcement officials to air complains and make suggestions.[65] Progress has been noted in those police departments whose top leadership (1) makes it clear to the rank and file that anti-lesbian/gay action is not to be tolerated[66] and (2) institutes training sessions in which officers and recruits become familiar with lesbian/gay issues.[67] The police departments in Boston, New York, Los Angeles, and San Francisco have taken measures to recruit lesbians and gay men for officer candidacy and to make bias crime a priority in its enforcement practices.[68]

Feeling the support of community networks and organizations, lesbians and gay men as individuals have become more assertive in bringing legal suits against police officers for misconduct and unnecessary violence.[69] Several cases have been won.[70]

Lesbians and gay men, however, are reluctant to accept such indications of progress as either complete or permanent. Gains have been partial and only within particular urban areas.[71] Police raids, involving unnecessary violence, still occur.[72] Training sessions are "often wedged in among a catchall minority training . . . and could be more effective," according to Trish Donahue, a law enforcement specialist with the San Francisco-based Human Rights Resource Center.[73] And if improved relations with the police typically follow upon the election of politicians who support the rights of lesbians and gay men, should not future periods of bad relations be expected when unsympathetic politicians are placed in office? The fragility characteristic of relations with the police is illustrated by a series of events following the assassination and asence of Mayor Moscone from the political scene in San Francisco. Journalist Warren Hinckle writes:

Since the deaths of Moscone and Milk, their protector and champion gays in San Francisco, have complained of increasing police harassment under the less liberal regime of Moscone's successor, Dianne Feinstein, whom gays with decreasing affection refer to as the Ayatollah Feinstein. Moscone was barely in his grave when the cops raided the Mabuhay Gardens, a punk nightclub police have been itching to bust, and crashed the Crystal Hotel in the Tenderloin, where they subjected the drag-queen tenants to the ministrations of nightsticks. "Why should you care? They're just a bunch of fruits," the sergeant in charge told the hotel's owner when he protested.

Moscone had frowned upon police poking their clubs into the business of consenting adults. Mayor Feinstein seems to hear the sound of another drummer. In a recent interview with the *Ladies Home Journal*, the attractive, ritually bebowed lady mayor said: "The rights of an individual to live as he or she chooses can become offensive—the gay community is going to have to face this."[74]

That arrests and attacks are still timed and used for political advantage and publicity is evident from events contemporaneous with the 1981 municipal and provincial elections in Ontario. A report by a gay lobby group states:

Prior to the last provincial election, the NDP and some members of the provincial Liberal Party supported the inclusion of sexual orientation in Ontario's Human Rights Code.

The timing of the bath raids [February 5, 1981] to coincide with the provincial election, coupled with a perceived right-wing swing in the electorate, appeared to many members of the public to be a use of the police by the Tory Party to embarrass both the Liberals and the NDP over the gay rights issue and to strengthen the Party's hold in its rural, conservative constituency in Southern Ontario.[75]

Experience has shown lesbians and gay men that recognition and visibility can be both denied and celebrated within a proximate time and space. Perhaps Arthur Bell captured the uncertainty, fragility, or illusion of progress in his report of incidents occurring in New York City on September 29, 1983, the date that "will go down in gay history as the night of contrasts." He writes:

Gay politics has come a long way in the 13 years since the drag queens told the cops to fuck off at Stonewall—as witness the black-tie, $150-a-plate Human Rights Campaign Fund dinner at the Waldorf last Wednesday. Yet the issue of freedom for gays hasn't moved an inch—perhaps regressed a few thousand years—as witness the police assault on the black gay bar, Blue's, on West 43rd street and the savage beating of its patrons at the very same hour [U.S. presidential Democratic nominee] Walter Mondale was giving his humdrum human rights speech at the Waldorf.[76]

Reported increases in police violence at political demonstrations by lesbian/gay people in 1989 are, also, cause for caution.[77] Unconvinced that equal rights and protection have become policy, lesbians and gay men understand the gains that have been made as isolated or single threads that have not become part of the political fabric.

Hustlers and Anti-Gay Violence

Hustlers in the gay world are boys and men who engage in sexual activity with other men for money.[1] Some are gay identified; others are not.[2] Because anti-gay violence is defined as the physical assault of a gay person by a nongay person because the victim is perceived as gay, this discussion considers only straight-identified hustlers.[3]

Some perpetrators of anti-gay violence, particularly those whose motive is robbery, pose as hustlers. They sell or offer to sell sexual activity, but only as a means to enter the customer's home and/or to subdue him. They typically forgo the agreed-upon sexual encounter, physically restrain and/or injure their supposed customer, and remove from his person or residence money or property.[4] Because these perpetrators are not technically hustlers, they are not to be so considered here.

Albert J. Reiss, Jr., in his 1961 sociological study of male homosexual prostitution, finds that hustlers who are self-identified heterosexuals tend to be lower-class, career-oriented delinquents.[5] Unlike gay-identified hustlers, these boys think of themselves as neither homosexuals nor hustlers. They "see themselves as 'getting a queer' only as a substitute activity or as part of a versatile pattern of delinquent activity." They are not career-hustlers, but career-delinquents, for whom hustling is one of several delinquent activities in which they engage to get money. It is a "transitory activity," eventually replaced by adult delinquency or by getting a job and getting married.[6]

Reiss finds that the activity is peer-sanctioned, "an institutionalized aspect of the organization of lower-class delinquency-oriented groups"[7]: "The peer-group actually serves as a school of induction for some of its members. The initiated boy goes with one or more of his peer group for indoctrination and his first experience."[8] Before a boy has his first experience with a client, he has been told by members of his peer-group how to make contacts, how to collect money when a client resists paying, and how to behave during the encounter.[9] Boys are trained to seek out clients. Hardly innocent, vulnerable children who are taken advantage of by overpowering, more highly sophisticated adults, these boys are fully aware of what they are doing and how to succeed at doing it.[10]

The training by the peer group includes passing on the four norms governing transactions. They are:

1. The sexual activity is for making money; the client must always pay and the boy must seek a transaction for the sole purpose of financial gain, never for sexual gratification.
2. Sexual activity is limited to mouth-genital fellation, with only the adult as fellator.
3. Both the boy and adult must remain affectively neutral during the transaction.
4. No violence may be used, unless the client violates any of the above norms.[11]

Violence tends to be avoided because it would disrupt the organization of the system. If violence and danger were the repeated experience and expectation of clients, the system could not exist. Since both the boys and the clients understand themselves to be delinquents and involved in delinquent activity, neither wants to behave in a manner that would draw the attention of the police. Secrecy and smooth, private transactions are in the interest of and to the benefit of both parties. Although robbers often target gay men because they perceive them to be vulnerable and lacking access to police protection, the primary concern of hustlers is their own vulnerability to arrest and incarceration. Clients, too, fearing exposure, rarely risk pushing the boys beyond that to which they are agreeable.[12]

When the boys in Reiss's study do use violence, "they always reported some violation of the subcultural expectations" (i.e., of the norms established and passed on within the peer group).[13] Reiss concludes that such violence functions (1) to control and combat behavior that violates the expectations and norms of the peer group and (2) to protect the nonhomosexual, "masculine" identity of the boys.[14] If the client decides not to pay because he thinks the boy either enjoys the sex or likes him, the boy must correct him. The boy's action is not directed at the gay identity of the client as much as it preserves the nongay identity of the boy. It is not technically anti-gay because it is not directed at the person because that person is gay; it also lacks the offensive and premeditated pursuit characteristic of most anti-gay violence. But the clearest indicator of its not being anti-gay, at least in the minds of the hustler, is that the violent reaction is motivated primarily by the client's withholding an agreed-upon fee. Reports show that the boys react with violence most often when money is withheld and much less frequently when sexual norms are violated.[15] Although separating the financial components from the sexual is impossible, the boys see the transaction as solely for money. They are most prone to attack their clients when they are not paid.

However, some hustlers, when in need of finances that exceed the usual amount of payment for sexual activity, have been known to bypass their own occupational guidelines. They have robbed and physically attacked clients with whom they have an ongoing business arrangement.[16] These attacks typically take the form of the boy's visiting the home of a client with an accomplice. Sexual activity may be offered as a pretense, but the means and purpose of the encounter are to outnumber and overpower with threats and physical injury the client until a demanded sum of money or property is relinquished. Although such actions fall outside of the usual hustler–client transaction, they take advantage of the hustler–client relationship that has been established. Technically the boy is acting as a robber, not a hustler; but the robbery is predicated on the boy's knowledge of the victim as his client. Although the attack appears to be anti-gay, in that the victim is selected because the perpetrator knows that he is, as a gay man, vulnerable to the attack and not likely to report to the police, the hustler steps out of his role to be the robber.

Studies do not show whether or not this deviation from business as usual is frequent enough to constitute yet another typical pattern of anti-gay violence. If it is not frequent, a conclusion can tentatively be made: while violence may occur within the hustling scene, as noted and discussed in the Reiss study, its purpose appears to be to enforce payment and not to be anti-gay. Violence that does appear to be anti-gay is carried out by the hustler, but in violation of his own peer-defined occupational guidelines (i.e., as a robber, not as a hustler).

Results of Comstock's Survey of Ninety-seven First-Year College Students

Each of the various groupings of respondents in all tables reported the following rank order of those who have influenced their thoughts and feelings about homosexuality: **peers, friends, parents. Popular culture** and **siblings** were next in order for all, female, and male groups of respondents. For nonviolent men, **teachers** were fourth; for violent men, the **church** was fourth.

TABLE E.1

Anti-Gay/Lesbian Verbal Harassment, Graffiti, Violence

	Respondents		
Responses	Total (%) (N = 97)	Female (%) (N = 54)	Male (%) (N = 43)
Ever verbally harassed:			
lesbians	11	9	14
gay men	22	9	37
Ever written anti-lesbian/gay graffiti in public place	10	4	19
Ever physically attacked lesbians or gay men	8	2	16
Specifically: thrown objects			
lesbians	0	0	0
gay men	1	0	2
chased/followed			
lesbians	2	2	2
gay men	3	0	7
hit/kicked/beat			
lesbians	0	0	0
gay men	4	0	9
robbed			
lesbians	0	0	0
gay men	1	0	2

NOTE: No "weapon assault" or "vandalism of property" was reported.

TABLE E.2

Attitudes, Opinions, Interaction, Socialization

	Respondents		
Responses	Total (%) (N=97)	Female (%) (N=54)	Male (%) (N=43)
Self-ranking of attitudes toward homosexuality:			
very approving	3	4	2
approving	5	7	2
neutral	34	37	30
disapproving	29	31	26
very disapproving	25	15	37
Upbringing (re:homosexuality)			
to accept	39	52	23
to disapprove	61	48	77
Support lesbian/gay rights:			
full equality	45	52	37
rights in some areas	36	35	37
Total (some kind of rights)	81	87	74
Talked to lesbian or gay man	70	74	65
Know any lesbians or gay men	45	52	37
Lesbians or gay men who are:			
friend	10	11	9
relative	8	9	7
acquaintance	31	39	21
teacher	12	13	12
neighbor	3	4	2
other	22	22	21
Ever tried to befriend:			
lesbians	8	7	9
gay men	20	24	14
Ever read about homosexuality; if yes, material was:	57	63	49
approving	4	6	0
disapproving	20	12	33
both	76	82	67
Ever read material written by lesbian or gay man	29	22	37
Ever listened to speech by lesbian or gay man	20	19	21
Think lesbians and gay men should try to be heterosexual	51	52	49

Attitudes, Opinions, Interaction, Socialization According to Anti-Gay/Lesbian Behavior (Graffiti, Verbal Harassment, and Violence) of Male Respondents

	Male Respondents		
Responses:	*Nonviolent* (N=21) 49%	*Graf/verb/vio* (N=22) 51%	*Violent* (N=7) 16%
Self-ranking of attitudes toward homosexuality:			
very approving	0	5	0
approving	5	0	0
neutral	32	29	33
disapproving	36	14	0
very disapproving	23	52	67
Upbringing (re:homosexuality)			
to accept	32	14	17
to disapprove	68	86	83
Support lesbian/gay rights:			
full equality	45	33	33
rights in some areas	32	43	34
Total (some kind of rights)	77	76	67
Talked to lesbian or gay man	59	76	100
Know any lesbians or gay men	32	43	83
Lesbians or gay men who are:			
friend	9	10	0
relative	0	14	33
acquaintance	23	14	33
teacher	9	14	17
neighbor	0	5	0
other	18	24	17
Ever tried to befriend:			
lesbians	14	5	17
gay men	18	10	17
Ever read about homosexuality;	32	62	83
If yes, material was:			
approving	0	0	0
disapproving	14	38	60
both	86	62	40
Ever read material written by lesbian or gay man	18	57	33
Ever listened to speech by lesbian or gay man	23	19	33
Think lesbians and gay men should try to be heterosexual	41	52	67

Comstock's Interview with a
Former Perpetrator

People who disapprove of homosexuality may find it easy to accept, and may welcome, the findings that perpetrators are typically people with whom they regularly associate—brothers, sons, fathers, and other male relatives and friends. Those who do not feel negatively about homosexuality and who make efforts to support lesbians and gay men may resist the notion that perpetrators are likely to be "one of us" and not "different from us." In his work on social labeling and deviant behavior, sociologist Edwin M. Schur observes that "many people seem to draw a certain comfort from the belief that violent acts are committed predominantly by 'sick individuals' "; such beliefs are held by middle-class people in particular because they " 'are functional for maintaining [their] customary moral and cognitive world.' "[1] In other words, we are not comfortable with the notion that we or those like us are either capable of committing or actually do commit those acts that we find tasteless or wrong. We prefer to consider the origin, arena, and actors for such activity to be other than or outside of that with which we are familiar and for which we are responsible. The tenacity of the desire to want perpetrators to be unlike or separate from ourselves in spite of information showing otherwise was illustrated for me in a conversation I had with a former student.

During the time of my research and well after I had discovered the sociological "averageness" of perpetrators, I had the occasion to meet and talk with a man who had been a student of mine when I taught in a secondary school. During a lull in the conversation, I casually asked if he knew any people who engage in violence against lesbians and gay men. Without hesitation he answered affirmatively and matter-of-factly said that in high school he and his male friends would drive into San Francisco's gay/lesbian neighborhoods and shout names, insults, and threats from the car windows at gay men walking on the sidewalks. On another occasion, while waiting in line to see a movie, he had pushed a gay man who was standing in front of him. He also told me that during his college years, a time when he became acquainted with and accepting of lesbians and gay men, he gave a party at which his father bullied, pushed, and forced a gay man to leave.

I was less surprised by the description of events given by my former student than by never having considered that I might personally know and be friends with perpetrators of anti-gay/lesbian violence. High school students and their parents with whom I had been on friendly terms and with whom I maintained contact after graduation were, in fact, the likely subjects of my research. The conversation showed me that the findings of my research alone had not been sufficient to dislodge my preconceptions that perpetrators are "other" and socially distanced from me. More recently, any remaining resistance to my accepting the averageness of perpetrators was finally abated; in an informal survey of college freshmen I was teaching, 16 percent of the male students report having engaged in anti-gay/lesbian violent acts (see appendix E).

That my former student and his male friends were athletic, healthy, upper-middle-class, average-to-good students in a suburban private school and that their parents were established community members and business leaders correlate further with my findings that perpetrators are for the most part neither socially nor economically marginal. The boys and their parents, supporting such causes as ecological responsibility, tended to be broad-minded on social issues. The boys liked and talked about cars, partying, rock music, and girls. They would be accepted into selective colleges; most would finish; and some would go on to advanced degree programs. They were known for their exuberance and "being rowdy," but they did not stand out as troublemakers. Other than an occasional traffic ticket and alcohol use that was not unusual among students generally, the boys demonstrated that which was considered acceptable adolescent masculine behavior. Unknown to me, such behavior included attacking gay men.

When I asked my former student why they had attacked gay men, he gave a variety of reasons. They had driven into San Francisco's gay neighborhoods for adventure, "something to do," relief from boredom, and excitement. He said he had pushed the gay man in the movie line because "I thought homosexuality was wrong." When I prodded for other reasons, he suggested that he and his friends "were probably attacking something within ourselves." When I asked why, if they were attacking something within themselves, they targeted other people, especially people they did not like, he said they were attacking people to whom "we were actually attracted." When I repeated his statement in the form of a question—"You were attracted to the gay men you attack? —, he said, "Yes." I responded by saying that I would have thought they would have simply attacked any gay man without regard for particular features and looks they found attractive; he suggested that the victims "were more carefully selected than that, that not any gay man was a likely target." When I said that attacking others to attack something within themselves and attacking those to whom they were attracted did not make sense to me, he said, "It isn't a rational matter." He said that it did not make sense to him either and wondered why it had to make sense. The reason he gave for his father's attacking the gay man at his party was that "my father thought he was protecting me." When I said I could better comprehend his father's motive, he said, "I don't really understand it."

Unwittingly, he provided a summary of the range of reasons usually given by young perpetrators for their attacks. They most readily acknowledge the recreational, adventuresome aspect of pursuing, preying upon, and scaring lesbians and gay men, and secondarily and less frequently they offer the "wrongness of homosexuality" as a further rationale. The latter is usually couched in vague or general terms, such as "I did it because 'the Bible,' 'the church,' 'my parents,' or 'society' say it's wrong," and is offered less as an explanation or social commentary and analysis than as a simply stated justification or permission. They do not always express their reasons clearly nor seem to understand their motives completely, especially when acknowledging that feelings of confusion around sexuality and personal attraction are related to their attacks. At no point did my former student mention that he and his friends had felt personal dislike for lesbians and gay men.

Older perpetrators, like the young man's father, are less likely to seek out victims than they are "to protect" themselves and/or their families within their own domains from "invasions," assertiveness, or visibility of lesbians and gay men. Dan White's assassination of fellow supervisor Harvey Milk in the political arena of city hall and Tyacks' confessed slaying of two gay men who had moved into "his" neighborhood (see table 3.18, in chapter 3) illustrate the "protection" motive, as does the tendency for other older perpetrators to be (1) husbands or male lovers who are "losing" their wives or girlfriends to lesbian relationships and

(2) male parents who prevent lesbian/gay people from associating with their children or who physically punish and try to correct their lesbian/gay children. Older perpetrators, more than the younger, seem to understand more readily and/or articulate more clearly their reasons and motives.

Notes

INTRODUCTION

1. U.S. Congress, House Subcommittee on Criminal Justice, Committee on the Judiciary, *Anti-Gay Violence,* pp. 1–2.

2. Robin Tower, "Senate, 92 to 4, Wants Data on Hate Crimes Spawned by Bias," *New York Times,* February 9, 1990, p. A17; and Andrew Rosenthal, "President Signs Law for Study of Hate Crimes: Gay Rights Leaders Go to First Official Event," *New York Times,* April 24, 1990, p. B6.

3. Sheila D. Collins, "The Familial Economy of God," *Theology in the Americas Documentation Series* 8 (New York: Theology in the Americas, 1979).

4. See, for example, Robert McAfee Brown, *Theology in a New Key: Responding to Liberation Themes* (Philadelphia: Westminster Press, 1978).

1. A HISTORICAL OVERVIEW

1. See, for example, Donald Vining, *A Gay Diary, 1933–1946* (New York: Pepys Press, 1979), pp. 284–287, 324–325, 336–338, 347–348; William Hazlett, "Terror in the Streets: Hoods Seeking Kicks Mean Danger to All," pp. 8–11; " 'Queer Hunting' Among Teenagers," *Mattachine Review,* June 1961, pp. 6–15; and John D'Emilio, *Sexual Politics, Sexual Communities: The Making of a Homosexual Minority in the United States, 1940–1970,* pp. 51, 201, 207.

2. See, for example, Alfred C. Kinsey, Wardell B. Pomeroy, and Clyde E. Martin, *Sexual Behavior in the Human Male,* p. 384; William A. Westley, "Violence and the Police," pp. 37–38; Maurice Leznoff and William A. Westley, "The Homosexual Community," pp. 259, 262; Albert J. Reiss, Jr., "The Social Integration of Queers and Peers," pp. 262, 272; and Edwin M. Schur, *Crimes Without Victims. Deviant Behavior and Public Policy; Abortion, Homosexuality, Drug Addiction,* p. 83.

3. For scholarly work, see, for example, D'Emilio, *Sexual Politics;* Jonathan

Katz, ed., *Gay American History: Lesbians and Gay Men in the U.S.A.: A Documentary;* Salvatore J. Licata and Robert P. Petersen, eds., *The Gay Past: A Collection of Historical Essays;* Keith Vacha, *Quiet Fire: Memoirs of Older Gay Men;* Margaret Cruikshank, ed., *The Lesbian Path;* Judy Grahn, *Another Mother Tongue: Gay Words, Gay Worlds;* Vito Russo, *The Celluloid Closet: Homosexuality in the Movies,* pp. 61–179, 261–262; and collective projects, such as the oral history project of the Lesbian Herstory Archives of New York City and the San Francisco Lesbian and Gay History Project.

For film, see Nancy Adair and Casey Adair, *Word Is Out: Stories of Some of Our Lives.*

For the work of journalists, see, for example, Donn Teal, *The Gay Militants;* and Randy Shilts, *The Mayor of Castro Street: The Life and Times of Harvey Milk.*

For the writings of activists, see Barbara McDonald with Cynthia Rich, *Look Me in the Eye: Old Women, Aging and Ageism* (San Francisco: Spinsters, Ink, 1983); Ruth Simpson, *From the Closet to the Courts: The Lesbian Transition;* and Ginny Vida, ed., *Our Right to Love: A Lesbian Resource Book,* pp. 34–35, 124–128, 230, 232.

4. D'Emilio, *Sexual Politics,* pp. 24, 27, 38. See also Andrea Weiss and Greta Schiller, *Before Stonewall: The Making of a Gay and Lesbian Community,* pp. 31–36; and Shilts, *The Mayor of Castro Street,* p. 50.

5. D'Emilio, *Sexual Politics,* pp. 24–29. See also William C. Menninger, *Psychiatry in a Troubled World: Yesterday's War and Today's Challenge* (New York: Macmillan, 1948), pp. 227–228; Weiss and Schiller, *Before Stonewall,* pp. 32–35; Donald Webster Cory, *The Homosexual in America: A Subjective Approach,* pp. 76–78; Vacha, *Quiet Fire,* p. 171; Merle Miller, "What It Means to Be a Homosexual," p. 48; Adair, *Word Is Out,* pp. 57–58; and War Department, *Sex Hygiene Course: Officers and Officer Candidates, Women's Army Auxiliary Corps,* Pamphlet No. 35–1 (Washington, D.C., 1943), pp. 3, 24–28.

6. See D'Emilio, *Sexual Politics,* pp. 38, 100; Russo, *The Celluloid Closet,* pp. 99–106; Susan Estabrook Kennedy, *If All We Did Was to Weep at Home: A History of White Working-Class Women in America* (Bloomington: Indiana University Press, 1979; Midland Book, 1981), pp. 199–201; Weiss and Schiller, *Before Stonewall,* pp. 36–47; John D'Emilio, "Gay Politics, Gay Community: San Francisco's Experience," pp. 80–81; Menninger, *Psychiatry in a Troubled World,* pp. 229–231; Barbara Stephens, "Homosexuals in Uniform," *Ladder,* June 1959, p. 17; Jonathan Ned Katz, *Gay/Lesbian Almanac: A New Documentary,* pp. 616–618, 630–631; Adair, *Word Is Out,* pp. 60–61; Vacha, *Quiet Fire,* p. 173; Del Martin and Phyllis Lyon, *Lesbian/Woman* (San Francisco: Glide Publications, 1972), pp. 200–208; Allan Berube and John D'Emilio, "The Military and Lesbians During the McCarthy Years," in Estelle B. Freedman, Barbara C. Gelpi, Susan L. Johnson, and Kathleen M. Weston, eds., *The Lesbian Issues: Essays from "Signs"* (Chicago: University of Chicago Press, 1985), pp. 279–295; and Colin J. Williams and Martin S. Weinberg, *Homosexuals and the Military: A Study of Less than Honorable Discharge* (New York: Harper & Row, 1971), pp. 45–47, 53.

7. See D'Emilio, *Sexual Politics,* pp. 32–33, 58; Weiss and Schiller, *Before Stonewall,* pp. 36–37, 51–53; Vacha, *Quiet Fire,* p. 199; Martin and Lyon, *Lesbian/Woman,* p. 203; Shilts, *Mayor of Castro Street,* p. 51; Salvatore J. Licata, "The Homosexual Rights Movement in the United States: A Traditionally Overlooked Area of American History," in Licata and Petersen, eds., *The Gay Past,* p. 166.

8. See Kinsey, *Behavior in the Human Male,* pp. 625, 627, 659–660; D'Emilio, *Sexual Politics,* pp. 34–35; Weiss and Schiller, *Before Stonewall,* pp. 37–38.

9. Henry P. Van Dusen, "The Moratorium on Moral Revulsion," *Christianity and Crisis,* June 21, 1948, p. 81.
See also Katz, "1948, January 14: *N.Y. Times Book Review; Time; Parents' Magazine:* Alfred Kinsey's and others' *Sexual Behavior in the Human Male,*" *Gay/Lesbian Almanac,* pp. 630–631.

10. For commentary on the popular media, see Cory, *The Homosexual in America,* pp. 176–177, 313; Russo, *The Celluloid Closet,* pp. 18, 31, 45, 66, 68, 73, 75, 78, 79, 86, 92–96, 97, 100–108, 110, 112–115, 135, 241–242, 247–260; D'Emilio, *Sexual Politics,* pp. 134–136; and Katz, *Gay/Lesbian Almanac,* pp. 651–652.

11. D'Emilio, *Sexual Politics,* pp. 40, 44.

12. See D'Emilio, *Sexual Politics,* pp. 42, 46–47, 49; U.S. Senate, 81st Congress, 2d Session, Committee on Expenditures in Executive Departments, *Employment of Homosexuals and Other Sex Perverts in Government* (Washington, D.C., 1950); Cory, *The Homosexual in America,* pp. 269–280; Gerard Sullivan, "A Bibliographic Guide to Government Hearings and Reports, Legislative Action, and Speeches Made in the House and Senate of the United States Congress on the Subject of Homosexuality," in John P. DeCecco, ed., *Bashers, Baiters and Bigots: Homophobia in American Society* (New York: Harrington Press, 1985), pp. 135–189; Katz, *Gay American History,* pp. 105–109; Weiss and Schiller, *Before Stonewall,* pp. 38, 42–44; John Gerassi, *The Boys of Boise: Furor, Vice and Folly in an American City;* and Katz, *Gay American History,* pp. 109–119.

13. See Cory, *The Homosexual in America,* pp. 281–292; D'Emilio, *Sexual Politics,* p. 14, 17, 18; [Jon J. Gallo et al.], "The Consenting Adult Homosexual and the Law: An Empirical Study of Enforcement and Administration in Los Angeles County," pp. 663–668, 681–685; Vacha, *Quiet Fire,* p. 173; Vida, *Our Right to Love,* p. 35; Katz, *Gay American History,* pp. 162–207; Adair, *Word Is Out,* pp. 3–13, 29–41; Vacha, *Quiet Fire,* p. 173; and Sara Diamond, "Still Sane," pp. 30–35.

14. See Sullivan, "A Bibliographic Guide to Government Hearings and Reports, Legislative Action, and Speeches Made in the House and Senate of the United States Congress on the Subject of Homosexuality," in DeCecco, ed., *Bashers, Baiters and Bigots,* pp. 135–189.

15. Shilts, *Mayor of Castro Street,* p. 50.

16. See D'Emilio, *Sexual Politics,* p. 52; U.S. Senate, 67th Congress, 1st Session, Committee on Naval Affairs, *Alleged Immoral Conditions at Newport*

(R.I.) Naval Training Station (Washington, D.C., 1921); and Katz, *Gay American History*, p. 579, n. 74.

17. D'Emilio, *Sexual Politics*, pp. 15–22. See also Katz, *Gay American History*, pp. 258–279.

18. See D'Emilio, *Sexual Politics*, p. 52; Erwin J. Haeberle, "A Movement of Inverts: An Early Plan for a Homosexual Organization in the United States," in DeCecco, ed., *Bashers, Baiters and Bigots*, pp. 127–133; Katz, *Gay American History*, pp. 385–397: Weiss and Schiller, *Before Stonewall*, pp. 12–30; Katz, *Gay/Lesbian Almanac*, pp. 428–436, 438–440, 553–566; and Licata, "The Homosexual Rights Movement in the United States," in Licata and Petersen, eds., pp. 161–189.

19. D'Emilio, *Sexual Politics*, pp. 11–13. See also Lee Rainwater, "Some Aspects of Lower Class Sexual Behavior," *Journal of Social Issues* (1966) 22:105–106.

20. D'Emilio, *Sexual Politics*, pp. 40, 52.

21. Others besides Kinsey were reevaluating homosexuality positively and advocating tolerance of lesbians and gay men; for example, in psychiatry, Clara Thompson, "Changing Concepts of Homosexuality in Psychoanalysis," *Psychiatry* (1947) 187:183–189, Menninger, *Psychiatry in a Troubled World*, pp. 222–231, and Evelyn Hooker, 1956 (work cited in D'Emilio, *Sexual Politics*, pp. 112–113, n. 12); and in sociology, Gordon Westwood, *Society and the Homosexual*, and Leznoff and Westley, "The Homosexual Community," pp. 257–263.

22. Shilts, *Mayor of Castro Street*, p. 51. See also Licata, "The Homosexual Rights Movement in the United States," in Licata and Petersen, eds., *The Gay Past*, p. 166.

23. See Martin and Lyon, *Lesbian/Woman*, p. 55; Licata, "The Homosexual Rights Movement in the United States," in Licata and Petersen, eds., *The Gay Past*, p. 166; and Shilts, *Mayor of Castro Street*, p. 51.

24. D'Emilio, *Sexual Politics*, p. 32.

25. See Westwood, *Society and the Homosexual*, p. 126; Grahn, *Another Mother Tongue*, pp. 28–33; D'Emilio, *Sexual Politics*, pp. 49–51; Teal, *The Gay Militants*, p. 115; Jess Stearn, *The Grapevine* (Garden City, N.Y.: Doubleday, 1964), pp. 183–194; Vida, *Our Right to Love*, p. 124; [Gallo et al.], "Consenting Adult Homosexual and the Law," pp. 718–179; Martin S. Weinberg and Collin J. Williams, *Male Homosexuals: Their Problems and Adaptations* (New York: Oxford University Press, 1974), pp. 26, 33, 49–50; Peter Fisher, *The Gay Mystique: The Myth and Reality of Male Homosexuality* (New York: Stein and Day, 1972), p. 139.

26. D'Emilio, *Sexual Politics*, p. 33. See also Vida, *Our Right to Love*, p. 35.

27. See Martin and Lyon, *Lesbian/Woman*, p. 215; D'Emilio, *Sexual Politics*, pp. 57–74, 88–90, 195, 200–202, 227, 231–232; Katz, *Gay American History*, pp. 406–420; Teal, *The Gay Militants*, pp. 40–43, 195–202; and Weinberg and Williams, *Male Homosexuals*, p. 54.

28. See [Gallo et al.], "Consenting Adult Homosexual and the Law," pp.

719–725; Vida, *Our Right to Love,* p. 124; and Miller, "What It Means to Be a Homosexual."

29. Reported by D'Emilio in *Sexual Politics,* p. 157.

30. See Vida, *Our Right to Love,* p. 124. Not all encounters with the police happened in bars and in lesbian/gay neighborhoods. For an account of illegal apprehension and detention of a high school–age lesbian in Denver in 1948, see Barbara Grier, "The Garden Variety Lesbian," in Cruikshank, *The Lesbian Path,* pp. 172–173.

31. For a discussion and case study of a municipal police force's illegal use of violence in general and specifically directed against homosexuals, see Westley, "Violence and the Police."

32. D'Emilio in *Sexual Politics,* p. 15, cites the following example: "A New York City magistrate, writing in 1951, described how the court attendant's 'normally stentorian voice drops to a whisper' when reading a homosexual-related complaint, while judges commonly directed gratuitous, abusive language at defendants."

33. D'Emilio, *Sexual Politics,* p. 51. See also Howard Brown, *Familiar Faces, Familiar Lives: The Story of Homosexual Men in America Today,* pp. 223–225; Cory, *The Homosexual in America,* 1951; " 'Queer Hunting,' " *Mattachine Review,* June 1961, pp. 6–15; and Hazlett, "Terror in the Streets," pp. 8–11.

34. D'Emilio, *Sexual Politics,* p. 51. Grahn, in *Another Mother Tongue,* p. 31, remembers that going to gay/lesbian bars "had considerable dangers." For example; "Sailors lurked in the alleys outside waiting to prove their 'manhood' on our bodies; more than once they beat someone I knew—dike or faggot—on her or his way home. A brick crashed through the front window one night, scattering glass splinters over the dance floor."

35. D'Emilio, in *Sexual Politics,* p. 51, describes an example of "blaming the victim:" "In 1954 the murder of two homosexuals in Miami by 'queerbashers' who had picked up their victims in a gay bar led the mayor to reverse a longstanding policy of closing his eyes to the existence of the establishments. Police made sweeps of the bars and beefed up their patrols of Bay Front Park and other meeting places. Like prostitutes, who also violated conventional sexual morality, gay men were subjected to VD inspections and verbal abuse by the police. In a strange twist, the individuals most in need of protection had become the targets of the police." See also Vacha, *Quiet Fire,* p. 175.

36. Simpson, *From the Closets to the Courts,* p. 27, 30. See also Vida, *Our Right to Love,* p. 35.

37. For a historical summary of violence against lesbians and gay men in America, see Katz, *Gay American History,* p. 11.

Several works that focus on violence entirely or provide a serious consideration of the topic amid other concerns of lesbian herstory and gay history in Western civilization are Louis Crompton, "Gay Genocide: From Leviticus to Hitler," in Louie Crew, ed., *The Gay Academic* (Palm Springs, Calif.: ETC Publications, 1978), pp. 67–91, and "Homosexuals and the Death Penalty in Colonial America," *Journal of Homosexuality* (1976) 1:277–293; Arthur Evans, *Witchcraft and the Gay Counterculture: A Radical View of Western Civilization and Some of the People It Has Tried to Destroy;* Louis Crompton, "The Myth of Lesbian Impunity: Capital Laws from 1270 to 1791," pp. 11–25, Brigette Eriksson, trans., "A Lesbian Execution in Germany, 1721: The Trial Records," pp. 27–40, E. William Monter, "Sodomy and Heresy in Early Modern Switzerland," pp. 41–68, and Robert F. Oaks, "Defining Sodomy in Seventeenth-Century Massachusetts," pp. 79–83, in Licata and Petersen, eds., *The Gay Past;* and Thorkil Vanggaard, *Phallos: A Symbol and Its History in the Male World* (Denmark: 1969; New York: International Universities Press, trans. ed., 1972), pp. 165–180. See also John Boswell, *Christianity, Social Tolerance, and Homosexuality: Gay People in Western Europe from the Beginning of the Christian Era to the Fourteenth Century* (Chicago: University of Chicago Press, 1980), pp. 282–283, 292, 295.

Crompton, Evans, and Boswell make different claims for the historical continuity of anti-gay/lesbian violence. Although all three agree that a dramatic increase in hostility toward gay people occurred between 1150 and 1350, they disagree as to the prevalence of and locus of authority for anti-gay legislation and enforcement before this time. Evans and Crompton claim that considerable violence did occur regularly, whereas Boswell says that the evidence does not support such a position.

Crompton states that laws condemning homosexuals to death "first enter the statute books with the coming to power of Christianity in the fourth century A.D." and continue to influence legal policy in Christian Europe until the French Revolution. He does not, however, document incidents from 390 A.D., the date of Emperor Theodosius's "law condemning homosexuals to be burnt at the stake," to 1270, when the *Establissments* of St. Louis prescribed that "if anyone be suspected of *bouguerie,* he shall be taken to the Bishop, and if he is proved guilty, he shall be burned."

For Evans, the persecution of lesbians and gay men predates the Christian era but attains official policy status and is systematically enforced only when the Roman Empire embraces Christianity. He traces the emergence of war-making governments, which replace matriarchal religions (based on nature, women, sexuality, and sharing) with patriarchal religions (based on commerce, men, fighting, and domination). The Roman Empire was the most advanced achievement and example of such government. Because there was a close link between the old religions' nature worship and the practice of homosexuality, the state and church's attacks against pagan practices usually included the persecution of lesbians and gay men; and woven into the church's consistent attacks on heresy, paganism, and the ancient women-centered religions, Evans finds a legacy of anti-homosexuality. He cites the Council of Elvira, 300 A.D., with its denial of last rites to anyone guilty of pederasty, as a turning point from which "for the next several hundred years, numerous church synods [would] condemn the continued practice of pagan rites and the survival of nature worship." For example, the Council of Toledo in 447 A.D. established the doctrine of the Devil, who was identified with the Celtic horned god, and in 693 A.D. condemned male homosexuality; and Charlemagne, in 787 A.D., decreed that anyone making sacrifices to the Devil should be put to death and later outlawed sodomy.

Boswell forgoes both patriarchy and Christianity to identify the "increasing absolutism of government," both in the late Roman Empire and in the thirteenth and fourteenth centuries, as causing increased anti-gay hostility. He claims that the "scope of such laws [as cited by Evans and Crompton] and the severity of punishment they imposed were decided anomalies in early medieval justice" and that "their influence was negligible." He proceeds to justify the Council of Toledo in terms of secular efforts to unite a Visigothic Spain with which the Church cooperated reluctantly, to qualify Theodesius's law as forbidding only "forcing or selling males into prostitution," and to reveal Charlemagne's proscriptions against homosexuality as forgery. His tendency to think it "doubtful that the laws were consistently enforced" sustains a bias for seeing the church as harmless or not responsible. His apology for the church is evidenced by (1) his willingness to forgive its participation in Spain not only because it reluctantly, "under direct orders from the monarchy," enacted a "conciliar decree stipulating degradation from holy orders and excommunication for clerics . . . and excommunication, 100 stripes, and exile for a lay person" convicted of homosexual behavior, because such punishment was a "dramatic mitigation of the penalty under civil law"; (2) his tempering the impact of the Theodosian Code by speculating on the degree to which the populace agreed with it; and (3) although providing evidence for the forgery of Charlemagne's decree, his not accounting for those forces in the ninth century which would require and execute a redaction which so "severely punish[es] homosexual acts." In addition to "increasingly oppressive legislation passed against [Jews and gay people] throughout the sixth and seventh centuries" by civil authorities in Spain, he does recognize that homosexuality was not approved of officially elsewhere in Europe in the early Middle Ages. He sees the disapproval, however, as similar to that of other sexual sins: "Homosexuality is thus reduced to a simple form of fornication, i.e., the release of seed in an improper way." I am not sure why homosexuality as one sin among others makes the punishment for it any less oppressive; and Evans would say that the church's legislation of sexuality in general is precisely where one needs to begin to understand the persecution of lesbians and gay men. Boswell's appraisal of later times, when harsher laws were on the books, sustains his optimism: "Extremely few instances of capital punishment for the simple crime of sodomy are known from published sources. Unpublished materials may some day yield more information, but there seems little reason to imagine that they will dramatically alter present understanding." Given a tradition of disapproval of varying magnitude and the evidence of some capital punishment, both of which he acknowledges, how many executions would Boswell require before he would be able to imagine that lesbians and gay men may have been in mortal danger?

Whether passed by civil or ecclesiastical authorities, all three writers provide evidence of anti-homosexual legislation, often prescribing physical punishment and death, from the time of the late Roman Empire to the nineteenth century in Europe and America.

38. Accounts of incidents leading up to and including Nazi efforts to exterminate homosexuals include Lillian Faderman and Brigette Eriksson, eds. and

trans., *Lesbian-Feminism in Turn-of-the-Century Germany: An Anthology* (Tallahassee, Fla.: Naiad Press, 1982); Erwin J. Haeberle, " 'Stigmata of Degeneration': Prisoner Markings in Nazi Concentration Camps," pp. 135–139, and Rudiger Lautmann, "The Pink Triangle: The Persecution of Homosexual Males in Concentration Camps in Nazi Germany," pp. 141–160, in Licata and Petersen, eds., *The Gay Past;* Heinz Heger, *The Men with the Pink Triangle* (Boston: Alyson Publications, 1980); Richard Plant, "The Men with the Pink Triangle," *Christopher Street,* February 1977, pp. 4–10, and *The Pink Triangle: The Nazi War Against Homosexuals* (New York: Henry Holt, 1986); Frank Rector, *The Nazi Extermination of Homosexuals* (New York: Stein and Day, 1981); Martin Sherman, *Bent* (New York: Avon Books, 1979; Bard, 1980); James D. Steakley, *The Homosexual Emancipation Movement in Germany* (New York: Arno Press, 1975); Ian Young, *Gay Resistance: Homosexuals in the Anti-Nazi Underground* (Toronto: Stubblejumper Press, 1985); "Lesbians in Pre-Nazi Germany: Sixty Places to Dance, Talk and Play," with excerpts from first-person accounts, "Lesbians in the Butzow Concentration Camp" and "Marte and Olga in Berlin," in the "Global Lesbianism" issue of *Connexions: An International Women's Quarterly* (1982), 3:16–18; Eugen Kogon, *The Theory and Practice of Hell: The German Concentration Camps and the System Behind Them,* Heinz Norden, trans. (New York: Farrar, Straus and Cudahy, 1950; Berkley Book, Berkley Publishing Group, 1980), pp. 34–35; Detlev J. K. Peukert, *Inside Nazi Germany: Conformity, Opposition and Racism in Everyday Life,* Richard Deveson, trans. (New Haven: Yale University Press, 1987), pp. 199, 203, 208, 209, 219–220; and Pieter Koenders, *The Homomonument,* Eric Wulfert, trans. (Amsterdam, The Netherlands: Menne Vellinga Produkties and Walter van Opzeeland Publishing Consultancy, 1987).

39. Decrees and the enforcing of antihomosexual laws prescribing physical punishment in Europe are listed chronologically in Evans, *Witchcraft and the Gay Counterculture,* pp. 157–169; by Crompton, "Gay Genocide;" in *The Gay Academic,* pp. 85–91; and by Ellen M. Barrett, "Legal Homophobia and the Christian Church," *Hastings Law Journal* (1979), 30:1021–1022.

See also Vanggaard, *Phallos,* pp. 176–177; Barrett, "Legal Homophobia and the Christian Church," p. 1022; Meredith Gould, "Lesbians and the Law: Where Sexism and Heterosexism Meet," in Trudy Darty and Sandee Potter, eds., *Women-Identified Women,* pp. 150–151; and Katz, *Gay American History,* pp. 20–23.

40. See Katz, *Gay American History,* pp. 22–23; Crompton, "Gay Genocide," in *The Gay Academic,* p. 71; and Katz, *Gay/Lesbian Almanac,* pp. 68–70, 73–82, 84–89, 91–125, 127–128, 130–131, 133.

41. Katz, *Gay American History,* p. 12.

42. See Katz, *Gay American History,* pp. 23–24; Vanggaard, *Phallos,* pp. 173, 176; and Crompton, "Gay Genocide: From Leviticus to Hitler," in *The Gay Academic,* p. 73.

43. Crompton, "Gay Genocide," *The Gay Academic,* p. 71.

44. See Cory, *The Homosexual in America,* pp. 281–292; Hugh M. Hefner, ed., "The Playboy Philosophy," Part 16 (including chart, Penalties for Sex

Offenses in the U.S.), *Playboy* (HMH Publishing Company, reprint 1964); Gould, "Lesbians and the Law," in Darty and Potter, eds., *Women-Identified Women*, pp. 149–162; Thomas B. Stoddard, E. Carrington Boggan, Marilyn G. Haft, Charles Lister, and John P. Rupp, appendix A, "Criminal Statutes Relating to Consensual Homosexual Acts Between Adults," *The Rights of Gay People* (New York: Bantam Books, 1975; revised ed., 1983), pp. 131–166; and Privacy Project, National Gay and Lesbian Task Force, "Privacy Project Fact Sheet."

However, castration and clitoridectomy were discussed, prescribed, legally sanctioned, and carried out by various individuals and schools of thought within the medical profession. See Katz, *Gay/Lesbian Almanac*, pp. 185–187, 200–201, 241–243, 245–247, 254–256, 492–493, 536–637.

45. Westwood, *Society and the Homosexual*, p. 80; and Crompton, "Gay Genocide," *Gay Academic*, p. 71.

46. As quoted in Westwood, *Society and the Homosexual*, p. 80.

47. Randolph Trumbach, ed., "The Phoenix of Sodom, or the Vere Street Coterie (1813)," *Sodomy Trials: Seven Documents*, Number 7 (New York: Garland, 1986), n.p.

48. Quoted in Katz, *Gay American History*, p. 53; see also p. 48.

49. See Katz, *Gay American History*, pp. 43; 45–47; 48–49; 87; 88; 575, n. 42; and Katz, *Gay/Lesbian Almanac*, p. 235.

50. Katz, *Gay/Lesbian Almanac*, pp. 452–453.

51. Luvenia Pinson, "The Black Lesbian—Times Past, Times Present," p. 8. See also "Women Who Pass for Men," *Jet*, February 28, 1954, pp. 22–24.

52. F. A. McHenry, "A Note on Homosexuality, Crime and the Newspapers," pp. 533–548. The examples discussed in his article occurred in New York, Los Angeles, Boston, and Norfolk, Virginia.

53. See Katz, *Gay/Lesbian Almanac*, pp. 571–584, who cites Gershon Legman, "The Language of Homosexuality," pp. 1149–1179 in George Henry, *Sex Variants: A Study of Homosexual Patterns* (New York: Hoeber, 1941).

54. Charles McCabe, "Riverside Drive, 1932," *San Francisco Chronicle*, April 7, 1978. Compare, for example, with report by Churchill, *Homosexual Behavior Among Males*, pp. 194–197, of an incident in San Francisco in 1961 in which a man was perceived as gay and beaten to death by four young men: "About this case [the] Inspector . . . commented to the press, 'They said they considered [the victim's] death justifiable homicide.' He added, 'They seem to regard the beating-up of whomever they consider sex deviates as a civic duty.' . . . These young men admitted that the beating they gave [the victim] was not the first they had ever administered to a person whom they deemed to be in the 'unfortunate category.' There had been many other such nights. . . . When they left their friends that . . . evening they felt quite free to announce their intention of seeking prospective victims without the slightest fear of losing face. They said they knew of at least fifty other youths within the brief confines of their own neighborhood who participated in similar attacks upon 'queers.' . . . It had been affirmed by the young vigilantes that they 'keep watch on establishments patronized by homosexuals, then track down the patrons as potential victims for attack.' "

55. For accounts of the Stonewall rebellion, see D'Emilio, *Sexual Politics,* pp. 231–233, 246–247; Licata, "The Homosexual Rights Movement in the United States," in Licata and Peterson, eds., *The Gay Past,* pp. 178–179; Shilts, *The Mayor of Castro Street,* pp. 41–42; Toby Marotta, *The Politics of Homosexuality,* pp. 71–76; and Robert Amsel, "Back to Our Future?: A Walk on the Wild Side of Stonewall," *Advocate* (Los Angeles), September 15, 1987, pp. 36–39, 44–49.

56. Licata, "The Homosexual Rights Movement in the United States," in Licata and Petersen, eds., *The Gay Past,* p. 178.

An article by Lucian Truscott IV, "Gay Power Comes to Sheridan Square," *Village Voice,* July 3, 1969, p. 18, quoted extensively in D'Emilio, *Sexual Politics,* p. 232, and in Marotta, *Politics of Homosexuality,* pp. 72–73, reports that when the last bar patron, a lesbian, was led from the bar to the police car, "she put up a struggle from car to door to car again," at which moment "the scene became explosive. Limp wrists were forgotten. Beer cans and bottles were heaved at the windows and a rain of coins descended on the cops. . . . Almost by signal the crowd erupted into cobblestone and bottle heaving. . . . From nowhere came an uprooted parking meter—used as a battering ram on the Stonewall door. I heard several cries of 'let's get some gas,' but the blaze of flame which soon appeared in the window of the Stonewall was still a shock." Allen Ginsberg is noted in the article as saying, "You know, the guys there were so beautiful. They've lost that wounded look that fags all had ten years ago."

57. D'Emilio, in *Sexual Politics,* pp. 159–160, 165, 175, 234–235, observes that whereas the achievement of the 1960s for the gay/lesbian community was publicity, visibility, and recognition, as reflected in the first appearance by a gay activist on television and the first demonstrations at the White House, gains made in the late 1960s and 1970s would hinge on militant confrontations and community organizing. See also pp. 58, 185.

58. See interview with Barbara Gittings in Katz, *Gay American History,* pp. 420–433. For an account of Kameny's confrontations with and his efforts to organize demonstrations against the federal government, see D'Emilio, *Sexual Politics,* pp. 150–157.

59. From a speech by Frank Kameny, quoted in D'Emilio, *Sexual Politics,* p. 154.

60. For examples and a discussion of the gains achieved during the 1960s, see D'Emilio, *Sexual Communities,* pp. 159–160, 165, 175, 185, 189–190, 195, 213, 215, 218–219, 234–235.

61. Shilts, in *The Mayor of Castro Street,* p. 41, observes that, coming as it did on the same weekend as the funeral of Judy Garland—a person reputedly held in reverence by gay men and "who seemed the metaphor for their existence: put-upon and therefore self-destructive, a victim with a nebulous vision of Oz over the rainbow"—the Stonewall rebellion signaled an end to accepting the status of victims and launched the fight for equality. See also John Rechy, *The Sexual Outlaw: A Documentary: A Non-Fiction Account, with Commentaries, of Three Days and Nights in the Sexual Underground,* pp. 186–189.

62. D'Emilio, *Sexual Politics,* pp. 237–238, 246.

63. The following statement by Marotta in *Politics of Homosexuality*, p. 159, provides an example of the new confrontational politics and arenas of protest: "As planned, the loud and colorful picket line staged outside GOP headquarters attracted the attention of reporters and photographers. Those inside vowed not to leave until they were granted a public interview with the Republican state chairman. Five of GAA's [Gay Activists Alliance] leaders stayed until they were arrested, becoming the first gay political activists ever to be arrested in the course of duty. During July and August, the trial . . . became a focus for well-publicized demonstrations aimed at establishing that homosexuals were a minority with legitimate political grievances."

The unprecedented assertiveness by lesbians and gay men in the political arena as well as the unprecedented recognition that some politicians gave to their concerns are reflected in the following remarks by Miller, "What It Means to Be a Homosexual," p. 60: "When Arthur J. Goldberg paid what was to have been a routine campaign visit to the intersection of 85th and Broadway [in New York City], more than three dozen members of G.A.A. [Gay Activists Alliance] were waiting for him. They shook his hand and asked him if he was in favor of fair employment for homosexuals and of repeals of the state laws against sodomy. Goldberg's answer to each question was, 'I think there are more important things to think about.'

But before the election Goldberg had issued a public statement answering yes to both questions, promising as well to work against police harassment of homosexuals. Richard Ottinger and Charles Goodell also issued statements supporting constitutional rights for homosexuals. Of course, Rockefeller and Buckley, the winners, remained silent on those issues, but Bella Abzug, one of the earliest supporters of G.A.A., won, and so did people like Antonio Olivieri, the first Democrat elected in the 66th District in 55 years. Olivieri took an ad in a G.A.A. benefit program that served to thank the organization for its support."

64. D'Emilio, *Sexual Politics*, p. 206.

65. D'Emilio, *Sexual Politics*, pp. 206, 207, 238. See also Marotta, *Politics of Homosexuality*, pp. 324–325; and Evans, *Witchcraft and the Gay Counterculture*, p. 1.

66. See Marotta, *Politics of Homosexuality*, pp. 153–157.

67. Simpson, *From the Closets to the Courts*, p. 127, 129. See also Martin and Lyon, in *Lesbian/Woman*, p. 254.

68. Russo, *The Celluloid Closet*, p. 62, quotes Barbara Gittings, a pre-Stonewall lesbian activist, as saying, "The first gay meeting which grew into the gay liberation movement was held in 1950 in someone's apartment in Los Angeles, and the door was locked and the blinds were drawn and there was a lookout posted because they thought it was illegal to talk about homosexuality."

See Simpson, *From the Closets to the Courts*, p. 165; Kevin Berrill, "Anti-Gay Violence: Causes, Consequences, Responses," a White Paper by the Violence Project of the National Gay and Lesbian Task Force (Washington, D.C.), p. 1, submitted to U.S. Congress, House Subcommittee on Criminal Justice of Committee on the Judiciary, *Anti-Gay Violence*, 99th Cong., 2d Session, 1986; William Paul, "Minority Status for Gay People: Majority Reaction and Social

Context," in William Paul, James D. Weinrich, John C. Gonsiorek, and Mary E. Hotvedt, eds., *Homosexuality: Social, Psychological, and Biological Issues*, p. 360; and " 'Anita for President': Another Gay Church Hit by Vandals," *Advocate* (Los Angeles), October 19, 1977.

69. Simpson, *From the Closets to the Courts*, pp. 132–134, reproduces from newsletters of the Gay Activist Alliance accounts of demonstrators' being beaten by police "without any provocation" and of arrested demonstrators being beaten in their cells by police. See also Rechy, *The Sexual Outlaw*, pp. 181–183; and Teal, *The Gay Militants*, pp. 70–73, 200.

70. For accounts of the incident and two similar perspectives on the resistance of the district attorney's office to arrest and prosecute, see Calvin Trillin, "A Few Observations on the Zapping of the Inner Circle," pp. 64–69; and Michael Kramer, "Fireman's Brawl," pp. 6–7.

71. See, for example, Michael Blaine, "GAA/Inner Circle: The Charge Is Mayehem," *Village Voice* (New York), May 4, 1972; Lacey Foxborough, in *New York Times*, "Maye Held as Harasser in Gay Alliance Fracas," May 23, 1972, p. 30; "Witness Testifies: City Aide Says Union Chief Stomped Protester at Hotel," June 24, 1972; "Court Told Maye Beat Homosexual," June 27, 1972; "Attack Charges Denied by Maye: Never Kicked Homosexual, He Testifies in Defense," June 28, 1972, p. 46; Joseph P. Fried, "Maye Asserts Gay Activists Intentionally Set up Incident," *New York Times*, May 24, 1972; Joseph Kahn, in *New York Post*, "Gay Beatings—DA Probes Maye Role" and "The Hilton Beatings—Two Attachers Known," April 20, 1972; "Demands Maye's Arrest in Beating," April 22, 1972, p. 2; "Inner Circle: Still No Action," April 22, 1972; "3d Official Links Maye to Beating," April 24, 1972; "Ready Report on Beatings," April 26, 1972, p. 36; "Saw Maye Assault Activist: Official," April 28, 1972; "Rap DA's Probe of Beatings," May 2, 1972, p. 17; "Gays Going to Court in Maye Case," May 5, 1972, p. 10; Joseph Kahn and George Arzt, "Grand Jury Weighs Case of Gay Beatings," *New York Post*, May 10, 1972, p. 10; Judith Michaelson, in *New York Post*, "Charge Police Ignored Beatings at Hilton Gala," April 18, 1972, pp. 4, 54; "Prepared to Testify: A 3d Witness Accuses Maye," April 19, 1972; Joe Nicholson, Jr., "Maye Not at Fault: Fire Officers' Boss," *New York Post*, April 27, 1972; Eric Pace, "Official Accuses Maye of Assault: City Aide Says He Saw Gay Intruder Being Attacked," *New York Times*, April 25, 1972; Mike Pearl, "Maye Stomped Gay, Trial Told," *New York Post*, June 23, 1972; William Proctor, in *New York Daily News*, "City Aide Testifies to Attack by Maye," June 24, 1972; "Struck Gay After He Grabbed Me: Maye," June 28, 1972, p. 20; "Fireman Maye Acquitted in Hilton Hassle," July 6, 1972; William Proctor and Paul Meskil, "May Hit with a Rap in Gay Tiff," *New York Daily News*, May 23, 1972; and Robert Vare, "Maye Set to Tell His Story," *New York Post*, June 27, 1972.

72. See, for example, Pete Hamill, "The Inner Circle," *New York Post*, April 7, 1972; and press release, "Statement Regarding the Charges Against Allen Roskoff," issued by New York City Councilmen Eldon R. Clingan, Carter Burden, and Charles Taylor.

73. See Kramer, "Fireman's Brawl," pp. 6–7.

74. Edward I. Koch, "Law, Order, and Justice," *Congressional Record-House*, April 24, 1972, p. H-3478.

75. Koch, "Law, Order, and Justice," p. H-3478.

76. Another example of surprise and outrage by non-lesbian/gay people, when exposed to violence against lesbians and gay men, is reported by D'Emilio, *Sexual Politics*, p. 194; Weinberg and Williams, *Male Homosexuals*, p. 49; Vida,. *Our Right to Love*, p. 127; and Martin and Lyon, *Lesbian/Woman*, pp. 239–240. Here the incident involved liberal church ministers who worked with lesbians and gay men in San Francisco.

77. For an account of the repeal of gay and lesbian rights legislation in these various areas, see Shilts, *Mayor of Castro Street*, pp. 212–219. For an analysis of organized efforts to stop the repeal in Eugene, Oregon, see Gay Rights Writer's Group, *It Could Happen to You: An Account of the Gay Civil Rights Campaign in Eugene, Oregon* (Boston: Alyson Publications, 1983).

78. For an account of the growth of opposition by the religious right, see Shilts, *Mayor of Castro Street*, pp. 214–219. Gay Rights Writer's Group, *It Could Happen to You*, p. 35, reports that a poll taken in Eugene in advance of the day of voting found an "average pro-gay voter to be young, single, Democrat, having at least one gay friend, and not attending church regularly. An average anti-gay voter lived in a nuclear family, was older, Republican or politically conservative, denied knowing any gay people, and attended a fundamentalist church."

79. In Gay Rights Writer's Group, *It Could Happen to You*, p. 66, lesbian and gay organizers in Eugene point out that fundamentalist Christians were not the main force behind the repeal effort. Significant support came from small and medium-sized businesses.

80. "Harassment of Gays Increases Since Dade County Referendum," *GayLife* (Chicago), August 19, 1977.

81. "Anita Sued for Death," *Sioux City Journal* (Iowa), July 2, 1977, p. 4A. See also Bill Sievert, "The Killing of Mr. Greenjeans," *Mother Jones*, September–October 1977, pp. 39–42, 46–48.

82. For example, see the introductory paragraphs of Warren Hinckle, "Dan White's San Francisco," *Inquiry*, October 29, 1979, pp. 3–4.

83. For an account of the campaign to defeat the Briggs Initiative, see Shilts, *Mayor of Castro Street*, pp. 221–223, 230–231, 238–250. See also Sievert, "The Killing of Mr. Greenjeans," pp. 42, 46.

84. Shilts, *Mayor of Castro Street*, p. 160.

85. Shilts, *Mayor of Castro Street*, p. 160.

86. Gay Rights Writer's Group, *It Could Happen to You*, p. 74.

87. Shilts, *Mayor of Castro Street*, p. 348. See also Robert W. Peterson, "Remembering a Dark Night: San Franciscans Gather on the Tenth Anniversary of Harvey Milk's Murder," *Advocate* (Los Angeles), January 3, 1989, pp. 14–15.

88. David J. Thomas, "San Francisco's 1979 White Night Riot: Injustice, Vengeance, and Beyond," in Paul, Weinrich, Gonsiorek, and Hotvedt, eds., *Homosexuality*, pp. 350–357.

Shilts, *Mayor of Castro Street,* p. 302, reports that after the assassination police officers were observed wearing T-shirts on which was printed the slogan, "Free Dan White." He states further: "Within a week of the killings, Dan White had become a cause celebre for police officers who never had much use for either Harvey Milk or his liberal ally, George Moscone. . . . Gays were enraged at the news that police and fireman had raised a reported $100,000 for White's defense fund." White was a former policeman and fireman.

89. Shilts, *Mayor of Castro Street,* p. 331.

90. Peter Freiberg, "Community United Against Violence," *Advocate,* October 28, 1986, pp. 10–11.

91. Kevin Berrill, "Safety Begins at Home: Building a Local Anti-Violence Project," *Task Force Report* (National Gay and Lesbian Task Force), January–February 1983.

92. Kevin Berrill, "Safety Begins at Home: The United, Madison," *Task Force Reprt* (National Gay and Lesbian Task Force), May–August 1983.

93. Originally founded in 1973 as the National Gay Task Force (NGTF) with headquarters in New York City, this national gay and lesbian civil rights organization moved its offices to Washington, D.C., in 1985 and changed its name to the National Gay and Lesbian Task Force (NGLTF).

94. See, for example, Diana Christensen, "Testimony on Anti-Gay Violence," prepared by the executive director of Community United Against Violence, San Francisco, and Kevin Berrill, "Anti-Gay Violence: Causes, Consequences, Responses," A White Paper submitted to the Committee on the Judiciary, in U.S. Congress, House Subcommittee on Criminal Justice, Committee on the Judiciary, *Anti-Gay Violence,* 1986, pp. 32–75; D'Emilio, "Gay Politics, Gay Community," p. 102; and William R. Greer, "Violence Against Homosexuals Rising, Groups Seeking Wider Protection Say," *New York Times,* November 23, 1986, p. 36.

95. Violence Project, National Gay and Lesbian Task Force, "Anti-Gay Violence, Victimization and Defamation in 1988," p. 11. The release of similar findings by the Boston Police Department is reported in "Gaybashing Complaint Filed Against Boston Firefighters," *Our Paper* (Portland, Maine), March 1987, p. 3; see also "Ethnoviolence in Boston: The Boston Police Department Study, 1983–1987," *Forum* (Newsletter of National Institute Against Prejudice and Violence), September 1989, pp. 1, 5.

2. EMPIRICAL DATA ON VICTIMS

1. See, for example, Ruth Simpson, *From the Closet to the Courts: The Lesbian Transition,* pp. 34–35, 37–38, 173; Evelyn Torton Beck, ed., *Nice Jewish Girls: A Lesbian Anthology,* pp. 126, 160; Barbara Smith, ed., *Home Girls: A Black Feminist Anthology,* pp. xlvi–xlvii; and David Kopay and Perry Deane Young, *The David Kopay Story: An Extraordinary Self-revelation,* pp. 15, 42, 53, 57, 224–226.

2. See, for example, John Rechy, *The Sexual Outlaw: A Documentary: A Non-Fiction Account, with Commentaries, of Three Days and Nights in the*

Sexual Underground, pp. 29, 30, 54, 57, 98–99, 100, 120, 180–183, 220–230; and Susan Cavin, *Lesbian Origins,* pp. 161–178.

3. See, for example, Gloria Naylor, *The Women of Brewster Place;* Noel Ryan, "Stavrogin," in Michael Denneny, Charles Ortleb, and Thomas Steele, eds., *First Love/Last Love: New Fiction from "Christopher Street,"* pp. 135–150; Martha Shelley, "Affair with a Married Woman," in Beck, ed., *Nice Jewish Girls,* pp. 161–163; and Harvey Fierstein, *The Torch Song Trilogy.*

4. For sections in books, see, for example, Martin S. Weinberg and Collin J. Williams, *Male Homosexuals: Their Problems and Adaptations,* pp. 49–50, 54, 66; and Alan P. Bell and Martin S. Weinberg, *Homosexualities: A Study of Diversity Among Men and Women,* pp. 78, 79, 190, 191, 193, 307.

For articles in journals, see, for example, Ted S. Bohn, "Homophobic Violence: Implications for Social Work Practice," pp. 91–112; Pam Chamberlain, "Homophobia in Schools or What We Don't Know Will Hurt Us," p. 3; Joseph Harry, "Derivative Deviance: The Cases of Extortion, Fag-Bashing and the Shakedown of Gay Men," pp. 546–563; Leonore Gordon, "What Do We Say When We Hear 'Faggot'?" pp. 25–27; Brian Miller and Laud Humphreys, "Lifestyles and Violence: Homosexual Victims of Assault and Murder," pp. 169–185.

5. See, for example, in the Bibliography to this book listings for articles in *Gay Community News* (Boston) and *Advocate* (Los Angeles).

6. See, for example, in the Bibliography the listings for Peter Freiberg, Rick Harding, and Robert W. Peterson, in *Advocate* (Los Angeles).

7. Arthur Bell, *Kings Don't Mean a Thing: The John Knight Murder Case;* and Randy Shilts, *The Mayor of Castro Street: The Life and Times of Harvey Milk.*

8. See, for example, in the *Village Voice* (New York), the following articles by Arthur Bell: "Midnight Ramble Roundup: Chasing the Bat Pack," pp. 1, 11; "Gay-Bashing Spree in the Village," p. 18; "Death Comes Out," pp. 1, 11–12; "Shooting at Ghosts: Ronald Crumpley's Lethal Odyssey," pp. 1, 20, 21; "Bell Tells," p. 24; "Black Tie and Blood," pp. 1, 11–12, 14. See also Randy Shilts, "Gay Attacked by Four Youths on Polk Street Dies of Injuries," *San Francisco Chronicle,* August 2, 1984; and Bertram A. Workum, *Kentucky Post,* cited by Ed Hicks, "Cohen Murdered," *Gaybeat* (Cincinnati), August 1986, p. 5.

9. See, for example, Jim Bray, "Woman Says Police Beat Lesbian Lover," *St. Louis Globe-Democrat,* July 11, 1978; Foster Church, "Probe of Firebomb Stirs Questioning: Of Unwanted Sort Gay Commune Gets Attention," pp. 1A, 1B; "Four Beaten, Robbed in Reverchon Park," *Dallas Morning News,* July 11, 1986, p. 23A; Lacey Fosburgh, "Maye Held as Harasser in Gay Alliance Fracas," *New York Times,* May 23, 1972, p. 30; Veronica Fowler, "Gay Teens Harassed by Peers," *Ames Tribune* (Ames, Iowa), November 13, 1983, pp. 1,7; Erik Gunn, "Gays Wonder If Fear Led to Gresty's Murder," *Rockford Register-Sun* (Rockford, Ill.), December 6, 1979, p. 3B; Marita Hernandez, "Prosecution in Gay Murders Urged," *Los Angeles Times,* September 5, 1981, p. 26I; Bob Holliday, "Men Claim Neighbors' Taunting Forced Move," p. 2A; Joseph Kahn, "Gays Going to Court in Maye Case," *New York Post,* May 5, 1972, p.

10; Bill McAuliffe, "Bouza Cites Diligence in Probes of Crimes Against Gays," p. 6D; John Rawlinson, "Outside Northside Tavern: 4 Teenagers Charged in Beating Death," *Arizona Daily Star* (Tucson, Ariz.), June 8, 1976, pp. 1B, 9B; Irene Sege, "Northampton's Gays Fight Back: Reports of Harassment Trigger Action," pp. 47, 52; Tux Turkel, "Our of Fear Comes a Killing: Homosexual's Harassment Ends with a Tragedy," p. 1A; Kristi Vaughan, "Lesbians Uneasy in Northampton," pp. 1H–2H.

10. See, for example, "Justice Not Served," *Arizona Daily Star* (Tucson, Arizona), October 27, 1976; Ira Glasser, "The Yellow Star and the Pink Triangle," *New York Times*, September 10, 1975; Peter Hamill, "Kings Go Forth," *New York Post*, April 20, 1972; Robert Lipsyte, "The Closet, a Violent and Subtle Prison"; Courtland Milloy, "Closet Life, Phobia and Foul Play"; Roger Simon, "Playing It Straight in Crimes on Gays," p. 4; "Solidarity with Gays," *Boston Globe*, February 1, 1987.

11. For articles from magazines, see, for example, Michael Reese, "The Growing Terror of 'Gay Bashing,' " *Newsweek*, March 3, 1981; and Laurence Zuckerman, "Open Season on Gays: AIDS Sparks an Epidemic of Violence Against Homosexuals," *Time*, March 7, 1988, p. 24.

For television shows, see, for example, Betsy Aaron, "Violence Against Gays"; Phil Donahue, "Queerbashing"; Kathy McManus and John Stossel, "Homophobia"; and Oprah Winfrey, "Homophobia."

12. Those articles that have focused on violence have dealt with the social work aspect of providing services to victims; see, for example, Craig L. Anderson, "Males as Sexual Assault Victims," pp. 145–162; and Bohn, "Homophobic Violence," pp. 91–112.

13. Surveys have been conducted by lesbian/gay organizations alone and in conjunction with municipal offices and agencies. For examples of the latter see Office of the Mayor, Kevin H. White, City of Boston, Executive Summary, *The Boston Project: Toward an Agenda for Gay and Lesbian Citizens;* Office of the Governor, Anthony S. Earl, State of Wisconsin, "Governor's Council of Lesbian and Gay Issues: Violence Survey Final Report"; Edward Peeples, Jr., Walter W. Tunstall, Everett Eberhardt, and the Research Task Force with technical assistance from the Commission on Human Relations, City of Richmond, *A Survey of Perceptions of Civil Opportunity Among Gays and Lesbians in Richmond, Virginia;* San Francisco Board of Supervisors, Committee on Fire, Safety and the Police, "Four-Hour Public Hearing on Queerbashing," October 9, 1980 (transcript of testimony edited for broadcast on KSAN-FM's Gay Life Program and aired October 18, 19 and November 8, 9, 16 of 1980, available from Lesbian and Gay Associated Engineers and Scientists, Sunnyvale, Calif.); and "New Orleans Gays Report Bashing, Bias," *Advocate* (Los Angeles), October 10, 1989, p. 21.

For studies and reports based on self-reporting by victims, see NYC Commission on Human Rights, *Gay and Lesbian Discrimination Documentation Project;* Van de Kamp, *Attorney General's Commission on Racial, Ethnic, Religious and Minority Violence;* Dick Stingel, "CUAV Assault Report Survey and Analysis 01/79–02/80"; and Carmen Vasquez, *Quarterly Reports: January–March*

1984 to January–March 1986; U.S. Congress, House Subcommittee on Criminal Justice of the Committee on the Judiciary, *Anti-Gay Violence,* pp. 76–85, 147–151; North Carolinians Against Racist and Religious Violence, "Homophobic Violence in North Carolina: 1983–1984," and Mab Segrest, "Responding to Bigoted Violence in North Carolina," *North Carolina Forum* (Raleigh, N.C.), 1985; Greg Kelner and Project Understanding, *Homophobic Assault: A Study of Anti-Gay Violence;* and Violence Project of the National Gay and Lesbian Task Force, "Anti-Gay Violence and Victimization in 1985" (includes reports collected from organizations and anti-violence projects representing forty-four communities throughout the United States; see subsequent reports for 1986, 1987, and 1988).

14. See comments by Peeples, in *Survey . . . of Richmond, Virginia,* pp. 3–4; Gregory D. Stanford, "Violence Rife, Gays Tell Panel," *Milwaukee Journal,* June 3, 1984, pp. 1, 13; Tom McNaught, in "Survey Methodology," in White, *Boston Project,* p. 67; Identity, Incorporated, *One in Ten: A Profile of Alaska's Lesbian and Gay Community,* p. 2; New Jersey Lesbian and Gay Coalition "Discrimination Against Lesbians and Gay Men in New Jersey," p. 4; Vermonters for Lesbian and Gay Rights, "Discrimination and Violence Survey of Lesbians and Gay Men in Vermont," p. 1; and Susan Cavin, "Rutgers Sexual Orientation Survey: A Report on the Experiences of Lesbian, Gay, and Bisexual Members of the Rutgers Community; New Brunswick, New Jersey," p. 13.

15. Total equals more than the number of surveys because several surveys used more than one resource for gathering data. Distribution and gathering techniques are not available for three of the surveys: Cauthern, Des Moines, and Minnesota.

16. Responses for my survey were gathered as follows:

I pilot-tested the questionnaire at the June 1986 meeting of Ulster County GALA (Gay and Lesbian Alliance) in Kingston, N.Y. Twenty-five people attended. More than half were women. Two were black. A group discussion followed the completion of questionnaires by all individuals present. Suggestions resulted in my simplifying some questions and adding others to accommodate anti-woman violence experienced by lesbians.

Using the *Gayellow Pages: USA and Canada,* Frances Green, ed., a national guide to gay and lesbian businesses, organizations, publications, activities, and events, I selected and wrote to 120 organizations. I chose at least one from each state with preference for those involving lesbians and people of color. My letter described my research project and asked for their cooperation in distributing questionnaires to members of their organization. I explained that each questionnaire would be accompanied by a return-addressed, stamped envelope; leaders of organizations, therefore, would be responsible for distributing questionnaires but not for having them returned. I enclosed a return-addressed, stamped postal card with my letter for their response. Each postal cared was coded, so a message was not required unless an organization wanted to receive more than five questionnaires.

Many groups not only asked for more than five, but expressed appreciation and encouragement for my work. Some colleagues in the anti-violence movement had warned me that without a woman's name and signature on my introductory letter the response from lesbian organizations would be minimal. However, not only were expressions of support written more frequently by women, but the response rate from exclusively lesbian groups was 50 percent (25 of 50) compared to 43 percent (30 of 70) from men's and mixed groups.

In response to returned postal cards, I sent 550 questionnaires to fifty-five organizations. I also distributed fifty and collected twenty-four questionnaires at a meeting of Poughkeepsie (New York) GALA in October 1986, and I distributed 100 and collected seventy-four questionnaires at the registration table of the national convention of Black and White Men Together (BWMT) at Union Theological Seminary in New York City, July 3, 1986. A total of 700 questionnaires was distributed and 294 returned from July to December 1986, for a response rate of 42 percent. Responses were received from ninety-nine cities and towns in thirty-one states and Washington, D.C.

17. Bell and Weinberg, *Homosexualities,* pp. 78, 79, 190, 191, 193, 307.

18. Cynthia Cauthern, "900 Black Lesbians Speak," p. 12.

19. Joseph Harry, *Gay Children Grown Up: Gender Culture and Gender Deviance,* p. 166.

20. White, *Boston Project.*

21. Ames Civil Rights Task Force, "Results and Analysis of the Ames Civil Rights Task Force of Ames Area Lesbians and Gay Men."

22. New Jersey Lesbian and Gay Coalition, "Discrimination Against Lesbians and Gay Men in New Jersey: 1977–1983."

23. Peeples, *Survey . . . of Richmond, Virginia.*

24. Felice Yeskel, *The Consequences of Being Gay: A Report on the Quality of Life for Lesbian, Gay and Bisexual Students at the University of Massachusetts at Amherst.*

25. Des Moines Gay and Lesbian Democratic Club, as reported in Kevin Berrill, "Anti-Gay Violence: Causes, Consequences, Responses," A White Paper by the Violence Project of the National Gay and Lesbian Task Force, Prepared by Kevin Berrill, Violence Project Director, Submitted to the Committee on the Judiciary, Subcommittee on Criminal Justice, Washington, D.C., Fall 1986, p. 24 (included in U.S. Congress, House Subcommittee on Criminal Justice, Committee on the Judiciary, *Anti-Gay Violence,* 99th Cong., 2d sess., 1986, p. 66).

26. Greater Louisville Human Rights Coalition, "A Survey of Anti-Gay Discrimination in the Greater Louisville Area," 1985.

27. Wayne Steinman, "Information Collected from Questionnaire 'Answer 16 Questions for Gay/Lesbian Rights,' " Survey conducted by New York State Lesbian and Gay Lobby, Albany, New York, January 1985; and Wayne Steinman and Peter McNight, "Testimony [by chairperson and coordinator] on behalf of the New York State Lesbian and Gay Lobby given at the State Task Force on Gay Issues' Public Hearings on Discrimination Based upon Sexual Orientation," January 17, 1971.

28. Identity, Inc., *One in Ten.*

29. Cavin, "Rutgers Sexual Orientation Survey."

30. Anthony R. D'Augelli, "Gay Men's and Lesbian Women's Experiences

of Discrimination, Harassment, Violence, and Indifference" (University Park: Pennsylvania State University, Department of Individual and Family Studies, May 1, 1987).

31. Dallas Gay Alliance, "Dallas Gay Alliance Survey of Activism, Violence and Discrimination in the Dallas Gay Community," 1986.

32. Vermonters for Lesbian and Gay Rights, "Discrimination and Violence Survey of Lesbians and Gay Men in Vermont."

33. "Some Results from a Youth Survey," *Lavender Network* (Eugene, Ore.), August 1989, p. 42; and Robin Madell and Maureen Burke, "Lesbian and Gay Youth Support Needs Survey; Eugene–Springfield, Oregon."

34. Miller and Humphreys, "Lifestyles and Violence," pp. 169–185.

35. Diana Sepejak, "The Willingness of Homosexuals to Report Criminal Victimization to the Police."

36. Harry, "Derivative Deviance," 546–563.

37. Legislative and Social Action Ministry, Lesbian and Gay Interfaith Council of Minnesota, "Data Concerning Violence and Harassment Directed Against Gay Men and Lesbian Women and Their Communities."

38. William Paul, "Minority Status for Gay People," in William Paul, James D. Weinrich, John C. Gonsiorek, and Mary E. Hotvedt, eds., *Homosexuality: Social, Psychological, and Biological Issues* (Beverly Hills, Calif.: Sage Publications, 1982), p. 60, cites an informal pilot survey of fifty gay men in San Francisco by McDonough, "Anti-Gay Violence and Community Organization" (M.A. dissertation, San Francisco State University, 1981).

39. Office of the Governor, Earl, "Violence Survey Report."

40. National Gay Task Force, *Anti-Gay/Lesbian Victimization: A Study by the National Gay Task Force in Cooperation with Gay and Lesbian Organization in Eight U.S. Cities.*

41. Steven K. Aurand, Rita Addessa, and Christine Bush, *Violence and Discrimination Against Philadelphia Lesbian and Gay People: A Study by the Philadelphia Lesbian and Gay Task Force.*

42. Maine Civil Liberties Union, Maine Lesbian/Gay Political Alliance, and University of Southern Maine Department of Social Welfare, "Discrimination and Violence Survey of Gay People in Maine."

43. Steve Wheeler, "Results of Survey Released by GLRA," p. 42; also, personal correspondence from Steve Wheeler, including tally sheets, photographs, maps, and drawing.

44. Deborah Anne Potter, "Violence, Self-Definition and Social Control: Gay and Lesbian Victimization."

45. Gregory Herek, "Sexual Orientation and Prejudice at Yale: A Report on the Experience of Lesbian, Gay, and Bisexual Members of the Yale Community."

46. Lesbian Rights Task Force of Maryland NOW, "Maryland Anti-Lesbian/Gay Violence and Discrimination Documentation Project: Results of a Project Completed by the Lesbian Rights Task Force of Maryland NOW."

47. Kenneth B. Morgen, *The Prevalence of Anti-Gay/Lesbian Victimization in Baltimore: 1988.*

48. Originally founded in 1973 as the National Gay Task Force (NGTF)

with headquarters in New York City, this national gay and lesbian civil rights organization moved its offices to Washington, D.C., in 1985 and changed its name to the National Gay and Lesbian Task Force (NGLTF).

49. The demographic information for the respondents (294) in my survey is as follows:

Gender:
female	42.5% (125)	
male	56.5% (166)	
		(3 missing information)

Race
Native American	1.0%	(3)
Asian	3.1%	(9)
Hispanic	7.9%	(23)
Black	11.3%	(33)
White	76.6%	(223)

(3 missing information)

Race and gender:
Native American woman	1	Native American men	2
Asian woman	1	Asian men	8
Hispanic women	4	Hispanic men	19
Black women	5	Black men	29
White women	114	White men	108

(3 missing information)

Financial income:
under $5,000	5.6% (15)
$5,000–$10,000	14.2% (38)
$10,001–$15,000	12.7% (34)
$15,001–$20,000	19.4% (52)
$20,001–$25,000	13.4% (36)
over $25,001	34.7% (93)

(26 missing information)

Occupations:
Service providers	16.4% (47; 23 women, 24 men)
Clericals, technicians	15.0% (43; 15 women, 28 men)
Managers, administrators	13.6% (39; 19 women, 20 men)
Students	10.5% (30; 18 women, 12 men)
Laborers, transporters	8.4% (24; 10 women, 14 men)
Teachers, professors	7.3% (21; 6 women, 15 men)
Writers, artists	7.0% (20; 11 women, 9 men)
Salespeople, consultants	6.3% (18; 5 women, 13 men)
Lawyers, engineers, etc.	5.2% (15; 7 women, 8 men)
Researchers, archivists	4.9% (14; 5 women, 9 men)
Business executives	3.1% (9; 5 women, 4 men)

Unemployed		1.4% (4; 1 women, 3 men)
Retired		0.7% (2; both men)
		(8 missing information)

Class background:

lower class	26.6% (75)	
middle class	64.2% (181)	
upper class	9.2% (26)	(12 missing information)

Age:

20 under	4.8% (14)	
21–30	39.2% (114)	
31–40	38.3% (111)	
41–50	12.0% (35)	
51–60	4.3% (13)	
61–70	1.0% (3)	(4 missing information)

Location:

Responses were received from ninety-nine cities in thirty-one states and Washington, D.C. The states (in alphabetical order) with numbers of respondents from each are as follows: Arizona (3), Arkansas (4), California (12), Colorado (1), Connecticut (5), Florida (6), Georgia (7), Hawaii (2), Idaho (1), Illinois (15), Indiana (12), Kansas (2), Kentucky (5), Maine (5), Maryland (4), Massachusetts (10), Michigan (14), Minnesota (3), Montana (4), New Hampshire (5), New Jersey (4), New Mexico (12), New York (60), North Dakota (5), Ohio (12), Pennsylvania (9), Texas (25), Utah (5), Virginia (5), Washington, D.C. (22), Washington (3), West Virginia (1), Wisconsin (3), missing (3).

---

50. Gender composition is provided by the following surveys: Cauthern (100% female); Vermont (64% female, 36% male); Cavin-Rutgers (61% female, 39% male); Potter (60% female, 40% male); Alaska (56% female, 44% male); Madell/Burke and Yeskel-UMass (51% female, 49% male); Philadelphia (48% female, 52% male); Maine (46% female, 54% male); Herek-Yale (45% female, 55% male); Comstock (43% female, 57% male); Morgen (42% female, 58% male); D'Augelli-PennState (37% female, 63% male); Richmond (36% female, 64% male); Wisconsin (35% female, 65% male); Louisville and Sepejak (34% female, 66% male); Ames and NGLTF (32% female, 68% male); Bell/Weinberg (30% female, 70% male); New Jersey (29% female, 71% male); Wichita (25% female, 75% male); Boston (19% female, 81% male); Dallas (13% female, 87% male); Harry-1and-2, McDonough, and Miller/Humphreys (100% male). Only Alaska, Philadelphia, Comstock, Richmond, Wichita, Sepejak, NGLTF, and Bell/Weinberg organized and interpreted data according to gender composition.

Racial composition is provided by surveys as follows: Comstock (23% people of color, 77% white); Maryland (23% color, 61% white); Madell/Burke, Richmond and Bell/ Weinberg (18% color, 82% white); Morgen (15% color, 83%

white); NGLTF (15% color, 85% white); Alaska (12% color, 88% white); Yeskel-UMass, Louisville, Harry-1 (10% color, 90% white); Harry-2 (9% color, 91% white); Boston, Wichita, Wisconsin (7% color, 93% white); Dallas (4% color, 94% white); Philadelphia (3% color, 97% white); Cauthern (100% color); and Sepejak (100% white). Only Comstock, Richmond, and Bell/Weinberg organized and interpreted data according to racial composition.

Composition by economic status or financial income is provided by Maine, Vermont, Louisville, Richmond, Ames, Sepejak, and Harry-1 (all with approximately two thirds of respondents *under* $15,000 per year) and by Alaska, Dallas, Maryland, and Comstock (two thirds *over* $15,000). Madell/Burke reports that over two thirds of its respondents (all under twenty-two years of age) are from middle-, upper-middle-, and upper-class families. Only Comstock organized and interpreted data in terms of yearly financial income.

Composition by age is provided by twenty-five surveys. The respondents of most, with the exceptions of those with student samples, range from teenage to late sixties. Bell/Weinberg has the most balanced distribution. Richmond, Harry-2, Philadelphia, New Jersey, Alaska, NGLTF, Boston, McDonough, Maine, Vermont, Louisville, Morgen, Dallas, Maryland, and Comstock each have an average age ranging between thirty and thirty-five; Sepejak, Ames, Potter, and Wisconsin average in the late twenties; Wichita, D'Augelli-PennState, in the early twenties; and Yeskel-UMass, Madell/Burke, and Harry-1, with primarily student samples, between nineteen and twenty. None of the surveys organized and interpreted data by age; however, Madell/Burke, with its sample of under-twenty-three-year-olds, does provide a picture of violence in the lives of lesbian/gay youth.

51. New Jersey restricted reporting incidents to the past seven years; Morgen, Dallas, and Philadelphia, to both past-year and lifetime incidents; and Herek-Yale, Cavin-Rutgers, and D'Augelli-PennState to incidents during time as a student.

52. Some surveys restricted reporting to incidents that had happened within the immediate location (Yeskel-UMass, Herek-Yale, Cavin-Rutgers, D'Augelli-PennState, Alaska, Boston, Louisville, Minnesota, New Jersey, Dallas, New York State, Maryland, and Richmond), with Wichita's focusing on a particular park, and Maine-1 and Philadelphia-1's asking for incidents experienced both locally and elsewhere.

53. Herek-Yale, D'Augelli-PennState, Cavin-Rutgers, Morgen, Wisconsin, Dallas, Vermont, Miller/Humphreys, Maryland, and Sepejak do not use or compute a general anti-gay/lesbian violence category.

54. Compare Wichita, New Jersey, New York, Yeskel-UMass, Minnesota, Louisville, Boston, Dallas, and Philadelphia-1 with Philadelphia-2, Maine, Madell/Burke, and Comstock.

55. Compare McDonough, Harry-1 and-2, Dallas, and Bell/Weinberg with Philadelphia-2, Maine-2, Madell/Burke, and Comstock.

56. Three surveys (Alaska, 61 percent; Cauthern, 90 percent; and NGLTF, 94 percent) broaden their general violence category to include verbal harassment.

For a summary of surveys that shows consistently high rates of anti-gay/ lesbian verbal harassment among respondents (60 to 90 percent of respondents), see Berrill, "Anti-Gay Violence," pp. 23–24. In my survey 89 percent of the respondents (261 of 294 respondents) reported verbal harassment, which included "anti-gay/lesbian names, insults, and threats of violence directed at you by heterosexual people because of your sexual orientation." For a summary of the findings on verbal harassment from my survey, see appendix A.

57. National Gay Task Force, *Anti-Gay/Lesbian Victimization,* pp. 10, 31–32, summarizes its findings as follows: "In nearly half the questions, there are no statistically significant differences between cities in rates of response. All eight cities are much alike in the rates at which assailants throw object at respondents, vandalize or set fire to their property, sexually harass or assault them, and abuse them in school. Respondents in all survey locations also show similar rates of knowing others who have been victimized because of their sexual orientation.

Where there are significant city differences in response to questions, they vary much less consistently than differences by sex, and usually only one or two cities depart from the norm."

58. For newspaper accounts of incidents occurring in rural areas, see Laura Allen and Peter Kropotkin, "Happyless Valley," *Valley Advocate* (Springfield, Mass.), February 23, 1983, pp. 3, 9; Barbara LeBlanc, "Amherst Democrats Support Area Homosexual Community," *Daily Hampshire Gazette* (Hampshire, Mass.), March 11, 1983, pp. 1+; Jil Clarke, "Harassment of Northampton Lesbians Continues," *Gay Community News* (Boston), April 2, 1983, p. 1; Sege, "Northampton's Gays Fight Back," pp. 47, 53; Karen Lee Ziner, "Trouble in Paradise: The Lesbians of Northampton Under Attack," pp. 1, 6–7, 24; Ima Dyke, "Lesbian Community Harassed," *Valley Women's Voice* (Northampton, Mass.), June 1983, pp. 1, 3; Vaughan, "Lesbians Uneasy in Northampton," pp. H1–H2; Maureen Fitzgerald, "Man Jailed for Threats to Lesbians," *Daily Hampshire Gazette* (Hampshire, Mass.), October 11, 1983, pp. 1–3; Stephanie Kraft, "Terror by Phone: The Kremensky Trial Exposes the Upheaval in Northampton's Changing Social Setting," *Valley Advocate* (Springfield, Mass.), October 19, 1983, pp. 3, 9; Barry Bearak, "Slaying of Openly Gay Man Raises Troubling Questions for Quiet Town," *Des Moines Register,* August 14, 1984, p. 1A; Foster Church, "Probe of Firebomb Stirs Questioning: Of Unwanted Sort Gay Commune Gets Attention," pp. 1A, 1B; and Dave Walter, "Nevada Ghost Town Is Site of New Gay City," *Advocate* (Los Angeles), December 23, 1986, pp. 15–16.

For accounts of incidents in suburban areas, see "Attacks Begin in Suburbs," *Gay Life* (Chicago), September 26, 1976; Scott Richardson, "Gay Bloomington Homeowner: Harassment Turns Dream into Nightmare," p. 3A; Bob Holliday, "Men Claim Neighbors' Taunting Forced Move," p. 2A; "Harassment! in Mastic," *Long Island Connection,* January 20, to February 2, 1983, pp. 12–13, 15; and David Behrens, "Tracing Violence Against Gays," p. 6.

59. Cauthern's findings would tend to support a higher rate of victimization among lesbians of color also. Cauthern and NGLTF are the only surveys that include verbal harassment in their general violence categories and do not limit

reporting of incidents to time and place. Their percentages (90 and 94, respectively) appear similar and comparable, but Cauthern's includes only victimization of black lesbians by black men. A still higher rate would be expected if victimization by white perpetrators were included as it is in NGLTF.

60. The following accounts provide information about anti-gay/lesbian violence in the lives of poor people: For a newspaper article about poor gay men, see Donna Severin, "Gay and Poor: Portraits of Two Gay Couples," *New York Native,* November 3, 1986, pp. 23–24. For accounts of violence against homeless gay men, see City of New York, *Gay and Lesbian Discrimination,* pp. 48, 96, 97, 98. For the story of a working-class man's ordeal with teenagers who harassed and assaulted him for a period of months, see Peter Freiberg, "A Killing in Maine," *Advocate* (Los Angeles), March 4, 1986, pp. 10–12.

61. Bureau of Justice Statistics, *Crime Victimization in the United States, 1984: A National Crime Survey Report* NCJ-100435, Washington, D.C., U.S. Department of Justice, May 1986, pp. 2, 14.

62. Although the lack of uniformity across all the surveys limits comparisons of the various findings to some general and suggestive observations, the similar design of Philadelphia, Maine, Wisconsin, Yale, Rutgers, PennState, and Comstock after NGLTF yields a body of six surveys with comparable categories and information.

Vermont, Morgen, and Madell/Burke also use some, but not all, of these subcategories; but only those surveys that use all the standardized subcategories are considered here for comparison. Those percentages found by Vermont, Morgen, and Madell/Burke are, however, identical or similar to those found by the other surveys: Vermont (followed or chased, 32%; objects thrown at, 21%; vandalism or arson, 19%; punched, hit, kicked, or beaten, 16%; weapon assault, 5%; sexual assault, 14%), Morgan (objects thrown at, 24%; punched, hit, kicked, or beaten, 17%; weapon assault, 10%; other 28%), and Madell/Burke (two percentages are given for "in-school" and "out-of-school" experiences, respectively: chased or followed, 37% and 31%; property damage, 26% and 31%; sexual assault, 9% and 11%; physical violence, 26% and 31%).

Maryland uses all categories, but limits reporting of incidents to those that occurred within the state (followed or chased, 12%; objects thrown at, 4%; punched, hit, kicked, or beaten, 9%; vandalism, 12%; spit at, 7%; weapon assault, 7%; and sexual assault, 9%).

63. *Women.* Among the literature on the raping of women by men, the rape of lesbians is rarely discussed or mentioned. Exceptions are Kathleen Boyle, "Lesbians," in Linda Tschirhart Sanford and Ann Fetter, eds., *In Defense of Ourselves* (New York: Doubleday, 1979), pp. 148–151, and Pauline B. Bart and Patricia H. O'Brien, *Stopping Rape: Successful Survival Strategies* (New York: Pergamon Press, 1985), pp. 62–64. In telephone conversations and written correspondence with various programs, projects, and organizations working against rape across the United States, I learned that no one has turned his or her attention to research and writing about anti-lesbian rape.

Rape Crisis centers report few, if any, instances of victims' identifying as lesbians (e.g., the coordinator of Womankind Counseling Center in Concord,

New Hampshire, in a letter to me [October 1986], says that during her two-year tenure, the Center has "not had any referrals of lesbians who were dealing with a recent rape." The director of the Rape Intervention Program, St. Luke's-Roosevelt Hospital Center, New York City, in an interview with me (September 11, 1986), estimates that, at most, 3 percent of their clients are lesbians. She adds that most lesbians are "smart enough to use services available to women without self-identifying and risking anti-lesbian discrimination, especially from hospital emergency rooms and law enforcement agencies."

The research by Bart and O'Brien may suggest that there is a lower rate of victimization among lesbians than among women in general. Of six self-identified lesbians in a sample of ninety-four women, five report having stopped their rapes. "Mindful of the small number of women," the authors claim that the "fact that only one out of six lesbians was raped—and her situation was one in which no other woman was able to escape—gives further support for the feminist analysis: In order to avoid rape it is helpful to transcend traditional 'feminine' socialization and style." Of the total sample of ninety-four women, thirteen resisted their rapes, six avoided rape, and seven did not. Five of the six were lesbians. (See also Judith McDaniel, "Present Danger"; Michaele Uccella and Melanie Kaue, "Survival Is an Act of Resistance"; Denslow Tregarten Brown, "Lesbian Consciousness and Male Violence"; Rita Frenzel, "Claiming My Rights"; Donna Allegra, "Butch on the Streets"; Thrace, "Action Proposal for Lesbian Revolutionary Movement from a Lesbian Separatist's Position"; and Sidney Spinster, "Warriors of the Luniform Shield: Lesbians and Direct Action," in Frederique Delacoste and Felice Newman, eds., *Fight Back! Feminist Resistance to Male Violence*, pp. 3–25, 28–30, 39–41, 44–45, 301–311.

Susan Cavin, in *Lesbian Origins*, pp. 83, 86–87, 116–117, 169–174, extends this appreciation for the protective power of women's independence and communal support into a speculative historical analysis relating rates of rape to the "sex ratios" of various societies and environments. She argues that high-female/low-male sex ratios diminish, control, and/or eliminate sexual violence against women. Her thesis is supported by the empirical work by Beth E. Schneider, "Consciousness About Sexual Harassment Among Heterosexual and Lesbian Woman Workers," *Journal of Social Issues* (1982), 38:85, who examines sexual harassment, not specifically rape, and finds that "those in a workplace with a predominance of men report more incidents than those in female-dominated workplaces. For example, 17 percent of lesbians in workplaces with 80 percent or more women were approached by co-workers, while 73 percent in workplaces with 80 percent or more men were approached by co-workers."

Although some would argue that lesbianism, understood not only as personal self-identification but as supportive networking with other lesbians and women, protects women and deters rape, Ralph H. Gundlach, in "Sexual Molestation and Rape Reported by Homosexual and Heterosexual Women," *Journal of Homosexuality* (Summer 1977), 2:367–384, finds that lesbians who are raped subsequently develop such woman-identified networks or strengthen those with which they are currently involved. On the basis of data "gathered from questionnaires and interviews of 48 lesbians and 30 heterosexual women who had been the object of rape or attempted rape," he concludes that the "adult heterosexual women tended to accept the rape as one of the hazards of choosing whom to be with and whom to avoid. Those who later or already were lesbians found themselves disgusted by the sexuality and violence of these men, felt dirtied by the rape, and strongly turned toward the gentleness of other women."

For materials that advocate sensitivity for and provide training to counselors of rape victims, see Rape Intervention Program, St. Luke's-Roosevelt Hospital Center, *Advocate Training Manual,* New York (n.d.), p. 32; Lesbian Feminist Liberation, "Not All Women Who Are Raped Are Heterosexuals," New York (n.d.); Harriet Malinowitz, "Lesbians and Sexual Assault," *Newsline* (Newsletter of the New York City Gay and Lesbian Anti-Violence Project) (n.d.), pp. 4–5; and brochure by the New York City Gay and Lesbian Anti-Violence Project, *Sexual Assault of Lesbians.*

Although the preceding resources do not consistently distinguish between lesbians who are raped because they are women (i.e., the perpetrator does not know about the victim's sexual orientation) and victims of anti-lesbian rape, the following do: Abigail Norman, "The Problem of Violence," *Catalyst* (1981), 12:85; Abby Tallmer, in *Task Force Report* (Newsletter of National Gay Task Force), "Defining Anti-Lesbian Violence," September–October 1983, pp. 4, 7, and "Sexual Assault of Lesbians: Some Issues," March–April 1984; and Jacqueline Schafer, "Lesbian and Gay Sensitivity Training Workshop Guide" and "Outline for Lesbian and Gay Sensitivity Training Workshop," prepared by the Lesbian and Gay Issues Committee, New York City Task Force Against Sexual Assault (n.d.). Tallmer's second article outlines and discusses the clinical issues for survivors of anti-lesbian rape. Schafer provides role-plays and training materials for counselors to victims. Tallmer's first article together with Norman's provides the following patterns of rape that are characteristically anti-lesbian: (1) *Assault by cabdrivers:* "Because lesbians in many urban areas are afraid to travel alone on mass transit late at night, they are particularly vulnerable to attack by cabdrivers who park their cars in front of lesbian bars, waiting for potential victims. Very often rape is the ultimate object of this particular pattern of assault" (Tallmer, p. 4). (2) *Assault by a man or group of men upon leaving a lesbian bar:* "A man or group of men wait around a women's bar for a victim to emerge who is tired or intoxicated. They drag her into a car or cab or follow her home, where she is raped or gang raped" (Norman, p. 85). (3) *Attack of a couple by a single man:* "A man follows a lesbian couple home or ascertains where they live, often in his neighborhood or building. He gains entry, ties up one woman and forces her to watch while he rapes the other" (Norman, p. 85). (4) *Assault of a lesbian by a "gay" man:* "In this pattern, straight male rapists pose as gay men, often in settings such as mixed gay bars. They make friends with otherwise suspicious women, saying things like, 'Don't worry, I'm gay, too." Once they gain the woman's trust, they accost and rape her" (Tallmer, p. 4). (5) *Rape by ex-lover, ex-husband, or acquaintance:* A woman comes out to an ex-lover, ex-husband, or a man who's been interested in her. He apprehends her or comes to her home and rapes or abuses her, saying, 'All you need is a good fuck. This will teach you to be straight' " (Norman, p. 85). See also Dorothy I. Riddle and

Barbara Sang, "Psychotherapy with Lesbians," *Journal of Social Issues* (1978), 34:94. (In my survey, one woman wrote on her questionnaire, "I was raped in 1982 in my own home by a man under the delusion that a lesbian wouldn't be a lesbian if the woman had a good man, which he believed himself to be.")

Rape used as a corrective for lesbianism was sanctioned by the criminal justice system as reported in the following incident in Ohio: "Last year. . . , a 19 year-old lesbian, was kidnapped by her father and three others and subjected to 'deprogramming' from 'lesbian mind control,' a process that included being deprived of food and sleep and repeatedly raped. When she was released from her 'treatment,' [she] returned to her lover and filed charges against her parents and deprogrammers. The parents defended their actions on the grounds that her lover was exerting 'mind control' over her, and they acted out of love for her when they arranged the kidnapping and 'treatment.' They paid 8000 dollars and were fully aware of the methods used.

"The Judge dismissed charges of sexual battery, assault and kidnapping, and deleted all references to forced heterosexual acts as rape, redefining this as 'heterosexual activity meant to sway [her] from her lesbianism.' " ["Court Condones Rape of Lesbian," *Peace News* (Nottingham, Great Britain), July 23, 1982, p. 5; see also Heidi Silver, "Ohio Court Allows Brutal Anti-Lesbian Persecution," *Workers World* (New York), June 18, 1982, p. 11.]

A series of incidents of verbal harassment and physical assaults against lesbians in Northampton, Massachusetts, occurring over a one-year period, October 1982 to October 1983, were marked by the rapes of three women because they were lesbians, one of whom "received a threatening phone call from a male *while she was recovering in the hospital after the rape*," as reported by Ima Dyke, "Lesbian Community Harassed," *Valley Women's Voice* (Northampton, Mass.), June 1983, p. 1. See also Sege, "Northampton's Gays Fight Back," p. 47; Clarke, "Harassment of Northampton Lesbians Continues," p. 1; Ziner, "Trouble in Paradise: The Lesbians of Northampton Under Attack," p. 1; Vaughan, "Lesbians Uneasy in Northampton," p. H1; Toni Dickerson, Abigail Norman, Robin Omata, Lydia Dean Pilcher, Afua Kafi-Akua, Daresha Kyi, producers and directors, in Diana Agosta, ed., *Just Because of Who We Are: Working Tapes,* interviews with Bet Birdfish, Kim Christensen, and Kiriyo Spooner (New York: Heramedia, 1986).

See also the following newspaper articles: "Lesbians and Rape: Protection Under the Law?" *Off Our Backs* (Washington, D.C.), June 1986, p. 17; "Lesbian Raped, Repeatedly Harassed," *Another Voice* (Huntington, N.Y.), December 18, 1985, p. 13; Kim Westheimer, "Lesbian Survivor of Rape Harassed Again," *Gay Community News* (Boston), April 12, 1986, p. 2; "Lesbian Activist Protests Police Actions," *Out!* (Madison, Wis.), March 1984, p. 3; Sue Burke and Brooks Egerton, "Plot Sickens in Racine Rape Case," *Out!* (Madison, Wis.), April 1984, p. 3; Jenning, "Homosexual Assaults Produce Defensive Countermeasures," p. 1.

Men. Social consciousness about rape of men by men not in institutions, encouragement and support for victims to report rapes, and services for recovering victims appear to be increasing. See, for example, Abigail Van Buren, ("Dear

Abby," syndicated column) "Male Rape Victims Must Report Crimes," *Daily Freeman* (Kingston, N.Y.), March 4, 1986, p. 11; Stephen Donaldson, "Sexual Assault of Men: A Hidden Crime," *Newsline* (Newsletter of New York City Gay and Lesbian Anti-Violence Project) (n.d.), p. 3; N. Douglas Elwood and Bruce Larson, eds., *Same-Sex Assault: A Handbook for Intervention Training* (Minneapolis: Park Avenue Clinical Services, 1981) (published and distributed in cooperation with Minnesota Program for Victims of Sexual Assault, Minnesota Department of Corrections); Rape Intervention Program, St. Luke's-Roosevelt Hospital Center, *Advocate Training Manual*, pp. 22–24; and brochure by New York City Gay and Lesbian Anti-Violence Project, *Male Sexual Assault*.

Studies estimate that 10 percent of identified sex crime victims are men; see, for example, Elwood and Larson, *Same-Sex Assault*, p. 2. Diana E. H. Russell, *Sexual Exploitation: Child Sexual Abuse and Workplace Harassment* (Beverly Hills, Calif.: Sage Publications, 1984), p. 71, cites studies from the early 1970s that give smaller percentages (4 and 5 percent). A study of male college students finds that as many as 30 percent of respondents reported "at least one act of criminally forced sodomy" perpetrated against them; Schultz and DeSavage, cited in Russell, *Sexual Exploitation*, p. 71.

Available research maintains that victims and assailants are overwhelmingly heterosexual; see, for example, Nicholas Groth and Ann Wolbert Burgess, "Male Rape: Offenders and Victims," p. 809; Arthur Kaufman, Peter Divasto, Rebecca Jackson, Dayton Voorhees, and Joan Christy, "Male Rape Victims: Noninstitutionalized Assaults," p. 223; and Stephen Donaldson, "Thinking About Rape of Males," 2nd ed., prepared for use by the Committee on Male Survivors of Rape, New York City Task Force Against Sexual Assault, February 6, 1986, p. 1. Nicholas Groth, in *Men Who Rape*, pp. 124–125, finds that defining sexual lifestyle of offenders as homosexual or heterosexual is problematic because, "in general, their interpersonal relationships lacked such qualities as empathy, mutuality, and reciprocity," and they tended to possess a "rather ambiguous and undefined sexuality that was more self-centered that interpersonal."

The victims tend to be young (see Donaldson, p. 2), with ages ranging from sixteen to twenty-eight years (see, for example, Groth and Burgess, p. 807).

For clinical observations of victims and offenders and narratives descriptive of incidents, see Groth, *Men Who Rape*, pp. 120–140; Groth and Burgess, pp. 807–808; and Kaufman, Divasto, Jackson, Voorhees, and Christy, p. 22. Russell, *Sexual Exploitation*, p. 72, criticizes the available social science literature as lacking in sufficient data (Groth and Burgess' sample being "small and highly unrepresentative") and also criticizes Groth and Burgess' tendency to combine information about offenders gathered from offenders with that gathered from victims.

The literature about the raping of men by men only occasionally mentions homophobia as an underlying motivating force and addresses the specific issues of anti-gay rape. The exceptions are Anderson, "Males as Sexual Assault Victims," pp. 91–112, who addresses the setup, attack, and aftermath pattern of assault and subsequent crisis intervention needs; and "A Male Survivor's Story,"

Newsline (Newsletter of the New York City Gay and Lesbian Anti-Violence Project), p. 2.

See also these newspaper articles: Tommi Avicolli, "Man Raped by 2 Men and Boy," *Philadelphia Gay News,* August 22–28, 1986, p. 1; "26-year-Old Man Reports Sexual Assault by 3 Men," *Des Moines Register* (Des Moines, Iowa), February 3, 1986, p. 14A; "Faggot Haters Rape California Male," *Gay Chicago News,* August 1977; "Crimes Against Gay Men Continue in Boston's Back Bay Section," *Gay Community News* (Boston), September 30, 1978; "Iowa City, Iowa," *Advocate* (Los Angeles), October 1, 1985, p. 26; "Male Rapes Reported in Iowa," *Equal Time* (Minneapolis), September 18, 1985, p. 2; Tom Knudson, "3 Men Raped in Iowa City," *Des Moines Register* (Des Moines, Iowa), August 13, 1985, p. 3M.

64. San Francisco Board of Supervisors, Committee on Fire, Safety and the Police, "Four-Hour Public Hearing on Queerbashing," pp. H4–H5.

65. Conversation with Mertz recorded in Berrill, "Anti-Gay Violence," p. 8.

Dick Stingel, testifying at San Francisco Board of Supervisors, Committee on Fire, Safety, and the Police, "Four-Hour Public Hearing on Queerbashing," p. H2, states that of the incidents reported to the Community United Against Violence (CUAV) in San Francisco "40% of the assaults involved deadly weapons, 10% involved such things as knives, ice picks, broken bottles and razors. 20% involve the use of blunt instruments such as bats, two-by-fours, sticks, bottle, rocks, and clubs. 7% involve such weapons as automobiles, ropes, chains, and 3% of the assaults reported to us involved the use of guns. The results of the assaults, the consequences to the victim are that almost none of the victims escaped unscathed, more than 40% requried medical treatment ranging from stitches and splints to major surgery. Two assaults reported to us resulted in the death of the victims. One murder near Buena Vista Park was of a 22 year old Gay man, recently arrived from Fresno, killed by a gunshot to the head. The second involved a man whose body was thrown out of a car on Highway 101 near San Mateo. He had been beaten so severely that he literally had no face left."

According to Vasquez, *Quarterly Statistical Analyses: January 1984 to March 1986,* the quarterly rate for reported incidents in which weapons are used is 34 percent and the rate for those in which medical treatment is required is 32 percent.

66. Other than Miller/Humphreys, see Frank W. Kiel, "The Psychiatric Character of the Assailant as Determined by Autopsy Observations of the Victim," pp. 263–271; Donal E. J. MacNamara and Edward Sagarin, *Sex, Crime, and the Law,* pp. 156–157; Joseph C. Rupp, "Sudden Death in the Gay World," pp. 189–191; and Victoria Lynn Swigert, Ronald A. Farrell, and William C. Yoels, "Sexual Homicide," pp. 391–401.

Miller/Humphreys, pp. 170–172, find the last three studies lacking in substantial data, and state that "both MacNamara and Sagarin's study and Rupp's study ... constitute, at best, speculative essays with a few examples cited to substantiate the author's claims having been acquired through fortuitous circumstances."

Although I agree that these studies are limited, the Swigert, Farrell, and Yoels study of sexual homicide and MacNamara and Sagarin's use of the President's Commission on Law Enforcement and Administration of Justice Study do suggest a disproportionately high incidence of anti-gay murder. The President's Commission, for example, "set out to study (as part of its determination of the extent and impact of crime) all crimes reported for one week in one police precinct in Chicago (a precinct with a heterogeneous social and ethnic makeup)." I agree with MacNamara and Sagarin that "it may be only coincidence [that] the one homocide reported was of [an anti-]homosexual nature," but it, also, suggests a high rate of incidents of this kind, especially when considered with the other study. Swigert, Farrell, and Yoels, after reviewing 444 homicide cases from a nineteen-year period in one psychiatric facility, found that of the five cases that qualified as sexual homicides (murders involving a sexual encounter with the victim) two were anti-homosexual in nature. In spite of small numbers in each study, the findings of both are consistent in suggesting that the frequency of anti-gay murders is higher than that of murders among the general population.

67. See, for example, James Coates, "Minneapolis Cops Take New Look at String of Homosexual Slayings," *San Francisco Examiner,* October 26, 1986. "Authorities Search for Body Linked to Disappearances of Homosexuals," *Louisville Courier-Journal* (Kentucky), June 15, 1978, p. 12D. In *Another Voice* (Huntington, N.Y.), "Police Alert Gays to Killer," December 18, 1985, p. 5; and "Serial Killer of Gay Men in Queens," May 7, 1986, p. 3. Marita Hernandez, "Prosecution in Gay Murders Urged," *Los Angeles Times,* September 5, 1981, p. I-26. Lisa White, "Tarheel Killing Fields: Gay men Keep Turning Up Dead— But Activists Fear Police Indifference to Fag-Bashing," *Philadelphia Gay News,* February 14–20, 1986, pp. 1, 27. "Man Confesses Killing 6 Homosexuals in Atlanta," *New York Times,* November 30, 1986, p. 30. "Homos Fear Rise in Gay Murders," *New Crusader* (Chicago), December 20, 1975, pp. 1, 3. "Gay Slayings," *Ames Tribune* (Ames, Iowa), October 20, 1983, p. 4. Tracie Cone, "Murdering the Gay Everyman, Part II," p. 5. Lou Siegel, "Violence Against Gays/Police Against Gays," p. 8. John Ward, "Police Suspect Gay Angle to Murder," *Philadelphia Gay News,* July 18, 1985, pp. 1, 23. David Morris, "Another Gay Man Murdered Here," *Gay Community News* (Boston), January 31, 1981, p. 1. Kim Westheimer, "Two Gay Men Killed: Hub Police Deny Link in Recent Anti-Gay Violence," *Gay Community News* (Boston), June 29 to July 5, 1986, p. 1. In *Gay Community News* (Boston), "Six Slain This Year: Bay Area Police Continue Investigations," November 11, 1978; "Washington Police Investigate Increase in Murders of Gays," August 5, 1978, p. 3; "Three DC Murders," March 11, 1978.

68. *CUAV Dish* (Newsletter by and for the Volunteers of Community United Against Violence, San Francisco), February 1987, reports that "there have been 17 gay-related homicides in San Francisco in the last 13 months." Mab Segrest, in "Responding to Bigoted Violence in North Carolina," reports that "at least five men have been murdered in the past two years because their attackers perceived them to be gay." Kathleen Sarris, president, Justice, Incorporated, in her testimony in U.S. Congress, House, Subcommittee on Criminal Justice of

Committee on the Judiciary, *Anti-Gay Violence,* says that her organization "became involved in the violence issue in 1983, when a member pointed out that over a two (2) year period of time at least 14 gay men, from Indianapolis, had been murdered." See examples of regularly published announcements by the New York City Gay and Lesbian Anti-Violence Project in *New York Native,* "Help Sought in Gay Murder," August 18, 1986, pp. 7–8; "Anti-Violence Project Seeks Information on Murder Victim," June 15, 1987, p. 9; and Mike Salinas, "Anti-Violence Project Seeks Information on Murder: Suspect Tied to Robbery Spree," March 23, 1987, p. 10. See also Frank Broderick, "The Ugly Reality of Anti-Gay Violence in Phila. Area," *Au Courant* (Philadelphia), August 14, 1989, pp. 1, 7, for an account of seven murders of gay men within a two-month period.

Although no accurate figure can be calculated to show what percentage of anti-gay/lesbian violence involves murder, documentation by anti-violence projects shows that approximately 5 percent of reported incidents of physical assaults are murders. Sources for my computation are Kevin Berrill, "Crisisline: Expanded Activity, Violence Reports, AIDS Discrimination, Caller Profiles," *Task Force Report* (Newsletter of the National Gay Task Force) (September–October 1983), p. 3; Violence Project, National Gay and Lesbian Task Force, "Anti-Gay Violence and Victimization in 1985," Washington, D.C., 1985, p. 2; "Anti-Gay Violence, Victimization and Defamation in 1986," Washington, D.C., 1987, p. 3.

69. Some law enforcement agencies have begun to record the anti-gay/lesbian nature of crimes. See, for example, District Attorney's Office (Manhattan), County of New York, unpublished collection and summaries of "some of the cases involving gay or lesbian victims which have been prosecuted by the Manhattan District Attorney's Office between 1980 and May 1985" (known as *80 Case Memo*) (May 1985); Robert M. Morgenthau, *Report of District Attorney, County of New York, 1983–1984,* pp. 12, 14–15; U.S. Congress, House Subcommittee on Criminal Justice of the Committee on the Judiciary, *Anti-Gay Violence,* pp. 108–146; Alice T. McGillon, deputy commissioner, "Release 38" (announcement of formation of Bias Incident Investigating Unit), Public Information Division, Police Department, City of New York, December 19, 1980; Arlo Smith, district attorney, San Francisco County, "Dealing with Anti-Gay Violence: 'Homosexual Panic' Defense Is Bigotry in Action," *Bay Area Reporter* (San Francisco), November 3, 1983, pp. 1, 11; Commission on Racial, Ethnic, Religious and Minority Violence, Office of the Attorney General, John K. Van de Kamp, State of California, *Attorney General's Commission on Racial, Ethnic, Religious and Minority Violence Final Report, April 1986,* Sacramento, California, Office of the Attorney General, 1986; and Francis M. Roache, police commissioner, "Community Disorders Unit," Special Order Number 87 to all bureaus, districts, etc., of Boston Police Department.

As of 1989, state legislation requiring the collection of statistics on bias-related crimes, including those against victims because of their sexual orientation, has been passed in Connecticut (Pub. Act 87-279, passed 1987), Minnesota (H2340, S2124, passed 1988), and Oregon (SB 606, passed 1989). See Arthur S.

Leonard, "Gay and Lesbian Rights Protections in the U.S.: An Introduction to Gay and Lesbian Civil Rights" (Washington, D.C.: National Gay and Lesbian Task Force, 1989); Violence Project, National Gay and Lesbian Task Force, "Anti-Gay Violence, Victimization and Defamation in 1988," pp. 30–33; and Don Powell and Fred Neal, "Gay Bashing Outlawed, Tracked: A Look Back at the 1989 Legislative Session," *Right to Privacy Political Action Committee Newsletter* (Portland, Oregon), September 1989, pp. 1–3.

In 1989 the U.S. House of Representatives and in 1990 the U.S. Senate approved legislation requiring the federal government to collect statistics on crimes motivated by bias based on race, ethnicity, religion, or sexual orientation. The President subsequently signed the bill into law.

70. Miller/Humphreys, p. 183. My research supports this finding; see, for example, the following books by journalists: Bell, *Kings Don't Mean a Thing;* Shilts, *Mayor of Castro Street;* and Weiss, *Double Play.*

For magazine articles see Janet Cotton, "Murder and the Cathedral," *Macleans,* August 4, 1980, p. 18; Hinckle, "Dan White's San Francisco," pp. 3–20; Doug Ireland, "The New Homophobia: Open Season on Gays," pp. 207–210; Philip Plews, "The Evil That Boys Do," pp. 60, 62–63, 86, 88–89, 91–92; Brian Shein, "Gay-Bashing in High Park," pp. 37–39, 64–69; Bill Sievert, "The Killing of Mr. Greenjeans," pp. 39–42, 46–48; and Thomas Szasz, "How Dan White Got Away with Murder and How American Psychiatry Helped Him Do It," pp. 17–21.

For newspaper articles, see Barry Adkins, "Accused Priest Killer Alleges Sexual Advances: 'Father Fred' Mourned in Brooklyn," *New York Native,* June 2, 1986, p. 8; Tommi Avicolli, "Police Identify Bodies Found in Bucks County," *Philadelphia Gay News,* July 25–31, 1986, pp. 1, 10; Barry Bearak, "Slaying of Openly Gay Man Raises Troubling Questions for Quiet Town," p. 1A; Bell, "Death Comes Out," pp. 1, 11–12; Fred Berger, "Community Reacts to Bangor Murder," *Our Paper* (Portland, Maine), pp. 1, 8; David Brill, "Police Investigate Murders and Beatings: Violence Mars Start of New Year in Boston," *Gay Community News* (Boston), January 13, 1979; Fox Butterfield, "Slaying of Homosexual Man Upsets Confidence of Bangor, Me.," *New York Times,* July 25, 1984; Peg Byron, "Anti-Gay Killings in Bangor: Will Kids Get Away with Murder in Maine?" *New York Native,* July 30 to August 12, 1984, pp. 9, 10; Peter Canellos, "A City and Its Sins: The Killing of a Gay Man in Bangor"; Dwight Cathcart, "Assessing the Legacy of Charlie Howard: The Impact of a Gay Man's Murder," p. 1ff; Linda Clark, "Five Teens Plead Guilty in Park Beating Death," pp. A1, A2 (also, other articles on this incident to December 4, 1985); Gregory Douthwaite, "MCC Pastor in Stockton Murdered: Police Believe Killing Was Gay-Related; No Suspects," *Bay Area Reporter* (San Francisco), February 20, 1986, p. 17; Rachel Duell, "Outpouring at Jersey City Memorial: Hospital Workers Condemn Murder of Gay Union Brother," *Workers World* (New York), January 11, 1980, p. 6; Peter Freiberg, "Youth Acquitted in Bludgeoning Murder: Kalamazoo Gays Outraged; Judge Publicly Disagrees with Verdict," *Advocate* (Los Angeles), April 1, 1986, pp. 12–13; Charles Hallam, "Rushville Man to Stand Trial for Monmouth Resident's Murder," *Rock Island*

Argus (Rock Island, Ill.), May 15, 1979; Rick Harding and Lisa M. Keen, "Son Shoots Mother, Friend," *Washington Blade* (Washington, D.C.), May 2, 1986, p. 10; Mike Hippler, "Anatomy of a Murder," *Advocate* (Los Angeles), February 17, 1987, pp. 42–49; Andrew Lesk, Ken Poppert, and Ric Taylor, "Boys Will Be Boys," *Body Politic* (Toronto), January 1986, pp. 13–15; Charles Linebarger, "S.F. 'Fag Bashers' Convicted of Murder," *Advocate* (Los Angeles), January 21, 1986, p. 16; Eugene McCarthy, "Sold Rifle to Accused, Clerk Tells Murder Trial," *Kitchener-Waterloo Record* (Ontario), September 10, 1985, pp. 1A, 2A (also, articles on this incident to October 4, 1985); Jeff Maclin, "Oak Lawn Beating Victim Dies: 2 Men Sought in Plano Man's Death," *Dallas Morning News,* July 23, 1986, p. 18A; George Mendenhall, "Justice in Bakersville: Gays Murdered, Protestor Fired, Case Dismissed," *Bay Area Reporter* (San Francisco), January 27, 1983; Gary Oakes, "5 'Average' Teens Get 9 Years for Killing Librarian," *Toronto Star,* November 27, 1985, pp. 1A, 4A; Steve Pokin, "Leads Develop in Wood Murder," *Mt. Vernon Register News* (Mt. Vernon, Ill.), July 31, 1980; John Preston, "Bangor Tragedy No Isolated Incident," *Weekly News* (Miami, Fla.), October 24, 1984, pp. 3, 22; John Rawlinson, "Outside Northside Tavern: 4 Teenagers Charged in Beating Death," *Arizona Daily Star* (Tucson), June 8, 1976, pp. 1B, 9B; Harry Ring, "Bigots Kill Gay Man in Maine," *Militant* (New York), August 10, 1984, p. 7; Dion B. Sanders, "Murder in Maine Prompts Public Outrage: Judge Frees Three Teenagers Who Confessed to Killing Gay Man," *Bay Area Reporter* (San Francisco), August 2, 1984, p. 14; Mark Scott, "Gay-Related Murder in Prince George's County," *Washington Blade* (Washington, D.C.), July 27, 1984, p. 6; Heidi Silver, "Murderer of Gay Man Gets Slap on Wrist," *Workers World* (New York), February 29, 1980, p. 2; Carol Stengel, "Youths Attack Bar Patrons: Nebraska Man Beaten to Death Here," *Arizona Daily Star* (Tucson), June 7, 1976; Kim Westheimer, "Two Gay Men Killed: Hub Police Deny Link in Recent Anti-Gay Violence," *Gay Community News* (Boston), June 29 to July 5, 1986, p. 1; Allen White, "Gays Outraged: Bakersfield Murderer All But Goes Free," *Bay Area Reporter* (San Francisco), June 17, 1982, pp. 1, 16; Maureen Williams, " 'Swishy' Gay Man Drowned by Three Teens: Bangor Gay Man Fatally Queerbashed," *Gay Community News* (Boston), July 21, 1984, pp. 1, 6.

71. Miller/Humphreys, pp. 173–174, used the following criteria for assessing which cases qualified for their study: (1) strong evidence that the victim was homosexual; (2) crime related to victim's sexual orientation; (3) elimination of cases of homosexual inmates murdered in prison; and (4) exclusion of cases in which nature of victim's life-style was not indicated or was unclear. Twenty-three cases were eliminated because of insufficient or obscure data, as were thirty-two victims of arson, forty-eight victims of mass murders, and six murders that took place in England. Fifty-two cases of individual Canadian and American homosexual males were retained.

For examples of anti-lesbian murder found in my research, see "Son Shoots Mother and Suspected Lesbian Lover," *Off Our Backs* (Washington, D.C.), June 1986, p. 17; "Recommend Jail for Daughter Who Helped Kill Lesbian Mother," *Pekin Times* (Pekin, Ill.), July 25, 1979 (Belton, Texas, UPI release); "Could the

Police Have Prevented Donna Smith's Death?" *Gay Chicago News*, December 19, 1975; Peter Freiberg, "A Victim Tells Her Story: Survivor Talks About the Antigay Shooting that Killed Her Lover," *Advocate* (Los Angeles), January 3, 1989, pp. 18, 21; and Victoria A. Brownworth, "Survivor Talks," p. 17.

72. Miller/Humphreys, pp. 179–180.

73. Frank W. Kiel, "The Psychiatric Character of the Assailant as Determined by Autopsy Observations of the Victim," *Journal of Forensic Sciences* (1965), 10:269. See also Shilts, *Mayor of Castro Street*, pp. 162–163.

74. "Gang Beats Two Gays," *Washington Blade* (Washington, D.C.), July 27, 1984, p. 8 (quote from *Miami Herald*).

75. Of the other surveys, only New Jersey provides comparable data. Its findings (p. 15)—that 30 percent of the respondents "reported being attacked at a lesbian/gay establishment or en route to or from a lesbian/gay establishment" and that "nearly 15 percent of the respondents experienced violence actually at or near their homes or on the street"—are similar to my findings of 27 percent for "outside lesbian and/or gay bar, disco, or baths" and 17 percent for "at one's own home."

76. Although "cruising" (i.e., intentionally looking for a sexual partner) may occur anywhere, certain areas are more frequently used than others. For example, abandoned areas, public spaces after dark when not frequented by the general public, landscaped areas that afford protection and privacy, and buildings such as bus terminals that maximize anonymity are typically used for cruising. See Bell/Weinberg, pp. 73–80, 299–307, for frequencies of cruising among lesbians and gay men.

For the purposes of my survey and the current discussion, "areas known for cruising" do not include bars, homes, schools, or areas covered by the other settings used. In those cases in which settings may overlap, respondents were expected to decide which setting was appropriate for reporting. For more information on activity in cruising areas, see Edward William Delph, *The Silent Community: Public Homosexual Encounters* (Beverly Hills, Calif.: Sage Publications, 1978).

For a journalistic account of the physical dangers encountered by gay men in cruising areas, see Rechy, *The Sexual Outlaw*. Rechy focuses on police practices.

For sociological studies see Humphreys, *Tearoom Trade;* Jay Corzine and Richard Kirby, "Cruising the Truckers: Sexual Encounters in a Highway Rest Area," pp. 171–192; Troiden, "Homosexual Encounters in a Highway Rest Stop," in Goode and Troiden, *Sexual Deviance and Sexual Deviants*, pp. 211–228. Both Humphreys (pp. 49, 83–84, 97–99) and Troiden (pp. 216, 218) cite the need for a look-out person to detect the approaches of teenage "toughs" and police. Corzine and Kirby (pp. 183, 186) note that "cruisers are aware of the threat of physical violence if they offend a driver"; although they do not mention problems with teenagers, they find that "of those who may be present in settings, only state police or the employees at the rest areas are seen as potential threats by cruisers."

For a study of male prostitution in cruising areas, see Albert J. Reiss, Jr., "The Social Integration of Queers and Peers," pp. 249–278.

For a newspaper account of the arrest of two women for having sex in a public park, see "DA Charges Lesbians, Frees Married Couple," *Out!* (Madison, Wis.), August 1984, p. 2. For a literary account of lesbians' cruising in public restroom settings, see Anne Francis, "Toilet Love," *New York Native*, December 22, 1986, p. 23.

77. Of the other surveys, only Philadelphia (pp. 28–29) and Morgen (p. 4) present comparable data for settings and these are limited to schools. Philadelphia's percentages, although reflecting the differences found by my survey in rates of victimization between men and women in high school, are lower than mine. Its percentages for college neither reflect the differences between men and women in my survey nor are numerically similar to mine. Morgan presents percentages for men and women together (junior high school, 6%; high school, 6%; and college, 2%), but notes, "The lesbians in our sample were less than half as likely to be called names, threatened with violence, and assaulted in high school as their male counterparts because they were gay. Only in college did the climate improve somewhat for both sexes." Morgen, therefore, finds less incidence of violence in schools than I do, a similar difference between lesbian and gay victimization in junior and high school but not in college.

	Philadelphia % of Respondents (N = 167)		Comstock % of Respondents (N = 291)	
	Men	Women	Men	Women
junior high school	3	0	8	0
senior high school	6	1	13	2
college	0	0	8	15

78. Physical violence from parents in the home setting is a problem especially for some lesbian and gay youth; see Bruce Kogan, "Investing in Our Future," *New York Native*, September 15, 1986, p. 23, and Robert W. Peterson, "In Harm's Way: Gay Runaways Are in More Danger than Ever, and Gay Adults Won't Help," pp. 8–10. For an account of a gay youth's familial experiences with violence in a small town, see Howard Brown, *Familiar Faces, Hidden Lives*, pp. 89–95. See also Jim Rusnak, in Ann Heron, ed., *One Teenager in Ten: Testimony by Gay and Lesbian Youth* (Boston: Alyson Publications, 1983; New York: Warner Books, 1986), pp. 33–40; Keith Hefner and Al Autin, eds., *Growing Up Gay* (Ann Arbor: Youth Liberation Press, 1978); and Committee of Educators for Lesbian and Gay Concerns, Panel discussion on "Lesbians and Gays in the Public School," panel member Paula Hogan, Kathy Bliss, Arthur Lipkind, Brian Mooney, Pam Chamberlain, David Crowder, and Lisa George, moderated by Rinaldo Discologne and Liz Heron, Harvard Graduate School of Education, April 4, 1983.

The Institute for the Protection of Lesbian and Gay Youth in New York City reports that of the clients who have applied for services, 37 percent had experi-

enced violence from family members; see testimony prepared and delivered by
the executive director and the director of social work service of the Institute for
the Protection of Lesbian and Gay Youth in U.S. Congress, House Subcommittee
on Criminal Justice of Committee on the Judiciary Committee, *Anti-Gay Violence*, pp. 147–151. The Institute reports, also, that 8 percent of gay male youths
and 11 percent of lesbian youths "had need of emergency housing because of
family reactions to their sexual orientation. . . . The need for emergency housing
was usually connected to reports of abuse"; see National Gay Task Force,
"NGTF at Federal Hearings on Police Misconduct, Family Violence," *News
from NGTF* (Newsrelease) (New York) December 12, 1983.

79. For newspaper accounts of anti-gay/lesbian violence in high school set-
tings, see the following: Veronica Fowler, in *Ames Tribune* (Ames, Iowa), "Gay
Teens Harassed by Peers," November 13, 1984, pp. 1, 7; and "Gay Teens Still
Being Harassed," November 20, 1984, p. 1. Jenny Bower and Nancy Ostendorf,
"Students, Administration Tired of 'Non-Conformist' Issue," *Ames High Web*
(Ames, Iowa), November 30, 1984, p. 3. Nancy Gamon, "Assemblies Give
Opposing Views on Homosexuality," *Ames High Web* (Ames, Iowa), May 17,
1985, p. 7. "Lesbian Students Threatened," *Washington Blade* (Washington,
D.C.), April 12, 1985, p. 10.

For newspaper articles concerning the relationship between secondary school
educational policy and anti-gay/lesbian violence, see Mike Salinas, "Philadelphia
Board of Ed. Rejects Proposals on High School Homophobia: School District
Denies Problem," *New York Native*, May 11, 1987, pp. 8, 35; Lenny Giteck,
"School Days, School Days. . . ," *Advocate* (Los Angeles), September 1, 1987, p.
6; Peter Freiberg, in *Advocate* (Los Angeles), "Sex Education and the Gay Issue:
What Are They Teaching About Us in the Schools?" September 1, 1987, pp.
42–43, 45, 47–49, and "A Light in the Blackboard Jungle," April 25, 1989, pp.
50–52; and Robert W. Peterson, "Seattle Report: School Is Tough for Young
Gays," *Advocate* (Los Angeles), February 14, 1989, p. 15.

80. For newspaper and magazine accounts of anti-gay/lesbian violence on
college and university campuses, see Patricia Roth, " 'Not Going Away' at
Wheaton," *Bay Windows* (Boston), June 26, 1986, pp. 8, 13. "College Group
Wins Harass Battle," *New York Native*, June 9, 1986, p. 7. "Lesbian Students
Pushed Out of Closet," *Another Voice* (Huntington, N.Y.), February 5, 1986, p.
12. Carol Kirchenbaum, "Instant Activism: A Moment of Truth for Austin's
Gays," pp. 80–81. John Wolfe, "Gay Students Find Tolerance Losing Ground,"
Sunday News Journal (Wilmington, Delaware), February 17, 1985, p. C1. Jeff
Morgan, "Officials Express Concern over U of I Anti-Gay Graffiti," *Iowa State
Daily*, October 11, 1984, pp. 1, 2. "Freedman Upset by Graffiti," *Des Moines
Register* (Des Moines, Iowa), October 10, 1984, p. 6M. Cecilia C. Lyons (letter),
"Anti-Gay Violence on Blue Jeans Day at U. of L.," *Lavendar Letter* (Louisville,
Kentucky), December 1986, p. 15. Frank Elam, "Brigham Young U.: Mormons
Stake Out Gays," *Guardian* (New York), October 17, 1979, p. 9. John Ward, in
Philadelphia Gay News, " 'Students Against Faggots Everywhere' at U of Del.:
Campus Spawns Phobes," October 25, 1984, p. 5; "At University of Delaware:
Homophobia Still Growing," November 22, 1984, pp. 3, 6; and "At University

of Delaware: Anti-Gay Push Continues," December 20, 1984, pp. 4, 5. Tommi Avicolli, in *Philadelphia Gay News*, "Awareness Week Marked by Vigil and Vandalism" and "Gay Students Stage 'Flaunt-In,' " 18–24 April 1986, pp. 3, 6, 13; "Penn Student Plans to File Complaint," May 2–8, 1986, pp. 3, 27. Sue Dockstader, "GALA Receives Threats," *Women's Press* (Eugene, Ore.), November–December, 1985, p. 1. Jim, "Confrontations Mar Pride Week," *Women's Press* (Eugene, Ore.), July–August 1986, p. 3 (reprinted from *Lavendar Network*, June 1986). "GALA Reports Campus Harassment—Stony Brook," *Another Voice* (Huntington, N.Y.), August 6, 1986, p. 7. "Gay Students: Continued Harassment," *Guardian* (New York), April 28, 1982, p. 10. "Sparks Fly over Anti-Gay Letter," *Out!* (Madison, Wis.), April 1984, p. 3. Peter Freiberg, in *Advocate* (Los Angeles), "Out on Campus," June 9, 1987, pp. 10–12, 21; and "Students Cite Hate Attacks in Michigan," July 4, 1989, pp. 13, 16; and "Why Johnny Can't Tolerate Gays," March 14, 1989, pp. 8–9. Lorraine Bennett, in *Los Angeles Times*, "Athletes to Be Benched After Attack on Gay," March 13, 1981; and "Students Assail UC Riverside Handling of Attack on Gay," April 25, 1981. Paul Zwickler, "Members of 'Iron Fist' Expelled from University of Chicago for Anti-Gay Harassment: Reactionary Group Held Responsible for Hate Mail Directed at Gay People and Other 'Liberals,' " *New York Native*, August 3, 1987, p. 10. In *Advocate* (Los Angeles), "University of Hartford," February 16, 1988, p. 23; and "Rutgers University," March 1, 1988, p. 20. Eric Wong, "Rock-throwers Disrupt GLAD Slideshow, Hit Three Students," *Yale Daily News*, April 10, 1986, p. 1. Lee A. Daniels, "Prejudice on Campuses Is Feared to Be Rising," *New York Times*, October 31, 1988, p. A12, Fred M. Hechinger, "Fresh from Success in New York, Vartan Gregorian Pursues a Mission at Brown," *New York Times*, September 13, 1989, p. B11. "Harassing Letters Upset Students at Dartmouth," *New York Times*, October 19, 1989, p. B9. "Connecticut Campus Reports Bias Incidents," *New York Times*, October 16, 1989, p. B8.

See also Campus Environment Team, Pennsylvania State University, "Campus Climate and Acts of Intolerance: Report of the Campus Environment Team" (University Park, Pa.), October 1988.

81. Because its respondents are under twenty-three years of age and mostly in college or high school, Madell/Burke gives a more accurate picture of violence in the lives of lesbian/gay youth. Its findings show nearly equal, but slightly lower, frequencies for violence at school than for out of school: physical violence (26% in school, 31% out of school), property damage (26% in school, 37% out of school), followed or chased (37% in school, 31% out of school), and sexual assault (9% in school, 11% out of school).

82. Bureau of Justice Statistics, *Crime in the United States, 1984: A National Crime Survey*, pp. 6, 62–63.

83. For examples of attacks directed at gay men of color in a public lesbian/gay area, see Barry Adkins, "Minorities Attacked in Village," *New York Native*, September 1, 1986, p. 10.

84. Dick Stingel, testifying for the Community United Against Violence at San Francisco Board of Supervisors, Committee on Fire, Safety and the Police,

"Four-Hour Public Hearing on Queerbashing," October 9, 1980, pp. H2–H3, states: "Though anti-gay or lesbian violence occurs throughout San Francisco as indicated on the map [demonstrated], each dot on that map is the location of a single event of the 280 we have documented so far, the heaviest concentration is found in an area bounded by Duboce, Diamond, 20th, and Dolores St. If you want to know where it is on the map look for the red block. There are so many dots in that area that I didn't have room for them all. 40% of the assaults reported to us occur in our 'golden ghetto.' "

According to Vasquez, *Quarterly Statistical Analyses: January 1984 to March 1986,* the quarterly rate of reported incidents in public lesbian/gay areas is 70 percent.

85. Harry-2, p. 555.

86. Richmond, table 43.

87. Schneider, in "Consciousness About Sexual Harassment Among Heterosexual and Lesbian Women Workers," p. 85, however, finds that for sexual harassment (which does not include sexual assault, but involves pinching and grabbing, jokes about body and appearance, and sexual propositions and requests for dates) "in those instances where differences exist between [open and closed lesbians], it is always the closed lesbians who have more incidents; the more closed a lesbian is at work, the more she is thought to be single and heterosexual. Openness interestingly sets some limits but certainly not many. Lesbians are as a rule more open with co-workers, usually people who are or can be close friends, not with those in power; there are no differences among lesbians in the frequency of incidents with bosses or supervisors." Reporting on her study elsewhere, Schneider, "Peril and Promise: Lesbians' Workplace Participation," in Trudy Darty and Sandee Potter, eds., *Women-Identified Women,* pp. 211–230, says, "Ironically enough, the lesbians who tended to be secretive about their sexual identity (therefore presumed to be heterosexual) were more often sexually approached in these particular ways than the more open lesbians" (pp. 223–224).

See the following for examples of violence directed at a lesbian and gay man after each took public positions in support of lesbian/gay issues: "Vermont," *Advocate* (Los Angeles), May 23, 1989, p. 17, reports about "a lesbian who spoke in favor of a proposed state gay rights bill at a statehouse public hearing [and] was harassed and her home was burglarized following her testimony;" and Rick Harding, "Springfield's Shame: A Student's Home Is Torched in a Squabble Over a College Play," *Advocate* (Los Angeles), December 19, 1989, pp. 8–9, reports an incidence of arson of the house of a gay man who had advocated the public performance of the play *The Normal Heart,* by gay playwright Larry Kramer.

88. Smith, *Home Girls,* pp. xlvi–xlvii.

89. National Gay Task Force, "NGTF Survey Indicates Widespread Anti-Gay/Lesbian Violence" (news release), July 12, 1984.

90. Yeskel-UMass, p. 5. See also Campus Environment Team, Pennsylvania State University, "Campus Climate and Acts of Intolerance: Report of the Campus Environment Team," University Park, Pa., October 1988, p. 6, which re-

ports that "of the incidents [of acts of intolerance] reported, gays and lesbians were the most likely to be the victims of intolerance, directly."

91. These percentages can be confirmed by the findings (4 percent for women and 6 percent for men) in Bureau of Justice Statistics, *Crime Victimization in the United States, 1984*, p. 14.

92. Philadelphia, p. 33. In my survey, in addition to incidents of anti-gay/ lesbian violence, women were asked to report violence that had been directed against them because they are women, and people of color were asked to report incidents of violence directed against them because of their racial identities. Thirty-five percent of the women report having been the victims of anti-woman violence; 19 percent of the people of color report having been the victims of racist violence.

93. Philadelphia, p. 13; confirmed in Bureau of Justice Statistics, *Crime Victimization in the United States, 1984*, p. 2.

94. Philadelphia, p. 13; confirmed in Bureau of Justice Statistics, *Crime Victimization in the United States, 1984*, p. 2.

3. EMPIRICAL DATA ON PERPETRATORS

1. See, for example, Carmen Vasquez, *Quarterly Statistical Analyses: January 1984 to March 1986;* Office of the Mayor, Kevin H. White, City of Boston, *Executive Summary, The Boston Project: Toward an Agenda for Gay and Lesbian Citizens;* Greg Kelner and Project Understanding, *Homophobic Assault: A Study of Anti-Gay Violence;* City of New York, Commission on Human Rights, *Gay and Lesbian Discrimination Project;* and National Gay and Lesbian Task Force, *Anti-Gay Violence, Victimization and Defamation in 1986*, Washington, D.C., 1987.

2. For magazine articles, see, for example, Doug Ireland, "The New Homophobia: Open Season on Gays," pp. 207–210; Carol Kirschenbaum, "Instant Activism: A Moment of Truth for Austin's Gays," pp. 80–81; Frances Fitzgerald, "The Castro," Part I, pp. 34–38, 43–44, 46, 51–70, and Part II, 44, 46–63; Michael Reese, "The Growing Terror of 'Gay Bashing,' " *Newsweek*, March 3, 1981, p. 30; and Laurence Zuckerman, "Open Season on Gays: AIDS Sparks an Epidemic of Violence Against Homosexuals," *Time*, March 7, 1988, p. 24.

For newspaper articles, see, for example, Lorraine Bennett, "Athletes to Be Benched After Attack on Gay," *Los Angeles Times*, March 13, 1981; Steve Brewer, " 'Gay-bashing' Worsens Since AIDS Epidemic," pp. B1 +; Jeanne Curran, "Police Fear Homosexuals Not Reporting Criminal Acts Performed Against Them," *Bangor Daily News* (Bangor, Maine), July 10, 1986; David Jackson, "Robber, Sadist, Sometimes a Killer: Gay Hustler: A Violent Threat," *Chicago Daily News*, February 28, 1976, p. 1; Steve Jenning, "Homosexual Assaults Produce Defensive Countermeasures," and " 'Gay Bashing' Emerges as Vicious Crime of Hard Times," pp. B1, B7; and Kristi Vaughan, "Lesbians Uneasy in Northampton," pp. H1–H2.

For television coverage, see Kathy McManus, producer, and John Stossel, "Homophobia," p. 5.

3. See, for example, Phil Nash, "A Gaybasher Says 'I'm Sorry,' " *Bay Windows* (Boston), June 26 to July 2, 1986, pp. 1, 9–10; Eric Rofes, "Queer Bashing: The Politics of Violence Against Gay Men," pp. 8–9, 11; Eric Weissman, "Kids Who Attack Gays," *Christopher Street*, August 1978, pp. 9–13; Seymour Kleinberg, *Alienated Affections: Being Gay in America*, pp. 197–202; and Oprah Winfrey, "Homophobia."

4. See, for example, the following books: Arthur Bell, *Kings Don't Mean a Thing: The John Knight Murder Case*; Randy Shilts, *The Mayor of Castro Street: The Life and Times of Harvey Milk*; and Mike Weiss, *Double Play: The San Francisco City Hall Murders*.

For magazine articles, see, for example, Warren Hinckle, "Dan White's San Francisco," pp. 3–20; and Bill Sievert, "The Killing of Mr. Greenjeans," pp. 39–42, 46–48.

For newspaper articles, see, for example, Peter Canellos, "A City and Its Sins: The Killing of a Gay Man in Bangor," *Boston Phoenix*, November 13, 1984; and Linda Clark, "Five Teens Plead Guilty in Park Beating Death," *Globe and Mail* (Toronto), November 25, 1985, pp. A1, A2.

For a documentary film, see Robert Epstein and Richard Schmeichen, *The Times of Harvey Milk*.

5. For entries in books, see, for example, Wainwright Churchill, *Homosexual Behavior Among Males: A Cross-Cultural and Cross-Species Investigation*, p. 197; and Laud Humphreys, *Tearoom Trade: Impersonal Sex in Public Places* pp. 83–84, 98–99.

For entries in journal articles, see, for example, Ted S. Bohn, "Homophobic Violence: Implications for Social Work Practice," pp. 93–94; Ben R. Huelsman, "Southern Mountaineers in City Juvenile Courts," pp. 49–54; and Brian Miller and Laud Humphreys, "Lifestyles and Violence: Homosexual Victims of Assault and Murder," pp. 179–181.

6. For statements by law enforcement officials, see, for example, Robert J. Johnston, Jr., chief, New York City Police Department, in U.S. Congrfess, House Subcommittee on Criminal Justice of Committee on the Judiciary, *Anti-Gay Violence*; Robert M. Morgenthau, "Testimony of Robert M. Morgenthau, District Attorney of New York County, In Support of Intro 2, before the New York City Council," March 11, 1986; and "State of California, Office of the Attorney General, John K. Van de Kamp (announcement of intention to "propose civil rights legislation to impose criminal penalties for hate violence directed against minorities and gays"), April 17, 1986.

For remarks by school officials and teachers, see Veronica Fowler, "Gay Teens Harassed by Peers," *Ames Tribune* (Ames, Iowa), November 13, 1984, pp. 1, 7; and Leonore Gordon, "What Do We Say When We Hear 'Faggot'?" *Interracial Books for Children Bulletin* (1983), 14:25–27.

7. National Gay Task Force, *Anti-Gay/Lesbian Victimization: A Study by the National Gay Task Force in Cooperation with Gay and Lesbian Organizations in Eight U.S. Cities*; and Deborah Anne Potter, "Violence, Self-definition and Social Control: Gay and Lesbian Victimization."

8. Kenneth B. Morgan, *The Prevalence of Anti-Gay/Lesbian Victimization*

in Baltimore: 1988 (Towson, Md.: Chesapeake Psychological Services, 1988); Steven K. Aurand, Rita Addessa, and Christine Bush, *Violence and Discrimination Against Philadelphia Lesbian and Gay People: A Study by the Philadelphia Lesbian and Gay Task Force;* and Maine Civil Liberties Union, Maine Lesbian/Gay Political Alliance, and University of Southern Maine Department of Social Welfare, "Discrimination and Violence Survey of Gay People in Maine."

9. See Vasquez, *Quarterly Statistical Analyses;* Dick Stingel, "CUAV Report Survey and Analysis 01/79–02/80," San Francisco, Community United Against Violence, Inc. (n.d.); Diana Christensen, in U.S. Congress, House Subcommittee on Criminal Justice of Committee on The Judiciary, *Anti-Gay Violence;* Greg Kelner and Project Understanding, *Homophobic Assault: A Study of Anti-Gay Violence.*

10. Kevin Berrill, in "Crisisline: Expanded Activity, Violence Reports, AIDS Discrimination, Caller Profiles," *Task Force Report* (Newsletter of the National Gay Task Force), September–October 1983, pp. 3, 7, reports a similar finding from the cases logged by the NGTF Violence Project: "A clear majority (65%) did not know their assailants." Potter, p. 39, reports that 85 percent of the perpetrators in her study are "strangers and not known to those they attacked."

11. Of the surveys discussed in chapter 2, only three report respondents' experiences of physical violence by police: 1 percent of both female and male respondents in the Philadelphia-2 survey, 15 percent of the Maine-2 respondents, and 2 percent of Morgen's respondents report physical assaults by police officers. Other surveys, however, do report a broader category of "physical and verbal" harrassment by the police. These are Alaska, 6 percent of female respondents, 11 percent of male respondents, and 8 percent of all respondents; Vermont, 8 percent of all respondents; Philadelphia-2, 16 percent of female respondents and 24 percent of male respondents; NGLTF, 20 percent of all respondents; Maine-2, 48 percent of all respondents; and Wisconsin, 24 percent of all respondents.

12. See also, "Could the Police Have Prevented Donna Smith's Death?" *Gay Chicago News,* December 19, 1975; "Conviction of Murder Is Upheld," *Champaign Courier* (Champaign, Ill.), September 19, 1978; City of New York, *Gay and Lesbian Discrimination,* p. 58; and Philadelphia Lesbian and Gay Task Force, "Excerpts from Case Studies," p. 4.

13. National Gay Task Force, *Anti-Gay/Lesbian Victimization,* p. 26. The findings, compared with mine, are as follows:

	% Respondents NGLTF			% Respondents Comstock		
Physical Abuse By:	*Male*	*Female*	*All*	*Male*	*Female*	*All*
father	4.3	2.1	3.6	3	0	2
mother	1.4	2.9	1.9	0	0	0
sister	1.1	0.5	1.0	0	2	1
brother	3.6	2.7	3.3	9	2	6
other relatives	1.7	1.6	1.7	0	4	3

14. Morgen, pp. 5–6, reports that because of their sexual orientation 10 percent of the women in his survey and 6 percent of the men had been assaulted by family members.

15. U.S. Congress, House Subcommittee on Criminal Justice of Committee on the Judiciary, *Anti-Gay Violence,* pp. 147–151. See also Peter Freiberg, "Helping Gay Street Youth in New York," pp. 10–12; and Frank A. Conway, "Joyce Hunter," *Christopher Street,* 123 (1988), pp. 52–53.

16. The 117 incidents involve 262 perpetrators and 176 victims, which can be broken down approximately as follows:

Perpetrators of color = 92 (victims = 48; incidents = 37)
White perpetrators = 170 (victims = 128; incidents = 80)
Female perpetrators = 10 (victims = 6; incidents = 5)
Male perpetrators = 252 (victims = 170; incidents = 112)

As the information about perpetrators is organized according to demographic variables, these figures will change slightly. Because perpetrators sometimes attack in interracial and mixed-gender groups, the tallies of victims according to the racial identities and genders of perpetrators will yield higher numbers of victims than reported above. Each participating gender or racial identity in a single attack is credited with the total number of victims of the attack.

17. Potter, p. 39, reports that 89 percent of the incidents in her study involve only male assailants.

18. For anecdotal data, see Ruth Simpson, in *From the Closet to the Courts,* p. 173.

19. Exceptions have been reported. For example, in District Attorney's Office (Manhattan), County of New York, unpublished collection and summaries of "some of the cases involving gay or lesbian victims which have been prosecuted by the Manhattan District Attorney's Office between 1980 and May, 1985" (hereafter referred to as *80 Case Memo*), May 1985, p. 2, the following is reported: "People v. Valerie Slater. During the afternoon of October 5, 1984, as the victim was walking east on Christopher Street, a prostitute, for no apparent reason, smashed him in the face with a pair of metal tipped high heeled shoes causing a large gash on his forehead and lacerating his cheek."

20. The following newspaper articles report incidents in which women assisted or accompanied male perpetrators: "Recommend Jail for Daughter Who Helped Kill Lesbian Mother," *Pekin Times* (Pekin, Ill.), July 25, 1979; "Lesbian Attacked," *Off Our Backs* (Washington, D.C.), November 1985, p. 14; and Ed Hicks, "Killer's Trial Tells Sordid Tale," *Gaybeat.* (Cincinnati), May 1, 1985, pp. 1, 4, 6. See also District Attorney's Office (Manhattan), *80 Case Memo,* p. 7.

21. Potter, p. 39, finds that perpetrators reported in her study "tended either to be teenagers (23%) or young adults (49 percent were 18 to 24 years old)."

However, a wide range of ages for perpetrators is reported in my survey and elsewhere. See, for example, Gordon, "What Do We Say When We Hear 'Faggot'?", pp. 25–27; letter to the editor in the *San Francisco Chronicle* quoted by Hinckle, "Dan White's San Francisco," p. 11; Stanley Kauffmann, "Harsh Contradictions," p. 24; and Cynthia R. Cauthern, "900 Black Lesbians Speak," p. 12.

22. Vasquez, *Quarterly Statistical Analyses: January 1984 to March 1986;* Stingel, "CUAV Report Survey and Analysis 01/79–02/80," p. 2, and Testimony by Stingel at San Francisco Board of Supervisors, Committee on Fire, Safety and the Police, "Four-Hour Public Hearing on Queerbashing," October 9 (transcript of testimonies edited for broadcast on KSAN-FM's Gay Life Program and aired October 18, 19 and November 9, 16, of 1980; available from Lesbian and Gay Associated Engineers and Scientists, Sunnyvale, Calif.), p. H2.

See also Ruben Rosario, "Anti-Gay Violence Probed: Homosexuals Join Those Aided by Cop Unit as Attacks Based on Race, Beliefs Increase," p. 31.

23. CUAV, too, finds that in reports of anti-gay violence: "most of the victims . . . are in their late twenties" and "most assailants are . . . under twenty years of age." See also U.S. Congress, House Subcommittee on Criminal Justice of Committee on the Judiciary, *Anti-Gay Violence,* pp. 72–75.

24. Bureau of Justice Statistics, *Criminal Victimization in the United States, 1984,* pp. 5, 50.

25. Cauthern, "900 Black Lesbians Speak," p. 12.

26. Findings from my survey compared to findings from Vasquez, *Quarterly Statistical Analyses: January 1984 to March 1986;* Berrill, "Crisisline," pp. 3, 7; Bureau of Justice Statistics, *Criminal Victimization in the United States, 1984,* pp. 5, 49, 54, are as follows:

| | | CUAV | | Bureau of Justice | |
Race	Comstock (%) (N=116)	(%) (N=1417)	NGLTF (%) (N=208)	Single-off. (%) (N=4,219,850)	Multi-off. (%) (N=1,637,960)
white	73	43	70	69	50
black	28	32	12	26	34
Hispanic	5	20	2	4[a]	5[a]
Native American	1	0	16[a]		
Asian	0	5			
multiracial	6	7			10

[a] Other.

Although CUAV's findings may reflect San Francisco's larger percentages of Hispanic and Asian people not represented by the national sample, all three— CUAV, NGLTF, and my survey—find that the majority of perpetrators are white, approximately one third are black, and Hispanics rank third. These percentages also reflect national statistics for all crimes of violence. With the exception of NGLTF, all report a percentage for black perpetrators that is similar and larger than the percentage of black people in the general population.

27. See Fitzgerald, "The Castro," Part I, pp. 34–38, 43–44, 46, 51–70; Part II, pp. 44, 46–63; Stingel, "CUAV Report Survey and Analysis 01/79–02/80,"

pp. 1, 2, and Testimony, San Francisco Board of Supervisors, "Four-Hour Hearing on Queerbashing," pp. H2, H3; Vasquez, *Quarterly Statistical Analyses: January 1984 to March 1986;* U.S. Congress, House Subcommittee on Criminal Justice of Committee on the Judiciary, *Anti-Gay Violence,* pp. 72–75; and Mike Hippler, "Anatomy of a Murder Trial," pp. 42–49.

The Commission on Social Justice, Archdiocese of San Francisco, provides the following information in its *Homosexuality and Social Justice: Report of the Task Force on Gay/Lesbian Issues,* 1983, p. 21: "On April 26, 1980, CBS Reports broadcast a controversial program entitled, 'Gay Power, Gay Politics.' Immediately following the airing of the CBS Report, CUAV reported a 400% increase in Incident Reports of Violence directed toward the gay/lesbian community. Prior to this programming, the trend of violent acts against the gay/lesbian community had gone down in comparison to the statistics of 1979." In his testimony before San Francisco Board of Supervisors, "Four-Hour Hearing on Queerbashing," p. H2, Stingel notes that the "trend was reversed and has been up since then."

William Paul, "Minority Status for Gay People: Majority Reaction and Social Context," in William Paul, James D. Weinrich, John C. Gonsiorek, and Mary E. Hotvedt, eds., *Homosexuality: Social, Psychological, and Biological Issues,* p. 369, n. 4, reports: "Mutual cooperation between Black and Gay communities in San Francisco led to cooperative development of a community center [citing *San Francisco Examiner,* January 29, 1982, p. A3]. Anti-Gay violence in that city elicited a cooperative effort from Latino groups led by Centro de Cambio, working with Gay and Lesbian community groups in 1981. Many such efforts have emerged recently, usually without media coverage."

28. The apparent lack or paucity of Native American perpetrators reported by anti-violence projects and surveys may reflect the lack of data gathering in geographical areas in which sizable Native American populations reside. A few incidents occurring on Indian reservations have been reported; see, for example, Will Roscoe, "Gay American Indians: Creating an Identity from Past Traditions," *Advocate* (Los Angeles), October 29, 1985, pp. 45–48.

The scarcity of reports may also indicate that anti-gay/lesbian violence is practiced less by Native American people than by members of other racial groups; see, for example, Walter L. Williams, in his anthropological study, *The Spirit and the Flesh: Sexual Diversity in American Indian Culture,* p. 38, 40–41, 52, 144, 147, 175–200, 209, 227, 210–212; Judy Grahn, *Another Mother Tongue: Gay Words, Gay Worlds,* pp. 49–72, 68–69; Jonathan Katz, "Native Americans/Gay Americans: 1528–1976," *Gay American History: Lesbians and Gay Men in the U.S.A.: A Documentary* Part IV, pp. 281–334; Arthur Evans, *Witchcraft and the Gay Counterculture: A Radical View of Western Civilization and Some of the People It Has Tried to Destroy,* pp. 100–111; Kenneth Steffenson, *Manitoba Native Peoples and Homosexuality: Historical and Contemporary Aspects* (Winnipeg, Manitoba: Council on Homosexuality and Religion, 1985); Edward Westermarck, *The Origin and Development of the Moral Ideas,* vol. 2 (London: Macmillan, 1908), pp. 456–489; Paula Gunn Allen, *The Sacred*

Hoop: Recovering the Feminine in American Indian Traditions, pp. 1–7, 194–208, 245–261.

29. Brewer, " 'Gay-bashing' Worsens Since AIDS Epidemic," p. B1, interviews Paul Seidler, the San Francisco Police Department's liaison officer to the gay/lesbian community, who "said the attackers are most often out-of-town toughs who come to the city expressly to hunt homosexuals, or city residents resentful of homosexuals sharing their neighborhoods and public transportation." That the Castro, at the time when gay men and lesbians were beginning to move into it, was a deteriorating white working-class neighborhood undergoing the movement of families to the suburbs should be kept it mind. Gays were not displacing a population; they were repopulating a dying neighborhood. Gay men did in time move into the adjacent Fillmore and Mission Districts, but the thrust of anti-gay/lesbian violence has consistently been by perpetrators from outside the Castro coming into the neighborhood in search of victims. This point is made to dispel the commonly held notion that a prominent motive for anti-gay/lesbian violence is resentment over being pushed out of or having to share a neighborhood. Data suggest that incidents do not most frequently occur in the neighborhoods in which perpetrators live.

See, also, Kirschenbaum, "Instant Activism," p. 81.

30. Described also in an autobiographical short story by Raven Crone, "Heaven" (typewritten).

See also the statement by Maxine Feldman in Evelyn Torton Beck, ed., *Nice Jewish Girls: A Lesbian Anthology,* p. 126.

31. See, for example, the following media coverage: "White Supremacists Indicted in Fires Targeted at Gays, Jews (Hot Springs, Ark.)," *Des Moines Register,* April 26, 1985, p. 12T; Tom Knudson, "3 Men Raped in Iowa," *Des Moines Register,* August 13, 1985, p. 3M; "KKK March, Opponents Protest (Murfreesboro, Tenn.)," *Daily Freeman* (Kingston, N.Y.), July 5, 1987, p. 2; Anne-Christine d'Adesky, "Black Muslim Group Attacks Gays: Nation of Islam Makes Homophobic Threats," *New York Native,* August 10, 1987, p. 9; "North Carolina," *Advocate* (Los Angeles), February 2, 1988, p. 24, and December 5, 1988, p. 29; Rick Harding, "Jurors Acquit N.C. Neo-Nazis in Gay Deaths," *Advocate* (Los Angeles), July 4, 1989, p. 12; Peter S. Karasopoulos, "KKK Visits Maine Again," and Marjorie Love, "Klan Upstaged," *Our Paper* (Portland, Maine), July 1988, p. 7; Gene-Gabriel Moore, "North Carolina's War Against Gays," *Christopher Street,* 1988, 121:14–18; "South Carolina," *Advocate* (Los Angeles), June 6, 1989, p. 29; Peter Freiberg, in *Advocate* (Los Angeles), "A Hair Style to Die From: Skinheads Adopt Your Grade-School Haircut and a Violent, Antigay Doctrine," pp. 8–9, and "Upstate N.Y. Attacks Tied to Skinheads"; "Gay Bashing Conviction," *Lavender Network* (Eugene, Ore.), November 1989, p. 25; and Philip S. Gutis, "Attacks on U.S. Homosexuals Held Alarmingly Widespread," *New York Times,* June 8, 1989, p. A24. For an incident in the 1930s, see Jonathan Ned Katz, "1936, June: *N.Y. Times:* 'A Shouting, Jeering Mob,' " *Gay/Lesbian Almanac* (1983), pp. 523–524; 715, n. 52.

For data-gathering reports, see Chris Lutz and Center for Democratic Renewal, *They Don't All Wear Sheets: A Chronology of Racist and Far Right Violence—1980–1986*, pp. 25, 32, 35, 59; Peter Finn and Taylor McNeil, "The Response of the Criminal Justice System to Bias Crime: An Exploratory Review," submitted to National Institute of Justice, U.S. Department of Justice (Cambridge, Mass.: Abt Associates, October 7, 1987), p. 1; Mab Segrest, "Responding to Bigoted Violence in North Carolina"; National Gay and Lesbian Task Force, *Anti-Gay Violence, Victimization in 1985*, pp. 6–7, *Anti-Gay Violence, Victimization and Defamation in 1986*, pp. 11–12, *Anti-Gay Violence, Victimization and Defamation in 1987*, pp. 3, 15–16, and *Anti-Gay Violence, Victimization and Defamation in 1988*, pp. 18–19; and Commission on Social Justice, Archdiocese of San Francisco, *Homosexuality and Social Justice*, pp. 17–23.

32. *GayLife* (Chicago), February 10, 1978.

33. Katherine Bishop, "Neo-Nazi Activity Is Arising Among U.S. Youth," *New York Times*, June 13, 1988, p. A12.

34. Potter, p. 39, reports that respondents in her survey "were attacked by anywhere from 1 to 9 assailants, the average being 3."

CUAV reports that "65.6% of the attackers were joined by others as they attacked the victim." See citation of CUAV's report to the San Francisco Mayor's Criminal Justice Council, December 31, 1981, in Commission on Social Justice, Archdiocese of San Francisco, *Homosexuality and Social Justice*, p. 21.

35. Potter, p. 39, finds that most respondents in her survey "were attacked either when they were alone (45%) or with one other person."

See also Stingel, "CUAV Report Survey and Analysis 01/79–02/80," p. 1, who concludes, "There is, indeed, safety in numbers, . . . 71% of all assaults were directed against people walking or being alone. The odds of an assault are reduced by two thirds (66%) if a friend is with you, and reduced by 90% if two friends are with you. Assaults against groups of four or more are rare enough to allow us to conclude that assaults can be prevented altogether by constantly traveling with three or more friends."

36. Arthur Bell, "Midnight Ramble Roundup: Chasing the Bat Pack," p. 11, observes, "They follow a certain street ethic. Never attack a woman alone or two or more women because of possible rape charges. Never attack an old man alone because he's no challenge. Young men are good targets. Male couples are great targets. And someone really big is the best target to tackle. You can boast about it later."

37. Similar percentages (34 percent of incidents) for perpetrators' being armed are reported by CUAV. See Vasquez, *Quarterly Statistical Analyses: January 1984 to March 1986*.

38. See, for example, City of New York, *Gay and Lesbian Discrimination*, p. 50; and Rick Harding, "Now Hear This: Deaf Gays Discuss the Violence and Ostracism They Face," p. 11.

39. "Misleading" often takes the form of lying, as when a perpetrator engages the victim in "friendly" conversation by asking for directions and subsequently attacks her or him. See, for example, Rick Harding and Lisa M. Keen,

"Assault with a Caustic Fluid," *Washington Blade* (Washington, D.C.), June 6, 1986, p. 10.

Perpetrators also mislead victims by making sexual overtures to the victim (usually male) and then attacking after perpetrator and victim have retired to a private area. See, for example, Robert Lipsyte, "The Closet, a Violent and Subtle Prison."

Kelner, *Homophobic Assault*, pp. 43–44, reports that in eleven of twenty reported incidents entrapment or the "deliberate use of seduction or enticement" was used by perpetrators.

For examples of cases that have been adjudicated, see District Attorney's Office (Manhattan), *80 Case Memo*, "People v. Ronald Norman," p. 17, and "People v. Buddy Giles," p. 22.

40. For example, perpetrators have been known secretly to drop powerful sleeping chemicals into their would-be sexual-partner's drink and subsequently rob the victim's person or dwelling. Physical injury is sometimes inflicted. Commonly used drugs are scopalamine and lorazapan. For examples of incidents in newspaper articles, see David France, "Queerbashing and the Social Contract: A Report on Anti-Gay Violence," *New York Native*, July 15, 1984, p. 11; and "Robber Who Drugged Gays Sent to Prison," *San Francisco Chronicle*, June 3, 1982, p. 47. For summaries of adjudicated cases, see District Attorney's Office (Manhattan), *80 Case Memo*, "People v. Mark Galassi," p. 1, "People v. Saban Dreas," p. 12, and "People v. Nelson Gomez," p. 20.

41. For example, Kelner, *Homophobic Assault*, p. 43, report an incident preceded by verbal abuse of the "sort directed generally to women. . . . As the incident escalated, homophobic sentiments were included. The victim felt that she was being attacked because she had just left a gay club, and because she was not responding to the situation in the way that women are expected to."

A similar story, "Three Women Attacked," *GayLife* (Chicago), July 28, 1978, is reported from Chicago: "Three women were attacked after leaving [a lesbian bar]. . . . The incident began when several patrons from a neighborhood bar made anti-gay and anti-women remarks to the three women as they walked past. One patron chased the women on his bicycle and attacked them. . . ."

42. See, for example, City of New York, Commission on Human Rights, "NYC Commission on Human Rights Report on Discrimination Against People with AIDS, November 1983–April 1986," pp. 8, 41–43; City of New York, *Gay and Lesbian Discrimination*, pp. 20, 23, 87, 94; National Gay and Lesbian Task Force, *Anti-Gay Violence, Victimization and Defamation in 1986*, p. 5; and David M. Wertheimer, "The Rise in AIDS-Related Violence," pp. 1, 6, 9; U.S. Congress, House Subcommittee on Criminal Justice of Committee on the Judiciary, *Anti-Gay Violence*, pp. 72–75; and Randy Schell, "CUAV–Muni Muggers Attack Rider Who Has AIDs," *Bay Area Reporter* (San Francisco), September 27, 1984, p. 14.

For newspaper and magazine accounts of AIDS-related anti-gay/lesbian violence, see Richard J. Meislin, "AIDS Said to Increase Bias Against Homosexuals," *New York Times*, January 21, 1986, p. 4B; Anne-Christine d'Adesky,

"Suspect Arrested in Queens Double Killing, Beheadings: Motive for Grisly Murder Sought," *New York Native,* November 10, 1986, p. 8; Ruben Rosario, "AIDs Spurs Gay Attacks," p. 31; Brewer, " 'Gay-bashing' Worsens Since AIDS Epidemic," p. B1 +; Ruth Snyder, " 'Gay Bashing'—AIDS Fear Cited as Attacks on Male Homosexuals Grow," Part 1, pp. 3, 32; Craig Wilson, "Gay Bashing: Brutal AIDS Backlash," pp. 1D, 2D; Laurence Zuckerman, "Open Season on Gays: AIDS Sparks an Epidemic of Violence Against Homosexuals," *Time,* March 7, 1988, p. 24; Fitzgerald, "The Castro—Part II," p. 50; Robert W. Peterson, "Fire Guts Texas AIDS Homes: Arson Suspected in Blazes in Dallas, Austin," *Advocate* (Los Angeles), January 3, 1989, p. 16.

43. Kenneth B. Morgen, *The Prevalence of Anti-Gay/Lesbian Victimization in Baltimore: 1988,* p. 3.

Potter, p. 41, reports, "Two of the respondents mentioned with no prompting that their attackers specifically mentioned AIDS, saying such things as 'I hope you get AIDs.' It is possible that more than these 2 were attacked because of fear of AIDs; the survey did not ask respondents if their assailants mentioned AIDS."

44. Presidential Commission on the Human Immunodeficiency Virus Epidemic, *Final Report* (Washington, D.C.: Office of the President of the United States, Ronald Reagan, June 1988), p. 140.

See also, "Federal Policy: AIDS Medical Costs by 1992," *AIDS Policy and Law Newsletter* (Washington, D.C.: Bureau Publications), January 6, 1989.

45. See Toni Dickerson, Abigail Norman, Robin Omata, Lydia Dean Pilcher, Afua Kafi-Akua, Daresh Kyi, *Just Because of Who We Are: Working Tapes.*

46. See Fred Berger, "Grand Jury Refuses to Indict," *Our Paper* (Portland, Maine), January 1986, pp. 1, 3; Tux Turkel, "Out of Fear Comes a Killing: Homosexual's Harassment Ends with Tragedy," p. A1; and Peter Freiberg, "A Killing in Maine," *Advocate* (Los Angeles), March 4, 1986, pp. 10–12.

47. For accounts that describe the suddenness with which assaults are typically executed, see the narratives in the following: Joseph McQuay, "It Happened in Just a Split Second," *Weekly New* (Miami, Florida), July 4, 1984, p. 3; and Marc Lerro, "Violent Crime Up in Oak Lawn; Gays Often a Target," pp. 6–7.

48. Kelner, *Homophobic Assault.* pp. 42–43. See also, "Killing May Be 'Gay Bashing,' " *New York Native,* December 22, 1986, p. 9; and "Lesbian Attacked" in *Off Our Backs* (Washington, D.C.), November 1985, p. 14.

49. Reese, "The Growing Terror of 'Gay Bashing,' " p. 30. See also Jenning, " 'Gay Bashing' Emerges as Vicious Crime of Hard Times," p. B1.

50. Kirschenbaum, "Instant Activism," p. 80.

51. Interview by Rofes, "Queer Bashing," p. 8.

52. Interview by Rofes, "Queer Bashing," p. 9.

53. Interview by Nash, "A Gay Basher Says 'I'm Sorry,' " p. 9.

54. "Conviction of Murder Is Upheld," *Champaign Courier* (Champaign, Ill.), September 19, 1978.

55. "Court Condones Rape of Lesbian," *Peace News* (Nottingham, Great Britain), July 23, 1982, p. 5; and Heidi Silver, "Ohio Court Allows Brutal Anti-Lesbian Persecution," *Workers World* (New York), June 18, 1982, p. 11.

56. Information about this incident taken from "Four Beaten, Robbed in Reverchon Park," *Dallas Morning News,* July 11, 1986, p, 23A; Jim Zook, "Officer, Suspect Shot in Oak Lawn Park," *Dallas Morning News,* July 12, 1986, pp. 33A, 38A; Jerry Needham, "Suspect Set Free 36 Hours Before Police Shooting," *Dallas Times Herald,* July 12, 1986, pp. 23A, 29A.

57. Information about this incident taken from Jim Ryan, in *Gay Community News,* " 'Barbaric Behavior, Unprovoked Attack': District Gaybashers Given Light Sentences," May 26, 1984, p. 1; "Gaybashers' Sentences Enrage Washingtonians," June 2, 1984, p. 1; Lou Chibbaro, Jr., in *Washington Blade* (Washington, D.C.), "GAA Charges 'Misconduct' by Judge in Sentencing," May 18, 1984, pp. 1, 3; "Courts Must Respond to Violence, Say Activists," May 25, 1984, pp. 1, 11; "Victim Hits Two St. John's Teens with Civil Suits," August 24, 1984, pp. 7, 8; "Jury Orders Teens to Pay Assault Victim," May 30, 1986, pp. 1, 4; "Taking the Stand: A Gay Plaintiff in the Courtroom," June 6, 1986, pp. 1, 6; "Taking the Stand: When a Gay Plaintiff Goes on Trial," June 13, 1986, pp. 1, 7, in *Advocate* (Los Angeles), "Judge Under Fire for Remarks: Two D.C. Youths Get Probation for Brutal Attack on Gay Man," July 10, 1984, p. 16.

58. Information about this incident taken from George Mendenhall, " 'Nice Boys' Who Brutalized Russell Mills Are Sentenced," *Bay Area Reporter* (San Francisco), April 7, 1983, pp. 1, 13.

59. Information about this incident taken from Bell, "Midnight Ramble Roundup: Chasing the Bat Pack," pp. 1, 11; Ireland, "Rendezvous in the Ramble," pp. 39–42; and "One Pleads Guilty in New York," *Gay Community News* (Boston), January 6, 1979.

60. Information about this incident taken from Brenda Buchanan, in *Our Paper* (Portland, Maine), "Arrest Likely in Assault on Women," October 1986, pp. 1, 10; "Assault Case Goes to DA," November 1986, p. 15; "Charges Brought in Assault Case," December 1986, p. 1; "Trial Set for Assault Suspect," February 1987, p. 1; "Plea Bargain Ends Assault Case," March 1987, pp. 1, 6.

61. Using Vasquez, *Quarterly Statistical Analyses: January 1984 to March 1986,* I computed the following percentages for the "time of day" and "time of year" at which incidents occur based on information about 739 incidents reported to CUAV:

Time of Day	Time of Year
8 A.M.–2 P.M. 16% of incidents	Jan–Mar 22% of incidents
2 P.M.–8 P.M. 26% of incidents	Apr.–June 27% of incidents
8 P.M.–2 A.M. 40% of incidents	July–Sept. 29% of incidents
2 A.M.–8 A.M. 18% of incidents	Oct.–Dec. 22% of incidents

62. Weissman, "Kids Who Attack Gays," pp. 9–13.

63. Christopher L. San Miguel and Jim Millham, "The Role of Cognitive and Situational Variables in Aggression Toward Homosexuals," pp. 11–27. For the purposes of the experiment aggression is defined as a "negative evaluation"

of and the causing of an "actual loss of money to the target." This form of aggression does not involve physical assault and the experiment cannot be said to replicate the conditions and situation of actual anti-gay/lesbian violence. Its value rests primarily in showing that knowing lesbians and gay men and knowing about homosexuality does not necessarily lessen the likelihood of a young man's perpetrating violence against lesbians and gay men.

64. This notion is supported further by an interview with a former perpetrator on the nationally televised *Oprah Winfrey Show;* the young man stated that he and his friends had attacked lesbian/gay people because they had been bored and had nothing else to do. Oprah Winfrey, "Homophobia."

See also Tom Ammiano, who, in testimony at the "Four-Hour Hearing on Queerbashing," p. H15, reports about his experience in a program to discuss lesbian/gay issues with students in San Francisco's public schools. The enjoyment derived from attacking lesbians and gay men by perpetrators is captured in his following remark: "One of the kids responded to a question of ours, 'Why do you want to beat us up?' . . . He said, 'Because it makes me feel good.' "

65. Jenning, " 'Gay Bashing' Emerges as Vicious Crime of Hard Times," p. B1. Buchanan, in "Arrest Likely in Assault on Women," p. 1, reports that, according to a detective in the Portland, Maine Police Department, patrons of a straight bar, who had been harassing women who go to a nearby women's bar, "sit there talking about baseball and football and beating up gays. [Harassing the women] is a sporting event for them. That's just my opinion, but I'll bet I'm not far off."

66. Lee Ellenberg and Mental Health Department of Fenway Community Health Center, "Counseling Service for Gay and Lesbian Victims," Boston, February 5, 1986, p. 2. (Photocopied.)

See also Ireland, "Rendezvous in the Ramble," p. 39; and Brian Shein, "Gay-Bashing in High Park: A Tale of Homophobia and Murder," p. 39.

67. The constellation and variety of perpetrators' characteristics cited here are also observed and summarized by Churchill, *Homosexual Behavior Among Males,* pp. 196–198, and West, *Homosexuality Re-Examined,* pp. 204–205. Churchill describes incidents in which the perpetrators considered their acts "justifiable homicide" and a "civic duty"; they were not afraid to "admit" engaging in the practice of anti-gay/lesbian violence and said that lots of others do it; their attacks were planned and they studied homosexual hangouts. West's description includes the issues of parental support, peer pressure, legal sanction; the fact that perpetrators say attacking gays makes them "feel good"; and the surprise and regret expressed by some when they realize, upon being apprehended, the damage they have done.

68. See Kim Westheimer, "Boston Les/Gay Alliance to Sponsor Meetings on Violence: Gay Bashing Still a Popular Boston Sport," *Gay Community News* (Boston), December 7–13, 1986, p. 3; Charles Hallam, "Rushville Man to Stand Trial for Monmouth Resident's Murder," *Rock island Argus* (Rock Island, Illinois), May 15, 1979; "Son Shoots Mother and Suspected Lover," *Off Our Backs* (Washington, D.C.), June 1986, p. 17; "Gay Man Killed in Vermont,"

Another Voice (Huntington, New York), November 6, 1985, p. 9; Arthur Bell, "Death Comes Out," p. 12.

69. "Judge Binds Bangor 3 Over for Murder Trial," *Weekly News* (Miami, Florida), August 29, 1984, p. 3.

70. "Judge Binds Bangor 3 Over for Murder Trial," p. 3.

71. The combination of admitting guilt and expressing regret while maintaining innocence has been observed and reported by a number of journalists covering various incidents. Another example can be cited from an incident that occurred in Northampton, Massachusetts. Maureen Fitzgerald, in "Man Jailed for Threats to Lesbians," *Daily Hampshire Gazette* (Hampshire, Mass.), October 11, 1983, pp. 1, 3, quotes the twenty-three-year-old perpetrator who was sentenced to jail for three months after admitting that he made a number of violent threats against lesbians by telephone: "I don't know why I did it. It was pure stupidity. . . . I have a big mouth. . . . I did something wrong. . . . But I'm no big criminal. I've never even been in court before. I don't really know what this [holding up handcuffs] is going to prove. . . . I would like to know what the community thinks about this. I want to know what the Northampton natives think about this."

72. Miller and Humphreys, "Lifestyles and Violence," pp: 169–185.

73. Because the depth and style of reporting vary among journalists and publications, assembling a uniform and comprehensive list of characteristics for many incidents is not possible. Not only are facts reported and prioritized differently, but cases are frequently not covered through to their conclusion in the legal process.

74. See, for example, "Police Say Newspaper Heir May Have Known His Killer," *Chicago Sun-Times,* December 9, 1975, p. 34; and Bell, *Kings Don't Mean a Thing.*

75. See, for example, "Authorities Search for Body Linked to Disappearance of Homosexuals," *Louisville Courier-Journal* (Louisville, Kentucky), June 15, 1978, p. D12; "Man Eyed in Six Killings," *Chicago Sun-Times,* April 8, 1979; Janet Cotton, "Murder in the Cathedral," *Macleans,* April 8, 1980, p. 18; Arthur Howe and Nancy Kesler, "Asmus Murder Leads Police to Gay Community: Gays Quizzed in Asmus Case," *Morning News* (Delaware), April 1, 1977, pp. 1, 2; and Charles S. Farrell and Nancy Kesler, "Warrant Is Issued in Asmus Slaying," *Morning News* (Delaware), April 7, 1977, p. 3.

76. A notable exception, not only for its attention to an incident that would most likely be overlooked by the mainstream media because of its ordinary and nonspectacular characteristics, but also for its thoroughness and follow-through, is the coverage by Brenda Buchanan of an assault on lesbians, in *Our Paper* (Portland, Maine), "Arrest Likely in Assault on Women," October 1986, pp. 1, 10; "Assault Case Goes to DA," November 1986, p. 15; "Charges Brought in Assault Case," December 1986, p. 1; "Trial Set for Assault Suspect," February 1987, p. 1; "Plea Bargain Ends Assault Case," March 1987, pp. 1, 6.

77. Information about this incident taken from: "3 Accused of Killing Homosexual Sentenced," *Des Moines Register,* January 10, 1986, p. 2A; Randy

Shilts, "Gay Attacked by Four Youths on Polk Street Dies of Injuries," *San Francisco Chronicle,* August 2, 1984; Charles Linebarger, "S.F. 'Fag Bashers' Convicted of Murder," *Advocate* (Los Angeles), January 21, 1986, p. 16; Mike Hippler, "Anatomy of a Murder Trial," *Advocate* (Los Angeles), February 17, 1987, pp. 42–49; and "Murder Convictions Voided in Gay Man's Death," *New York Times,* August 28, 1989, p. A11.

78. Information about this incident taken from Shein, "Gay-Bashing in High Park," pp. 37–39, 64–69. Andrew Lesk, Ken Popert, and Ric Taylor, "Boys Will Be Boys," *Body Politic* (Toronto), January 1986, pp. 13–15. Philip Plews, "The Evil that Boys Do," *Toronto,* May 1986, pp. 60, 62–63, 86, 88–89, 91–92. Linda Clark, in *Globe and Mail* (Toronto); "Five Teens Plead Guilty in Park Beating Death," November 26, 1985, pp. A1, A2; "Teens Jailed 9 Years Each in Beating Death," November 27, 1985, pp. A1, A22; "Killing in the Park: What Possessed 5 'Average' Sensitive Youths to Beat a Man to Death," December 4, 1985, pp. A1, A18. Gary Oakes, "5 'Average' Teens Get 9 Years for Killing Librarian," *Toronto Star,* November 27, 1985, pp. A1, A4.

79. Information about this incident taken from *Arizona Daily Star* (Tucson), "Gays Call Death Outside Bar 'Part of Pattern of Violence,' " June 8, 1976, "Tragedy in Tucson" (editorial), June 10, 1976; "Youths Get Probation in June Killing: No 'Slap on Wrist,' Judge Tells Defendants," October 23, 1976; and "Justice Not Served" (editorial), October 27, 1976; *Tucson Daily Citizen,* "Judge Reduces Charges in Bar-Beating Death," July 10, 1976; "Teens Get Probation in Killing at Tavern," October 22, 1976; "Gays Criticize Sentence," October 23, 1976; and "A Tragic Tucson Example of Lost Justice" (early November) 1976, pp. 35–36; "Killers Get Probation," *Advocate* (Los Angeles), November 17, 1976; John Rawlinson, "Outside Northside Tavern: 4 Teenagers Charged in Beating Death," *Arizona Daily Star* (Tucson), June 8, 1976, pp. 1B, 9B; and Carol Stengel, in *Arizona Daily Star* (Tucson), "Youths Attack Bar Patrons: Nebraska Man Beaten to Death Here," June 7, 1976; and "Probation for Four Juveniles Criticized by Gay Coalition," October 14, 1976.

80. Information about this incident taken from Fox Butterfield, "Slaying of Homosexual Man Upsets Confidence of Bangor, Me."; John Preston, "Bangor Tragedy No Isolated Incident," *Weekly News* (Miami), October 24, 1984, p. 3; Canellos, "A City and Its Sins," pp. 1, 6–7, 22–23, 26, 28–29, 30–32; Dwight Cathcart, "The Importance of Truth: Crimes Against Gays," *R.F.D.* (Bakersville, N.C.), Fall 1986, pp. 20–22; Donna Turley, "Wrist-Slap for Murder Prompts Outcry," *Guardian* (New York), October 24, 1984, p. 5; and Office of Lesbian and Gay Concerns, Unitarian Universalist Association, "FYI: What You Should Know About the Charlie Howard Murder," Boston, June 1985.

81. Information about this incident taken from "Recommend Jail for Daughter Who Helped Kill Lesbian Mother" (Belton, Texas), *Pekin Times* (Pekin, Ill.), July 25, 1979.

82. For example, in the Howard incident, Canellos, "A City and Its Sins," reports, "According to testimony from the three boys and others at the party [they went to after the incident], the boys breathlessly told their friends that 'We jumped a fag and threw him in the stream.' Most of the kids laughed and asked

questions about the incident. Then the whole group settled down for a long night of partying."

83. The sexual-attraction ploy is, according to other sources, commonly used. For example, Curran, in "Police Fear Homosexuals Not Reporting Criminal Acts Performed Against Them," July 10, 1986, reports about a number of robberies of homosexuals that "involved a juvenile propositioning a homosexual" and taking the victim to an apartment "where a sexual relationship was begun with the perpetrator." A police detective is quoted as saying, "Sometime during the liaison, they would steal his slacks and wallet."

84. Information about this incident taken from "A San Francisco Jury . . . ," *GayLife* (Chicago), March 10, 1978; "Hillsborough Case Proceeds," *Advocate* (Los Angeles), January 25, 1978; Sievert, "The Killing of Mr. Greenjeans," pp. 39–42, 46–48; and Shilts, *Mayor of Castro Street,* pp. 154–155, 158, 162–165, 167–168.

85. "Justice Not Served," *Arizona Daily Star* (Tucson), October 27, 1976. See also Lou Chibbaro, Jr., "Youth Gets 6 to 20 Years Despite 'Sex Advance' Plea," *Washington Blade* (Washington, D.C.), June 22, 1984, p. 7, for a case in which a lower-class hustler did not win acquittal by using the "homosexual panic" defense as other middle-class perpetrators have.

86. For an in-depth account of the method of operation of a nongay pair of males who targeted gay men for robbery and assault, see Bell, "Death Comes Out," pp. 1, 11–12. The pair typically frequented gay bars to proposition gay men and accompany them to their apartments to rob and assault them. The assaults frequently resulted in death.

87. Information about this incident taken from "Could the Police Have Prevented Donna Smith's Death?" *Gay Chicago News,* December 19, 1975.

88. Information about this incident taken from Ed Hicks, "Killer's Trial Tells Sordid Tale," *GayBeat* (Cincinnati), May 1, 1985, pp. 1, 4, 6, and "Dawson Case Winds Up," *GayBeat* (Cincinnati) July 1985, p. 3.

89. Information about this incident taken from Mark Scott, "Murder Suspect Awaits Trial," *Washington Blade* (Washington, D.C.), September 7, 1986, p. 9; and Tracie Cone, "Murdering the Gay Everyman, Part Two."

90. Information about this incident taken from Rebecca Pierce, in *Kalamazoo Gazette* (Kalamazoo, Michigan), "Jurors to Consider What Weapon Used in Man's Death," January 18, 1986; "Trial Focuses on Who Struck Killing Blow," January 23, 1986; "Co-defendants May Be Called in Murder Trial," January 27, 1986, "Co-defendants Testify in Murder Trial," January 30, 1986; and "Jury and Judge Differ in Opinions on Murder Acquittal," February 7, 1986, pp. B1, B2; Al Jones, in *Kalamazoo Gazette* (Kalamazoo, Michigan), "Murder Trial Draws to a Close," February 5, 1986; and "Jury to Get Murder Case Today," February 6, 1986; Larry R. Carter, "Beating Victim's Family Still in Shock," *Kalamazoo News* (Kalamazoo, Michigan), February 21–27, 1986, pp. 1, 9; in *Kalamazoo News* (Kalamazoo, Michigan), "Gays Say Murderer Set Free: Human Rights Groups Plan Rally on Courthouse Steps," February 14–20, 1986, p. 1, and (editorial), February 21–27, 1986, p. 3; Peter Freiberg, "Youth Acquitted in Bludgeoning Murder: Kalamazoo Gays Outraged; Judge Publicly

Disagrees with Verdict," *Advocate* (Los Angeles), April 1, 1986, pp. 12–13; and Kris Hamel, "Kalamazoo Lesbians, Gays Slam Acquittal of Murdering Bigot," *Workers World* (New York), March 13, 1986, p. 11.

91. Information about this incident taken from Ed Hicks, in *GayBeat* (Cincinnati), "Cohen Murdered," August 1986, pp. 1, 5, 6; "Media: When a Gay Man Is Killed . . . ," September 1986, pp. 1, 7; "Murder Victim Put on Trial: Messmer Guilty of Aggravated Assault," December 1986, pp. 1, 5, 7; "Moore Guilty of Lesser Charges," December 1986, pp. 5, 7, 9, 10; and "Messmer Gets 40 Years," January 1987, p. 3. "Strange Bedfellows: Leis to Preside at Cohen Trial," *GayBeat* (Cincinnati), October 1986, p. 4.

92. Hustlers are male prostitutes who service other men sexually.

93. Information about this incident taken from "Conviction of Murder Is Upheld," *Champaign Courier* (Champaign, Illinois), September 19, 1978.

94. Information about this incident taken from Hinckle, "The Untold Story," pp. 8–20; Weiss, *Double Play,* pp. 4–9, 48–51, 58–71, 80–83, 88–89, 98–99, 116, 122–127, 142–143, 148–150, 152–161, 167–170, 172, 182–196, 212–213, 244–245, 254–255, 262–271, 276–279, 286–289, 292–312, 322–331, 334–337, 342–343, 348–351, 372–373, 415–416; Shilts, *The Mayor of Castro Street,* pp. 162, 184–185, 192–193, 197–200, 225–226, 257–258, 260–275, 278–279, 289, 304–306, 308–326, 342; Thomas Szasz, "How Dan White Got Away with Murder and How American Psychiatry Helped Him Do It," *Inquiry,* pp. 17–21; Epstein and Schmeichen, *The Times of Harvey Milk;* and Fitzgerald, "The Castro—Part I," pp. 51–70.

95. Information about this incident taken from Eugene McCarthy, in *Kitchener-Waterloo Record* (Ontario), "Sold Rifle to Accused, Clerk Tells Murder Trial," September 10, 1985, pp. 1A, 2A; "Schafer Shot at Close Range, Forensic Expert Tells Court," September 11, 1985, pp. 1A, 2A; "Kluke Trial Jury Out While Lawyers Argue," September 12, 1985, p. 1A; "Kluke Admitted Shooting Schafer, Court Told," September 13, 1985, pp. 1A, 2a; "Focus in Kluke Murder Trial Shifts to Defense," September 14, 1985, pp. 1B, 2B; " 'Never Meant to Hurt' Schafer, Kluke Says," September 16, 1985, p. 1A; "Kluke Admits Having 5 Homosexual Encounters," September 17, 1985, pp. 1A, 2A; "No Evidence that His Client Intended to Kill, Lawyer Says," September 18, 1985, p. 1B; "Kluke Murder Case Goes to the Jurors," September 19, 1985, p. 1A; "Kluke Jury Wants to See How Weapon Worked," September 20, 1985, p. 1B; and "Appeal Likely: Kluke Found Guilty of First-Degree Murder in Park Slaying," September 21, 1985, pp. 1A, 2A.

96. Information about this incident taken from Ed Hicks, in *GayBeat* (Cincinnati), "Van Hook Guilty," August 1985, pp. 1, 6; "Van Hook Sentenced to Die," September 1985, p. 1; "Equal Protection on Trial," September 1985, p. 4; and "Defense as Theatre," September 1985, pp. 2–3.

97. Information about this incident taken from Allen White, "Gays Outraged: Bakersfield Murderer All But Goes Free," *Bay Area Reporter* (San Francisco), June 17, 1982, pp. 1, 16; and George Mendenhall, "Justice in Bakersfield: Gays Murdered, Protester Fired, Case Dismissed," *Bay Area Reporter* (San Francisco), January 27, 1983.

98. Information about this incident taken from "2 Slain, 6 Wounded at N.Y. Gay Bars; Suspect Seized," *Chicago Tribune*, November 21, 1980. Arthur Bell, in *Village Voice* (New York), "Shooting at Ghosts: Ronald Crumpley's Lethal Odyssey," July 22–28, 1981, pp. 1, 20, 21; and "The Jungle" (Letter), August 5–11, 1981, p. 23; and France, "Queerbashing and the Social Contract: A Report on Anti-Gay Violence," *New York Native*, July 2–15, 1984, p. 12.

99. See also, in chapter 1, discussion of the 1972 incident involving forty-one-year-old Michael Maye, president of the Uniformed Firefighters Association, who was charged by a Manhattan grand jury with harassment because he "struck, shoved and kicked" a member of the Gay Activists Alliance who with other members entered a gathering of media people in the grand ballroom of the New York Hilton hotel to protest oppression of lesbians and gay men in the media. Both the boldness of demonstrators in "invading" a public meeting and the perpetration of violence by a middle-aged community leader appear to be unprecedented. For coverage of the incident, see Lacey Fosburgh, "Maye Held as Harasser in Gay Alliance Fracas," *New York Times*, May 23, 1972, p. 30; Eric Page, "Official Accuses Maye of Assault: City Aide Says He Saw Gay Intruder Being Attacked," *New York Times*, April 25, 1972, p. 11; Michael Kramer, "Fireman's Brawl," *New York*, May 22, 1972, pp. 5–6; and Calvin Trillin, "A Few Observations on the Zapping of the Inner Circle," *New Yorker*, July 15, 1972, pp. 64–69.

100. Bell, "Shooting at Ghosts," p. 20, reports, "On the witness stand, Crumpley spoke eloquently and at length. He was rarely asked to elaborate on a point by . . . his court-appointed counsel, and was never interrupted by [the] Assistant D.A. . . . or Judge. . . . Most murderers give tour-de-force performance under oath—anything to save their necks. Crumpley stuck his neck out—he didn't give a damn what happened to him. He wasn't acting and I doubt if he told a single lie. His testimony reduced the entire courtroom to silence. Crumpley ran longer than *Gone with the Wind* and was twice as mesmerizing."

101. Shilts, *Mayor of Castro Street*, pp. 310–311. See also Weiss, *Double-Play*, pp. 293–297; Szasz, "How Dan White Got Away with Murder," p. 20; and Hinckle, "The Untold Story," p. 14.

102. Since the purpose of a defense is not to portray the defendant accurately as much as it is to portray him favorably, those for White, Tyack, and Crumpley, as well as those in the Heakin, Zeller, and Howard cases in table 3.18, selected, accented, and interpreted various parts of the defendants' pasts.

Hinckle's research, reported in "The Untold Story," pp. 12–17, shows that, contrary to the image presented by the defense, White had not really been a wholesome athlete as a youngster, was not the working-class hero of his electoral district, nor the hard-working, devoted family man, the righter of social evils, and the protector of homespun, traditional values. See also Weiss, *Double Play*, pp. 143–145, 158–161, 185, 188–189, 193–195, 212–213, 278–403; and Fitzgerald, "The Castro—Part I," pp. 66–70.

Since prosecution attorneys demonstrated little interest or effect in challenging character references and the construction of character profiles in these cases, the value of defense arguments as a source of information about perpetrators rests more in their generating or provoking interest, inquiry, and research by journalists than in their contributing to the establishment of facts in court. See, for example, Shilts, *The Mayor of Castro Street,* pp. 314–316, 318–320; Shein, "Gay-Bashing in High Park," p. 65; Ryan, in *Gay Community News* (Boston), " 'Barbaric Behavior, Unprovoked Attack;' District Gaybashers Given Light Sentences," May 26, 1984, p. 1; and "Gaybashers' Sentences Enrage Washingtonians," June 2, 1984, p. 1.

103. The defendants were portrayed as having tried to be nice to their victims, who in turn were unreceptive and violated the kindness.

For Crumpley, see Bell, "Shooting at Ghosts," p. 20. For White see Weiss, in *Double Play,* pp. 123–127, 148–149, 172; Hinckle, "The Untold Story," p. 13, 15, 18; and John D'Emilio, "Gay Politics, Gay Community: San Francisco's Experience," pp. 97–98.

104. Bell, in "Shooting at Ghosts," *Village Voice* (New York), July 22–28, 1981, p. 20, reports that Crumpley seems either to contradict his own claims of or to acknowledge having changed his tolerance and concern for gay men when he admitted there had been times when "I'd attack [gay men], punch them, beat them" and recalled being "ticked off" when talking "about religion and gay things" with his father, an "African Methodist Episcopalian minister whose credo on the subject of homosexuality was live and let live."

105. See Hinckle, "The Untold Story," p. 18–19; and Shilts, *The Mayor of Castro Street,* pp. 198–199.

106. See Hinckle, in "The Untold Story," pp. 12–17; Weiss, *Double Play,* pp. 143–145, 153, 167, 212, 255; Shilts, *The Mayor of Castro Street,* pp. 193–195, 200, 254–255; Fitzgerald, "The Castro—Part I," pp. 69–70; and Dorothy Bryant, *A Day in San Francisco* (Berkeley, Calif.: Ata Books, 1982), pp. 49–54.

107. For a description of a time at which Milk's political career was at an all-time high and White's at an all-time low, see Weiss, *Double Play,* pp. 198–199. For an account of Milk's record as a supervisor, especially his ability to address the needs of different groups of people and to effect necessary changes, see Shilts, *The Mayor of Castro Street,* pp. 293–210. Shilts notes that after his death "leaders in the Chinese, black, Latino, environmental, labor, neighborhood, and Democratic Party groups . . . rallied behind Milk's powerful memory."

108. Shilts, *Mayor of Castro Street,* p. 342. See also Weiss, *Double-Play,* p. 418; Epstein and Schmeichen, *The Times of Harvey Milk;* and Szasz, in "How Dan White Got Away with Murder," pp. 20–21. Szasz discusses another part of the "diminished capacity" or mental illness defense, which was presented by a psychiatrist who "told the jury [according to *Newsweek,* June 4, 1979] that White's compulsive diet of candy bars, cupcakes and cokes was evidence of deep depression—and a source of excessive sugar that had aggravated a chemical imbalance in his brain." Szasz points out, however, that two weeks after his testimony the psychiatrist "flatly contradicted his own testimony" with the following remarks in an interview with a *San Francisco Chronicle* reporter: "Judges and juries should determine issues of guilt and innocence, sanity and insanity . . . psychiatrists are often pushed into making that decision for them.

. . . There is a tendency for psychiatrists to find mental illness in every instance of emotional stress. I personally resist this."

109. France, "Queerbashing and the Social Contract," p. 12.

110. See, for example, "Man Eyed in Six Killings," *Chicago Sun-Times,* April 8, 1979; "Authorities Search for Body Linked to Disappearances of Homosexuals," *Louisville Courier-Journal* (Louisville, Kentucky), June 15, 1978, p. D12; and Arthur Bell, in *Village Voice* (New York), "Bell Tells," January 13–19, 1982, p. 24; "How Many Murders," April 16, 1979, p. 6.

111. For examples other than those in tables 3.15–3.18, see "Authorities Make 'Clone Murder' Arrest," *Gay Community News* (Boston) January 13, 1979; Farrell and Kesler "Warrant Is Issued in Asmus Slaying," p. 3; Hallam, "Rushville Man to Stand Trial for Monmouth Resident's Murder," *Rock Island Argus* (Rock Island, Ill.), May 15, 1979; "This Man Is Dangerous," *GayLife* (Chicago), October 13, 1978; and "Robber Who Drugged Gays Sent to Prison," *San Francisco Chronicle,* June 3, 1982, p. 47.

112. Bureau of Justice Statistics, *Criminal Victimization in the United States, 1984,* pp. 4, 46. The Bureau presents statistics for single- and multiple-offender incidents. For purposes of comparison here and following, I use the single-offender statistics in the text and cite multiple-offender statistics in notes.

113. Bureau of Justice Statistics, *Criminal Victimization in the United States, 1984,* p. 48. See p. 52 for multiple-offender statistics (74% male, 8% female, 12% mixed).

114. Bureau of Justice Statistics, *Criminal Victimization in the United States, 1984,* pp. 5, 48. See p. 53 for multiple-offender statistics (40% under twenty-one).

115. Bureau of Justice Statistics, *Criminal Victimization in the United States, 1984,* pp. 5, 49. See p. 49 for multiple-offender statistics (50% white).

116. Bureau of Justice Statistics, *Criminal Victimization in the United States, 1984,* pp. 5, 50.

117. Bureau of Justice Statistics, *Criminal Victimization in the United States, 1984,* p. 58.

118. Bureau of Justice Statistics, *Criminal Victimization in the United States, 1984,* pp. 6, 67.

119. Bureau of Justice Statistics, *Criminal Victimization in the United States, 1984,* pp. 6, 68.

120. Examples from newsmedia coverage other than that used to construct tables 3:15–3:18 reinforce the conclusion that perpetrators occupy respectable positions within society. For example, there are reports of perpetrators who are athletes (Bennett, "Athletes to Be Benched After Attack on Gay"), firemen and policemen (Trillin, "A Few Observations on the Zapping of the Inner Circle," pp. 64–69; "Justice for Gays: Philly Cop Suspended, Boston Firefighter Convicted, in Gaybashing Incidents," *New York Native,* June 22, 1987, pp. 8–9; Buchanan, " 'Gaybashing Complaint Filed Against Boston Firefighters,' p. 3; and Elizabeth Pincus, "1979 Peg's Place Assault by Off-Duty S.F. Cops Goes to Trial," *Coming Up!* [San Francisco], June 1985), members of the armed forces

(Lou Chibbaro, Jr., "Two Accuse Marines of Harassment on Capitol Hill," *Washington Blade* [Washington, D.C.] August 3, 1984, pp. 7, 8), favored sons of the middle class (Lou Chibbaro, Jr., "Sons of Police Official Are Arrested in P St. Assault: U.S. Atty's Office Drops the Charges in Two Assaults," *Washington Blade* [Washington, D.C.], October 3, 1986, pp. 1, 11), a stockbroker (Phil Donahue, Tom Matarrese, Jan Matarrese, Troy Perry, Cal Thomas, and Kevin Berrill, participants in television show on "Queerbashing," *Donahue Transcript 04306*) and a mathematician at a missile base (George Mendenhall, "Three More Killers Plead 'I Panicked': 'Homosexual Panic' Defense Spreads Around State: S.F. Public Defender's 'Saturday Night Special' Takes Poll," *Bay Area Reporter* [San Francisco], October 27, 1983, pp. 1, 17).

121. Canellos, "A City and Its Sins."

122. "Killers Get Probation," *Advocate* (Los Angeles), November 17, 1976. See also "Teens Get Probation in Killing at Tavern," *Tucson Daily Citizen,* October 22, 1976.

123. Quoted by Chibbaro, "Judge Under Fire for Remarks: Two D.C. Youths Get Probation for Brutal Attack on Gay Man," p. 16.

124. Plews, in "The Evil that Boys Do," *Toronto,* May 1986, p. 62, observes, "Almost any group of humans larger than five sooner or later becomes a variation of the Sidney Poitier–Tony Curtis film, *The Defiant Ones,* full of contrary types unhappily shackled together. These eight lads, however, had much in common. They were all Swansea neighbors. Most were mediocre students who had failed a grade along the way—first at Swansea Public School and now at Western Technical Commercial where macho was almost a religion. They were jocks. Most came from blue collar families of Eastern European background. They were average. And after tonight they all had a terrible secret."

125. Plews, "The Evil that Boys Do," p. 63.

126. Linda Clark, "Killing in the Park: What Possessed 5 'Average, Sensitive Youths' to Beat a Man to Death," *Globe and Mail* (Toronto), December 4, 1985, p. A1.

127. Lesk, Popert, and Taylor, "Boys Will Be Boys," p. 14.

128. Gregory M. Herek, "Beyond 'Homophobia': A Social Psychological Perspective on Attitudes Toward Lesbians and Gay Men," *Journal of Homosexuality* (1984), 10:6. See also Laurie McClain, Ellen Greenlaw, Connie Newoman, Charles Spencer, and Shoshana Cohen (The Gay Writer's Group), *It Could Happen To You: An Account of the Gay Civil Rights Campaign in Eugene, Oregon* (Boston: Alyson Publications, 1983), p. 35.

129. Shein, "Gay-Bashing in High Park," p. 65.

4. UNDERSTANDING ANTI-GAY/LESBIAN VIOLENCE

1. Sheila D. Collins, "The Familial Economy of God," *Theology in the Americas Documentation,* Series 8 (New York: Theology of the Americas, 1979). See also Gerda Lerner, *The Creation of Patriarchy* (New York: Oxford University Press, 1986; Oxford University Press paperback, 1987), pp. 15–35.

2. For the Soviet Union, see David Remnick, "In Age of Glasnost, Homo-

sexuality Still Taboo in Soviet Union," *Washington Post,* March 9, 1989, pp. A27, A36. For Cuba see Allen Young, *Gays Under Cuba* (San Francisco: Grey Fox Press, 1981), p. 40. For South Africa see Peter Cummings, "A Double Bind for Black Gays: New Group Struggles to Win Support for Gay Rights Within Anti-Apartheid Movement," and Barry Ronge, "White and Gay: One South African's View of a Country in Transition," in *Advocate* (Los Angeles), December 22, 1987, pp. 28–30, 124–125. For New Zealand, see "New Zealand," *Advocate* (Los Angeles), October 10, 1989, p. 25. For the Netherlands see Henk van den Boogaard, *Flikkers Moeten We Niet: Mannen als Doelwit van Antihomoseksueel Geweld* (Amsterdam, The Netherlands: Uitgeverij SUA, 1987). For Great Britain see Anna Durell, "At Home," Julian Meldrum, "On the Streets," and Bruce Galloway, "The Police and the Courts," in Bruce Galloway, ed., *Prejudice and Pride: Discrimination Against Gay People in Modern Britain* (London: Routledge and Kegan Paul, 1983), pp. 1–18, 62–77, 102–124; and Quentin Crisp, *The Naked Civil Servant* (New York: Holt, Rinehart and Winston, 1977; New American Library, Plume Book, 1983), pp. 11, 16, 44, 54, 58–63. For Iran see "Iran," *Advocate* (Los Angeles), March 13, 1990, p. 29.

3. Lerner, *The Creation of Patriarchy,* p. 239. Collins, "The Familial Economy of God," p. 2, defines patriarchy as a "social system in which the status of women is defined primarily as wards of their husbands, fathers or brothers."

Gayle Rubin, "The Traffic in Women: Notes on the 'Political Economy' of Sex," in Rayna R. Reiter, ed., *Toward an Anthropology of Women* (New York: Monthly Review Press, 1975), pp. 167–168, notes that the term *patriarchy* should not be applied as a general term to any gender-stratified system, because it derives from a "specific form of male dominance" in which "one old man whose absolute power over wives, children, herds, and dependents, was an aspect of the institution of fatherhood, as defined in the social group in which he lived." She cites several anthropologists whose work shows, for example, that "many New Guinea societies are viciously oppressive to women[;] but the power of males in these groups is not founded on their roles as fathers or patriarchs, but on their collective adult maleness, embodied in secret cults, men's houses, warfare, exchange networks, ritual knowledge, and various initiation procedures."

4. See Robert H. Bremmer, John Barnard, Tamara K. Hareven, and Robert M. Mennel, eds., *Children and Youth in America: A Documentary History.* Vol. I: 1600–1865 (Cambridge, Mass.: Harvard University Press, 1970), pp. 27–63.

Collins, "The Familial Economy of God," p. 4, states: "This is basically the family model of biblical times, and its extension through history can be glimpsed in the marriage ceremony in which the father 'gives the bride away,' in laws which prohibit a widower from getting his wife's social security, and in the acceptance by women of their father's and husband's surnames. Since women were not expected to have an identity in their own right, daughters who could not be married off were literally expendable as people throughout much of history, and old women with no male protection were burned as witches."

5. Collins, "The Familial Economy of God," p. 5. Collins elaborates: "In the patriarchal family a girl is not expected to have the same access to power,

234 4. UNDERSTANDING ANTI-GAY/LESBIAN VIOLENCE

privilege and responsibility as her brother. In the event that she was the eldest child, the patrimony would skip her entirely to be inherited by a younger brother. Likewise, a wife did not share equal power, privileges and status with her husband. Indeed, whatever status and power she had was vicarious, through participation in her husband's title and property. This legacy continues in the discrimination against women in credit and housing and in the degradation with which welfare mothers are treated who are, in essence, wives without husbands to give them identity or status—hence, non-persons."

6. Collins, "The Familial Economy of God," pp. 6–7. Collins maintains that the role of the Alien or Slave is a "role which is generally not seen as one at all because it remains outside the family constellation entirely." She explains the historical connection between slavery and the subordination of women by noting that "Gunnar Myrdal in *An American Dilemma* has pointed out that when the early American slaveholders sought a legal and ideological justification for the practice of slavery, they turned to the English Common Law's definition of women as wards of their husbands and fathers." However, she also talks of an "important distinction" between the roles of Alien or Slave and Daughter:

"Unlike the role of Daughter in the patriarchal family, the role of Slave was a static, one, admitting of no change in status or power. Growing up within the family, the Daughter could at least look forward to being a Wife which, if this did not give her ultimate status or power, at least set her over others, namely the younger generation and slaves. Though in the American system of slavery subtle class distinctions arose as between house slaves and field hands, there was nevertheless the knowledge—even among the household servants—that one was outside the family entirely. Even the child of a master and his slave could claim no place at the family table.

"It was because of the unpaid, brutalized labor of slavery that the Daughter growing up within the dominant family got to enjoy whatever perquisites came with being a member of the Family. Upon assuming the role of Wife, her managerial capacity was bought at the expense of her black sisters over whom she ruled."

7. Rubin, "The Traffic in Women," pp. 160–161, provides the following summary of Karl Marx's theory of capitalism: "Briefly, Marx argued that capitalism is distinguished from all other modes of production by its unique aim: the creation and expansion of capital. Whereas other modes of production might find their purpose in making useful things to satisfy human needs, or in producing a surplus for a ruling nobility, or in producing to insure sufficient sacrifice for the edification of the gods, capitalism produces capital. Capitalism is a set of social relations—forms of property, and so forth—in which production takes the form of turning money, things, and people into capital. And capital is a quantity of goods or money which, when exchanged for labor, reproduces and augments itself by extracting unpaid labor, or surplus value, from labor and into itself. . . . The exchange between capital and labor which produces surplus value, and hence capital, is highly specific. The worker gets a wage; the capitalist gets the things the worker has made during his or her time of employment. If the total value of the things the worker has made exceeds the value of his or her

wage, the aim of capitalism has been achieved. The capitalist gets back the cost of the wage, plus an increment—surplus value. This can occur because the wage is determined not by the value of what the laborer makes, but by the value of what it takes to keep him or her going—to reproduce him or her from day to day, and to reproduce the entire work force from one generation to the next. Thus, surplus value is the difference between what the laboring class produces as a whole, and the amount of that total which is recycled into maintaining the laboring class."

8. Collins, "The Familial Economy of God," pp. 4–5. See also Catharine A. MacKinnon, *Sexual Harassment of Working Women: A Case of Sex Discrimination* (New Haven: Yale University Press, 1979), pp. 9–23; and Susan Estabrook Kennedy, *If All We Did Was to Weep at Home: A History of White Working-Class Women in America* (Bloomington: Indiana University Press, 1979; Midland Book, 1981).

9. See Collins, "The Familial Economy of God," pp. 5–8. See also David Brody, *Labor in Crisis: The Steel Strike of 1919* (Philadelphia: J. B. Lippincott, 1965), pp. 14–15; Stanley Aronowitz, *False Promises: The Shaping of American Working Class Consciousness* (New York: McGraw-Hill, 1973), pp. 158–166, 196–198, 307; Kenneth Keniston and Carnegie Council on Children, *All Our Children: The American Family Under Pressure* (New York: Harcourt Brace Jovanovich, 1977; Harvest/HBJ Book, 1978), pp. 44–45; Leslie Marmon Silko, *Ceremony* (New York: Viking Penguin, 1977; New American Library, 1978; Penguin Books, 1986; reprint ed., 1988), p. 115; Bremmer, Barnard, Hareven, and Mennel, eds., *Children and Youth in America*, p. 597; and Kennedy, *If All We Did Was to Weep at Home*, pp. 20–47.

10. See, for example, the account of Charles M. Schwab's rise to the presidency of the Carnegie Steel Company in Brody, *Labor in Crisis*, pp. 14–15.

11. See Judith Plaskow, "Anti-Semitism: The Unacknowledged Racism," in Barbara Hilkert Andolsen, Christine E. Gudorf, and Mary D. Pellauer, eds., *Women's Consciousness, Women's Conscience: A Reader in Feminist Ethics* (New York: Harper & Row, 1985; Perennial Library, 1987), pp. 76–77; Harold E. Quinley and Charles Y. Glock, *Anti-Semitism in America* (New York: The Free Press, 1979; Transaction, Incorporated, 1983), pp. xi, 11, 12–13, 19, 20, 185; Herman Feldman, *Racial Factors in American Industry* (New York: Harper & Row, 1931), pp. 132–188; Kennedy, *If All We Did Was to Weep at Home*, pp. 48–67; Aronowitz, *False Promises*, pp. 158–166; and Sheila D. Collins, *The Rainbow Challenge: The Jackson Campaign and the Future of U.S. Politics* (New York: Monthly Review Press, 1986), pp. 27–30.

12. See Susan Ehrlich Martin, *Breaking and Entering: Policewomen on Patrol* (Berkeley: University of California Press, 1980; paperback ed., 1982), pp. 59–75; Arthur Niederhoffer, *Behind the Shield: The Police in Urban Society*, p. 12; and appendix C.

Collins, "The Familial Economy of God," p. 9, writes: "Not only can these role patterns be discerned in specific workplace settings, but they can be seen operating on a broader scale in the relations between various sectors of the economy. Certain sectors of the economy like high finance and management

relate to other sectors, like the churches, as Father to Wife. Occupations dominated by women and minorities, such as service, sales and clerical work relate to
heavy industrial production as Daughter to Brother."

13. Popular rhetoric about gender-equality may suggest a yielding of the
man-and-wife tradition to spousal reciprocity; however, contraindicators reflecting public policy and actual practice are the defeat of the Equal Rights Amendment and statistics that show that women who have moved into wage-earning
positions (1) are paid lower wages than men for comparable work and (2) have
continued to bear the major share of household tasks as well. See Beverly
Wildung Harrison, "The Equal Rights Amendment: A Moral Analysis," in Carol
S. Robb, ed., *Making the Connections: Essays in Feminist Social Ethics* (Boston:
Beacon Press, 1985), pp. 167–173; Barbara Hilkert Andolsen, "A Woman's
Work Is Never Done: Unpaid Household Labor as a Social Justice Issue," in
Andolsen, Gudorf, and Pellauer, eds., *Women's Consciousness, Women's Con-
science,* pp. 3–18; and Jennifer A. Kingson, "Women in the Law Say Path Is
Limited by 'Mommy Track,' " *New York Times,* August 8, 1988, pp. A1, A15.

14. The discussion that follows is based on and the quotations used are taken
from Toni Morrison, *Sula* (New York: Alfred A. Knopf, 1973; New American
Library, Plume Book, 1982), pp. 80–83.

15. See Keniston, *All Our Children,* pp. 2–23; Angela Y. Davis, *Women,
Race and Class* (New York: Random House, 1981; Vintage Books, 1983), pp.
224–230; Aronowitz, *False Promises,* pp. 95–96, 205–206, 283; Harry Braverman, *Labor and Monopoly Capital: The Degradation of Work in the Twentieth Century* (New York: Monthly Review Press, 1974), p. 287; Joseph H.
Pleck, *The Myth of Masculinity* (Cambridge, Mass.: MIT Press, 1981), pp. 159–
160; Kennedy, *If All We Did Was to Weep at Home;* and John D'Emilio, *Sexual
Politics, Sexual Communities: The Making of a Homosexual Minority in the
United States, 1940–1970,* p. 29.

16. See Aronowitz, *False Promises,* p. 284; and Braverman, *Labor and Monopoly Capital,* pp. 271–283.

17. See D'Emilio, *Sexual Politics, Sexual Communities,* p. 38.

For information about the media and information systems see Aronowitz,
False Promises, pp. 95–111; Vito Russo, *The Celluloid Closet: Homosexuality
in the Movies* (New York: Harper & Row, 1981), pp. 61–179; Jonathan Ned
Katz, "1947, January 26: *N.Y. Times Book Review:* Ferdinand Lundberg and
Dr. Marynia F. Farnham's: *Modern Woman: The Lost Sex"*; "1947, June 9:
Newsweek: 'Homosexuals in Uniform' "; "1948, January 14: *N.Y. Times Book
Review; Time; Parents' Magazine:* Alfred Kensey's and others' *Sexual Behavior
in the Human Male",* "1949, June 19: *N.Y. Times Book Review:* Ward Thomas's *Stranger in the Land"*; and "1914, October 10: *Newsweek:* 'Queer People,' " *Gay/Lesbian Almanac,* pp. 612–613, 616–618, 630–632, 645–646,
651–652.

For information about government participation, see Aronowitz, *False Promises,* pp. 264–270; and Andrea Weiss and Greta Schiller, *Before Stonewall: The
Making of a Gay and Lesbian Community* (Tallahassee, Fla.: Naiad Press,
1988), pp. 42–53.

For information about public education, see Keniston, *All Our Children,* pp. 15–16; and Barverman, *Labor and Monopoly Capital,* p. 287.

For information about religious institutions, see Harrison, *Making the Connections,* pp. 83–166, 193–234; James B. Nelson, *Embodiment: An Approach to Sexuality and Christian Theology* (Minneapolis; Augsburg Publishing House, 1978; paperback ed., 1979), pp. 130–151; Roger L. Shinn, "Homosexuality: Christian Conviction and Inquiry," in Edward Batchelor, Jr. ed., *Homosexuality and Ethics* (New York: Pilgrim Press, 1980), pp. 3–13.

18. Pleck, *The Myth of Masculinity,* pp. 5, 8, 159–160. For an example of this school of thought, see Ferdinand Lundberg and Marynia F. Farnham, *Modern Woman: The Lost Sex* (New York: Harper & Row, 1946) as cited and discussed by Katz, *Gay/Lesbian Almanac,* pp. 612–613. Katz quotes Lundberg and Farnham as saying that "basic masculinity and femininity" were not "superficial" or predominant "characteristics" but "determined by the emotional attitude of any man or woman to his or her reproduction function."

19. Aronowitz, *False Promises,* pp. 198–199; and Keniston, *All Our Children,* pp. 7–12.

20. For an example of support provided by the dominant school of thought in the discipline of psychology, see Lundberg and Farnham, *Modern Woman,* as cited and discussed by Katz, *Gay/Lesbian Almanac,* pp. 612–613, who writes and quotes as follows:

"In the 1980s, Lundberg's and Dr. Farnham's authoritative formulation of a procreatively-defined masculinity and femininity may be seen as one expression of the post-war ideology of fecundity. Taken seriously and enacted by a large part of the population, this gave rise to the baby boom of the 1940s and '50s. The ideal of the true woman and man as prolific breeder is also reflected in the new, historically specific stress in the late 1940s on the homosexual as 'sterile.'

"In their book Lundberg and Dr. Farnham argued that it was 'superficial' to define 'masculinity' and 'femininity' in terms of the characteristics allegedly predominating in each sex. According to the authors' own 'deeply penetrating' definition, 'basic masculinity and femininity' was

determined by the emotional attitude of any man or woman to his or her reproductive function. Basic masculinity or femininity is impaired in proportion as acceptance and assertion of the reproductive function is in any way qualified or denied. . . .

Qualification may take the most basic form possible: refusal or inability to engage in heterosexual relations on any terms. Such inability is clearly seen in full-fledged homosexuals. The next most basic form [of qualification] is: engagement in heterosexual relations but with the complete intent to see to it that they do not eventuate in reproduction. . . . Bachelor and spinster both represent examples of impaired masculinity and femininity. . . .

Historically, bachelors 'were recognized as having among them a high percentage of masturbators and homosexuals.' "

21. See Robert H. Bremmer, John Barnard, Tamara K. Hareven, Robert M. Mennel, eds., *Children and Youth in America: A Documentary History.* Vol. 2: 1866–1932, Parts 1–6 (Cambridge, Mass.: Harvard University Press, 1971), p. 663; Aronowitz, *False Promises,* p. 284; William E. Schmidt, "Community

Colleges Emerge as Centers for Job Training" *New York Times* (national ed.), June 20, 1988, pp. 1, 10; and Keniston, *All Our Children*, pp. 14–15.

22. Mihaly Csikszentmihalyi, "The Pressured World of Adolescence," *Planned Parenthood Review*, Spring 1986, p. 3. See also Mary Ellen Goodman, *The Culture of Childhood: Child's-Eye Views of Society and Culture* (New York: Teachers College Press, 1970), pp. 145, 153; Mihaly Csikzentmihalyi and Reed Larson, *Being Adolescent: Conflict and Growth in the Adolescent Years* (New York: Basic Books, 1984), p. 12; Joseph F. Kett, *Rites of Passage: Adolescence in America, 1790 to the Present* (New York: Basic Books, 1977); Bremmer, Barnard, Hareven, and Mennel, eds., *Children and Youth in America*, Vol. I; James Garbarino and Andrew F. Kelly, "An Introduction to Troubled Youth in Troubled Families," Aaron T. Ebata, "Social Competence in Adolescence," and Teresa M. Cooney, "Behavior Problems in Adolescence," in James Garbarino, Cynthia J. Schellenbach, Janet M. Sebes, and associates, eds., *Troubled Youth, Troubled Families: Understanding Families At-Risk for Adolescent Maltreatment* (New York: Aldine de Gruyter, Division of Walter de Gruyter, 1986), pp. 13, 170, 172; Peter Blos, *The Adolescent Passage: Developmental Issues* (New York: International Universities Press, 1979), pp. 12–13; and Herant Katchadourian and Donald T. Lunde, *Fundamentals of Sexuality* (New York: Holt, Rinehart and Winston, 1972; 3d ed., 1980), pp. 243–257.

23. Csikszentmihalyi, "The Pressured World of Adolescence," p. 3.

24. See Keniston, *All Our Children*, pp. 32, 204; Commission on Minority Participation in Education and American Life, *One-Third of a Nation: A Report of the Commission on Minority Participation in Education and American Life* (Washington, D.C.: American Council on Education and Education Commission of the United States, May 1988); Commission on Youth and America's Future, *The Forgotten Half: Pathways to Success for America's Youth and Young Families* (Washington, D.C.: Commission on Youth and America's Future, 1988); Stuart Taylor, Jr., "Justices Uphold Fees for School Bus," *New York Times*, June 25, 1988, p. 8; and "Many in U.S. Face Bleak Job Outlook: Study Says a Lack of College Can Mean Lifetime Low Pay or Unemployment," *New York Times*, November 19, 1988, p. 8.

25. Csikszentmihalyi, "The Pressured World of Adolescence," p. 4. See also Csikszentmihalyi and Larson, *Being Adolescent*, p. 15.

For resources that discuss teenagers' needs and interests and parental responses, see Ruth Bell, *Changing Bodies, Changing Lives: A Book for Teens on Sex and Relationships* (New York: Random House, 1981); Jeanne Jacob Speizer, "The Teenage Years," in, Boston Women's Health Book Collective, ed. *Ourselves and Our Children: A Book by and for Parents* (New York: Random House, 1978), pp. 87–109; and Garbarino and Kelly, "The Challenge of Being Parent to an Adolescent" in chapter 1, "An Introduction to Troubled Youth in Troubled Families," in Garbarino, Schellenbach, and Sebes, eds., *Troubled Youth, Troubled Families*, pp. 12–16.

For resources that discuss teenage problem behaviors see Keniston, *All Our Children*, pp. 199–200; M. Joan McDermott, *Rape Victimization in 26 American Cities: Applications of the National Crime Survey Victimization and Atti-*

tude Data (Bureau of Justice Statistics, U.S. Department of Justice, Washington, D.C.), Analytic Report SD-VAD-6 (Albany, N.Y.: Criminal Justice Research Center, 1979), pp. 12–14; Leon Dash, "At Risk: Chronicles of Teen-Age Pregnancy" (six-part series) *Washington Post,* January 26–31, 1986; Tamar Lewin, "Fewer Teen Mothers, but More Are Unmarried," *New York Times,* March 20, 1988, p. II-6; Cooney, "Behavior Problems in Adolescence," in Garbarino, Schellenbach, and Sebes, eds., *Troubled Youth, Troubled Families,* pp. 179–180; and two fact sheets developed by National Council on Alcoholism and distributed by New York State Council on Alcoholism, "Facts on Alcoholism and Alcohol-Related Problems" and "Alcoholism and Other Alcohol-Related Problems Among Children and Youth"; and Division of Substance Abuse Services and Division of Alcoholism and Alcohol Abuse, Research Institute on Alcoholism, *A Double Danger: Relationships Between Alcohol Use and Substance Use Among Secondary School Students in New York State,* prepared by Blanche Frank, Douglas Lipton, Rozanne Marel, James Schmeidler, Grace M. Barnes, and John W. Welte (Albany, N.Y.: State of New York, Fall 1985).

26. Csikszentmihalyi and Larson, *Being Adolescent,* p. 244.

27. Csikszentmihalyi, "The Pressured World of Adolescence," p. 4. See also Csikszentmihalyi and Larson, *Being Adolescent,* pp. 251, 265, 267–269.

28. Keniston, *All Our Children,* p. 195. For information concerning teenagers who have more serious criminal activities and social problems, see Rita Kramer, *At a Tender Age: Violent Youth and Juvenile Justice* (New York: Henry Holt, 1988); and Elizabeth Marek, *The Children at Santa Clara* (New York: Viking Penguin, 1987; Penguin Books, 1988).

29. For example, when the young men who killed Charlie Howard were sentenced to less than a year in the Maine Youth Center, staff members there considered them to be "lightweights." Peter Canellos, "A City and Its Sins: The Killing of a Gay Man in Bangor," writes, " 'These kids, as far as I can see, are atypical from our average kid,' says youth center counselor James Irwin. 'They're social beings. Most of the kids we see are antisocial.' In other words, [Howard's assailants] committed their crime as a means of gaining acceptance into society —not as a means of rebelling against it. Adds Irwin, 'I think throwing a known homosexual off the bridge is something that would be a feather in their cap among kids at Bangor High.' As far as Irwin can tell, there was no single reason for their dislike of gays—they only treated gays as they thought most people did."

30. Pam Chamberlain, "Homophobia in Schools or What We Don't Know Will Hurt Us," p. 3, observes, "When Charlie Howard was killed in Bangor, Maine in 1984 by a group of teenage boys who beat him up and flung him off a bridge to drown, the Maine gay community had to lobby hard to get the public to take the action as a violent demonstration of hatred against gays and not just a childish prank gone sour. Missing from the debate was an inquiry into why these young men felt they could get away with such behavior."

31. Doug Ireland, "Rendezvous in the Ramble" (sidebar, "Gay-Bashers: The Exorcist Syndrome") *New York,* July 24, 1978, p. 41, quotes John Money, "a pediatrician and past president of the Society for the Scientific Study of sex . . .

professor of medical psychology at Johns Hopkins University, chief of its Gender Identity Clinic, and co-editor of the five-volume *Handbook of Sexology*," as saying: "The folkways of our culture fill our young people with images of homosexuals as sick, evil, less than human. There are so many signals from the home, the school, the church—and from the media—which make homosexuality the daily butt of television humor and have given such publicity to Anita Bryant and her gays-are-child-molesters campaign as to legitimize her views in the eyes of our youth. . . . At the same time, the law epitomizes this attitude. The very fact that our laws make homosexuality a crime validates the idea that 'queers' are animals."

Examples of anti-gay/lesbian statements by religious leaders and in religious tracts, may be found in Aaron Fricke, *Reflections of a Rock Lobster: A Story About Growing Up Gay*, p. 94; Enrique Rueda, *The Homosexual Network: Private Lives and Public Policy* (Old Greenwich, Conn.: Devin Adair Company, 1982), pp. 3–28; Congregation for the Doctrine of Faith, "Letter to the Bishops of the Catholic Church on the Pastoral Care of Homosexual Persons," adopted in an ordinary session of the Congregation on the Doctrine of the Faith; given at Rome, October 1, 1986; approved and ordered to be published by Pope John Paul II during an audience granted to Prefect Joseph Cardinal Ratzinger; also, bearing name of Alberto Bovone, Titular Archbishop of Caesarea in Numidia, Secretary (Vatican City, 1986); Dave Walter, "Falwell Finally Pays for Antigay Remark," *Advocate* (Los Angeles), October 28, 1986, p. 17; "Indiana," *Advocate* (Los Angeles), May 24, 1988, p. 21; William Paul, "Minority Status for Gay People: Majority Reaction and Social Context," in William Paul, James D. Weinrich, John C. Gonsiorek, and Mary E. Hotvedt, eds., *Homosexuality: Social, Psychological, and Biological Issues*, p. 363.

See also Bruce Kogan, "Sins of the Fathers: When Belfast Came to the Bronx," *New York Native*, March 16, 1987, pp. 17–18; Edgar K. Byham, president, Letter to Integrity Friends and Colleagues; Integrity, Incorporated; Washington, D.C.; Eastertide 1988; Evan Drake Howard, "Extremism on Campus: Symbols of Hate, Symbols of Hope," *Christian Century*, July 15–22, 1987, p. 627; and Kevin Berrill, National Gay Task Force Violence Project coordinator, " 'Anti-Gay Violence and the Church,' Support Statement for a Resolution Affirming Lesbian and Gay Lifestyles; Riverside Church, New York, NY," March 1985.

For public statements supporting lesbians and gay men, see NGLTF Anti-Violence Project, "Statements on Anti-Gay Violence by Religious, Political, and Law Enforcement Leaders: An Organizing Resource" (Washington, D.C.: National Gay and Lesbian Task Force, November 20, 1989). See also Martha R. Gottwals, "General Synod 17—Here's What Delegates Did," *United Church (of Christ) News* (Cleveland), July–August 1989, p. 7.

32. See, for example, Howard Brown, *Familiar Faces, Hidden Lives: The Story of Homosexual Men in America Today*, pp. 89–95; Fricke, *Reflections of a Rock Lobster*, pp. 64–65, 68, 77, 80–81; Chamberlain "Homophobia in Schools or What We Don't Know Will Hurt Us," pp. 3–6; Ann Heron, ed., *One Teenager in Ten: Testimony by Gay and Lesbian Youth* (Boston: Alyson Publi-

cations, 1983; New York: Warner Books, 1986); and U.S. Congress, House Subcommittee on Criminal Justice, Judiciary Committee, *Anti-Gay Violence,* pp. 147–151.

33. See, for example, entire issue entitled "Teen-age Pregnancy: The Search for Solutions," *Planned Parenthood Review,* September 1986; Chamberlain, "Homophobia in Schools or What We Don't Know Will Hurt Us," pp. 3–6; Rod Paul, "Sex Education Manual Prompts Moral Outrage," *New York Times,* April 24, 1988, section 1, p. 39; and Peter Freiberg, "School Sex Manual Creates N.H. Stir," *Advocate* (Los Angeles), June 21, 1988, pp. 16–17; and "New York," *Advocate* (Los Angeles), July 5, 1988, p. 21.

34. See, however, the following articles concerning the public statement by and censure of a judge: "Judge Apologizes for Remarks About Homosexuals," *New York Times,* December 23, 1988, p. A18; "Dallas Gays Protest Judge's Comments: Jurist's Notions About Gays Make Him Unfit for the Bench, They Say," *Advocate* (Los Angeles), January 31, 1989, p. 13; Robert W. Peterson, "Texans Blast Antigay Judge: Public Condemnation of Hampton Is Swift and Widespread," *Advocate* (Los Angeles), February 14, 1989, pp. 10, 12; and "Dallas Judge Censured for Slurring Homosexuals," *New York Times,* November 29, 1989, p. A28.

35. Csikszentmihalyi and Larson, *Being Adolescent,* p. 244; McDermott, *Rape Victimization in 26 American Cities,* pp. 12–14; Keniston, *All Our Children,* p. 195; and Garbarino, Wilson, and Garbarino, "The Adolescent Runaway," in Garbarino, Schellenbach, and Sebes, *Troubled Youth, Troubled Families,* p. 43.

36. I use the term *socialization* to mean the formal and informal shaping of people within a particular social, political, cultural, economic structure. Direct instruction and education within formal environments—such as schools, families, and churches—as well as the prevailing behavioral and social patterns to which people adapt and adjust are part of the process. The "hidden curriculum" (a term used by professor of religious education John H. Westerhoff III), consisting of the expectations, attitudes, interactions, and roles that are socially dominant but not explicitly, intentionally, or consciously communicated by adults to children, are considered stronger forces in the socialization process than the covert messages and lessons designed for the instruction of children. In other words, children are more likely to be influenced by and to model that which they see adults doing rather than that which they are told to do by adults. See John Westerhoff III, *Will Our Children Have Faith?* (New York: Seabury Press, 1976), pp. 16–19.

I use the term *gender role* instead of *sex role* to signify that these behaviors and traits are not biological but culturally formed and learned. In social science literature, both terms are used, often interchangeably with the same meaning. Pleck, in *The Myth of Masculinity,* p. 12, notes the increased usage of the term *gender role.* Pleck (pp. 10–11) defines *sex role* (and here I would find his definition suitable for my preferred term, *gender role*) as the "set of behaviors and characteristics widely viewed as (1) typical of men and women *(sex role stereotypes),* and (2) desirable for women or men *(sex role norms)."* He adds,

"The behaviors and characteristics comprising sex roles include aspects of personality (traits, dispositions) and social roles (especially activities performed at the job and in the family). In personality, the male role may be characterized as aggressive, achievement oriented, and emotionally inexpressive. In specific social roles, it may be characterized by such terms as breadwinner, husband, and father." Pleck subsequently argues against the traditional view of "sex roles" that sees them as developing from within the self rather than being imposed from without.

See also Rubin, "The Traffic in Women," in Reiter, ed., *Toward an Anthropology of Women,* pp. 179–180; Ann Oakley, *Sex, Gender, and Society* (London: Maurice Temple Smith, 1972; New York: Harper & Row, 1972), pp. 173–188; and Inge K. Broverman, Susan Raymond Vogel, Donald M. Broverman, Frank E. Clarkson, and Paul S. Rosenkrantz, "Sex Role Stereotypes: A Current Appraisal," *Journal of Social Issues* (1972), 28:57–78.

37. See, for example, Dorothy I. Riddle and Barbara Sang, "Psychotherapy with Lesbians," *Journal of Social Issues* (1978), 34:85; Norma Costrich, Joan Feinstein, Louise Kidder, Jeanne Marecek, and Linda Pascale, "When Stereotypes Hurt: Three Studies of Penalties for Sex Role Reversals," *Journal of Experimental Social Psychology* (1975), 11:520–532; Pleck, *The Myth of Masculinity;* Ruth E. Hartley, "Sex-Role Pressures and the Socialization of the Male Child," in Deborah S. David and Robert Brannon, eds., *The Forty-Nine Percent Majority: The Male Sex Role* (Reading, Mass.: Addison-Wesley, 1976), pp. 235–244; and David M. Rorvik, "The Gender Enforcers: Seeing to It that Boys Will Be Boys," *Rolling Stone,* October 9, 1975, pp. 52–53, 67, 86.

See also the following social commentaries: Deborah S. David and Robert Brannon, "The Male Sex Role: Our Culture's Blueprint of Manhood, and What It's Done for Us Lately," and Lucy Komisar, "Violence and the Masculine Mystique," in David and Brannon, eds., *The Forty-Nine Percent Majority,* pp. 1–45, 201–215; Joseph H. Pleck and Jack Sawyer, eds., *Men and Masculinity* (Englewood Cliffs, N.J.: Prentice-Hall, Spectrum Book, 1974); Audre Lorde, "Man Child: A Black Lesbian Feminist's Response," in *Sister Outsider: Essays and Speeches* (Trumansburg, N.Y.: Crossing Press, 1984), pp. 72–80; Claude Brown, *Manchild in the Promised Land* (New York: Macmillan, 1965; Signet, 1965); Bruce Kokopeli and George Lakey, "More Power Than We Want: Masculine Sexuality and Violence," in New Society Publishers, ed. *Off Their Backs . . . And on Our Own Two Feet* (Philadelphia: New Society Publishers, 1983), pp. 1–8; Mike Bradley, Lonnie Danchik, Marty Fager, and Tom Wodetzki, *Unbecoming Men: A Men's Consciousness-Raising Group Writes on Oppression and Themselves* (Albion, Calif.: Times Change Press, 1971); and Jack Litewka, "The Socialized Penis," *Liberation,* March–April 1974, pp. 16–25.

38. See, for example, Riddle and Sang, "Psychotherapy with Lesbians," p. 85; Broverman, Vogel, Broverman, Clarkson, and Rosenkrantz, "Sex Role Stereotypes," pp. 57–78; Charles Berger, "Sex Differences Related to Self-esteem Factor Structure," *Journal of Consulting and Clinical Psychology* (1968), 32:442–446; Rae Carlson, "Stability and Change in the Adolescents' Self-image," *Child*

Development (1965), 36:659–666; Beverly I. Fagot and Isabelle Litman, "Stability of Sex Role and Play Interests from Preschool to Elementary School," *Journal of Psychology* (1975), 89:285–292; and John Hollender, "Sex Differences in Sources of Social Self-esteem," *Journal of Consulting and Clinical Psychology* (1972), 38:343–347.

39. See study by Jeffrey Z. Rubin, Frank J. Provenzano, and Zella Luria, "The Eye of the Beholder: Parents' Views on Sex of Newborns," *American Journal of Orthopsychiatry* (1974), 44:512–519.

40. For a summary of research on gender-role socialization and preschool children, see Alice Sterling Honig, "Sex Role Socialization in Early Childhood," *Young Children,* September 1983, pp. 57–70.

41. See Oakley, *Sex, Gender, and Society,* p. 106.

42. See Marc Feigen Fasteau, Chapter 11, "Violence: The Primal Test," *The Male Machine* (New York: McGraw-Hill, 1974), pp. 144–157; David and Brannon, eds., *The Forty-Nine Percent Majority,* especially Lucy Komisar, "Violence and the Masculine Mystique," pp. 201–215, and Ruth E. Hartley, "Sex-Role Pressures and the Socialization of the Male Child," pp. 235–244; and John H. Gagnon, "Physical Strength, Once of Significance," in Pleck and Sawyer, eds., *Men and Masculinity,* pp. 139–149.

For comments about the role of sports in the socialization of males to behave violently, see Peter Candell, "When I Was About Fourteen . . .," in Pleck and Sawyers, eds., *Men and Masculinity,* pp. 17–18. David Kopay and Perry Deane Young, *The David Kopay Story: An Extraordinary Self-revelation.* Dave Meggysey, *Out of Their League* (San Francisco: Ramparts Press, 1971; Paperback Library, 1971). Warren Farrell, "Super Bowl"; Joseph Pleck, "My Male Sex Role—And Ours"; and James S. Coleman, "Athletics in High School," in David and Brannon, eds., *The Forty-Nine Percent Majority,* pp. 216–219, 253–269. Bradley, Danchik, Fager, and Wodetski, "Out in Right Field," and "Growing Up Popular," *Unbecoming Men,* pp. 36–46.

For comments about the role of the military in the socialization of males to behave violently, see "Life in the Military," in Pleck and Sawyer, eds., *Men and Masculinity,* pp. 127–129. Samuel S. Stouffer et al., "Masculinity and the Role of the Combat Soldier," in David and Brannon, eds., *The Forty-Nine Percent Majority,* pp. 179–183. Geraldine L. Wilson, "The Values Conveyed in Children's Toys," *Interracial Books for Children Bulletin* (1981), 12:3–9.

For comments about social expectations for males to be ready for violence and to defend themselves, see Brown, *Manchild in the Promised Land,* pp. 265–268. Fricke, *Reflections of a Rock Lobster.* Lorde, "Man Child," in *Sister Outsider,* pp. 72–80. Tommi Avicolli, "He Defies You Still: The Memoirs of a Sissy," *Radical Teacher* (n.d.), 24:4–5. Committee of Educators for Lesbian and Gay Concerns, Panel discussion on "Lesbians and Gays in the Public School," Panel members: Paula Hogan, Kathy Bliss, Arthur Lipkind, Brian Mooney, Pam Chamberlain, David Crowder, and Lisa George, Moderated by Rinaldo Discologne and Liz Heron, chairpersons (Cambridge, Mass.: Harvard Graduate School of Education, April 4, 1983). National School Safety Center, *Schoolyard Bully*

Practicum, Harvard University; Cambridge, Mass., May 12–13, 1987 (Encino, Calif.: National School Safety Center, a partnership of Pepperdine University and the United States Justice Department, 1987).

43. I find the distinction between *violence* and *aggression* made by Lionel Tiger in *Men in Groups* (New York: Random House, 1969), pp. 158–159, to be helpful here: " 'Aggression' is a social-organization term referring to a process, while 'violence' describes an event which is only one possible outcome of the aggressive process. Aggression occurs when an individual or group see their interest, their honour, or their job bound up with coercing the animal, human, or physical environment to achieve their own ends rather than (or in spite of) the goals of the object of their action. Violence may occur in the process of the interaction. Violence is most obvious when it is physical; unless noted otherwise, the term here will refer to coercion involving physical force to resolve conflict between coercer and coerced. For example, laundries may compete by advertising, service, and prices to secure contracts for servicing restaurants; in my sense, they are aggressing against their competitors. But Mafia-controlled laundries in the United States may use 'muscle,' window-breaking, arson, etc., to win laundry contracts from firms not employing these means of securing business. In this case, violence is an incident in the process of commercial (aggressive) competition."

Males are socialized to be coercive, which may at times "require" violence. The powerlessness felt by adolescent males (i.e., the lack of opportunity to exercise and develop coercive skills) may "necessitate" compensatory acts of violence toward those who are as powerless or less powerful.

44. See Garbarino, Wilson, and Garbarino, "The Adolescent Runaway," and Cooney, "Behavior Problems in Adolescence," in Garbarino, Schellenbach, and Sebes, eds., *Troubled Youth, Troubled Families*, pp. 43, 183.

45. See Carlson, "Stability and Change in the Adolescent's Self-image," pp. 659–666; and Wilson H. Guertin and Sidney M. Jourard, "Characteristics of Real-Self–Ideal-Self Discrepancy Scores Revealed by Factor Analysis," *Journal of Consulting Psychology* (1962), 26:241–245.

46. See Broverman, Vogel, Broverman, Clarkson, and Rosenkrantz, "Sex-Role Stereotypes," pp. 64–65, 69; Costrich, Feinstein, Kidder, Marecek, and Pascale, "When Stereotypes Hurt," pp. 520–530; Berger, "Sex Differences Related to Self-esteem Factor Structure," pp. 442–446; David M. Connell and James E. Johnson, "Relationship Between Sex-Role Identification and Self-esteem in Early Adolescents," *Developmental Psychology* (1970), 3:Hollender, "Sex Differences in Sources of Social Self-esteem," pp. 343–347. Carlson, "Stability and Change in the Adolescent's Self-image," p. 660, refers to "self-esteem" as the "correspondence between one's present concept of self and his[/her] self-ideal."

47. Jesus Rangel, "Rutgers U., in Wake of a Student's Death, to Curb Fraternities," p. 9.

48. See Judith V. Becker, Jerry Cunningham-Rathner, and Meg S. Kaplan, "Adolescent Sexual Offenders: Demographics, Criminal and Sexual Histories, and Recommendations for Reducing Future Offenses," *Journal of Interpersonal*

Violence (December 1986), 1:431–445; and Marie Fortune, *Sexual Violence: The Unmentionable Sin* (New York: Pilgrim Press, 1983), pp. 181–183.

49. See McDermott, *Rape Victimization in 26 American Cities,* p. 12. For findings concerning the benign regard for date rape demonstrated by teenagers, see Laurel Fingley, "Teenagers in Survey Condone Forced Sex," *Ms.,* February 1981, p. 23.

50. Information obtained from interview with Donald J. Bromberg, captain and commanding officer, and Carl A. Zittell, sergeant, Bias Incident Investigating Unit, Police Department, City of New York, September 18, 1986. See also Ruben Rosario, "Anti-Gay Violence Probed: Homosexuals Join Those Aided by Cop Unit as Attacks Based on Race, Beliefs Increase," p. 31; Peter Finn and Taylor McNeil, *The Response of the Criminal Justice System to Bias Crime: An Exploratory Review,* submitted to National Institute of Justice, U.S. Department of Justice, Contract No. OJP-86-002 (Cambridge, Mass.: Abt Associates, October 7, 1987), pp. 1–2; Don Terry, "6 White Men Attack Black Man with Bats and Sticks on S.I. Street," *New York Times,* June 23, 1988, p. B2; Thomas J. Lueck, "Police Say Attack Is Bias-Related: Sanitation Worker Is Injured by White in Race Assault on Bronx Street Corner," *New York Times,* July 17, 1988, section 1, p. 24; and "3 Youths Charged in Defacement of Rutgers Jewish Student Center," *New York Times,* August 27, 1989, section 1, p. 32.

Within a single year, 1989, in New York City, four separate incidents of sexist, racist, and anti-Semitic violence by groups of teenage males received national attention in the newsmedia. The first incident involved the gang rape of a young woman who was jogging in Central Park; see Michael T. Kaufman, "Park Suspects: The Troubling Ties," *New York Times,* April 26, 1989, pp. A1, B24; and Joan Morgan, "The Pro-Rape Culture: Homeboys—of All Races—Stop You on the Street," *Village Voice* (New York), May 9, 1989, pp. 39, 52. The second incident involved the killing of a young black man by white youths; see Kirk Johnson, "Racism and the Young: Some See a Rising Tide," *New York Times,* August 27, 1989, section 1, p. 32; Howard W. French, "Hatred and Social Isolation May Spur Acts of Racial Violence, Experts Say," *New York Times,* September 4, 1989, p. 31; and Mark Bauman and Samme Chittum, "Married to the Mob: The Wiseguy Wannabees," *Village Voice* (New York), September 5, 1989, pp. 40, 42–43. The third incident involved the beating of three Jewish students by a gang of white teenage men; see Michael Freitag, "Three Jewish Students are Attacked by 20 White Men in Brooklyn," *New York Times,* October 9, 1989, pp. B1, B3; David E. Pitt, "Clues to Ethnic Attack Sought in Party," *New York Times,* October 10, 1989, p. B3; James C. McKinley, Jr., "Police Identify Man as Suspect in Beating Jews: 18-Year-Old Turns in Himself in Brooklyn," *New York Times,* October 11, 1989, p. B3; and James C. McKinley, Jr., "3 Teen-Agers Are Arrested in Bias Attack: More Are Sought in Beating of 3 Jewish Students," *New York Times,* October 12, 1989, pp. B1, B4. The fourth incident, involving the gang rape of a retarded teenage woman by fellow male high school students, occurred in nearby suburban New Jersey; see Robert Hanley, "Sexual Assault Shatters a New Jersey Town," *New York Times,* May 26, 1989, pp. B1, B4; Lisa W. Foderaro, "Glen Ridge Worries It Was Too

Forgiving to Athletes," *New York Times,* June 12, 1989, pp. B1, B4; and Robert Hanley, "2 More Charged in Glen Ridge Attack," *New York Times,* August 19, 1989, p. 26.

51. For discussion of legal rights and the law, see Thomas B. Stoddard, E. Carrington Boggan, Marilyn G. Haft, Charles Lister, and John P. Rupp, *The Rights of Gay People* (New York: Bantam Books, 1975; revised ed., 1983); Robert G. Bagnall, Patrick C. Gallagher, and Joni L. Goldstein, "Burdens of Gay Litigants and Bias in the Court System: Homosexual Panic, Child Custody, and Anonymous Parties," pp. 497–559; and Meredith Gould, "Lesbians and the Law: Where Sexism and Heterosexism Meet," in Trudy Darty and Sandee Potter, eds., *Women-Identified Women,* pp. 152–160; and Arthur S. Leonard, "Gay and Lesbian Rights Protections in the U.S.: An Introduction to Gay and Lesbian Civil Rights" (Washington, D.C.: National Gay and Lesbian Task Force, 1989).

The constitutionality of state laws prohibiting homosexuality was recently upheld by the U.S. Supreme Court decision in 1986 in the *Bowers* v. *Hardwick* case; for full text of the decision without footnotes, see *Bowers vs. Hardwick: The Supreme Court and Sodomy* (also, "The Constitution and Sodomy, A Commentary," and "The Nature of Rights," by Jim Peron) (San Francisco: Free Forum Books). For commentary, see Peron; Arthur S. Leonard, "Getting Beyond *Hardwick,*" *New York Native,* September 1, 1986, p. 20; and Linda Vance, "Gay Sex in the Sights of the Right: Intimate Inequality in the Minds of the Supreme Court," *Gay Community News* (Boston), Summer 1986.

For articles dealing with lesbian and gay marriage, see Harvard Law Review Staff, "Homosexual Marriage" in "Development in the Law—The Constitution and the Family," *Harvard Law Review* (1980), 93:1283–1289; Thomas B. Stoddard, "Gay Marriages: Make Them Legal," *New York Times,* March 4, 1989, p. 27; Peter Freiberg, "Wedding-Bell Blues: Some Gays Aren't Wedded to the Idea of Same-Sex Marriage," *Advocate* (Los Angeles), August 1, 1989, pp. 16–17; Sheila Rule, "Denmark Permits Gay 'Partnerships,' " *New York Times,* October 2, 1989, p. A8; and Philip S. Gutis, "Small Steps Toward Acceptance Renew Debate on Gay Marriage," *New York Times,* November 5, 1989, section 4, p. 24. See also Peter Freiberg, "Two Gays Can Be a Family, Court says: New York Rent-Case Ruling Is the First of Its Kind," *Advocate* (Los Angeles), August 15, 1989, pp. 12–13; and "Canadian Judge Rules Gays in Prison Entitled to Conjugal Visits," *TAGALA* (Newsletter of Toledo, Ohio, Gay and Lesbian Affiliation), December 1989, p. 1.

For articles dealing with child custody, see Donna Hitchens, "Social Attitudes, Legal Standards, and Personal Trauma in Child Custody Cases," *Journal of Homosexuality* (Fall–Winter 1979/80), 5:89–96; Rose A. Basile, "Lesbian Mothers I," *Women's Rights Law Reporter* (December 1984):3–18; Nancy Polikoff and Nan D. Hunter, "The Custody Rights of Lesbian Mothers: Legal Theory and Litigation Strategy," *Buffalo Law Review* (1976), 25:691–733; Mary L. Stevens, "Lesbian Mothers in Transition," in Ginny Vida, ed., *Our Right to Love: A Lesbian Resource Book* pp. 207–211; Riddle and Sang, "Psychotherapy with Lesbians," p. 91; and Wendell Ricketts, "Quietly Making

History: Lesbian Rights Project Creates New Sense of Family for Gays," *Advocate* (Los Angeles), pp. 46–48.

For articles dealing with adoption and foster-parenting, see Georgia Dullea, "Gay Couples' Wish to Adopt Grows, Along with Increasing Resistance," *New York Times,* February 7, 1988, section 1, p. 26; and Mary E. Hotvedt and Mandel, "Children of Lesbian Mothers," in Paul, Weinrich, Gonsiorek, and Hotvedt, eds., *Homosexuality,* p. 283.

Those organizational bodies that have been most explicit in issuing and enforcing restrictions on employment are the various branches of the U.S. military and most mainstream religious denominations; and their policies have tended to become more restrictive over the past twenty years.

Concerning employment in the military, see Katherine Bishop, "Court to Rehear Challenge to Army's Homosexual Ban," *New York Times,* June 10, 1988, p. A10; "Lesbian Struggles to Serve Army," *New York Times,* August 10, 1989, p. A14; C. Robert Zelnick, "The Navy Scapegoats a Dead Seaman," *New York Times,* September 11, 1989, p. A21; Stoddard, Boggan, Haft, Lister, and Rupp, *The Rights of Gay People;* Gould, "Lesbians and the Law," in Darty and Potter, eds., *Women-Identified Women,* p. 158; Joseph Schreiner, "Barriers to Achievement," Chicago, NOGLSTP (National Organization of Gay and Lesbian Scientists and Technical Professionals), 1986; Elaine Sciolino, "Report Urging End of Homosexual Ban Rejected by Military," *New York Times,* October 22, 1989, pp. 1, 24.

Concerning employment in religious denominations, see Gerald Renner, "Homosexuals Find Doors to Ordination Tightly Closed," *Hartford Courant* (Hartford, Conn.), January 27, 1986, pp. A1, A10; Peter Freiberg, "Congregation Ousts Mich. Gay Priest *[sic],*" *Advocate* (Los Angeles), December 22, 1987, pp. 16–17; Gary David Comstock, "Aliens in the Promised Land?" *USQR: Union Seminary Quarterly Review* (1987), 41 (3–4):93–104; W. Evan Golder, "Homosexual Candidates for Ministry Challenge UCC Ordination Polity," *United Church News,* February 1988, p. 8; Zalmon O. Sherwood, *Kairos: Confessions of a Gay Priest* (Boston: Alyson Publications, 1987); Joan L. Clark, "Coming Out: the Process and Its Price," *Christianity and Crisis,* June 11, 1979, pp. 146–153; Marvin M. Ellison, "Faithfulness, Morality, and Vision: Questions for a Justice-Seeking Church," *Christianity and Crisis,* November 9, 1987, pp. 381–383; Rose Mary Denman," Looking Forward, Looking Back," *Christianity and Crisis,* February 1, 1988, pp. 7–8; James L. Franklin, "Methodist Minister Faces Dismissal as Lesbian," *Boston Globe,* May 19, 1987; David Perry, "Lutheran Seminarians Face 'New Inquisition,' " *Advocate* (Los Angeles), July 5, 1988, pp. 37–39; and Stephen F. Morin and Ellen M. Garfinkle, "Male Homophobia," *Journal of Social Issues* (1978), 34:29–47.

Recruiting procedures by police and police departments traditionally screen out and discourage lesbian/gay applicants, also. See appendix C.

Among surveys of lesbians and gay men (see chapter 2), the majority of respondents report that they must conceal their sexual orientation to avoid discrimination in employment, and one third of respondents have experienced discrimination in hiring, promotion, termination, evaluation, and loss of clients.

See Edward H. Peeples Jr., Walter W. Tunstall, and Everett Eberhardt, *A Survey of Perception of Civil Opportunity Among Gays and Lesbians in Richmond, Virginia,* p. 15; Maine Civil Liberties Union, "Discrimination and Violence Survey of Gay People in Maine"; Vermonters for Lesbian and Gay Rights, "Discrimination and Violence Survey of Lesbians and Gay Men in Vermont"; New Jersey Lesbian and Gay Coalition, "Discrimination Against Lesbians and Gay Men in New Jersey: 1977–1983"; Aurand, Addessa, and Bush, *Violence and Discrimination Against Philadelphia Lesbian and Gay People,* pp. 14–15; Identity, Incorporated, *One in Ten: A Profile of Alaska's Lesbian and Gay Community,* p. 15; Alan P. Bell and Martin S. Weinberg, *Homosexualities: A Study of Diversity Among Men and Women,* pp. 141–148.

For articles dealing with instances of discrimination in employment, see Stuart Taylor, Jr., "C.I.A. Worker's Dismissal Subject to Review, Supreme Court Rules," *New York Times,* June 16, 1988, p. A1, D24; Peter Freiberg, "Gay Teachers: Lesbians Battle Prejudice in the Blackboard Jungle," *Advocate* (Los Angeles), October 2, 1984, pp. 21–23; and Judith M. Hedgpeth, "Employment Discrimination Law and the Rights of Gay Persons," *Journal of Homosexuality* (Fall–Winter 1979/1980), 5:67–78.

52. See "Occupations," n. 49, chapter 2. In my survey of lesbians and gay men, only one male respondent listed his occupation as "hairdresser," one as "dancer," and none as "interior decorator." See also Edwin M. Schur, *Crimes Without Victims: Deviant Behavior and Public Policy; Abortion, Homosexuality, Drug Addiction,* p. 93; Howard S. Becker, *Outsiders: Studies in the Sociology of Deviance* (New York: The Free Press, 1963; paperback ed., 1966), pp. 34, 35–36; and Edwin M. Schur, *The Politics of Deviance: Stigma Contests and the Uses of Power* (Englewood Cliffs, N.J.: Prentice-Hall, 1980), p. 92.

See Eugene E. Levitt and Albert D. Lassen, "Public Attitudes Toward Homosexuality: Part of the 1970 National Survey by the Institute for Sex Research," *Journal of Homosexuality* (1974), 1:29–43, who find that the public ranks from most acceptable to least acceptable the following occupations for gay men: florist, musician, artist, beautician, government official, medical doctor, minister, schoolteacher, court judge.

53. Maurice Leznoff and William A. Westley, "The Homosexual Community," pp. 257–263.

54. Martin S. Weinberg and Colin J. Williams, *Male Homosexuals: Their Problems and Adaptations,* pp. 223–229.

55. Laud Humphreys, *Out of the Closets: The Sociology of Homosexual Liberation,* p. 34.

56. Cynthia Crossen, "A Lingering Stigma," *Wall Street Journal,* March 20, 1987, p. 28D. Similar findings are reported by Keith Bradsher, "Young Men Pressed to Wed for Success," *New York Times,* December 13, 1989, pp. C1, C12. See also Arthur Lazere, "Up Front in the Executive Suite," *New York Native,* January 4, 1988, p. 23.

57. Gould, "Lesbians and the Law," in Darty and Potter, eds., *Women-Identified Women,* p. 157. See also Esther Newton, "Academe's Homophobia:

It Damages Careers and Ruins Lives," *Chronicle of Higher Education,* March 11, 1987, p. 104.

58. Robert L. Shinn, "Homosexuality: Christian Conviction and Inquiry," in Edward Batchelor, Jr., ed., *Homosexuality and Ethics,* p. 4, writes concerning the "victimization of homosexuals": "Whatever our final judgment about homosexuality, there is something peculiarly unhealthy in the zeal of its persecutors. Our is a culture that, by and large, tolerates much. We are not a people among whom 'all hearts are open, all desires known, and from whom no secrets are hid.' We permit and encourage considerable anonymity. The common life abounds in material for rumor and innuendo, and gossip is far from rare. Yet noblesse oblige works to neutralize some insinuations and to protect their victims.

"The exception is homosexuality. In high echelons of public life careers have been ruined by episodes of homosexuality. The hint of homosexual behavior is an absolute barrier to numerous public and private jobs."

59. The following are the percentages of respondents reporting anti-gay/lesbian violence by family members in my survey and in the survey by the National Gay and Lesbian Task Force (NGLTF):

Respondents:	Lesbians (%)	Gay men (%)	All (%)
NGLTF survey			
by fathers	2.1	4.3	3.6
by brothers	2.7	3.6	3.3
by mothers	2.9	1.4	1.9
by sisters	0.5	1.2	0.8
Comstock's survey			
by fathers	0	3	2
by brothers	2	9	6
by mothers	0	0	0
by sisters	2	0	1
by former husbands	4		

60. A gay man who forfeits his privilege and position in the family and workplace may be perceived by Brothers as disloyal or even stupid; but he can be let go or dismissed from the Brotherly ranks without injury to them. A lesbian's coming out affects differently the social order and those whom women serve; she, of course, gives up privilege and position (although she has less to give up than the gay man), but more significantly, Fathers and Brothers lose a subordinate and supporter. Her moving out of (or being moved out of) the position of household Wife or workplace Daughter to that of Alien does not, of course, move her into or above the ranks of household Father or workplace Brother. She gains no new power, nor advances, but her refusal to be a helpmate for a household Father and her being less appreciative of, less responsive to, and less easily managed in a workplace organized according to patriarchy

(male dominance in heterosexual relations and in the family) undermines the authority, position, and material needs of men who have power over her. Empirical studies of attitudes toward and dislike of lesbians and gay men tend to confirm this line of reasoning. For example, Mary Reige Laner and Roy H. Laner, "Sexual Preference or Personal Style? Why Lesbians Are Disliked," *Journal of Homosexuality* (Summer 1980), 5:339–356, in their study of 511 junior-college students, find that "hypofeminine" lesbians are disliked more than "hyperfeminine" or "feminine" lesbians; however, Michael D. Storms, "Attitudes Toward Homosexuality and Femininity in Men," *Journal of Homosexuality* (1978), 3:257–263, in his study of 258 college students, finds that respondents dislike "masculine" homosexual men more than "feminine" homosexual men. That lesbians would violate appropriate gender-role behavior at all appears to be a cause for the most serious dislike of them; however, that gay men might not readily appear deviant, and therefore not be easily identified and dismissed from the ranks of "real" men, seems to be the cause for the most serious dislike of them. Another study by Christopher L. San Miguel and Jim Milham, "The Role of Cognitive and Situational Variables in Aggression Toward Homosexuals," pp. 11–27, a simulated experiment involving 156 male college students, finds that "homosexuals who are perceived by a heterosexual as personally similar to himself are likely to experience heightened rather than diminished aggressiveness from that person."

Lesbian theologians Carter Heyward and Mary E. Hunt, "Roundtable Discussion: Lesbianism and Feminist Theology," *Journal of Feminist Studies in Religion* (1986), 2:97, write, "Lesbianism is the enemy of the dominant social order, for it embodies the potential collapse of power relations structured to secure men's control of women's bodies, and thereby, women's lives. Whether or not she intends to represent the demise of heterosexism (i.e., is a 'political' lesbian) or is conscious of being a representative of women's power (i.e., is a feminist), the lesbian woman signals that which our society does not gladly tolerate: women who submit willingly to men's definitions of 'women.' As representatives of women whose creativity is generated and whose power is called forth in relation to women, the lesbian is outlaw in heterosexist society. This is why the social (and internalized) pressures are formidable to keep lesbians in the closet—ashamed, afraid, silent."

See also Adrienne Rich, "Compulsory Heterosexuality and Lesbian Existence," pp. 631–660; Lorde, "Scratching the Surface," pp. 45–52; and Beth Schneider, "Peril and Promise: Lesbians' Workplace Participation," in Darty and Potter, eds., *Women-Identified Women*, pp. 211–230, and "Consciousness About Sexual Harassment Among Heterosexual and Lesbian Women Workers," *Journal of Social Issues* (1982), 38:75–98.

Ruth Simpson, *From the Closets to the Courts: The Lesbian Transition*, p. 69, adds the concern about women as child producers that is perceived by patriarchal standards to be threatened by lesbianism. In her discussion of women "who had 'confessed' their lesbianism to their priests and had been met with crushing denunciation," she reports: "It is painfully interesting to note that while the middle-aged lesbian women who had raised their families and were in some instances past childbearing age were more or less ignored by their clergymen, the younger women—their child-bearing years still ahead of them—were frequently exposed to damaging verbal abuse."

The tendency for lesbians to be less enamored with and to be less likely to copy patriarchal practices in organizations and business is captured by Frances Fitzgerald, "The Castro—Part I" (San Francisco's most visible and prosperous lesbian/gay neighborhood), pp. 59–60: "While gay men built businesses, gay women built communes, both literally and figuratively speaking; that is, while gay-male organizations tended to be rationalized and, in the case of businesses, hierarchical, women's organizations were structured for cooperation and the melding of individuals into the collective enterprise. The most businesslike of lesbian organizations would build in encounter-group techniques as a management strategy; the emotions, they understood, always had to be considered. Liberated gay women, in other words, turned out to be archetypically women, and gay men in the Castro archetypically men—as if somehow each gender had been squared by isolation from the other."

61. Note, for example, the greater frequency of discrimination in the workplace reported by lesbians compared to gay men in Aurand, Addessa, and Bush, *Violence and Discrimination Against Philadelphia Lesbian and Gay People*, pp. 14–15; and Bell and Weinberg, *Homosexualities*, p. 363. See also Schneider, "Consciousness About Sexual Harassment Among Heterosexual and Lesbian Women Workers," pp. 75–98.

62. See Ida B. Wells, in Alfreda M. Duster, ed., *Crusade for Justice: The Autobiography of Ida B. Wells* (Chicago: University of Chicago Press, 1970; reprint ed., 1972); and James Elbert Cutler, *Lynch-Law: An Investigation into the History of Lynching in the United States* (New York: Longmans, Green, 1905; reprint ed., Montclair, N.J.: Patterson Smith Publishing Corporation, 1969).

63. For a historical summary of violence in labor strikes in the United States, see Philip Taft, "Violence in American Labor disputes," in Marvin E. Wolfgang, ed., *Patterns of Violence* in *Annals of the American Academy of Political and Social Science* (1966), 365:127–148; for an account of the steel strike of 1919, see Brody, *Labor in Crisis*. For general histories of the labor movement, see Gordon F. Bloom and Herbert R. Northrup, *Economics of Labor Relations* (Homewood, Ill.: Richard D. Irwin, 1950; 7th ed., 1973), pp. 33–69; and Aronowitz, *False Promises*.

64. See Gunnar Myrdal, *An American Dilemma: The Negro Problem and Modern Democracy* (New York: Harper & Row, 1944; 20th anniversary ed., 1962), pp. 560–568; Wells, *Crusade for Justice*, pp. xix, 47–52, 70–71; Davis, *Women, Race, and Class*, pp. 110–126; and Studs Terkel's interview with C. P. Ellis, " 'Why I Quit the Klan,' " *Southern Exposure* (Durham, N.C.), Summer 1980, pp. 95–100.

65. See, for example, Brody, *Labor in Crisis*, pp. 132–133, 149–154, 158, 160–163; Richard Edwards, *Contested Terrain: The Transformation of the*

Workplace in the Twentieth Century (New York: Basic Books, 1979), pp. 53, 58–59, 63–65, 175; Aronowitz, *False Promises,* pp. 264–290, and Braverman, *Labor and Monopoly Capital,* pp. 284–289.

The movement of marginalized or Alien men into and/or through Daughter-type employment has historically created tension and insecurity within the economy. Marginalized or Alien men employed as Daughters attempt in time to exercise the patriarchal privilege associated with their gender. They seek to become Brothers. Immune to the shifting of low-paying jobs among Daughters and Aliens, established Brothers are free to compete among themselves for higher-paying, higher-status, more secure jobs. Competition among Brothers in the professional, managerial, technical, and heavy industry realm is acceptable behavior; but when Daughters or Aliens attempt to enter the competition, violence to repel them is acceptable.

66. Fitzgerald, "The Castro—Part I," pp. 69–70.

67. As noted in the Conclusion of chapter 1, community leaders and directors of anti-violence projects have claimed for a number of years that the rate of anti-gay/lesbian violence has been increasing. See, for example, Violence Project, National Gay and Lesbian Task Force, "Anti-Gay Violence, Victimization and Defamation in 1987," pp. 6–7; William R. Greer, "Violence Against Homosexuals Rising, Groups Seeking Wider Protection Say," *New York Times,* November 23, 1986; and James Kim, "Are Homosexuals Facing an Ever More Hostile World?" *New York Times,* July 3, 1988, section 4, p. 16. Their claims have been based for the most part on impression and increased self-reporting by victims, but not on longitudinal studies of representative samples of lesbians and gay men. However, an updated study by Larry Gross, Steven K. Aurand, and Rita Addessa, *Violence and Discrimination Against Lesbian and Gay People in Philadelphia and the Commonwealth of Pennsylvania: A Study by the Philadelphia Lesbian and Gay Task Force,* June 1988, p. 36, compares rates of violence for 1983–1984 using a sample of lesbians and gay men in Philadelphia with rates of violence for 1986–1987 using a similar sample. The study finds that rates increased from 24 percent to 46 percent of gay men and from 10 percent to 20 percent of lesbians sampled. See also Dick Stingel, "CUAV Assault Report Survey and Analysis, 01/79–02/80," (San Francisco: Community United Against Violence), who reports under "Hospital Data" the following: "Dr. Fleming, head of the Primary Care Unit (Emergency Room) at Franklin Hospital [in San Francisco], reports that his statistics reflect a *105% increase* in cases related to anti-Gay assaults from January to February 1980." San Francisco District Attorney Arlo Smith, "Dealing with Anti-Gay Violence: 'Homosexual Panic' Defense Is Bigotry in Action," *Bay Area Reporter,* November 3, 1983, pp. 1, 11, also reports, "While the overall number of street attacks in San Francisco has been declining, the number of attacks on Lesbians and Gays has been increasing."

See also Violence Project, National Gay and Lesbian Task Force, "Anti-Gay Violence, Victimization and Defamation in 1988" p. 11, which reports, "In New York City, the police Bias Incident Investigating Unit documented a 79% rise in the number of reported anti-gay crimes in 1988, *the largest increase of any type of bias crime in that city last year.*" Statistics showing decreases in incidents against black people, but not against Asian people and lesbians and gay men, were reported for 1986 in "Gaybashing Complaint Filed Against Boston Firefighters," *Our Paper* (Portland, Maine), March 1987, p. 3.

68. The discussion in chapter 1 highlights an incident in 1972 involving forty-one-year-old Michael Maye, president of the Uniformed Firefighters Association, who was subsequently charged by a Manhattan grand jury with harassment because he "struck, shoved and kicked" a member of the Gay Activists Alliance at a public event in the New York Hilton Hotel. For coverage of the case, see Lacey Fosburgh, "Maye Held as Harasser in Gay Alliance Fracas," *New York Times,* May 23, 1972; Eric Pace, "Official Accuses Maye of Assault: City Aide Says He Saw Gay Intruder Being Attacked," *New York Times,* April 25, 1972; Michael Kramer, "Fireman's Brawl," *New York,* May 22, 1972, pp. 6–7; and Calvin Trillin, "A Few Observations on the Zapping of the Inner Circle," pp. 64–69.

69. See, for example, as cited in notes in chapter 3 Carmen Vaszuez, *Quarterly Reports: January 1984 to March 1986* (San Francisco: Community United Against Violence), whose statistics show that over a twenty-six-month period the monthly rates of perpetrators by age are approximately the same: 46 percent (under twenty years of age), 27 percent (twenty to thirty years of age), 16 percent (over thirty years of age), and 11 percent (ages unknown). An earlier report by Stingel, "CUAV Assault Report Survey and Analysis 01/79–02/80," p. 2, shows that only 3 percent of reported perpetrators were over thirty years of age. This comparison must be made with the understanding that CUAV's data gathering, statistical analysis, and reporting procedures changed significantly from the time of the earlier report to the time of Vazquez's reports; Stingel's figures do not include anti-property (arson, robbery, vandalism) perpetrators.

The most recent statistics from CUAV, as reported in *The CUAV Dish* (Newsletter for the Friends of Community United Against Violence), April 1988, p. 2, show that for the third and fourth quarters of 1987, 52 percent and 60 percent, respectively, of the perpetrators were twenty-five years of age or younger.

70. See, for example, as noted in chapters 2 and 3, the testimony of Dick Stingel, chairman of the Community United Against Violence (CUAV), at San Francisco Board of Supervisors, Committee on Fire, Safety and the Police, "Four-Hour Public Hearing on Queerbashing," October 9, 1980 (transcript of testimony edited for broadcast on KSAN-FM's Gay Life Program and aired October 18, 19; November 9, 16 of 1980, available from Lesbian and Gay Associated Engineers and Scientists; Sunnyvale, California). Stingel states that CUAV believes that the increase is due in part to the "greater awareness of suburbia of us [lesbians and gay men] and of the [newly developing lesbian/gay neighborhood in] the Castro area [of San Francisco]." He, also, observes that the rate of reported incidents leaped at the end of April, perhaps not coincidentally with the airing of the CBS special "Gay Power, Gay Politics" on April 26, 1980. The program's focus on the lesbian/gay community in San Francisco and its negative portrayal of lesbian/gay life-styles are considered by gay/lesbian activists to be related to this increase in reports of violence.

A gay friend, who lived in Minneapolis at the time of the city council's passing a gay/lesbian rights ordinance, told me that attacks by young men on the street, subsequent to passage, became so frequent that to go out for a violence-free night of recreation he and friends would go to the clubs in nearby St. Paul, which did not have such an ordinance.

71. See Thomas Morgan, "Mainstream Strategy for AIDS Group," *New York Times,* July 22, 1988, pp. B1, B4; and Jason DeParle, "Rash, Rude, Effective, ACT-Up Gains AIDS Shifts," *New York Times,* January 3, 1990, pp. B1, B4.

72. See Peter Freiberg, "Frankly, Scarlett . . . Gay concerns Fail to Catch Fire at the Democrats' Atlanta Convention," *Advocate* (Loss Angeles), August 30, 1988, pp. 11–13; and "Elections in Brief" and Chris Bull, "Gays Bask in Dinkins Win: New York Mayor-Elect took Several Pro-Gay Positions," *Advocate* (Los Angeles), December 19, 1989, pp. 14–15.

73. See Roger A. Edmonson, "Just Doing His Thing: Mayor Gerald Ulrich Is a Reluctant Celebrity," *Advocate* (Los Angeles), April 25, 1989, pp. 44–46; Peter Freiberg, "Albany Man May Be First Black Gay City Official," *Advocate* (Los Angeles), October 24, 1989, p. 16; Mark O'Neill, "Parliamentary Procedure: Svend Robinson, Canadian MP, Stages a Successful Coming Out," *Advocate* (Los Angeles), May 24, 1989, pp. 32, 34; and "Elections in Brief," *Advocate* (Los Angeles), December 19, 1989, p. 15.

Even a heterosexual politician may lose an election because he supports lesbian/gay rights. See, for example, the analysis by Mab Segrest, "Gay Baiting: Anatomy of an Election," *Gay Community News,* of the 1984 U.S. Senate race between North Carolina's two-term governor Jim Hunt and its senior senator Jesse Helms.

74. Alfred C. Kinsey, Wardell B. Pomeroy, and Clyde E. Martin, *Sexual Behavior in the Human Male,* p. 630.

75. Kinsey, Pomeroy, and Martin, *Sexual Behavior in the Human Male,* pp. 383–384, unlike their otherwise meticulously documented conclusions, offer the following without evidence of supporting data and by way of admitting that findings "indicate basic differences in attitudes toward [homosexual] activity; but we are not sure that we yet understand what these differences are": "The highest incidences of the homosexual . . . are in the group which most often verbalizes its disapproval of such activity. This is in the group that goes into high school but never beyond in its educational career. These are the males who most often condemn the homosexual, most often ridicule and express disgust for such activity, and most often punish other males for their homosexuality. And yet, this is the group which has the largest amount of overt homosexual activity. Their involvement may be due to curiosity, to the fact that one may profit financially by accepting homosexual relations, or to the fact that one may derive a sadistic satisfaction from beating up the partner after orgasm has been achieved in the homosexual activity. In a certain segment of this group the idea is more or less accepted that one may uphold their heterosexual mores while 'playing the queers,' provided one punishes them after orgasm is achieved in the homosexual relation. As a group these males may strenuously deny that their sexual contacts have anything to do with homosexuality; but the full and complete record

indicates that many of them have stronger psychic reactions to other males than they care to admit. When they no longer find themselves being paid for such contacts, many of them begin paying other males for the privilege of sexual relations."

See also Ireland, "Rendezvous in the Ramble," p. 41, for comments by John Money, "a pediatrician and past president of the Society for the Scientific Study of Sex, . . . professor of medical psychology at Johns Hopkins University, chief of its Gender Identity Clinic, and co-editor of the five-volume *Handbook of Sexology*," who is quoted as saying: "In every case of this type I've seen in 30 years of work in this field, I have found such young men, on the one hand, attracted to homosexuality *and* acting it out. On the other, they try to destroy it. I call this the 'exorcist syndrome.' . . . The folkways of our culture fill our young people with images of homosexuals as sick, evil, less than human. There are so many signals from the home, the school, the church—and from the media —which make homosexuality the daily butt of television humor and have given such publicity to Anita Bryant and her gays-are-child-molesters campaign as to legitimize her views in the eyes of our youth. . . . At the same time, the law epitomizes this attitude. The very fact that our laws make homosexuality a crime validates the idea that "queers" are animals. . . . So . . . when teenagers see something evil about themselves, one way to get rid of the evil is to destroy it." Recounting a case from early in his research involving a gang of youths attacking lone gay men, he says, "These kids had already had sex with the men, but those who serviced them were objects, not people. By the way, I have stayed in touch with those kids, now men, for a quarter of a century. They are married with children, and their families do not know to this day that these men still seek out and engage in homosexual activity." Money's caseload does not necessarily represent the full range of perpetrators and is likely to include only the most severe cases, that is, those who come to the attention of law enforcement and social service agencies.

See also Katz, "1949, Summer: James Baldwin: A 'Panic . . . Close to Madness,' " *Gay/Lesbian Almanac*, p. 647, who writes, "An essay title "Preservation of Innocence; Studies for a New Morality" was published in Tangier, Morocco, in a small-circulation journal, *Zero*, by the twenty-five-year-old James Baldwin. . . . Baldwin points to a link between an uneasy, unfulfilled masculinity and violence, naming a 'panic . . . close to madness' caused not, certainly by 'homosexuality,' but by terror at 'sexual activity between men.' That terror is still too little understood in this society; it is the horror of the male who must annihilate the homosexual in order to destroy that possibility in himself." Bibliographic information is given, p. 719 n. 55, as follows: James Baldwin, "Preservation of Innocence: Studies for a New Morality," *Zero* (Tangier, Morocco), 1(2):14–22.

Most perpetrators give as the reason for their actions "going along with the crowd" or "because everyone else was doing it." See Eric Rofes, "Queer Bashing: The Politics of Violence Against Gay Men," pp. 8–9, who interviews two former perpetrators, one a currently self-identified gay man, the other a man who has never self-identified as gay. The former states: "I guess I was so afraid of people knowing the truth about me that I had to prove I wasn't a fag by beating up fags in the neighborhood. . . . Those days are behind me, thank God. It was the only way I could deal with myself in Brooklyn, by going along with the crowd. I feel bad that I joined in the beatings but if I didn't they'd call me queer too. I couldn't have taken that." According to Rofes, the latter "when asked if he harbors any homosexual feelings himself . . . claims to have never been sexually involved with a man and, furthermore, 'I wasn't doing it because I was homosexual, but because everyone else was doing it.' "

76. See, for example, Rofes, "Queer Bashing," pp. 8–9, 11, for the following information from his interviews with former perpetrators: "Another ex-queer basher, Jack Olson, grew up in Chicago, did his share of queer bashing, got married, and is now living in Chicago's North Shore suburbs with his wife and two children. . . . Olson's queer bashing days ended in his early twenties when he 'got a real job' and settled down."

77. State of New York, *Governor's Task Force on Bias-Related Violence*, p. 97.

Findings from my survey of lesbians and gay men support the notion that lesbians and gay men are the most vulnerable of groups within the Alien Category. Lesbian/gay respondents of color were asked if they feared more for their physical safety because of their sexual orientation, their racial identity, or both equally. Forty-five percent said their sexual orientation put them at greater risk; 24 percent said their racial identity did; and 31 percent said that both did equally.

5. A BIBLICAL PERSPECTIVE

1. The latter four (all in the New Testament) involve only a single term (the meaning of which is unclear but appears to refer to some kind of homosexual activity) among a formulaic list of "vices." Two of the passages, both in the Letters of Paul, are often discussed as possible references to and disapproval of homosexuality. In the First Letter of Paul to the Corinthians (6:9–10) and in the First Letter of Paul to Timothy (1:9–10), the meaning of the Greek term *arsenokoites* (literally, "one who lies with a male") is not clear; the term is variously understood and translated by biblical scholars. Robin Scroggs, *The New Testament and Homosexuality: Contextual Background for Contemporary Debate* (Philadelphia: Fortress Press, 1983), pp. 101–109, 118–121, concludes that because of the term's immediate proximity to others that mean "effeminate callboy," "thieves," "male prostitute," and "slave-dealer," the disapproval expressed in these passages is not of "homosexuality in general, not even pederasty in general, but that specific form of pederasty which consisted of enslaving boys or youths for sexual purposes, and the use of these boys by adult males." See also Derrick Sherwin Bailey, *Homosexuality and the Western Christian Tradition* (London: Longmans, Green, 1955), pp. 37–40; John Boswell, *Christianity, Social Tolerance, and Homosexuality: Gay People in Western Europe from the Beginning of the Christian Era to the Fourteenth Century* (Chicago: University of Chicago Press, 1980; Phoenix, 1981), pp. 106–107; George R. Edwards,

Gay/Lesbian Liberation: A Biblical Perspective, pp. 81–85, 100–102; and John J. McNeill, *The Church and the Homosexual*, pp. 50–53.

2. See Bailey, *Homosexuality and the Western Christian Tradition*, pp. 29–61; Boswell, *Christianity, Social Tolerance, and Homosexuality*, pp. 91–117; Edwards, *Gay/Lesbian Liberation;* E. Lawrence Gibson, *The Sodom Syndrome* (New York: New York Gay News, 1978); McNeill, *The Church and the Homosexual*, pp. 37–66; Scroggs, *The New Testament and Homosexuality*, pp. 1–16; and Gerald T. Sheppard, "The Use of Scripture Within the Christian Ethical Debate Concerning Same-Sex Oriented Persons," pp. 13–35.

3. See Boswell, *Christianity, Social Tolerance, and Homosexuality*, pp. 113–117; Sheppard, "The Use of Scripture"; and Scroggs, *The New Testament and Homosexuality*, pp. 71–73.

4. Herbert G. May and Bruce M. Metzger, eds. *The New Oxford Annotated Bible with the Apocrypha*, Revised Standard Version (New York: Oxford University Press, 1977), pp. 145, 148.

5. See Boswell, *Christianity, Social Tolerance, and Homosexuality*, pp. 99–101; Edwards, *Gay/Lesbian Liberation*, pp. 54–64; Scroggs, *The New Testament and Homosexuality*, pp. 70–71; and George F. Genung, "The Book of Leviticus," *An American Commentary on the Old Testament* (American Baptist Publication Society, 1905), p. 80.

6. See Martin Noth, *Leviticus: A Commentary*, J. E. Anderson, trans., Old Testament Library (Philadelphia: Westminster Press, 1965), p. 1433.

7. See Deuteronomy 23:17; 1 Kings 14:24; 15:12; 22:45; 2 Kings 23:7; and Job 36:14; and commentary by Boswell, *Christianity, Social Tolerance, and Homosexuality*, pp. 99 and 101, n. 34; Bailey, *Homosexuality and the Western Christian Tradition*, p. 53; and Edwards, *Gay/Lesbian Liberation*, pp. 54–57. Edwards evidence that the male temple prostitutes performed homosexually because "under patriarchy, only male members of the congregation were participants in ritual proceedings" is contradicted within the book of Leviticus itself (e.g., the purification ritual prescribed for childbirth and menstruation [12:1–8; 15:19–30].

8. Boswell, *Christianity, Social Tolerance, and Homosexuality*, p. 114. See also McNeill, *The Church and the Homosexual*, pp. 42–50. Subsequent passages within scripture itself refer to Sodom for having violated standards of hospitality (Isaiah 1:10–23; Ezekiel 16:48–49; Matthew 10:14–15; and Luke 10:1–12) or for sexual sin in general, not same-sex activity specifically (Jeremiah 23:14; Zephaniah 2:8–11; 2 Peter 2:6–14).

9. Boswell, *Christianity, Social Tolerance, and Homosexuality*, p. 112. See also Bailey, *Homosexuality and the Western Christian Tradition*, pp. 40–41.

10. *The New Oxford Annotated Bible*, p. 1362.

11. See McNeill, *The Church and the Homosexual*, p. 57.

12. See Bernadette J. Brooten, "Paul's Views on the Nature of Women and Female Homoeroticism," in Clarissa W. Atkinson, Constance H. Buchanan, and Margaret R. Miles, eds., *Immaculate and Powerful: The Female in Sacred Image and Social Reality*, (Boston: Beacon Press, 1985), pp. 61–87.

Biblical scholars have not articulated a convincing explanation for the absence from the two verses in Leviticus of any mention of female homosexuality. See Edwards, *Gay/Lesbian Liberation*, pp. 26, 85–86; and Scroggs, *The New Testament and Homosexuality*, pp. 140–144. That the document is addressed to men or that women were invisible in ancient Hebrew society are inadequate because rules and penalties are elsewhere prescribed for women (e.g., for childbirth, menstruation, adultery, incest, bestiality, sorcery, harlotry [Leviticus 12; 15:19–30; 20:10, 11, 16, 27; 21:9]). With the exception of Romans 1:18–32, women are also excluded from the other possible biblical references to homosexuality.

13. For discussion of Jewish literature and rabbinical thought, see Brooten, "Paul's Views on the Nature of Women and Female Homoeroticism," in Atkinson, Buchanan, and Miles, *Immaculate and Powerful*, pp. 63–65; Scroggs, *The New Testament and Homosexuality*, pp. 76–78, 80, 81, 85–86, 88–89, 90; Bailey, *Homosexuality and the Western Christian Tradition*, pp. 61–63; and Ruben Schindler, "Homosexuality, the Halacha, and the Helping Professions," *Journal of Religion and Health* (1979), 18:132–138.

For discussion of post-Constantinian regulations, see Walter Barnett, *Sexual Freedom and the Constitution: An Inquiry into the Constitutionality of Repressive Sex Laws* (Albuquerque: University of New Mexico Press, 1973), pp. 78–81.

14. Schindler, "Homosexuality, the Halacha, and the Helping Professions," *Journal of Religion and Health* (1979), 18:134; and Brooten, "Paul's Views on the Nature of Women and Female Homoeroticism," in Atkinson, Buchanan, and Miles, *Immaculate and Powerful*, pp. 63–65.

15. Louis Crompton, "Gay Genocide: From Leviticus to Hitler," in Louie Crew, ed., *The Gay Academic* pp. 69, 70, 73–78, 85–91. See also Louis Crompton, "The Myth of Lesbian Impunity: Capital Laws from 1270 to 1791," and Brigette Eriksson, trans., "A Lesbian Execution in Germany, 1721: The Trial Records," in Salvatore J. Licata and Robert P. Petersen, eds., *The Gay Past: A Collection* (New York: Harrington Park Press, 1985), pp. 11–25, 27–40.

16. Crompton, "Gay Genocide: From Leviticus to Hitler," in Crew, ed., *The Gay Academic*, p. 71; Louis Crompton, "Homosexuals and the Death Penalty in Colonial America," *Journal of Homosexuality* (1976), 1:277–293; Jonathan Katz, *Gay American History: Lesbians and Gay Men in the U.S.A.: A Documentary*, pp. 20–22; Jonathan Ned Katz, *Gay/Lesbian Almanac: A New Documentary*, pp. 76–77, 78–82, 101, 107; and Robert Oaks, "Perceptions of Homosexuality by Justices of the Peace in Colonial Virginia," *Journal of Homosexuality* (Fall–Winter 1979/80), 5:35–41, and "Defining Sodomy in Seventeenth-Century Massachusetts," in Licata and Petersen, *The Gay Past*, pp. 79–83.

17. Crompton, "Homosexuals and the Death Penalty in Colonial America," pp. 285–289.

18. *Encyclopedia of Crime and Justice*, 1st ed., "Homosexuality and Crime," by Anthony Russo and Laud Humphreys. See also Barnett, *Sexual Freedom and the Constitution*, pp. 75, 81–82; and Alfred C. Kinsey, Wardell B. Pomeroy, and Clyde E. Martin, *Sexual Behavior in the Human Male*, pp. 465–466, 487.

19. Three diverse examples are illustrative:

1. In her 1969 study of America's sexual underground, Sara Harris interviews "John Sorenson of Miami, Florida . . . a leader of his community, a Baptist church deacon and former head of the Miami vice sqaud" and "one of the most sought-after speakers by neighborhood and PTA groups." Sorenson, who considers homosexuality the "supreme abomination in God's eyes," would "put the homosexual in prison . . . [to take] him out of circulation" and reinstate the death penalty to bring a "stop to this whole thing [social problem]." He cites Leviticus 20:13 to justify his position. Sara Harris, *The Puritan Jungle: America's Sexual Underground*, pp. 169–175.
2. In 1971 the California state assembly defeated a bill that would have decriminalized anal–genital and oral–genital contacts between consenting adults in private. "Representative arguments from the bill's opponents during floor debate . . . [invoked the Bible] citing Leviticus 18:22." Barnett, *Sexual Freedom and the Constitution*, pp. 91–92, n. 48.
3. In 1976 the "Virginia Supreme Court quoted Leviticus" in upholding a district court's decision that the state's crimes-against-nature statute could be applied to private homosexual relations between consenting adults. William Paul, "Minority Status for Gay People: Majority Reaction and Social Context," in William Paul, James D. Weinrich, John C. Gonsiorek, and Mary E. Hotvedt, eds., *Homosexuality: Social, Psychological, and Biological Issues*, p. 364. See also Donald C. Knutson, "Introduction" to special issue on "Homosexuality and the Law," *Journal of Homosexuality* (Fall–Winter 1979/80), 5:5–24; and *Doe* v. *Commonwealth's Attorney for the City of Richmond*, 403 F. Supp. 1199 (E.D. Va. 1975), aff'd, 425 U.S. 901 (1976), as discussed in *Encyclopedia of Crime and Justice*, 1st ed., s.v. "Homosexuality and Crime," by Russo and Humphreys.

20. Congregation for the Doctrine of the Faith, "Letter to the Bishops of the Catholic Church on the Pastoral Care of Homosexual Persons," adopted in an ordinary session of the Congregation on the Doctrine of the Faith; given at Rome, October 1, 1986; approved and ordered to be published by Pope John Paul II during an audience granted to Prefect Joseph Cardinal Ratzinger; also, bearing name of Alberto Bovone, Titular Archbishop of Caesarea in Numdia, Secretary (Vatican City: Congregation for the Doctrine of Faith, 1986), p. 6.

21. *"Bowers* v. *Hardwick"* [excerpts from *Bowers* v. *Hardwick*, 106 U.S. 2841 (1986)], in Christine Pierce and Donald VanDeVeer, eds., *AIDS: Ethics and Public Policy*, (Belmont, Calif.: Wadsworth Publishing Company, 1988), pp. 219–229.

22. Arthur S. Leonard, "Getting Beyond *Hardwick,*" *New York Native*, September 1, 1986, p. 20; and NGLTF, "Anti-Gay Violence, Victimization and Defamation in 1986" (Washington, D.C.: National Gay and Lesbian Task Force, 1987), p. 5.

23. Congregation for the Doctrine of the Faith, "Letter to the Bishops of the Catholic Church on the Pastoral Care of Homosexual Persons," pp. 8–9. For an example of this policy in practice see Ari L. Goldman, "Cardinal Faults Recent

Attacks on Gay People: Advocates Praise Stand as an Important Step," *New York Times*, September 12, 1988, p. B3.

24. See Jeannine Grammick, "Prejudice, Religion, and Homosexual People," in Robert Nugent, ed., *A Challenge to Love: Gay and Lesbian Catholics in the Church* (New York: Crossroad Publishing Company, 1983), p. 11; Eugene E. Levitt and Albert D. Klassen, "Public Attitudes Toward Homosexuality: Part of the 1970 National Survey by the Institute for Sex Research," *Journal of Homosexuality* (1974),1:41; and Kinsey, Pomeroy, and Martin, *Sexual Behavior in the Human Male*, pp. 483, 631.

25. Kinsey, Pomeroy, and Martin, *Sexual Behavior in the Human Male*, p. 487.

26. Scroggs, *The New Testament and Homosexuality*, pp. v–viii.

27. See Noth, *Leviticus*, pp. 146–151.

28. Noth, *Leviticus*, pp. 9–10, 136, 138–139, 146, 159, 162, 163, 165–166. See also Genung, *The Book of Leviticus* p. v.

The following terms occur with the following frequency: *statutes* (twenty-four times), 3:17; 7:34; 10:9, 11; 16:29, 32, 34; 17:7; 18:4, 5, 26; 19:37; 20:8, 22; 23:14, 21, 31; 23:41; 24:3; 25:18; 26:3, 15, 43, 46; *laws* (fifteen times), 6:25, 7:1, 7, 11, 37–38; 11:46; 12:7; 13:59; 14:2, 32, 54, 57; 15:3, 32; 26:46; *ordinances* (twelve times), 5:10; 9:16; 18:4, 5, 26; 19:37; 20:22; 25:18; 26:3, 15, 43, 46; *covenant* (ten times), 2:13; 24:8; 26:9, 15, 25, 42(3X), 44, 45; and *commandments* (five times), 22:31; 26:3, 14, 15; 27:34. They are decreed "forever," "throughout your generation," and/or "in all your dwelling places" in 3:17; 6:18, 22; 7:34, 36; 10:9, 15; 16:29, 32, 34; 17:7; 22:3; 23:14, 21, 31, 41; 24:2, 3, 4, 8, 9.

For examples of the introductory formula, see 1:1–2; 4:1–2; 7:22, 28; 11:1–2; 12:1–2; 15:1–2; 17:1–2; 18:1–2; 19:1–2; 20:1–2; 22:1–2, 17–18; 23:1–2, 9–10, 23–24, 33–34; 24:1–2, 13–15; 25:1; 27:1. It occurs twenty-one times. "And Yahweh spoke to Moses" appears without " 'Say to the people of Israel' " fourteen additional times: 5:14; 6:1, 8, 19, 24; 8:1; 13:1; 14:1, 33; 16:1, 2; 21:1, 16; 22:26.

For examples of the concluding formula see 7:38; 16:34; 22:31–33; 24:23; 26:46; 27:34. See also a more abbreviated form in 8:4, 5, 9, 21, 29, 34, 35; 10:13, 15, 18; 17:2; 24:2.

29. See S. R. Driver, "The Book of Leviticus," *The Sacred Books of the Old and New Testaments* (New York: Dodd, Mead, 1898), p. 97.

30. *The New Oxford Annotated Bible*, pp. 146, 147.

31. See, for example, Mordecai Rosenfeld, "Sodom and the Constitution," *New York Law Journal*, October 7, 1986; and Robert Morris, *Rethinking Social Welfare: Why Care for the Stranger?* (New York: Longman, 1986), pp. 65–81.

32. For references to term *ger*, see 16:29; 17:8, 10, 12, 13, 15; 18:26; 19:10, 33, 34(3X); 20:2; 22:18; 23:22; 24:16, 22; 25:6, 23, 45, 47(3X). See also *toshav*, which is sometimes identical with *ger*, e.g., 25:6 (verb form), 23, 35, 45 (verb form), 47(2X), and sometimes distinguished as less assimilated, e.g., 22:10,

40. For discussion of the term *ger,* see Noth, *Leviticus,* pp. 131, 144; Roland de Vaux, *Ancient Israel,* vol. 1, *Social Institutions* (New York: McGraw-Hill, 1961; 1965), pp. 74–76; Norman K. Gottwald, *The Tribes of Yahweh: A Sociology of the Religion of Liberated Israel, 1250–1050 B.C.E.* (Maryknoll, N.Y.: Orbis Books, 1979), p. 291; Mayer Sulzberger, *The Status of Labor in Ancient Israel* (Philadelphia: Dropsie College for Hebrew and Cognate Learning, 1923), pp. 16, 21–22, 49, 51, 63–65, 86, and particularly for discussion of advance in status from earlier to later times, 25–26, 117–121; John Peter Lange, "Exodus; or, The Second Book of Moses," Charles M. Mead, trans., *A Commentary on the Holy Scriptures,* vol. 2 (New York: Scribner, Armstrong and Company, 1876), p. 145; Driver, "The Book of Leviticus," *The Sacred Books of the Old and New Testaments,* p. 87; and A. R. S. Kennedy, *Leviticus and Numbers* (Edinburgh: T. C. E. and E. C. Jack, 1938), p. 122.

For references to "one law for both native and sojourner," see 16:29; 17:8, 10, 12, 13, 15; 18:26. The only exception suggesting different status between sojourner and native is in 25:46: "You may make slaves of them, but over your brethren the people of Israel you shall not rule, one over another, with harshness." See also Sulzberger, *The Status of Labor in Ancient Israel,* pp. 59–86, 117–121; and in Kennedy, *Leviticus and Numbers,* p. 162, references to Exodus 12:49; Numbers 9:14; 15:15, 29, and p. 132, reference to the *ger* as a "fellowworshipper of Israel's God."

The term *rea'* occurs four times in 19:13, 16, 18; 20:10. The term *'amit* occurs eleven times in 6:2(2X); 19:11, 15, 17; 24:19; 25:14(2X), 15, 17; A. T. Chapman and A. W. Streane, *The Book of Leviticus* (Cambridge: Cambridge University Press, 1914), p. 139, say it is an unusual Hebrew word occurring only once outside of Leviticus in Zechariah 13:7. See also Noth, *Leviticus,* pp. 48–50, 141–142; Gordon J. Wenham, *The Book of Leviticus,* New International Commentary on the Old Testament (Grand Rapids, Mich.: William B. Eerdmans, 1979), pp. 266–267; and Nathaniel Micklem, "The Book of Leviticus," *The Interpreter's Bible,* vol. 2 (Nashville, Tenn.: Abingdon-Cokesbury Press, 1953), p. 86.

For references to the term *zar* and *neykar,* see 22:10 ("An outsider shall not eat of a holy thing."), 22:12 ("If a priest's daughter is married to an outsider she shall not eat of the offering of the holy things."), 22:13 ("Yet no outsider shall eat of [the holy thing]."); and 22:25 ("Neither shall you offer as the bread of your God any such animals gotten from a foreigner").

33. Wenham, *The Book of Leviticus,* p. 18. See also Noth, *Leviticus,* pp. 16–17, 151, 160; Mary Douglas, *Purity and Danger: An Analysis of Concepts of Pollution and Taboo* (London: Routledge and Kegan Paul, 1966; 1979), pp. 49–51; Robert North, Sociology of the Biblical Jubilee, (Rome: Pontifical Biblical Institute, 1954), pp. 222–223; S. H. Kellogg, *The Book of Leviticus,* (London: Hodder and Stoughton, 1891), p. 503; James L. Mays, *Leviticus, Numbers* (London: SCM Press, 1963, pp. 55–66; Micklem, "The Book of Leviticus," *The Interpreter's Bible,* vol. 2, pp. 87, 88; and Kennedy, *Leviticus and Numbers,* pp. 124–125.

34. See its use also in 10:10 and 11:47. See also the term *nazer,* "to separate, restrain, or dedicate," in 15:31 and 22:2, and *cherem,* "devoted" or "most holy," in 27:28.

35. *The New Oxford Annotated Bible,* p. 148.

36. For other references to separation from other nations, see 18:24, 28; 20:23; 25:44; 26:33, 38, 45.

For discussion and commentary on "cleanness" regulations, see Noth, *Leviticus,* pp. 89–126; Wenham, *The Book of Leviticus,* pp. 161–238; Norman K. Gottwald, *The Hebrew Bible—A Socio-Literary Introduction* (Philadelphia: Fortress Press, 1985), pp. 473–477; Mays, *Leviticus, Numbers,* pp. 44–54; and Douglas, *Purity and Danger,* pp. 41–57.

A theme of "inside/outside," in which inside is good or holy and outside is bad or unholy, runs through Leviticus. For example: "outside the camp," 4:11– 12, 21; 6:11; 8:17; 9:11; 16:27 (waste from sacrifices); 10:4–5 (bodies of priests who erred); 13:46 (leper); 14:3 (priest to examine leper); 24:14, 23 (the one who cursed Yahweh); "into the camp," 14:8 (leper after cleansing); 16:26, 28 (after letting scapegoat go and bathing and washing clothes); "not to go out of sanctuary," 21:12 (chief priest to visit dead); "outside of the city," 14:40, 41, 45, 53 (infected parts of leper's house); "in the holy place" vs. "into the wilderness," 16:2–3 (Aaron), 20–22 (scapegoat); "vomit/cast out of the land those who defile themselves," 18:24–25, 28; 20:22, 23; "into the land of Canaan" (promised land), 14:34; 18:3; 20:22; 23:10; 25:2(2X); "out of the land of Egypt" (slavery), 11:45; 18:3; "come into, bring to, or bring before the tent of the meeting," 4:4, 5, 14, 16 (sacrifices); 9:23 (Moses and Aaron); 10:9 (no alcohol); 16:23 (Aaron after sending scapegoat away); 17:5; 19:21 (sacrifices); "not bringing to door of the tent of meeting," 17:4, 9 (blood guilt and cut off from people for not bringing sacrifice); "not to go out from door of the tent of the meeting," 10:7 (priest); "draw near," 9:5, 7, 8 (congregation to Moses, Aaron to Moses and altar); 10:3, 4, 5 (good sons draw near to Aaron bad ones taken out); 16:1 (bad sons of Aaron drew near to Yahweh and died); 21:18, 21, 23 (blemished priests may not draw near to altar); "bring within the veil," 16:2 (Aaron to come with sacrifice), 12, 15 (bad sons of Aaron may not, good sons may); 21:23 (blemished priests may not). Concerning 24:14, 23, a passage in which the one who curses Yahweh is brought outside the camp and stoned to death, see Micklem, "The Book of Leviticus," *The Interpreter's Bible,* vol. 2, p. 119, who writes, " 'the whole ceremony is purgative, not judicial,' i.e., the thought underlying it is not the fitting of the penalty to the crime but the removal, as it were, of a spot of infection from the community."

For references to "cutting off," see Leviticus 7:20, 21, 25, 27 (for "uncleanness" in eating); 17:4, 9, 10, 14 (for not bringing sacrifice to central place of worship and for eating blood); 18:29 (for any of "abominations" in chapter 18, mostly sexual, also wizardry and sacrificing to other god); 20:3, 5, 6, 17, 18 (similar to chapter 18); 22:3 (for approaching holy things while "unclean"); 23:29, 30 (for not afflicting oneself or for working on the day of atonement). See also Micklem, "The Book of Leviticus," *The Interpreter's Bible,* vol. 2, pp. 37–38; and Wenham, *The Book of Leviticus,* pp. 233, 241–242, 285–286.

37. North, *Sociology of the Biblical Jubilee,* pp. 114, 143–147, 155–158, 165–167, 173, 215; and Noth, *Leviticus,* p. 187.

Biblical passages quoted form *The New Oxford Annotated Bible,* pp. 97, 154.

For comparison of Exodus 23:10–11 and Leviticus 25:1–7 see Noth, *Leviticus,* pp. 185–189; and Kennedy, *The Book of Leviticus,* p. 172.

See H. Eberhard von Waldow, "Social Responsibility and Social Structure in Early Israel," *Catholic Biblical Quarterly* (1970), 32:182–204, who includes in his discussion a citation of the three-membered formula of sojourner–widow–orphan in Deuteronomy 10:18; 16:11, 14; 24:19–21; Jeremiah 7:6; 22:3; Ezekiel 22:7; Psalm 94:6; 146:9.

Provisions for feeding the poor *(ani)* are mentioned in Leviticus only in 19:10 and 23:22, but widows and orphans are not mentioned specifically. See Mays, *Leviticus, Numbers,* p. 59; and Genung, "The Book of Leviticus," *An American Commentary on the Old Testament,* p. 80.

Allowances for those "who cannot afford" to participate in cultic practices are prescribed in Leviticus 5:7–13; 12:8; 14:21–32; and 27:8.

38. See Gottwald, *The Hebrew Bible,* pp. 414, 433; Noth, *Leviticus,* pp. 10–15, 129–130; Chapman and Streane, *The Book of Leviticus,* pp. xi–xiii, 156–173; and Martin Noth, *A History of Pentateuchal Traditions,* Bernhard W. Anderson, trans. (Englewood Cliffs, N. J.: Prentice-Hall, 1972), pp. 8–9, 46–62, 271–272.

Among the evidence of the lateness and P characteristics of Leviticus are the following:

1. The appropriation of early legislation and the embellishment of its "original strict phrasing"; for example, Exodus 21:17, "Whoever curses his father or his mother shall be put to death," compared to Leviticus 20:9, "For everyone who curses his father or his mother shall be put to death; he has cursed his father or his mother, his blood is upon him." See Noth, *Leviticus,* pp. 149–150.
2. The expression "the 'anointed' or 'high' priest," which occurs only in Hebrew scripture in Leviticus and signifies the end of the Jewish monarchy and the passing of "anointing" from the king "to the chief priest in Jerusalem who was the remaining representative of the still existing community." Noth, *Leviticus,* pp. 38, 56–57, 126, 153–157. See also Kennedy, *Leviticus and Numbers,* p. 24. For references to the chief priest, see 16:32; 21:10; "anointing," see 4:3, 5, 16; 6:20, 22; 7:36; 8:2, 10, 12, 30; 10:7, 16:2; "consecration," see 7:35, 37; 8:10, 11, 12, 15, 30; and "ordination," see 8:22, 28, 31, 33.
3. Several other references and subject matter that from the perspective of the sojourn at Sinai are anachronistic, presupposing, for example, settled, walled cities after the entry into Canaan (14:33–53; 25:32–34); the sacrifice of animals not available in the wilderness of Sinai (e.g., 1:14–17;

5:7; 12:8); and the socioeconomic conditions of the postmonarchy exile itself (e.g., 24:1–9; 26:27–39) and the period after the exile (e.g., 26:40–45). See Noth, *Leviticus*, pp. 110, 131–132, 176–177, 185, 190, 200, 201; and Micklem, "The Book of Leviticus," *The Interpreter's Bible*, vol. 2, pp. 3, 18, 94.

4. Pervasive throughout the document are "the priest" and "Aaron's sons the priests," those who convey and carry out the instructions. The phrase "and the priest shall" occurs 122 times: 1:12, 13, 15, 17; 2:2, 8, 9, 16; 3:11, 16; 4:6, 7, 10, 17, 20, 25, 26, 30, 31(2X), 34, 35(2X); 5:6, 8, 10, 12, 13, 16, 18; 6:1, 10, 12, 26; 7:5, 7, 8, 31; 12:8; 13:3(2X), 4, 5,(2X), 6(2X), 8(2X), 10, 11, 13, 15, 17(2X), 20(2X), 21, 22, 23, 25(2X), 26, 27(2X), 28, 29(2X), 31, 33, 34, 36, 37, 39, 43, 50, 54, 55; 14:3(2X), 4, 5, 11, 12, 14(2X), 15, 17, 18, 19, 20(2X), 24(2X), 25, 26, 28, 31, 36(2X), 38, 39, 40, 44, 48; 15:15(2X), 30(2X); 17:6; 19:22; 22:15; 23:11, 20; 27:8(2X), 12, 14, 18, 21, 23. An additional mention of "the priest" is made forty-three times: 7:6, 14; 12:6–7, 13:7(2X), 9, 12, 16, 19, 21, 26, 31, 36, 44, 49, 53, 56; 14:1, 13, 18, 23, 29, 35, 36, 48; 15:14, 29; 16:33; 17:5; 21:1, 7, 9, 21; 22:11, 12, 13, 14; 23:10, 20; 27:8, 11, 12, 14. The phrases "Aaron's sons the priests," "Aaron and his sons," and "Sons of Aaron" occur forty-eight times: 1:5, 7, 8, 11; 2:2, 3, 10; 3:2, 5, 8, 13; 6:9, 14, 16, 18, 19, 22, 24; 7:10, 31, 33, 34, 35; 8:2, 13, 14, 18, 22, 27, 30(2X), 31, 36; 9:1, 9, 12, 18; 10:1, 12, 16; 13:2; 21:1, 16, 24; 22:2, 17; 24:9. In 16:3, 6, 8, 9, 21, 23, the phrase "And Aaron shall" appears; the chapter ends with "the priest shall" in 16:32–33.

39. For discussion of the dating of Leviticus, see Noth, *Leviticus*, pp. 10–16, 18, 36, 53, 54, 64, 65, 68–69, 75–76, 91–92, 93, 117–118, 127–128, 136, 138, 140, 146, 149, 153–155, 166–168, 176–177, 179, 185; Driver, "The Book of Leviticus," p. 57; Mickelm, "The Book of Leviticus," *The Interpreter's Bible*, vol. 2, pp. 3–4; Mays, *Leviticus, Numbers*, p. 55; Kennedy, *Leviticus and Numbers*, pp. 15–16, 166; de Vaux, *Ancient Israel: Social Institutions*, vol. 1, p. 48, and *Ancient Israel: Religious Institutions*, vol. 2, p. 482.

For discussion of the P source in Leviticus, see Gottwald, *The Hebrew Bible*, pp. 202–203, 207; Noth, *A History of Pentateuchal Traditions*, pp. 8–9, 271–272; Chapman and Streane, *The Book of Leviticus*, pp. 136, 172–176; Kennedy, *Leviticus and Numbers*, pp. 20–31; Driver, *The Book of Leviticus*, pp. 56–58; and Noth, *Leviticus*, pp. 10–15.

For discussion of the fall of Jerusalem and Cyrus' decree, see Noth, *The History of Israel*, pp. 280–356.

40. Gottwald, *The Hebrew Bible*, p. 423. See also Martin Noth, *The History of Israel* (New York: Harper & Row, 1958; 2d ed., 1960), pp. 282–296.

41. See Gottwald, *The Hebrew Bible*, pp. 424–425, 428–429, 432; and Noth, *The History of Israel*, pp. 302–307, 318.

42. See Gottwald, *The Hebrew Bible*, pp. 437, 460–462, 491.

43. Gottwald, *The Hebrew Bible*, p. 437. See also Noth, *The History of Israel*, pp. 314–315, 317–318, 322–323, 330, 333, 338–339.

44. See Noth, *Leviticus,* pp. 131–132, 179, 187; Gottwald, *The Hebrew Bible,* pp. 424–427, 429–430, 431; and Noth, *THe History of Israel,* pp. 284–286, 289, 291–292, 308, 310, 317, 322, 326–330.

45. See Noth, *The History of Israel,* pp. 297, 330, 314–316, 333, 336–337; Noth, *Leviticus,* pp. 129–130, 165–166, 176–177, 185, 200–201; Gottwald, *The Hebrew Bible,* pp. 424–425, 460–463; and North, *Sociology of the Biblical Jubilee,* pp. 143–144, 158, 222–223.

46. See North, *Sociology of the Biblical Jubilee,* pp. 45, 158, 175; and Noth, *Leviticus,* pp. 140, 183–189.

47. In chapter 23, the "day of atonement," which is discussed in detail in chapter 16, is added to the ancient religious feasts (passover, feast of unleavened bread, and feast of weeks or offering of first fruits) as outlined in Exodus 23:14–17; 34:18, 22, 23 (also, preserved in Deuteronomy 16). These feasts are a "threefold group . . . closely bound up with the natural yearly cycle of agriculture and harvest." By inserting the sabbath law awkwardly into an otherwise coherent catalog of holidays (Leviticus 23:1–3), Leviticus reshapes their schedule and purpose according to a *seven-fold* structure whose aim is sacramental and legislative. Their occurrence is indicated numerically rather than seasonally (e.g., on the "fourteenth day of the month" and "on the morrow after the sabbath" rather than at times of planting and harvesting) and their celebration is ritualized (e.g., "the priest" and "the holy convocation" are introduced and prominent). Having established the *seven-day* sabbath as the scheduling principle for religious holidays, the "feast of weeks" is then discussed and set according to a *seven-week* plan. The next, being Leviticus's own contribution of the "day of atonement," is set to occur in the *seventh month* of the year. The "feast of booths" follows in the same month; its placement here and its rehearsal of Israel's living in booths or tents during the wilderness days of exodus are intended to lend historical credibility to the day of atonement. The progressive scheduling of holidays according to counting by sevens in days, weeks, and then months is completed in chapter twenty-five with the "sabbath of solemn rest for the land" in the *seventh year* and the Jubilee in the year after "seven weeks of seven years, *seven times seven years* . . . forty-nine years." The progression is unified by the Jubilee's commencement on the day of atonement in that year. See Chapman and Streane, *The Book of Leviticus,* pp. 125–128, 172–173; Noth, *Leviticus,* pp. 165–168, 183–185; and North, *Sociology of the Biblical Jubilee,* pp. 3, 38, 45, 86.

The prominence of the number 7 throughout Leviticus and its concentration in chapter 23 (23 percent of total references) accustoms and prepares the reader for its normative use in cultic scheduling. When one gets to chapter 25, counting by 7 to establish the jubilee year is familiar and expected. See Leviticus 4:6, 17; 8:33(2X), 35; 13:4, 5(2X), 6, 21, 26, 27, 31, 32, 33, 34, 50, 51; 14:7, 8, 9, 16, 38, 39, 51; 15:13, 19, 24, 28; 16:14, 19, 29; 22:27; 23:3, 6, 8(2X), 15, 16, 18, 24, 27, 33(2X), 36, 39(2X), 40, 41,(2X), 42; 25:4, 5, 8(4X), 9, 20; 26:18, 21, 27.

The term *yobel,* most often translated as "jubilee" but more accurately as "release" (noun, see North, *Sociology of the Biblical Jubilee,* pp. 176, also 2,

96–108), occurs in Hebrew scripture only in Leviticus; and here its mention is limited to chapter 25 (fourteen times) with echoes in chapter 27 (six times). See Leviticus 25:10, 11, 12, 13, 15, 28(2X), 30, 31, 33, 40, 50, 52, 54; 27:17–18(3X), 21, 23, 24.

Also, three verbs and two nouns, which are not otherwise used in Leviticus, dominate chapters 25 and 27. The verbs are *return (shavab)*, *redeem (ga'al)*, and *release (yatza)*, and their subject and objects are *property (achaza)* and *family (mishpata)*. Two other terms, *land (eretz)* and *field (sadeh)*, occur with considerably greater frequency than earlier in the document.

For *return*, see Leviticus 25:10(2X), 13, 27, 28, 41(2X); 27:24. For *redeem*, see Leviticus 25:24, 25, 26(2X), 29((2X), 30, 31, 32, 33, 48(2X), 49(3X), 51, 52, 54; 27:13, 15, 19, 20(2X), 26, 28, 31. For *release*, see Leviticus 25:28, 30, 31, 33, 50, 54; 27:21.

For *property*, see Leviticus 25:10, 13, 24, 25, 27, 28, 32, 33(2X), 34, 41, 45, 46; 27:16, 21, 22, 24, 28 [also, 14:34(2X)]. For *family*, see Leviticus 25:10, 25, 26(2X), 41, 47, 49, 54.

Land occurs thirty-seven times in chapters 23, 25, 26, and 27, compared to twelve times in the rest of the document; see Leviticus 14:34; 18:25(2X), 27, 28; 19:9, 23, 29(2X), 31, 45; 26:1, 4, 5, 6(3X), 20(2X), 32, 33, 34(3X), 38, 39, 41, 42, 43; 27:24, 30(2X).

Field occurs thirteen times in chapters 23, 25, and 27, compared to twice elsewhere in the document; see Leviticus 19:9, 19; 23:22; 25:12, 31, 34; 27:16, 17, 18, 19, 20, 21, 22, 24, 28.

The term *yobel* first appears as follows: "And you shall hallow the fiftieth year, and proclaim liberty throughout the land to all its inhabitants; it shall be a jubilee [release] for you, when each of you shall return to his property and each of you shall return to his family" (Leviticus 25:10, *The New Oxford Annotated Bible*, p. 154). Chapters 23–27, which develop the concept, provisions, and application of the Year of Release, are replete with efforts to establish historical precedence for it, as evidenced by the greater frequency of references to Egypt, Sinai, the ancient covenant with Yahweh, and the original sabbath law.

Egypt is referred to seven times, compared to five in the rest of the document; see Leviticus 11:45; 18:3; 19:34, 36; 22:33; 23:43; 24:10; 25:38, 42, 55; 26:13, 45. Notice especially the following pattern in chapter 25 for the three cases of "when your brother becomes poor"; (1) condition of poverty stated, (2) resolution prescribed in terms of help by family member, and (3) invocation of jubilee or exodus (25:28, 38), or both (25:40–42, 50–55).

Sinai is referred to three times, compared to twice elsewhere; see Leviticus 7:38(2X); 25:1; 26:46; 27:34. See Noth, *Leviticus*, p. 185, who writes, "Joined immediately to the introduction [25:1, 2], where the name of the mountain at Sinai is unusual and remarkable, and indicates the fundamental quality of the following ordinances, are [verses 2–7], which give the regulations for the sabbatical year."

Covenant is referred to nine times, compared to once elsewhere; Leviticus 2:13; 24:8; 26:9, 15, 25, 42(3X), 44, 45. See especially 26:42, in which the term is repeated with the names of individual patriarchs: "I will remember my covenant with Jacob, and I will remember my covenant with Isaac and my covenant with Abraham."

Sabbath is referred to eighteen times, compared to three times elsewhere. Notice especially the insistence and bombast of the language; for example, *"Every* sabbath day Aaron shall set it in order before Yahweh *continually* on behalf of the people of Israel as a covenant forever" (my underlines, Leviticus 24:8).

48. Kennedy, *Leviticus and Numbers,* p. 164. For statements concerning the uncertainty of origins, see Driver, *The Book of Leviticus,* p. 98; and Micklem, "The Book of Leviticus," *The Interpreter's Bible,* vol. 2, pp. 121–122. For arguments favoring ancient origins, see Noth, *Leviticus,* pp. 184–185; Chapman and Streane, *The Book of Leviticus,* p. 139; Genung, *The Book of Leviticus,* p. 97; and Kennedy, *Leviticus and Numbers,* p. 164. For refutation of these arguments, see North, *Sociology of the Biblical Jubilee,* pp. 100–102; and Wenham, *The Book of Leviticus,* p. 319.

49. Such speculation is supported by the following:

1. The Year of Release, as both the reformulation of sabbatical law and the recognition of Cyrus' decree, effectively combines Jewish law and the secular authority of Persia and satisfies the condition on which the exiles were allowed and encouraged to return to Jerusalem.

2. Reflecting the expectations that many had of Cyrus, one of the exiled Judaeans, the prophet known as "Deutero-Isaiah" (Isaiah 40–55), incorporated him by name into Israel's continuing prophecy that Yahweh intervenes in all of history (Isaiah 44:24–47:7, Cyrus is named twice). Because Cyrus was seen as God's instrument who would fell Babylon and return them to Jerusalem, the casting of his decree as anticipated at Sinai and fulfilling sabbath law is not unusual. See Noth, *The History of Israel,* p. 301; and Bruce C. Birch, *Singing the Lord's Song: A Study of Isaiah 40–55* (Cincinnati: United Methodist Church, 1981), pp. 89–108.

3. Leviticus does not discuss the Year of Release as an event that was to be repeated every forty-nine years. See Driver, *The Book of Leviticus,* p. 98; North, *Sociology of the Biblical Jubilee,* pp. 206–209; and Kennedy, *Leviticus and Numbers,* p. 164. The insistence in other chapters that the statutes are to be obeyed "forever," "throughout your generations," and "in all your dwelling places" is absent here. It would appear to be a special, single, fixed date rather than cyclically observed. Ownership is allowed "in perpetuity," but only in the special cases of a dwelling house within a walled city that has not been redeemed (25:30); the common fields belonging to the cities of Levites (25:34); and slaves bought from sojourners who have been born in one's land and inherited from one's father (25:46). These exceptions come after Yahweh's statement in 25:23 that the "land shall not be sold in perpetuity, for the land is mine."

50. See Noth, *The History of Israel,* pp. 302–316; Gottwald, *The Hebrew Bible,* pp. 437, 461–462, 479–480; and deVaux, *Ancient Israel. Religious Institutions,* vol. 2, pp. 387–397.

51. See Noth, *Leviticus*, pp. 56–57, 153–163; and chapters 6, 7, 21, and 22 in Leviticus.

52. For example:

1. The cultic inferiority of the female gender is indicated by (a) the two-week period of uncleanness assigned a woman after the bearing of a female compared to one week for bearing a male (12:1–5); (b) the greater financial valuation of males in religious dedications (27:1–7); and (c) the superiority of male animals in sacrifices, as revealed in the distinction between the male goat that "the ruler" is to offer and the female goat that "the common people" are to offer (4:23, 28; also, 1:3, 10; 4:3; 5:15, 18; 6:6). See Noth, *Leviticus*, pp. 97, 204–205; Kennedy, *Leviticus and Numbers*, p. 177; and Chapman and Streane, *The Book of Leviticus*, p. 176.

2. In social and cultic regulations, virginity and harlotry are indicated as virtue and vice, respectively, for women, but not for men (19:29; 21:7, 9, 13–15). The possible exception is a vague reference in 17:7 in which men are forbidden to "slay the sacrifices for satyrs, after whom they play the harlot."

3. The ruling body, the organization of priests, consists of the male descendants of Aaron (a) who must be physically unblemished (neither blind, lame, deformed, diseased, nor with crushed testicles [21:18–24], (b) who must marry a virgin (neither a widow, harlot, defiled woman, nor divorcee [21:7, 13–15]), (c) whose sons only may eat of the "most holy" cereal, sin, and guilt offerings (6:18, 29; 7:6), and (d) whose daughters are burned for playing the harlot (see Martin Noth, *The Old Testament World*, Victor I. Gruhn, trans. [Philadelphia: Fortress Press, 1966], p. 168), forbidden to eat of holy things if they marry an outsider, and become the property of another family when they marry and have children (21:9; 22:12–13).

4. The jubilee law itself is intended "to be in force for all the 'inhabitants' of the land [25:10], meaning here in a precise sense all those who were settled on and had a stake in the land, in practice the heads of families" (Noth, *Leviticus*, p. 187). It is "essentially an effort to hold the family together" (North, *Sociology of the Biblical Jubilee*, pp. 165–167), a family being a wife, children, hired servants, and slaves headed by a property-owning man (22:10; 25:10, 25, 44–46; 26:26). See also Genung, *The Book of Leviticus*, p. xiii; Micklem, "The Book of Leviticus," *The Interpreter's Bible*, vol. 2, pp. 37–38, 129.

53. See, for example, Kennedy, *Leviticus and Numbers*, p. 126; and Wenham, *Thee Book of Leviticus*, p. 254.

54. Judith Lewis Herman and Lisa Hirschman, *Father–Daughter Incest* (Cambridge, Mass.: Harvard University Press, 1981), p. 61.

55. A neighbor's or son's wife is not a blood relative; and the phrasing "father's wife" instead of "one's mother" would seem to indicate further that ownership, not relationship, is that which should not be violated. A much lesser punishment prescribed in 19:20 supports this interpretation. Here, for "lying

carnally" with a slavewoman, who is "designated for [acquired or gained by] another man but not ransomed or given her freedom," one needs only to make a guilt offering, for which forgiveness ritually follows. Because neither the man nor woman is "put to death, because she was not [yet] freed" (i.e., not officially or completely possessed by another man), that which qualifies sexual behavior as wrong would appear to be the lack of ownership by the perpetrator.

56. The phrase appears twice in the ten commandments in Exodus 20:2, 5, and subsequently in Deuteronomy 5:6, 9. Within Leviticus it appears fifty-two times; all but two of these are within the Holiness Code section (chapters 17–26), and 50 percent of these are in chapters 18, 19, and 20. See Leviticus 11:44, 45; 18;2, 4(2X), 6, 21, 30; 19:2, 3, 4, 10, 12, 14, 16, 18, 25, 28, 30, 31, 32, 34, 36, 37; 20:7, 8, 24, 26; 21:8, 12, 15, 23; 22:2, 3, 8, 9, 16, 30, 31, 32, 33; 23:22, 43; 24:22; 25:17, 38, 55; 26:1, 2, 13, 44, 45. See also Kennedy, *Leviticus and Numbers*, pp. 124–125; Chapman and Streane, *The Book of Leviticus*, p. xlviii; Micklem, "The Book of Leviticus," *The Interpreter's Bible*, vol. 2, p. 86; and Wenham, *The Book of Leviticus*, pp. 250–251.

57. See Noth, *Leviticus*, pp. 134–136, 146–151. The same can be said for the list of social regulations in chapter 19; see pp. 138–144.

58. Douglas, *Purity and Danger*, p. 124; see also, as cited in Wenham, *The Book of Leviticus*, pp. 222–224.

59. Gottwald, *The Hebrew Bible*, pp. 413, 473.

60. For social commentary, see Audre Lorde, "Grenada Revisited: An Interim Report," *Sister Outsider: Essays and Speeches* (Trumansburg, N.Y.: Crossing Press, 1984), pp. 176–190; Saul Landau, "Imperialism, Bush-Style," *New York Times*, December 22, 1989, p. A39; and R. W. Apple, Jr., "As Two Worlds Warm, A Post-Postwar Order Awaits," *New York Times*, December 24, 1989, section 4, p. 1.

61. Benjamin Friedman, *Day of Reckoning: The Consequences of American Economic Policy Under Reagan and After* (New York: Random House, 1988), pp. 20, 50, 90–91. Friedman, p. 29, reports: "On average during the prior three decades, we invested 3.3 percent of our total income in net additions to the stock of business plant and equipment. . . . Net business capital formation was 3 percent of total income on average during the fifties, 3.5 percent during the sixties, and 3.3 percent during the seventies. Thus far during the 1980s, the average has been just 2.3 percent. In no single year since 1981 have we achieved even 3 percent."

62. Friedman, *Day of Reckoning*, pp. 4, 6, 39–41, 65–74, 80–81, 99. See p. 39 for information on borrowing: "During the country's peak period of foreign borrowing for industrial expansion in the late 1860s and early 1870s . . . borrowing averaged 2.2 percent of America's annual income. . . . In 1987 it was 3.5 percent [with] no equivalent to the [previous century's] expanding railroad system or the new steel industry . . . only higher levels of consumer spending compared to our income than ever before."

See p. 73 for information on international investment: "Foreign direct investment in America . . . trebled while our direct investment abroad has increased by only one fifth. . . . Foreigners' 1986 real holdings in this country added up to $377 billion versus only $311 billion of American holdings abroad."

63. Friedman, *Day of Reckoning,* pp. 76–84. See p. 6 for information about the United States owing nearly half of its debt to foreign lenders: "At the beginning of the 1980s, foreigners owed Americans far more than we owed foreigners. The balance in our favor, amounting to some $2,500 per family, made the United States the world's leading creditor country, enjoying the advantages of international influence and power that have always accompanied such a position. Today, after a half a dozen years in which our government has borrowed record sums on our behalf, we owe foreigners far more that they owe us. The balance against us, already amounting to more than $7,000 per family, now makes the United States the world's largest debtor. Foreigners have already begun to settle these debts by taking possession of office buildings in American cities, houses in American suburbs, farm land in the heartland, and even whole companies."

64. Friedman, *Day of Reckoning,* pp. 4, 76, 109–110.

65. Friedman, *Day of Reckoning,* pp. 39–44, 97. See Gordon Allport, *The Nature of Prejudice* (Reading, Mass.: Addison-Wesley, 1954). For evidence of the defining of boundaries and sharpening of conflicts, see, for example, "Polls Find Majority Believe Race Prejudice Is Still Strong," *New York Times,* August 9, 1988, p. A13; Constance L. Hays, "Hispanic Population Suffering Along with Massachusetts Economy," *New York Times,* December 25, 1989, p. 18; and Peter Applebome, in *New York Times,* "Two Sides of the Contemporary South: Racial Incidents and Black Progress," November 21, 1989, p. A22, and "Bombings Echo Past, But Experts Hear Different Undertones," December 26, 1989, p. A20.

66. Friedman, *Day of Reckoning,* pp. 84–85.

67. For criticism of Friedman's position, see Charles R. Morris, *The Coming Global Boom: How to Benefit from Tomorrow's Dynamic Economy* (New York: Bantam, 1990); and "Let's Stop Worrying About the Budget Deficit" [Letters], *New York Times,* February 19, 1989, sec. 4, p. 18.

68. Polls show, for example, that public tolerance of homosexual relations between consenting adults was affected by public concern over AIDS. See Michael R. Kagay, "Homosexuals Gain More Acceptance: Poll Shows Rise in Tolerance of Private Acts Involving Gay Consenting Adults," *New York Times,* October 25, 1989, p. A24, who quotes the vice president of the Gallup Organization as saying: "Tolerance of homosexuals fell when Americans first started worrying about getting AIDS. But as people's fear of getting AIDS themselves has diminished, tolerance of homosexuality has rebounded to previous levels." Forty-five percent of those polled in 1982 favored legalizing homosexual relations. The percentage decreased in subsequent years to a low 33 percent in 1987. In 1988 the percentage rose to 47.

69. See Beverly Harrison, "The Equal Rights Amendment: A Moral Analysis," in Carol S. Robb, ed., *Making the Connections: Essays in Feminist Social Ethics* (Boston: Beacon Press, 1985), pp. 167–173.

70. See Arthur S. Leonard, "Gay and Lesbian Rights Protections in the U.S.: An Introduction to Gay and Lesbian Civil Rights" (Washington, D.C.: National Gay and Lesbian Task Force, 1989).

71. See Rick Simonson and Scott Walker, eds., "Introduction," *The Gray-wolf Annual Five: Multi-Cultural Literacy* (Saint Paul: Graywolf Press, 1988), pp. ix–xv.

72. See Hyman Bookbinder, "Did the War on Poverty Fail?" *New York Times,* August 20, 1989, section 4, p. 23; Leonard Silk, "Now, to Figure Why the Poor Get Poorer," *New York Times,* December 18, 1988, section 4, pp. 1, 5; and "Poverty Is Perceived as Increasing and State of the Poor Unimproved," *New York Times,* August 23, 1989, p. A14.

73. See Lorde, "Grenada Revisited," pp. 176–190; R. M. Koster, "In Panama, We're Rebuilding Frankenstein," *New York Times,* December 29, 1989, p. A35; Tom Wicker, "Beyond the Jackpot," *New York Times,* January 22, 1990, p. A15; R. W. Apple, "Panama Invasion Costly in a Far Wider Theater," *New York Times,* January 25, 1990; and John B. Oakes, "Bush in Panama: A Tragicomedy," *New York Times,* January 26, 1990, p. A3.

74. See Sanford Lakoff and Herbert F. York, *A Shield in Space?: Technology, Politics, and the Strategic Defense Initiative: How the Reagan Administration Set Out to Make Nuclear Weapons 'Impotent and Obsolete' and Succumbed to the Fallacy of the Last Move* (Berkeley: University of California Press, 1990).

75. See Flora Lewis, "The Earth Comes First," *New York Times,* July 30, 1989, section 4, p. 23; and Bill Green, "Earth to NASA," *New York Times,* August 27, 1989, section 4, p. 19.

76. See Linda Greenhouse, "The Court's Shift to the Right," *New York Times,* June 7, 1989, pp. A1, A22; and "Court Expands Right of Wardens to Censor Inmates' Reading," *New York Times,* May 16, 1989, p. A17.

77. See Lee A. Daniels, "Prejudice on Campuses Is Feared to Be Rising," *New York Times,* October 31, 1988, p. A12; "Wide Harassment of Women Working for U.S. Is Reported," *New York Times,* July 1, 1988, p. B6; Apple-bome, "Two Sides of the Contemporary South: Racial Incidents and Black Progress," *New York Times,* November 21, 1989, p. A22; William Greer, "Violence Against Homosexuals Rising, Groups Seeking Wider Protection Say," *New York Times,* November 23, 1986, p. 36; and Jason De Parle, "1989 Surge in Anti-Semitic Acts Is Reported by B'Nai B'Rith," *New York Times,* January 20, 1990, p. 10.

78. In 1590 Geneva was at war with the Duke of Saxony and the defendants captured were Turks; in 1610 a prominent official's homosexuality was related to his being arrested for high treason; and nearly all the homosexual defendants in Calvin's Geneva between 1555 and 1569 were foreigners. This latter period was a time when "Calvin's political allies finally took control of Geneva's magistracy" and were intent on establishing their power amidst waves of foreign refugees. See E. William Monter, "Sodomy and Heresy in Early Modern Switzerland," in Licata and Petersen, *The Gay Past,* pp. 41–53.

The economic demise of Holland and Germany are easily documented (see, for example, Thomas Colley Grattan, chapter 21, "From the Peace of Utrecht to the Incorporation of Belgium with the French Republic, A.D. 1713–1794," *Holland: The History of the Netherlands* (New York: Peter Fenelon Collier, 1899), pp. 325–339; and Detlev J. K. Peukert, chapter 2, "The Rise of National

Socialism and the Crisis of Industrial Class Society," *Inside Nazi Germany: Conformity, Opposition, and Racism in Everyday Life,* Richard Deveson, trans. [New Haven: Yale University Press, 1987], pp. 26–46.) but not so that of England in the early nineteenth century. Its rise to power was, in fact, beginning. However, the threat of Napoleonic invasion caused a national fear and insecurity that may have been taken out, in scape-goat fashion, on "outsiders" within the country (see, for example, William Strang, chapter 7, "The French Revolution and Napoleon," *Britain in World Affairs: The Fluctuation in Power and Influence from Henry VIII to Elizabeth II* [Westport, Conn.: Greenwood Press, 1976], pp. 85–96).

79. See Katz, *Gay American History,* pp. 12, 20–23; and Katz, *Gay/Lesbian Almanac,* pp. 23–133.

80. See Katz, "1778: George Washington; The Court Marshall of Lieutenant Frederick Gotthold Enslin"; "1810: Davis versus Maryland; 'Seduced by the Instigation of the Devil' "; and entries for 1915–1966, *Gay American History,* pp. 24, 26–27, 33–52.

81. See also Richard Plant, chapter 1, "Before the Storm," *The Pink Triangle: The Nazi War Against Homosexuals* (New York: Henry Holt, 1986), pp. 21–52.

82. Noth, *A History of Pentateuchal Traditions,* p. 47.

83. Noth, *A History of Pentateuchal Traditions,* pp. 47–62. See Michael Walzer, *Exodus and Revolution* (New York: Basic Books, 1985).

84. See Exodus 1:8–12 (J), 13–14(P), 15–22(E); 2:11–15(J), 23–24(P); 3:7–8(J), 9–12(E), 16–22(J); 4:27–31(J); 5:1–6:1(J); 6:2–13(P); 13:20–22(J). Source assignments taken from Noth, *A History of Pentateuchal Traditions,* pp. 267–271. Concerning contents and literary form of the book of Exodus, see Martin Noth, *Exodus: A Commentary,* J. S. Bowden, trans. Old Testament Library (Philadelphia: Westminster Press, 1962), pp. 9–17.

85. *The New Oxford Annotated Bible,* pp. 69–70.

APPENDIX C. THE POLICE AS PERPETRATORS

1. Carmen Vasquez, *Quarterly Statistical Analyses: January 1984 to March 1986,* San Francisco, Community United Against Violence, April 1984 to May 1986.

The Dallas Gay Alliance report for 1985 shows that 11 percent of reported incidents (fifteen of 138) involved "police harassment/negligence." See William W. Waybourn, director of social justice, Dallas Gay Alliance, in letter to Kevin Berrill, violence project coordinator, National Gay and Lesbian Task Force, February 11, 1986.

A study based on telephone calls to the Philadelphia Lesbian and Gay Task Force reveals that between February 1985 and February 1987, "more than 20% of the callers asserted they had been subjected to violence or harassment by police." See "Philadelphia, Pennsylvania," *Advocate* (Los Angeles), May 26, 1987, p. 26.

The Violence Project of the National Gay and Lesbian Task Force, in its report "Anti-Gay Violence, Victimization and Defamation in 1986," Washington, D.C., 1987, p. 3, shows that 8 percent of reported incidents (410 of 4,946 incidents) involved victimization of lesbians and gay men by the police. The victimization in 3 percent of all incidents (160 of 4,946 incidents) was "verbal/physical abuse"; in 5 percent of all incidents (250 of 4,946 incidents) the victimization was "harassment/negligence," which "includes police entrapment, unequal enforcement of the law, deliberate mishandling of cases, failure to take reports, etc." See also Kevin Berrill, "Criminal Justice Subcommittee: Hearing on Police Practices—Testimony Submitted by Kevin Berrill, Violence Project Director of the National Gay Task Force," November 28, 1983, p. 2.

2. See, for example, "Lesbians Prepare Suit Against Police," *Washington Blade* (Washington, D.C.), December 20, 1985, p. 12; "Lesbians Arrested in Subway Assault: Morgenthau Asks Bronx D.A. to Investigate Possible Police Brutality," *New York Native,* January 26, 1987, p. 6; Allen White, "Mayor's Aide Bagged: New Wave of After Hours Arrests on Castro; Reports of Police Violence in Mission Station Persist," *Bay Area Reporter* (San Francisco), July 29, 1982, pp. 1, 4; William Burks, "Chicago Police Sued for $15 Million: Suit Filed Against Officers in Drug Raid," *New York Native,* December 29, 1986, p. 6; David Brill, "Analysis: Questions Remain in South Station Cinema Raid," *Gay Community News* (Boston), January 27, 1979, pp. 6, 7; Alan MacLean, "Cops Beat Me Up, Gay Man Charges," *Body Politic* (Toronto), August 1979, p. 10; Peg Byron, "Blue's in the Night: Two Years After Raid, Police to Take No Action on Brutality," *New York Native,* (September 10–23, 1983; Elizabeth Pincus, "1979 Peg's Place Assault by Off-Duty S.F. Cops Goes to Trial," *Coming Up!* (San Francisco), June 1985; Diane Feinberg, "Cops Beat Black Lesbian," *Workers World* (New York), September 24, 1982, p. 11; Stephanie Hedgecoke, "Albuquerque Lesbians on Trial after Police Attack," *Workers World* (New York, October 10, 1985, p. 11; Debbie Bender, "Persistence Pays Off as Lesbians Win Suit," *Workers World* (New York), July 4, 1985, p. 12; Sharon Ayling, "Houston Cop Kills Gay Activist," *Workers World* (New York), July 4, 1980, p. 5; Gay Saskatchewan, "Toronto Gays Protest Raids," *Briarpatch,* March 1981, p. 17; Ken Popert and Brian Mossop, "Toronto the Good," *Canadian Dimension,* December 1981, pp. 4–6; Luis Lopez, "Manhattan Cops Attack Black Gay Bar," *Workers World* (New York), October 8, 1982, p. 11; David France, "Gay Bar Attacked by Police in N.Y.," *Guardian* (New York), October 20, 1982, p. 10; Arthur Bell, "Black Tie and Blood," *Village Voice* (New York), October 12, 1982, pp. 1, 11–12, 14; Sally McBeth, "Crown Steps in . . . Cop Gets Off Hook," *Toronto Clarion,* February 2, 1982, p. 5; "Will Submit Brief: Gays Tell Mayor of Police Brutality," *Ottawa Journal,* June 13, 1975, p. 3; Jim Bray, "Woman Says Police Beat Lesbian Lover," *St. Louis Globe-Democrat,* July 11, 1978; and Timothy Middleton, "Woman Testifies of Beating," *Metro-East Journal* (East St. Louis), July 11, 1978.

For other examples of incidents, see Dennis Altman, *The Homosexualization of America* (New York: St. Martin's Press, 1982; Boston: Beacon Press, 1983), pp. 45–46; Mike Weiss, *Double-Play: The San Francisco City Hall Killings,* p. 414; Martin S. Weinberg and Colin J. Williams, *Male Homosexuals: Their*

Problems and Adaptations (New York: Oxford University Press, 1974), p. 34; John Rechy, *The Sexual Outlaw: A Documentary: A Non-Fiction Account, with Commentaries, of Three Days and Nights in the Sexual Underground,* pp. 29–31; Randy Shilts, *The Mayor of Castro Street,* pp. 91–93; Berrill, "Criminal Justice Subcommittee," pp. 2–3; Lesbian and Gay History Group of Toronto, Appendix 1, "A History of the Relationships Between the Gay Community and the Metropolitan Toronto Police: A Brief Submitted to Arnold Bruner for His Study of Relations Between the Homosexual Community and the Police," pp. 6–17; and Coalition for Gay Rights in Ontario, "Discrimination Against Lesbians and Gay Men: The Ontario Human Rights Omission," pp. 7, 9–10, 24–25.

3. See, for example, David France, "Gay Bar Attacked by Police in N.Y.," *Guardian* (New York), October 20, 1982, p. 10; Arthur Bell, reporting the incident in "Black Tie and Blood," pp. 1, 11, 12; and William Burks, "Chicago Police Sued for $15 Million: Suit Filed Against Officers in Drug Raid," *New York Native,* December 29, 1986, p. 6.

4. See, for example, Elizabeth Pincus, "1979 Peg's Place Assault by Off-Duty S.F. Cops Goes to Trial"; Debbie Bender, "Persistence Pays Off as Lesbians Win Suit," *Workers World* (New York), July 4, 1985, p. 12; and Tim McCaskell, "Gays and Police," *Rikka* (Canada), Spring 1981, p. 38.

5. Greg Kelner and Project Understanding, *Homophobic Assault: A Study of Anti-Gay Violence,* pp. 25–26, 32, 33, 36, 47–53. See also Jim Merret, "Battery May Be Included: What Happens When You Report an Antigay Physical Attack," *Advocate* (Los Angeles), August 15, 1989, pp. 26–28, 30, 31.

In the Philadelphia Lesbian and Gay Task Force's two-year study of anti-gay/lesbian violence and discrimination documented through telephone calls to the Task Force's hotline, in twenty-five police-related cases "people complained about police refusing to take a report or [that police] dehumanized and degraded the person filing the complaint," the Task Force's executive director, Rita Addessa. See "Philadelphia, Pennsylvania," *Advocate* (Los Angeles), May 26, 1987, p. 26.

An example of blaming the victim is reported in "Mississippi," *Advocate* (Los Angeles), September 1, 1987, p. 26. To halt homophobic violence outside a gay bar in Meridian, Mississippi, the police chief suggested that the owner "close the bar and move out of town." The chief said, "The whole neighborhood is already feeling a sigh of relief. Several of the residents have called to tell me how happy they are."

An example of permitting violence to occur is reported by the Right to Privacy Committee in its "The Right to Privacy Committee's Brief to the City of Toronto Bruner Study in Relations Between Metropolitan Toronto Police and Toronto's Homosexual Community," p. 32: At a "gay community demonstration held on June 20, 1981" police "permitted violence to occur by failing to control a group of anti-gay agitators who harassed the demonstration throughout the evening. Police refused to hold a group of 30 or more anti-gay agitators until after the gay demonstrators had dispersed, despite repeated requests to do so by the demonstration's marshals. As a result, a group of the agitators attacked dispersing demonstrators. . . . The agitators were armed with sticks of wood taken from a nearby picket fence. Police were not in sight when the attack occurred and did not arrive for several minutes. By then the gay demonstrators had their attackers on the run. Police made no attempt to pursue and arrest the anti-gay agitators, many of whom remained nearby and visible to the demonstrators."

See also Judith Michaelson, "Charge Police Ignored Beatings at Hilton," *New York Post,* April 18, 1972, pp. 4, 54; Lisa White, "Tarheel Killing Fields: Gay Men Keep Turning up Dead—But Activists Fear Police Indifference to Fag-Bashing," *Philadelphia Gay News,* February 14–20, 1986, p. 1, 27; Laud Humphreys, *Out of the Closets: The Sociology of Homosexual Liberation,* p. 25; and Eric Gordon, "Police Inaction Questioned in Portland," *Our Paper* (Portland, Maine), December 1988, p. 6.

6. Dick Brown, "Johnston Speaks Out for 'My Gay Brothers, Sisters,' " pp. 1M, 2M.

7. William A. Westley, "Violence and the Police," p. 35.

8. Robert M. Morgenthau and Jacqueline C. Schafer, in U.S. Congress, House Subcommittee on Criminal Justice of Committee on Judiciary, *Anti-Gay Violence.* See also Right to Privacy Committee, "The Right to Privacy Committee's Brief to the City of Toronto Bruner Study in Relations Between Metropolitan Toronto Police and Toronto's Homosexual Community," pp. 39–40.

9. Westley, "Violence and the Police," pp. 34–41. The author writes: "The materials . . . are drawn from a case study of a municipal police department in an industrial city of approximately one hundred and fifty thousand inhabitants. This study included participation in all types of police activities, ranging from walking the beat and cruising with policemen in a squad car to the observation of raids, interrogations, and the police school. It included intensive interviews with over half the men in the department who were representative as to rank, time in service, race, religion, and specific type of police job."

10. Westley, "Violence and the Police," pp. 35–36. The author writes: "The apprehension and conviction of the felon is, for the policeman, the essence of police work. It is the source of prestige both within and outside police circles, it has career implications, and it is a major source of justification for the existence of the police before a critical and often hostile public. Out of these conditions a legitimation for the illegal use of violence is wrought.

"The career and prestige implication of the 'good pinch' elevate it to a major end in the conduct of the policeman. It is an end which is justified both legally and through public opinion as one which should be of great concern to the police. Therefore it takes precedence over other duties and tends to justify strong means."

11. Westley, "Violence and the Police," p. 35.

12. Westley, "Violence and the Police," p. 37.

13. Rechy, *Sexual Outlaw,* p. 57, quoting from *New West Magazine,* July 19, 1976. Rechy provides further analysis (p. 102): "It becomes clear that apart from providing cops a negative psychological outlet for their sexual frustrations, easy gay arrests, harassment, entrapment, and convictions—legally sanctioned sadism—disguise police inability to control violence. Boosted by the smashed

lives of homosexuals, statistics blur murders, rapes, muggings, robberies. (A well-known attorney claims to have found indications that, in one heavily gay area, the police have removed stalls between urinals in a public restroom in order to provide easier contact between males, and thereby increase arrests.)"

See also Humphreys, *Tearoom Trade*, pp. 93–96, for the author's self-report of being arrested in a public restroom even though he was neither engaging in nor soliciting sexual activity.

Berrill, "Criminal Justice Subcommittee," p. 2, reports that on a night in July 1983 in Florida, four women "were walking arm in arm out of a lesbian bar when a patrol car approached, slowed down and stopped. The officers got out of the car, accosted one of the women and called her a pervert. When [she] protested the remark, one officer threw her to the ground and sprayed mace in her face. Both she and [another] woman were then arrested for disorderly conduct and a liquor law violation."

See also "Lesbians Prepare Suit Against Police," *Washington Blade* (Washington, D.C.), December 20, 1985, p. 12; and Rich Harding, "Public Sex: As Arrest Numbers Rise, So Do the Human Costs," *Advocate* (Los Angeles), August 16, 1988, pp. 10–11.

14. As cited by John D'Emilio, *Sexual Politics, Sexual Communities: The Making of a Homosexual Minority in the United States, 1940–1970*, p. 202. The report, in the form of a twelve-page pamphlet titled "A Brief of Injustices: An Indictment of Our Society in Its Treatment of the Homosexual," was published by the Board of Trustees of the Council on Religion and the Homosexual, Incorporated, in 1965.

15. Westley, "Violence and the Police," p. 40.

16. Westley, "Violence and the Police," p. 40. Westley notes that "many men who held jobs in the police station rather than on beats indicated to the interviewer that their reason for choosing a desk job was to avoid the use of violence."

17. Westley, "Violence and the Police," p. 40.

Warren Hinckle, "The Untold Story: Dan White's San Francisco," *Inquiry*, pp. 11–12, provides the following statement by the former undersheriff of San Francisco who was in charge of Dan White in city jail after he confessed to assassinating Mayor Moscone and Supervisor Milk: "It all seemed very fraternal. One police officer gave Dan a pat on the behind when he was booked—sort of a 'Hey, catch you later, Dan' pat. Some of the officers and deputies were standing around with half-smirks on their faces. Some were actually laughing. I heard later they were telling Harvey Milk jokes. The joke the cops were telling was that Dan White's mother says to him when he comes home, 'No, you dummy, I said milk and baloney—not Moscone!'

"This was just a couple of hours after the mayor and supervisor had been shot down in cold blood. Some deputies—particularly the women deputies— were glaring at Dan White in disbelief and contempt, which is something you'd expect in such an extraordinary situation. But most of the policemen were acting like it was a routine occasion. They were even being chummy to Dan White. The attitude of the cops seemed to be that Dan White had done something they were not unhappy about—some of them seem elated—and they were in no way upset with him for doing it."

18. *Morand Report,* p. 184, quoted and discussed in Right to Privacy Committee, "The Right to Privacy Committee's Brief to the City of Toronto," pp. 41–43.

19. Westley, "Violence and the Police," *American Journal of Sociology* (1953), 59:40. See also, William A. Westley, "Secrecy and the Police," pp. 254–257.

20. Such shared disapproval is often corporately and publicly expressed. For example, as quoted by Edward H. Sebesta, "On Gaybashing: Its Politics, Method, and the Gay Challenge Against It; Circa 1978–1982," unpublished paper with appendices, San Francisco, April 7, 1984, p. 2, from the *San Francisco Policeman,* the official publication of the Police Officers Association, an article titled "Please Don't Touch or Bruise the Fruit," November 1979, states: "A new era is upon us. It is sad and almost incredible to see, but alas it is true! Decadence and immorality now crave respectability. A sickness that lurked in the shadows and behind closed doors is now engulfing this city. Like a blanket of plague it has started to cover our neighborhoods and ethnic districts, buying up property under the ruse of restoration and forcing the property values and old timers of this city—up and out. This coalition as you may have guessed by now is called homosexuality and is never more evident than on October 31st—Halloween night."

Secrecy and camaraderie among policemen is apparently violated, however, when one of the officers is identified as gay. See, for example, Peter Freiberg, "Michigan Cop Wins Antigay Bias Suit," *Advocate* (Los Angeles), May 10, 1988, p. 24, for an account of unnecessary assault and false arrest of an off-duty gay officer.

21. Arthur Niederhoffer, *Behind the Shield The Police in Urban Society.* On page v. the author writes: "This work is the crystallization of more than twenty years of police experience ranging from pounding the beat to instructing recruits at the Police Academy. To supplement personal experience I interviewed police officers from many parts of the country. Since retirement I have maintained close contact with law enforcement, and for several years I taught police administration courses in the Law Enforcement and Correctional Administration program at New York University Graduate School of Public Administration."

22. Niederhoffer, *Behind the Shield,* pp. 122–123. The rankings from most disliked to least disliked are as follows: cop-fighter, homosexual, drug addict, chronic letterwriter, annoying drunk, bookie, gang of juveniles, prostitute, known criminal, motorcycle group, psycho, motorist who double-parks, peddler, woman complainant, bohemian, minority group member.

Lesbian and Gay History Group of Toronto, "A History of the Relationship Between the Gay Community and the Metropolitan Toronto Police: A Brief Presented to Arnold Bruner for His Study of Relations Between the Homosexual Community and the Police," August 18, 1981, p. 4, states that in 1969 "Inspector Wilson [of the Toronto police force] casually commented that most of his officers were prejudiced against homosexuals and were revolted by homosexual acts."

23. Niederhoffer, *Behind the Shield,* p. 122, quoting Westley.

Hinckle, "The Untold Story: Dan White's San Francisco," pp. 11–12, provides the following statement by the former undersheriff of San Francisco and a professional criminologist: "There's a profound paranoia about gays in the police department. It's the sort of thing you see in macho subcultures of men. They both despise gays and are threatened by them. Perhaps it's the gays' free sexuality or the sense of enjoying breaking society's rules." Hinckle writes further that the former undersheriff "said that most police in his experience have the same attitude toward blacks and other minorities—anyone who deviates from the white male norm—but that gays in liberated San Francisco were so visible and up-front about their life style that it was a red flag to most orthodox cops."

24. [Jon J. Gallo et al.], "The Consenting Adult Homosexual and the Law: An Empirical Study of Enforcement and Administration in Los Angeles County," pp. 644–832.

The study is based on two phases of research—the first, data gathered from arrest reports, trials records, and probation reports from the Los Angeles County Superior Court records for the calendar years 1962–1964; and the second, "an extensive series of interviews with authorities in various related disciplines," including judges, private attorneys, chief deputy public defender, district administrator of the Department of Alcoholic Beverage Control, probations officers, and police departments. See pp. 799–802 for information about data-gathering methods.

Cited also by Weinberg and Williams, Male Homosexuals, pp. 24–25; Rechy, *The Sexual Outlaw,* p. 99; Humphreys, *Tearoom Trade,* pp. 87–88; D'Emilio, *Sexual Communities,* pp. 145–146, 183; and Joseph J. Bell, "Public Manifestations of Personal Morality: Limitations on the Use of Solicitation Statutes to Control Homosexual Cruising," pp. 98–101, 107–108.

Encyclopedia of Social Work, 18th ed., s.v. "Homosexuality: Gay Men," by Raymond M. Berger, argues against the "myth" that "most gay men today flaunt their homosexuality": "In fact, most gay men conceal their sexual orientation at least some of the time. Given the high likelihood of social ostracism, the threat of difficulties in employment and housing, and the prevalence of violence against openly gay men and women, it is not surprising that concealment is a way of life for many gay people." Berger is citing Weinberg and Williams, *Male Homosexuals: Their Problems and Adaptations,* chapter 13; A. P. Bell and M. S. Weinberg, *Homosexualities: A Study of Diversity Among Men and Women,* pp. 62–65; A. E. Moses and R. O. Hawkins, Jr., *Counseling Lesbian Women and Gay Men: A Life Issues Approach* (St Louis, Missouri: C. V. Mosby Company, 1982), p. 82. "Because gay men are generally indistinguishable from other men, public attitudes about gay men are formed on the basis of those who are most open about their sexual orientation. The popular media, in particular, tend to highlight the most extreme forms of public behavior, and, in the absence of more complete information about gay men, the public forms a biased view of male homosexuality."

Also, Mary Reige Laner and Roy H. Laner, "Sexual Preference or Personal

Style? Why Lesbians Are Disliked," *Journal of Homosexuality* (Summer 1980), 5:339–356, find that only a minority of the college students they sampled attributed "dangerousness" to lesbians and gay men.

25. [Gallo et al.], "The Consenting Adult Homosexual and the Law," pp. 795–796.

Bell, "Public Manifestations of Personal Morality," p. 108, reports the results of a more recent study in Los Angeles [B. Copilow and T. Coleman, *Report on the Enforcement of Section 647 (a) of the California Penal Code by the Los Angeles Police Department* (1972)] that further "indicates that complaints from members of the general public about conduct in violation of the solicitation laws are virtually nonexistent." Findings include the following: "Of the 662 arrests studied, 642 were made by plainclothes policemen, and 15 by uniformed officers. Only five involved complaints from private citizens, of whom two were actually private security officers. The remaining three complaints by private individuals were not for homosexual solicitation, but for lewd conduct of a heterosexual character. Both the original and a follow-up study [C. R. Toy, Update: *Enforcement of Section 647 (a) of the California Penal Code by the Los Angeles Police Department* (1972)] confirmed that although numerous private citizens file complaints for indecent exposure of a heterosexual nature, the complainants in all the homosexual conduct cases were plainclothes vice officers."

See also Richard R. Troiden, "Homosexual Encounters in a Highway Rest Stop," in Erich Goode and Richard R. Troiden, *Sexual Deviance and Sexual Deviants*, p. 218; and Jay Corzine and Richard Kirby, "Cruising the Truckers: Sexual Encounters in a Highway Rest Area," p. 187.

26. [Gallo et al.], "The Consenting Adult Homosexual and the Law," p. 698.

See also Brian Shein, "Gay-Bashing in High Park: A Tale of Homophobia and Murder," p. 68, who reports on the killing in a park of a gay man by teenage boys. Shein writes: "What of [the defense lawyer's] contention that cruising in High Park constitutes a provocation [for anti-gay violence], and his battle plan for 'cleaning up' the park? Metro Police Staff Inspector of 11 Division differs on the subject: 'If there were activity that the public found offensive, we'd certainly hear about it. The number of complaints is very, very small.' He good-naturedly points out that the park is so big that any sexual activity can be relatively discreet; the park, he implies, is big enough for everybody."

27. [Gallo et al.], "The Consenting Adult Homosexual and the Law," p. 707, n. 132. "Of the 475 misdemeanor arrests, 243 were made by decoys."

Del Martin and Phyllis Lyon, *Lesbian/Woman* (San Francisco: Glide Publications; revised ed., Toronto: Bantam Books, 1986), pp. 45–46, note that policewomen are also used as decoys.

Weinberg and Williams, *Male Homosexuals,* pp. 24–25, offer the following description of decoy activity by the police: "Police decoys . . . are police officers who intentionally lend themselves to receiving homosexual solicitation by walking, talking, and dressing as they think homosexuals do. The decoy will loiter in a public restroom, park, or street where homosexuals are known to congregate. Then, gestures, conversations, and so on by the apparent homosexual can be taken as evidence of solicitation and grounds for arrest. The U.C.L.A. study showed that in Los Angeles, 51 percent of the homosexual misdemeanor arrests (243 out of 475) were made by police decoys. Evidence centers around the officers' testimony that solicitation occurred, and corroboration is seldom asked for by the court. Behind this technique lies, of course, the issue of entrapment— was the enticement to commit the crime perpetrated by the officer or the defendant? Homosexual defendants frequently claim entrapment to be the case while the police just as frequently deny it; not surprisingly, the officer's story is believed in most cases. This technique is highly questionable in that the nature of the charge is extremely tenuous, the evidence is often suspect, and the whole procedure is open to abuse by the police."

Humphreys, *Tearoom Trade,* pp. 89–90, observes on the basis of interviews with men who engage in sexual activity with other men in public restrooms that "in regard to the blackmailing of tearoom participants: (1) most blackmailing is done by law enforcement personnel and as a result of decoy operations; (2) some blackmailing is practiced by those who pose as police officers; (3) a small amount is attempted (seldom with success) by close friends of the victims.

"Every respondent over the age of thirty whom I interviewed extensively had at least one story of police payoffs amounting to blackmail. With some, the police were paid off by sexual services rendered. In two instances, 'donations' were made to a 'charity fund' in return for release. One man alone—a prosperous married salesman who travels a great deal—has provided me with detailed accounts of eight instances in which he has 'bought off' decoys for amounts ranging from sixty to three hundred dollars. In each of these encounters with the law, the respondent had been 'led on' by the decoy."

See also Edwin M. Schur, *Crimes Without Victims: Deviant Behavior and Public Policy: Abortion, Homosexuality, Drug Addiction,* p. 83; Donald Rock, "Entrapment! To Have Tearoom Sex in the'50s Was to Risk Everything," pp. 50–51, 53; and Rick Harding, "Savannah Activists Charge Entrapment of Gays During Police Sting," *Advocate* (Los Angeles), March 15, 1988, p. 21.

28. [Gallo et al.], "The Consenting Adult Homosexual and the Law," p. 796.

See also Bell and Weinberg, "Cruising" and table 6, "Cruising," *Homosexualities,"* pp. 73–80, 299–307, for their findings from a survey of 1,077 lesbians and gay men: "The present investigation confirms . . . that public cruising is infrequent among lesbians and that, among homosexual men who cruise in public places, most conduct their sexual activity in the privacy of their homes. . . .

"Almost 40 percent of our male respondents either did no cruising at all or did it no more than once a month.

"The data also indicate that except for cruising on the streets, most of the homosexual males sought sexual partners in such relatively safe settings as the gay bar or bath, and few did much of their cruising in public rest rooms, movie theaters, or parks, where the danger of being arrested or physically assaulted is much greater. Perhaps this is why relatively few of them worried about the police or about being exposed or about being rolled and robbed. They were much more concerned about various aspects relating to their prospective partner."

29. For example Lesbian and Gay History Group of Toronto, "A History of the Relationship Between the Gay Community and the Metropolitan Toronto Police," p. 1, quotes Chief Constable John Chisholm, who said the following about homosexuality in 1957 before the Royal Commission on the Criminal Law Relating to Criminal Sexual Psychopaths: "The saddest feature of all . . . is that homosexuals corrupt others and are constantly recruiting youths of previous good character into their fraternity."

The following examples and studies show that young people who are homosexually active have rarely been recruited against their wishes.

John Gerassi, *The Boys of Boise: Furor, Vice and Folly in an American City*, pp. 35–36, writes about a public homosexual scandal in Boise, Idaho, in which the newsmedia and police expressed concern for the young people involved. Gerassi finds, however, that "only four or five youths were deeply involved. They knew who the homosexuals were, how to contact, and how to profit from their contact. They were juvenile delinquents, not homosexuals, and one phase of their delinquency was male prostitution. . . .

"Dr. [John] Butler [who submitted psychiatric findings for the cases] told me, '. . . that hard core of kids supposedly seduced by homosexuals were actually made up of tough gang members. . . . They were fully aware of what they were doing. They may have been only fifteen, sixteen and seventeen, but they were much too developed to be considered children. And, as it turned out, some of them became regular criminals."

See also Jonathan Katz, "1955: Anonymous; Witch-Hunt in Boise, Idaho; An Interview with a Victim, 'They Lit a Match to a Bonfire,'" *Gay American History: Lesbians and Gay Men in the U.S.A.: A Documentary*, p. 110. The interviewee states: "There was a hysteria about young teen-age boys being seduced by older men; that's what they conveyed to the public. The city paper, the *Idaho Daily Statesmen*, embellished on this. It kept emphasizing older men and young boys; it kept saying there was a sex ring of older men who were enticing these boys. There was no such thing; no such ring existed. The boys who were arrested in Boise all knew exactly what they were doing."

Two studies of young male prostitutes find that such boys are fully aware of their situation and that older men neither force nor coerce them. Donal E. J. MacNamara and Edward Sagarin, *Sex, Crime, and the Law*, p. 144, in their study of 162 young male prostitutes, find, "Not one of these men attributed his prostitutional activity to an early history of seduction or rape; in fact, a majority indicated that their initial homosexual experience was not only voluntary but self-initiated." Albert J. Reiss, Jr., "The Social Integration of Queers and Peers," in Hendrik M. Ruitenbeek, ed., *The Problem of Homosexuality in Modern Society*, in his study of lower-class, career delinquents finds, "Almost all lower-class boys reported they were solicited by a queer at least once. A majority refused the solicitation. Refusal is apparently easy since boys report that queers are seldom insistent."

30. Altman, *The Homosexualization of America,* p. 173; 204, n. 1.

31. Gerassi, *The Boys of Boise,* pp. 119–121.

32. Humphreys, *Tearoom Trade,* pp. 90–93.

33. Humphreys, *Tearoom Trade,* pp. 91–92.

34. Bell, "Public Manifestations of Personal Morality," pp. 97–114, finds: "Solicitation statutes have served to criminalize homosexual behavior that, among heterosexual behavior, would not be punishable. The courts have generally been reluctant to impose even civil sanctions on heterosexual importuning: 'Even the dire affront of inviting an unwilling woman to illicit intercourse has been held by most courts to be no such outrage as to lead to liability—the view being, apparently in Judge Magruder's well known words, that 'there is no harm in the asking' " [citing W. Prosser, *Law of Torts* 51 (4th ed. 1971), quoting Magruder, "Mental and Emotional Disturbance in the Law of Torts," *Harvard Law Review* (1936), 49:1033, 1055].

Rechy, *The Sexual Outlaw,* p. 102, for example, states: "In a city in which, in 1975, homicides rose over 600 for the first time—an increase of 17.5% over 1974—the Los Angeles Police Department was still able in 1976 to spare 103 men and over $100,000 to raid a gay bathhouse! Only 22.1% of all burglaries reported in 1974 were solved; yet, according to a 1974 *Los Angeles Times* account, the City Attorney's office was handling up to 500 gay-bar arrests yearly, many of those involving men merely holding hands or dancing together!" See also pp. 142–145, 279.

35. Alfred C. Kinsey, Wardwell B. Pomeroy, and Clyde E. Martin, *Sexual Behavior in the Human Male,* pp. 391–392.

36. Sherri Cavan, *Liquor License: An Ethnography of Bar Behavior* (Chicago: Aldine Publishing Company, 1966), pp. 70–72.

37. Diana Sepejak, "The Willingness of Homosexuals to Report Criminal Victimization to the Police" (M.A. dissertation, University of Toronto, 1977), p. 21.

38. Lesbian and Gay History Group of Toronto, "A History of the Relationship Between the Gay Community and the Metropolitan Toronto Police," pp. 3–4.

39. Niederhoffer, *Behind the Shield,* p. 12, quotes Dan Dodson, the director of the Center for Human Relations and Community Studies at New York University. Also cited is Joseph Lohman, Dean of the School of Criminology of the University of California at Berkeley, who says, "The police function [is] to support and enforce the interests of the dominant political, social, and economic interests of the town, and only incidentally to enforce the law."

See, for example, Arthur Leonard, "Getting Beyond *Hardwick,*" *New York Native,* September 1, 1986, p. 20, who notes in his review of the U.S. Supreme Court's decision in *Bowers* v. *Hardwick* to uphold Georgia's sodomy law: "Meanwhile, be careful, because there are scattered reports from around the country of stepped-up police harassment of gays as a result of the Court's opinion. And the fallout from *Hardwick* is not just in the press or in the street. One July 15, the Missouri Supreme Court cited *Hardwick* in upholding the state's criminal law against 'deviate' consensual sex, in a case arising from a highway rest-stop bust by a plainclothes cop."

See also Edwin M. Schur, *Labeling Deviant Behavior: Its Sociological Implications* (New York: Harper & Row, 1971), pp. 43–44, who shows a scale of public intolerance and rejection of "various kinds of deviators" (from least to most: intellectuals, former mental patients, atheists, ex-convicts, gamblers, beatniks, alcoholics, adulterers, political radicals, marihuana smokers, prostitutes, lesbians, homosexuals) which almost mirrors the scale of police attitudes toward their clientele (from least to most disliked: minority group member, bohemian, woman complainant, peddlar, motorist who double-parks, psycho, motorcycle group, known criminal, prostitute, gang of juveniles, bookie, annoying drunk, chronic letter writer, drug addict, homosexual, cop fighter) provided by Niederhoffer, *Behind the Shield*, p. 123.

40. Quoted in Berrill, "Criminal Justice Subcommittee: Hearing on Police Practices—Testimony Submitted by Kevin Berrill," p. 7.

41. Quoted in Berrill, "Criminal Justice Subcommittee: Hearing on Police Practices—Testimony Submitted by Kevin Berrill, p. 7.

42. Sebesta, "On Gaybashing," p. 2, quoting from "Shoveling Against the Tide," *San Francisco Policeman,* July 1979.

Sebesta also quotes from an article in the *San Francisco Chronicle,* February 1, 1982, in which a former San Francisco police officer trainee is interviewed: "He said that during his training in the police academy and in the field program instructors and other cadets routinely called him a 'faggot,' 'fruit,' and 'queer.' 'On a bathroom wall of the Northern Station,' Cady said, 'an officer had scrawled: "Cady and all faggots out of San Francisco." This graffiti was encircled by the words "Kill All Faggots," written three times.' "

See also Rick Harding, in *Advocate* (Los Angeles), "Not a Happy Trooper: Forced Out of His Job, a Florida Deputy Becomes an Unwitting Activist," June 20, 1989, pp. 8–9, 11, and "Forget It, Dallas Cops Tell Lesbian Job Seeker," August 29, 1989, pp. 13–14.

43. Susan Ehrlich Martin, *Breaking and Entering: Policewomen on Patrol* (Berkeley: University of California Press, 1980; paperback ed., 1982), p. 68.

44. Martin, *Breaking and Entering*, pp. 59–75; and Niederhoffer, *Behind the Shield*, p. 133.

45. Martin, *Breaking and Entering*, p. 59.

46. Martin, *Breaking and Entering*, p. 101.

See also Lewis M. Terman and Catharine Cox Miles, *Sex and Personality: Studies in Masculinity and Femininity* (New York: McGraw-Hill, 1936), pp. 164 (table 36, "Intercomparison of the Mean M-F Scores of 15 Occupational, Professional, and Vocational Groups"), 174–176, 456–458, who find on the rating scale for mental masculinity and femininity that among occupational groups the "policemen and firemen rate at the feminine limit of the occupational classes." They add that "to check the result 15 more policemen, members of a large California city, were given the M-F test" and the "average mean scores for the [policemen and firemen] group with these . . . men added" remained the same. I agree with Kinsey, Pomeroy, and Martin, *Sexual Behavior in the Human Male,* pp. 637–638, that the "Terman-Miles scale for determining the degree of masculinity or femininity of an individual is largely based upon . . . preconceptions [about homosexuality]"; femininity and masculinity are culturally defined and socially constructed, rather than innate or mental characteristics. However, the Terman-Miles M-F examination and scale do, I think, reflect the categorization of interests by social norms for appropriate behavior and thinking for men and women. That those who are policemen and firefighters, occupations which are socially considered to be quite masculine, have interests which are socially considered to be quite feminine suggests that those men compensate (and perhaps not consciously) by seeking employment in socially considered hypermasculine occupations. That their effort is successful (in terms of masking interests and feelings) is indicated by Terman and Miles' survey of psychologists who were asked to rank populations of various occupations on the M-F scale: "The most pronounced disagreement [with the actual findings about those within each occupational population] is the case of city policemen and firemen, who are ranked by both men and women [psychologists] as the most masculine occupational group, whereas they score among the lowest on the M-F test." The Terman-Miles findings support further the notion that police officers are very often low-status males (in terms of class background, previous employment, marital and parental status, education, and socially considered gender-appropriate interests) who seek to compensate for their social inferiority in a socially considered masculine occupation.

47. Martin, *Breaking and Entering,* pp. 84, 90.

For an inside view of the policeman's life, see William J. Caunitz, *Suspects* (New York: Crown Publishers, 1986; Bantam Books, 1987). Caunitz served in the New York City Police Department for thirty years before retiring as a detective lieutenant and writing this novel.

48. Martin, *Breaking and Entering,* p. 101.

49. Westley, "Violence and the Police," *American Journal of Sociology* (July 1953), 59:35.

50. Edward H. Peeples, Jr., Walter W. Tunstall, Everett Eberhardt, and the Research Task Force with technical assistance from the Commission on Human Relations, City of Richmond, *A Survey of Perceptions of Civil Opportunity Among Gays and Lesbians in Richmond, Virginia,* table 37.

See also Humphreys, *Out of the Closet,* p. 25; Rechy, *The Sexual Outlaw,* p. 29; Berrill, "Criminal Justice Subcommittee: Hearing on Police Practices—Testimony Submitted by Kevin Berrill," p. 4; James Credle, "Testimony of James Credle of Black and White Men Together, NYC for Congressional Hearings on Police Brutality," Brooklyn, New York, November 28, 1983, p. 2; Morgenthau and Schafer, in U.S. Congress, Subcommittee on Criminal Justice of Committee on Judiciary, *Anti-Gay Violence.*

51. Kelner, *Homophobic Violence,* p. 49, based on four of seven cases.

52. Morgenthau and Schafer, in U.S. Congress, Subcommittee on Criminal Justice of Committee on Judiciary, *Anti-Gay Violence.*

53. Robert J. Johnston, Jr., in U.S. Congress, House Subcommittee on Crim-

inal Justice, Committee on the Judiciary, *Anti-Gay Violence,* pp. 130–131, states, "This conclusion is based upon the fact that 50% of the incidents that the Bias Unit has investigated were not originally reported to the police at all. The complaints came to our attention informally through the Bias Unit's relationship with the N.Y.C. Gay/Lesbian Anti-Violence Project, a private organization active in the gay community."

See also Jeanne Curran, "Police Fear Homosexuals Not Reporting Criminal Acts Performed Against Them," *Bangor Daily News* (Bangor, Maine), July 10, 1986.

54. Forms of physical assault such as objects thrown at; chased or followed; spit at; punched, kicked, or beaten; assaulted or wounded with a weapon; arson or vandalism committed against property; robbed; and/or raped. See chapter 2 for data about these categories of physical assault.

55. Physical assaults include being punched, kicked, or beaten; being assaulted or wounded with a weapon; having arson or vandalism committed against property; being robbed; and/or being raped. See chapter 2 for data on the categories of physical assault.

See survey of 110 victims by Deborah Anne Potter, "Violence, Self-definition and Social Control: Gay and Lesbian Victimization (M.A. dissertation, Boston College, 1987), pp. 60–72, 121, for frequency of reporting according to the seriousness of the attack: "A physically traumatic or persistent attack was associated with making a report to the police. Over half of those who were punched, hit, kicked or beaten reported the incident. Less than one-third as many of those who did not experience these beatings reported. Similarly, approximately one-third of those who were chased (or followed) or were threatened made out reports compared to 10% or fewer of those who did not suffer from these traumatic attacks. Furthermore, over half of those who sustained injuries reported the attacks and only 19% of the rest did.

"Other situational variables such as number of attacks, whether the victims knew the attackers, or whether the victims were alone were not related to informing the police."

56. Other surveys offer these percentages of reporting: (Anthony D'Augelli, "Gay Men's and Lesbian Women's Experiences of Discrimination, Harassment, Violence, and Indifference," University Park, Pennsylvania State University, Department of Individual and Family Studies, May 1, 1987, pp. 24, 27) 93 percent of respondents did not report incidents to authorities; (Steven K. Aurand, Rita Addessa, and Christine Bush, *Violence and Discrimination Against Philadelphia Lesbian and Gay People: A Study by the Philadelphia Lesbian and Gay Task Force,* pp. 6, 25–27, 30, 34) 91 percent of male respondents and 61 percent of female respondents "who experienced criminal violence" did not report those crimes to the police; (Susan Cavin, "Rutgers Sexual Orientation Survey: A Report of Experiences of Lesbian, Gay, and Bisexual Members of the Rutgers Community," New Brunswick, New Jersey, Rutgers University, Women's Studies Department, April 1987, pp. 33–34) 88 percent of all incidents were not reported to Rutgers authorities; (Kenneth B. Morgen, *The Prevalence of Anti-Gay/Lesbian Victimization in Baltimore: 1988,* p. 8) 87 percent of both men

and women did not report incidents to the police; (Felice Yeskel, *The Consequences of Being Gay: A Report on the Quality of Life for Lesbian, Gay, and Bisexual Students at the University of Massachusetts at Amherst*, p. 16) "66.7% of student who have been victims of [queer jokes, anti-lesbian or gay slurs, pressure to be silent about sexual orientation, or vandalism of personal property] say they *have never reported* the incident to anyone"; (Gregory Herek, "Sexual Orientation and Prejudice at Yale: A Report on the Experience of Lesbian, Gay, and Bisexual Members of the Yale Community," Department of Psychology, April 3, 1986, pp. 2, 7) "of the 96 respondents who reported having been harassed or attacked, 90% said they had *not* reported at least one such incident to an appropriate Yale official (police, dean, supervisor, etc.)"; (Office of the Governor, Anthony S. Earl, State of Wisconsin, "Governor's Council on Lesbian and Gay Issues: Violence Survey Final Report," Madison, 1985) 75 percent of the victims had not gone to the police; (New Jersey Lesbian and Gay Coalition, "Discrimination Against Lesbians and Gay Men in New Jersey: 1977–1983," New Brunswick, 1983) "80% of the cases were not reported to the police"; and (Ames Civil Rights Task Force, "Results and Analysis of the Ames Civil Rights Task Force Survey of Ames Area Lesbians and Gay Men," Ames, Iowa, June 1984, pp. 6, 14, 18) "36% reported that they were reluctant to call for police protection because of their sexual orientation."

57. U.S. Congress, House Subcommittee on Criminal Justice of the Committee on the Judiciary, *Anti-Gay Violence*, pp. 147–151.

58. Bureau of Justice Statistics, *Criminal Victimization in the United States, 1984: A National Crime Survey Report* NCJ-100435 (Washington, D.C.: U.S. Department of Justice, May 1986), p. 85, table 94.

59. Percentages equal more than 100 percent because a single incident might require more than one response (e.g., the police could be both indifferent and competent).

The survey by Office of the Governor, Anthony S. Earl, State of Wisconsin, "Governor's Council on Lesbian and Gay Issues: Violence Survey Final Report," finds that of those who did go to the police, 50 percent said the police were indifferent, 24 percent said they were incompetent, 18 percent courteous or helpful, and 8 percent hostile.

In the survey by Yeskel, *The Consequences of Being Gay: A Report on the Quality of Life for Lesbian, Gay and Bisexual Students at the University of Massachusetts at Amherst*, pp. 7–8, 9, "80.1% of respondents state the Campus Police are inadequate in meeting their needs as lesbians, gays, or bisexuals"; if they were victims of harassment or discrimination, 68.9 percent of respondents report they would not go or would not go again to the Campus Police, 70.1 percent would not go to the Amherst town police, 62.2 percent would not go to the Dean of Students office, 63.6 percent would not go to the Ombuds Office, 62.9 percent would not go to faculty.

In the survey by Ames Civil Rights Task Force, "Results and Analysis of the Ames Civil Rights Task Force Survey of Ames Area Lesbian and Gay Men," Ames, Iowa, June 1984, pp. 6, 14, 18, "5% reported that they were refused services or aid by the police because of their sexual orientation[,] ... 16%

reported that they were treated with indifference by police[,] ... 9% were discouraged from pressing charges or following through on a complaint."

60. Percentages total more than 100 because some respondents indicated more than one reason for not reporting.

In the survey by Office of the Governor, Anthony S. Earl, State of Wisconsin, "Governor's Council on Lesbian and Gay Issues: Violence Survey Final Report," "of those who did not report an incident, the reasons most often given were that victims believed the police would be unsympathetic or hostile, that police or justice system would not pursue the case, or that they did not wish to identify themselves as homosexual."

In the survey by Herek, "Sexual Orientation and Prejudice at Yale: A Report on the Experience of Lesbian, Gay, and Bisexual Members of the Yale Community," pp. 2, 22, "the most common reasons cited for not reporting were the belief that the incident was not sufficiently serious and the fear that University authorities would respond negatively to the victims or would not take any action."

In the survey by New Jersey Lesbian and Gay Coalition, "Discrimination Against Lesbians and Gay Men in New Jersey: 1977–1983," cases were not reported by respondents "usually because of the catch 22 situation. ... If one does report harassment or discrimination to any authority (boss, landlord, police, etc.), one is most likely to experience more harassment or discrimination."

In the survey by Morgen, *The Prevalence of Anti-Gay/Lesbian Victimization in Baltimore: 1988*, p. 8, the reasons given for not reporting are that the victims "feared retaliation either by the police, their families or employers (51%), expected no help (12%) or other reasons (29%), such as the incident was ... not 'serious enough.' "

In the survey by Cavin, "Rutgers Sexual Orientation Survey," p. 64, reasons for not reporting are the following: not serious enough (30 percent), expected negative/hostile reaction (24 percent), feared exposure or further harassment (12 percent), felt nothing could be done (e.g., perpetrator caught) (12 percent), handled matter personally (12 percent), and not worth the trouble (9 percent).

Johnston, in U.S. Congress, House Subcommittee on Criminal Justice of Committee on the Judiciary, *Anti-Gay Violence*, 99th Cong., 2nd sess., 1986, states, "Possible reasons for this apparent under-reporting may be fear that the gay victim's family may find out, causing embarrassment or domestic problems; a fear that landlords or employers may find out, generating other forms of discrimination; or possibly a general fear and mistrust of the police."

Sepejak, in her survey of Canadian lesbians and gay men, "The Willingness of Homosexuals to Report Criminal Victimization to the Police" (M.A. dissertation, University of Toronto, 1977), p. 30, finds that "homosexuals are more willing to contact the police if victimized in a setting that would not identify them as homosexuals, as opposed to a setting that would identify them as such."

Philip Plews, in "The Evil That Boys Do," *Toronto*, May 1986, p. 60, reports that "according to Sergeant Pat McCullough of [Metropolitan Toronto's] 11th [Police] Division . . . there are few reported cases of 'queerbashing' because the victims dread coming forward."

Jim Zook, in "Officer, Suspect Shot in Oak Park," *Dallas Morning News,* July 12, 1986, pp. 33A, 38A, reports Sergeant Earl Newsom as saying, "A number of people who are robbed in the park don't want to report the crime. A number of the people are family people, bisexuals, closet gays. They don't want it known that they were in [the] Park in the middle of the night."

61. Bureau of Justice Statistics, *Criminal Victimization in the United States, 1984: A National Crime Survey Report* NCJ-100435, pp. 94–95, table 105. Six percent of victims of "all personal crimes" and 7.4 percent of victims of "all household crimes" did not report because "police would not want to be bothered"; 2.3 percent of victims of "all personal crimes" and 3.7 percent of victims of "all household crimes" said "police would be inefficient, ineffective, insensitive." The report states (p. 8), "The most frequent specific reason given by [these] victims for not reporting violent crimes to the police was that the event was a private or personal matter."

62. Peter Freiberg, "Gays and the Police: Old Problems, New Hope," *Advocate* (Los Angeles).

63. Berrill, "Criminal Justice Subcommittee: Hearing on Police Practices," p. 5.

64. Berrill, "Criminal Justice Subcommittee: Hearing on Police Practices," p. 5. A similar example is reported, p. 6, from Houston: "Until two years ago, gay people and members of other minority groups complained of numerous violations of their civil rights by the Houston Police Department. According to the Houston Gay Political Caucus, police harassment and violence against our community has decreased by 80% since 1982. The reason is simple: gay people helped elect Kathy Whitmire, who promised to use the full weight of her office to make the police deal fairly and responsibly with all minority groups, including the gay community. Since her election and the appointment of Chief of Police Lee Brown, a police liaison to the gay community has been appointed, gay and lesbian awareness training sessions are mandatory for new police recruits and a police advisory committee task force has been established to explore the relationship between the gay community and the Houston criminal justice system."

65. See, for example, Joseph Leary, "Stibich Meets with Gays Over Police Protection," *Chicago North Town News,* January 24, 1978. In *Out!* (Madison, Wisconsin), "Lesbian/Gay Leaders Talk to the Chief . . ."; Sue Burke, ". . . But Reports of Harassment Persist," December 1984, p. 3. Ed Hicks, in *GayBeat* (Cincinnati), "GayBeat Interviews Vice Squad Chief," March 1, 1985, pp. 1, 5–6; "More on Vice (Part II)," April 1, 1985, pp. 1, 6; "Vice Squad III," June 1985, pp. 1, 6; "Cincinnati Vice: IV; Continuing Our Interview with Lieutenant Harold Mills," July 1985, p. 1. Fred Berger, "Portland Police, Gays Open Dialogue: An Interview with Capt. Steve Roberts," *Our Paper* (Portland, Maine), November 1984, pp. 7, 11. "Gay/Police Pow-Wow," *GayBeat* (Cincinnati), July 1985, pp. 2, 7. "Gay Leaders Meet with Brooklyn D.A.: Holtzman Considers Adding Full-time Gay Liaison," *New York Native,* March 23, 1987, pp. 9–10. "California," *Advocate* (Los Angeles), August 4, 1987, p. 24. "Will Submit Brief: Gays Tell Mayor of Police Brutality," *Ottawa Journal,* June 13, 1975, p. 3. Forty-fourth War Assembly, Letter to Owners and Proprietors of Gay and

Lesbian Establishments re: "Police Protection and Services to Gay Persons," Office of Dick Simpson, alderman, City Council, City of Chicago, 1978. Eric Gordon, "Police Inaction Questioned in Portland" and "Violence Gives Birth to Rainbow Task Force," *Our Paper* (Los Angeles), December 1988, p. 6. Peter Freiberg, "NYC Cops: We Were Wrong; ACT UP Strip Searches Broke the Rules," *Advocate* (Los Angeles), May 23, 1989, p. 13.

See "Pennsylvania," *Advocate* (Los Angeles), December 8, 1987, p. 26, which reports that subsequent to the pressing of the Philadelphia Police Commissioner by the Philadelphia Lesbian and Gay Task Force's executive director "to combat antigay violence and to make his officers more sensitive to gay concerns," the Department "has hired a consultant to assess current training programs about minority issues—including those related to gay people—and to develop new programs."

66. See, for example, Francis M. Roache, police commissioner, Boston Police Department, Special Order Number 87, to all bureaus, districts, areas, divisions, offices, sections and units, Subject: "Community Disorders Unit," in which the following is stated to include "sexual orientation" in police protection policy: "It is the policy of the Department to ensure that all citizens can be free of violence, threats of harassment, due to their race, color, creed, sexual orientation, or desire to live or travel in any neighborhood." The Special Order goes on to include as one classification of "Community Disorder": "All crimes that are committed where there is evidence to support that the victim(s) were selected on account of sexual orientation, or incidents and situations precipitated by motives arising from sexual orientation."

67. See, for example, Berrill, "Criminal Justice Subcommittee: Hearing on Police Practices," pp. 8–9; Freiberg, "Gays and Police: Old Problems, New Hope," *Advocate* (Los Angeles); Johnston, chief, New York City Police Department, in U.S. Congress, House Subcommittee on Criminal Justice of Committee on the Judiciary, *Anti-Gay Violence*, pp. 8–12; and Ruben Rosario, "Anti-gay Violence Probed: Homosexuals Join Those Aided by Cop Unit as Attacks Based on Race, Beliefs Increase," p. 31.

68. For changes in recruiting policies, see "N.Y. Police Reach Out to Gay Recruits," *Advocate* (Los Angeles), November 13, 1984, p. 13. Steering Committee and Public Safety Committee, Boston Lesbian and Gay Political Alliance, "Proposal: Steering Committee and Public Safety Committee of the Boston Lesbian and Gay Political Alliance; Submitted to Mayor Raymond L. Flynn and Police Commissioner Francis M. Roache," February 17, 1987. Joe Sciacca and John Impemba, "Flynn Supports Hiring Gay Police," *Boston Herald*, February 4, 1987, p. 10. Steve Patterson, "The Herald Wants to Know Your View," *Boston Herald*, February 4, 1987, p. 10. Joe Sciacca, "Police Boss to Study Gay Recruiting" and "Gay Officer: Recruiting Eased Strain," *Boston Herald*, February 8, 1987. Beverly Ford, "Gay Activists Call for Boston Police Hiring Switch," *Boston Herald*, March 10, 1987. "Boston, Massachusetts," *Advocate* (Los Angeles), April 28, 1987, p. 25. Paula Charland, "Lesbians, Gay Men Urged to Try for Police Program," *Bay Windows* (Boston), July 9, 1987. See also, "California," *Advocate* (Los Angeles), April 26, 1988, p. 24, for Los Angeles Mayor

Tom Bradley's announcement at a March 10, 1988, news conference: "Not only have we adopted a policy of recruiting and promoting the employment of gays and lesbians in this city ... but the [Police] Commission just recently ... announced recommitment to that principle." The account also refers to his "outlining the formation of a hate-crimes unit in the city attorney's office and a task force to improve relations between police and the gay community."

For programs specifically oriented to "hate" crimes or bias-related violence, see Rosario, "Anti-gay Violence Probed: Homosexuals Join Those Aided by Cop Unit as Attacks Based on Race, Beliefs Increase," *New York Post*, February 16, 1986, p. 31; Interview with Donald J. Bromberg, captain and commanding officer, and Carl A. Zittell, sergeant, Bias Investigating Unit, Police Department, City of New York, September 18, 1986; and Peter Finn and Taylor McNeil, "The Response of the Criminal Justice System to Bias Crime: An Exploratory Review" (Cambridge, Mass.: Abt Associates, October 7, 1987), pp. 10–13.

69. See, for example, "Homosexuals and the Police," *St. Louis Post-Dispatch*, October 13, 1978; Elizabeth Pincus, "1979 Peg's Place Assault by Off-Duty S.F. Cops Goes to Trial," *Coming Up!* (San Francisco), June 1985; "Inquiry in Police Action at Gay Bar," *St. Louis Globe-Democrat*, July 18, 1979; Jim Marko, "Police Raid in Providence Brings Charges of Harassment," *Gay Community News* (Boston), December 23, 1978; William Burks, "Chicago Police Sued for $15 Million: Suit Filed Against Officers in Drug Raid," *New York Native*, December 29, 1986, p. 6; Christine Guilfoy, "Copy Faces Rights Complaint," *South End News* (Boston), April 9, 1987, pp. 1, 3; and Kim Westheimer, in *Gay Community News* (Boston), "Long Guang Huang Victory a Model for Organizing:Transsexual Charges Boston Police Brutality," February 22, 1986, and "Record of First Attack Disappears: Transsexual to Sue after 2nd Attack," March 8, 1986.

70. See, for example, the following newspaper articles concerning one case: In *Gay Community News* (Boston), "Gay Teenagers Brought Complaints: Boston Police Officers Accused of Abuse," May 27, 1978; "Youth Testifies in Hearings: Boston Charges Police Officers in Beatings," July 22, 1978; "Changing Signals" (Editorial), October 14, 1978. David Brill, in *Gay Community News* (Boston), "Officers Charged with Beating Youths: Defense in Boston Police Hearings Produces Witnesses," September 16, 1978; "Charged with Beating Youths: Comm. Jordan Suspends Police Officers," October 14, 1978, pp. 1, 8; "Boston Police Officers Appeal Suspensions in Beating of Youths," December 23, 1978. "Assaults on Gays Continue," *GPU News* (Milwaukee), September 1978, p. 4.

For other examples, see "Deputy Sheriff Found Guilty in Arkansas Transvestite Beating," *Gay Community News* (Boston), June 3, 1978; George Mendenhall, "Jury Finds Cop Guilty in Attacks on 2 Gay Men: Jurors Believe Victims, Not Police Officer; He's Free Until Sentencing April 12," *Bay Area Reporter* (San Francisco), March 21, 1985, pp. 1, 11; Anthony Glover, "Board Reprimands Police Captain in Arrests of Alleged Homosexuals," *St. Louis Post-Dispatch*, October 5, 1978; "Fort Worth Police to Stop Harassment," *GayLife* (Chicago), October 13, 1978.

71. See Freiberg, "Gays and Police: Old Problems, New Hope"; and Timothy Stirton, "Gay Cops, Good Cops," *Frontiers* (Los Angeles), July 13–27, 1988, pp. 54–55.

72. See, for example, William Burks, "Chicago Police Sued for $15 Million: Suit Filed Against Officers in Drug Raid," *New York Native*, December 29, 1986, p. 6. Mark Vandervelden, "Gay Bar 'Raids' in L.A. Spark Call for Probe," *Advocate* (Los Angeles), January 5, 1988, pp. 16–17. Peter Freiberg, in *Advocate* (Los Angeles), "Police Raid Syracuse Gay Bar, Arrest Four," March 1, 1988, pp. 14–15; and "Pittsburgh Raids Spark Lawsuit, Demonstration," May 24, 1988, pp. 17–18. Rick Harding, "W. Va. Police Admit Keeping List of Gays," *Advocate* (Los Angeles), May 24, 1988, pp. 28–19.

73. Freiberg, "Gays and Police: Old Problems, New Hope."

74. Hinckle, "The Untold Story: Dan White's San Francisco," p. 10.

75. Right to Privacy Committee, "The Right to Privacy Committee's Brief to the City of Toronto," p. 35.

76. Bell, "Black Tie and Blood," pp. 1, 11–12, 14. See n. 3 for details of this police raid of the bar.

77. See Rick Harding, "Blanketed in Anger: A Patchwork of Protests Upstages the AIDS Quilt," *Advocate* (Los Angeles), November 7, 1989, pp. 8–9; Brett Averill, "Castro Held Hostage: Many Injured as Police Sweep Bystanders from Sidewalk," *Bay Area Reporter* (San Francisco), October 12, 1989, pp. 1, 14–15, 23; and David Tuller, "S.F. Gays Demand Probe of Clash with Police," *San Francisco Chronicle*, October 9, 1989, p. A2.

APPENDIX D. HUSTLERS

1. See Donal E. J. MacNamara and Edward Sagarin's study of "Homosexual Prostitution," in their *Sex, Crime, and the Law*, pp. 142–149.

2. Martin Hoffman, "The Male Prostitute," p. 17, in his analysis of a study by Albert J. Reiss, Jr. (cited and discussed later in the text), concludes that a set of traditional guidelines enforced and passed on through lower-class delinquency groups permit boys in such peer groups "to engage in and derive a certain amount of sexual gratification from what are, behaviorally, homosexual acts *without thinking of themselves as being homosexual,* and therefore unmasculine. . . . The theoretical importance of the Reiss study is that it shows how sociological determinants, in this case the structuring of the relationship by the peer group norms, can serve to completely redefine "normal" expectations in an area even as highly charged with cultural taboos as male homosexual behavior."

3. Another example of anti-gay violence occurring in the hustling scene may be the victimization of a gay hustler by a nongay client. For example, male transvestites may engage in sexual activity with customers who react violently if and when the hustler's biological gender is discovered (see Tommi Avicolli, in *Philadelphia Gay News,* "Bucks County Police Seek Identity of Murdered Duo," July 18–24, 1986, p. 3; "Police Identify Bodies Found in Bucks County," July 25–31, 1986, p. 3; "Police Release Composites in Bucks County Murders," August 15–21, 1986, pp. 1, 29.). Because such reactions may be triggered by the

customer's feeling deceived, rather than by antagonism toward the supposed gay identity of the hustler, these incidents are perhaps not explicitly anti-gay.

4. See, for example, "Robber Who Drugged Gays Sent to Prison," *San Francisco Chronicle,* June 3, 1982, p. 47; David Jackson, "Robber, Sadist, Sometimes a Killer: Gay Hustler: A Violent Threat," *Chicago Daily News,* February 28, 1976, p. 1; Tommi Avicolli, "Police Seek Assault Suspect," *Philadelphia Gay News,* August 22–28, 1986, pp. 1, 23; "People v. Thomas and Lucille Hagen," District Attorney's Office (Manhattan), County of New York, Unpublished collection of "some of the cases involving gay or lesbian victims which have been prosecuted by the Manhattan District Attorney's Office between 1980 and May, 1985," May 1985, p. 7.

Ed Hicks, "Van Hook Found Guilty," *GayBeat* (Cincinnati), August 1985, pp. 1, 6, reports the following:

"Following his arrest, [the defendant] made a confession to the police. He told officers that he had gone to . . . 'a homosexual bar,' to get money. 'My method was to lure a homosexual to a place where I could rob the person. So I met this guy. . . . I told him I was expensive, I was looking for somebody to take care of me, I had expensive tastes. . . . I lured him on . . . to have sex with him.' [The defendant] drove his own car to [the victim's] apartment.

"Once in [the victim's] apartment, [the defendant] turned on the stereo, sat in a chair, and took out his penis to entice [the victim]. [The victim] walked over to him and, kneeling, reached up towards him. [The defendant] quickly grabbed and twisted his neck, put him in a choke hold, and strangled him. He held him on the floor until he stopped breathing. 'I don't know whether I broke his neck or not,' [the defendant] said, 'but that's what I intended to do.' He searched [the victim's] person for money, but found none. He went into the kitchen to look for food, but found no food either. Angry at the lack of money and food, he began to look for a knife. The only one he came across was a paring knife, though he tried to find one larger. With the knife he had he returned to [the victim], who was making 'gurgling' sounds in his throat. He cut [the victim] deep into his head, neck, chest and stomach. 'I tried to cut his head off,' [the defendant] said, 'but it wasn't working too well. . . . I cut his stomach open, and tried to work my way into his heart. . . .' Finally, [the defendant] began 'to get paranoid.' He smeared his fingerprints in the kitchen and on the stereo, stuck the knife into the hole he had cut in [the victim's] stomach—handle first, so as to cover fingerprints—and used a butter knife to open the front door. He took a few gold chains and a leather jacket with him as he left the apartment."

5. Albert J. Reiss, Jr., "The Social Integration of Queers and Peers," in Hendrik M. Ruitenbeek, ed., *The Problem of Homosexuality in Modern Society,* pp. 252–255, 259. Sex histories were obtained from all of the white Nashville boys who were resident in the Tennessee State Training School for Boys during the month of June 1958.

See also Hoffman, "The Male Prostitute," p. 17.

6. Reiss, "The Social Integration of Queers and Peers," in Ruitenbeek, *The Problem of Homosexuality in Modern Society,* pp. 250–251, 275–276.

See also John Gerassi, *The Boys of Boise: Furor, Vice and Folly in an American City*, pp. 33, 35; John Rechy, *The Sexual Outlaw: A Documentary: A Non-Fiction Account, with Commentaries, of Three Days and Nights in the Sexual Underground*, pp. 157–158; MacNamara and Sagarin, *Sex, Crime, and the Law*, p. 142; and Josh Thomas, "Appalachians, Hustling and Fag-Bashing," p. 7.

7. Reiss, "The Social Integration of Queers and Peers" in Ruitenbeek, ed., *The Problem of Homosexuality in Modern Society*, p. 262. He adds, "Boys who do not wish to be solicited are not vulnerable for another reason: they usually are members of groups which negatively sanction the activity. Such groups generally 'bug' boys who go out with fellators and use other techniques of isolation to discourage the transaction. There are also groups which look upon queers as 'fair game' for their aggressive activity. They beat them, roll, and otherwise put upon them."

8. Reiss, "The Social Integration of Queers and Peers," in Ruitenbeek, ed., *The Problem of Homosexuality in Modern Society,* pp. 259–260. See also Hoffman, "The Male Prostitute," *Sexual Behavior*, p. 17.

9. Reiss, "The Social Integration of Queers and Peers," in Ruitenbeek, ed., *The Problems of Homosexuality in Modern Society*, pp. 251, 260. See also Gerassi, *The Boys of Boise*, p. 33.

10. Gerassi, *The Boys of Boise*, pp. 35–36, investigates a public homosexual scandal in Boise, Idaho, in the mid-1950s. He observes: "Four or five youths were deeply involved. They knew who the homosexuals were, how to contact them, and how to profit from their contact. They were juvenile delinquents, not homosexuals, and one phase of their delinquency was male prostitution. . . .

Dr. [John] Butler [who offered psychiatric findings on cases that came to trial] told me . . . "that the hard core of kids supposedly seduced by homosexuals were actually made up of tough gang members. . . . They were fully aware of what they were doing. They may have been only fifteen, sixteen and seventeen, but they were much too developed to be considered children. And, as it turned out, some of them became regular criminals."

See also Jonathan Katz, "1955: Anonymous; Witch-Hunt in Boise, Idaho; An Interview with a Victim—'They Lit a Match to a Bonfire,' " in *Gay American History: Lesbians and Gay Men in the U.S.A.: A Documentary*, pp. 109–119. A victim of the scandal says (p. 110), "There was a hysteria in Boise about young teen-age boys being seduced by older men; that's what they conveyed to the public. The city paper, the *Idaho Daily Statesman*, embellished on this. It kept emphasizing older men and young boys; it kept emphasizing there was a sex ring of older men enticing these boys. There was no such thing; no such ring existed. The boys who were arrested in Boise all knew exactly what they were doing."

MacNamara and Sagarin, *Sex Crime, and the Law*, pp. 141–149, in their study of 162 male prostitutes, find (p. 144) that "not one of these men attributed his prostitutional activity to an early history of seduction or rape; in fact, a majority indicated that their initial homosexual experience was not only voluntary but self-inflicted."

11. Reiss, "The Social Integration of Queers and Peers," in Ruitenbeek, ed., *The Problem of Homosexuality in Modern Society*, pp. 264–271. See also Hoffman, "The Male Prostitute," *Sexual Behavior* (1972), 2:17–18.

12. Reiss, "The Social Integration of Queers and Peers," in Ruitenbeek, ed., *The Problem of Homosexuality in Modern Society*, pp. 255, 256, 258–259, 262. Reiss explains (p. 265), "From a sociological point of view, the peer–queer [boy-client] sexual transaction occurs between two major types of deviators— 'delinquents' and 'queers.' Both types of deviators risk negative sanctions for their deviant acts. The more often one has been incarcerated or arrested, the more punitive the sanctions from the larger social system for both types of deviators. At some point, therefore, both calculate risks and seek to minimize them, at least in the very short run. Each then becomes a means for the other to minimize risk."

13. Reiss, "The Social Integration of Queers and Peers," in Ruitenbeek, ed., *The Problem of Homosexuality in Modern Society*, p. 267.

14. Reiss, "The Social Integration of Queers and Peers," in Ruitenbeek, ed., *The Problem of Homosexuality in Modern Society*, p. 274.

15. For examples of incidents in which violence was used, see Lou Chibbaro, Jr., "Youth Gets 6 to 20 Years Despite 'Sex Advance' Plea," *Washington Blade* (Washington, D.C.), June 22, 1984, p. 7; Reiss, "The Social Integration of Queers and Peers," in Ruitenbeek, ed., *The Problem of Homosexuality in Modern Society*, pp. 271–274; Brian Miller and Laud Humphreys, "Lifestyles and Violence: Homosexual Victims of Assault and Murder," p. 177; Victoria Lynn Swigert, Ronald A. Farrell, and William C. Yoels, "Sexual Homicide: Social, Psychological, and Legal Aspects," *Archives of Sexual Behavior* (1976), 5:393; and MacNamara and Sagarin, *Sex, Crime, and the Law*, pp. 156–157. The most commonly reported disagreements and subsequent assaults concern payment. MacNamara and Sagarin, in their study of 162 male prostitutes, find (p. 157) that, "Assaults on an older male who promised financial compensation to a youth and then reneges (either before the sex act or after) do not seem to be rare. In our own interviews with hustlers, we were told of several such incidents. The respondents often claimed to have made felonious assaults or to have threatened the customer until money was produced; respondents also reported being told of such incidents by friends." For an interview with a former hustler who killed a client because the terms of the agreement were violated, see Seymour Kleinberg, *Alienated Affections: Being Gay in America* (New York: St. Martin's Press, 1980), pp. 197–202.

16. See, for example, Arthur Bell, *Kings Don't Mean a Thing: The John Knight Murder Case;* Tracie Cone, "Murdering the Gay Everyman, Part II." p. 5; Ed Hicks, in *GayBeat* (Cincinnati): "Killer's Sordid Tale," May 1, 1985, pp. 1, 4, 6; "Murder Victim Put on Trial: Messmer Guilty of Aggravated Murder," December 1986, pp. 1, 5, 7; "Moore Guilty of Lesser Charges," December 1986, pp. 5, 7, 9, 10.

APPENDIX F. INTERVIEW WITH A PERPETRATOR

1. Edwin M. Schur, *Labeling Deviant Behavior: Its Sociological Implications*, p. 47, who also quotes Thomas J. Scheff, *Being Mentally Ill* (Chicago: Aldine, 1966), p. 79.

See, for example, the following journalistic accounts of mass murderers: Ann Rule, *The Stranger Beside Me* (New York: W. W. Norton, 1980; New American Library, Signet, 1981); Tim Cahill and Russ Ewing, *Buried Dreams: Inside the Mind of a Serial Killer* (New York: Bantam Books, 1986); and Clifford L. Linedecker, *The Man Who Killed Boys* (New York: St. Martin's Press, 1980). In the preface to her account of the man responsible for the murder of several women, Rule writes, "Ted has been described as the perfect son, the perfect student, the Boy Scout grown to adulthood, a genius, as handsome as a movie idol, a bright light in the future of the Republican Party, a sensitive psychiatric social worker, a budding lawyer, a trusted friend, a young man for whom the future could surely hold only success." In their account of John Gacy, who murdered thirty-three boys, Cahill and Ewing, report (p. 88) that psychiatrists found that the "crimes [were] committed—and repeatedly committed—as a matter of free will and not as a result of any mental illness," and that neighbors were shocked (p. 8): "No, they said, the man never seemed insane. He drank now and again, no more than anyone else, and if he had one too many, which happened infrequently, he simply became a little louder, a little more friendly. He was proud of himself and his business, maybe even a bit of a braggart, and, sure, sometimes he bullied the teenage boys who worked for him, but the man himself regularly put in twelve- and sixteen-hour days. He pushed himself hard and obviously felt he had a right to revel in his accomplishments, to expect from his employees the same perfection he demanded of himself." Linedecker also reports that neighbors were stunned (pp. 193–194): "They could not understand how one man who had lived among them as a popular and trusted neighbor and friend could have committed crimes so atrocious as those of which he was accused."

See also Susan Schechter, "Toward an Analysis of Violence Against Women in the Family," *Women and Male Violence: The Visions and Struggles of the Battered Women's Movement* (Boston: South End Press, 1982), pp. 209–240, for a discussion of wife batterers. On pp. 211–213, she counters the understanding that perpetrators are psychologically unusual or abnormal: "Personality theories suggest that battering is about illness and poor impulse control rather than power. Poor impulse control is a grossly misleading term; many men are only violent with their wives in the privacy of their homes. Sometimes, they carefully select which area of a woman's body to abuse. They usually do not kill. Some exercise substantial control and stop their abuse when they are threatened with jail sentences. Although they act 'out of control,' most batterers know what they are doing." She also states: "In 'Psychological Aspects of Wife-Beating' [in Maria Roy, ed., *Battered Women: A Psychosociological Study of Domestic Violence* (New York: Van Nostrand Reinhold, 1977), pp. 114–115.], Natalie Shainess, a psychiatrist, maintains that men who batter may be under great stress and have no tools for handling it. Some of them are infantile, unable to tolerate frustration and therefore lash out. Although the descriptions may accurately portray some violent men, they still fail to explain why these men choose their wives as targets. It is easy to read backward into deprived childhoods to find the cause of violence, but many 'deprived' people are not violent. Indeed, men who were loved as children also learn to dominate and abuse women."

Empirical data, as cited by Marie Marshall Fortune, *Sexual Violence: The Unmentionable Sin* (New York: Pilgrim Press, 1983), pp. 176–190, have consistently shown that that which distinguishes perpetrators of sexist violence is not psychological illness and anti-social personalities, but their very averageness and ordinary behavior as typical male citizens. Accepting the notion that our friends and neighbors may be and are these very perpetrators is, of course, difficult and frightening; imagining and relegating perpetrators to the ranks of the "weird," "sick," and psychopathic provides us with the illusion of their minority and our safety and neutralizes the actual and dangerous behavior of men.

Selected Bibliography

Aaron, Betsy. "Violence Against Gays." Special Assignment for *ABC Nightly News*. October 21, 1986.

Adair, Nancy and Casey Adair. *Word Is Out: Stories of Some of Our Lives.* New York: Dell; San Francisco: New Glide Publications, 1978.

Aldridge, Chip. "Homophobic Violence: A Growing Epidemic." *Open Hands: Journal of Reconciling Congregation Program* (1987), 3(2):9–11.

Allen, Paula Gunn. *The Sacred Hoop: Recovering the Feminine in American Indian Traditions.* Boston: Beacon Press, 1986.

Allen, Scott. "Aftermath in Bangor: Was Charlie Howard's Murder an Isolated Incident or the Natural Outcome of Homophobia?" *Maine Times* (Topsham, Maine), August 10, 1984.

Ames Civil Rights Task Force. "Results and Analysis of the Ames Civil Rights Task Force of Ames Area Lesbians and Gay Men, June 1984." Ames, Iowa, 1984.

Anderson, Craig L. "Males as Sexual Assault Victims: Multiple Levels of Trauma." *Journal of Homosexuality* (1981–1982), 7:145–162.

Anti-Violence Project, National Gay and Lesbian Task Force. "Statements on Anti-Gay Violence by Religious, Political, and Law Enforcement Leaders: An Organizing Resource." Washington, D.C., November 20, 1989.

Aurand, Steven K., Rita Addessa, and Christine Bush. *Violence and Discrimination Against Philadelphia Lesbian and Gay People: A Study by the Philadelphia Lesbian and Gay Task Force.* December 1985.

Bagnall, Robert G., Patrick C. Gallagher, and Joni L. Goldstein. "Burdens on Gay Litigants and Bias in the Court System: Homosexual Panic, Child Custody, and Anonymous Parties." *Harvard Civil Rights–Civil Liberties Law Review* (1984), 19:497–559.

Bearak, Barry. "Slaying of Openly Gay Man Raises Troubling Questions for Quiet Town." *Des Moines Register,* August 14, 1984, p. 1A.

Beck, Evelyn Torton, ed. *Nice Jewish Girls: A Lesbian Anthology.* Crossing Press Feminist Series. Trumansburg, N.Y.: Crossing Press, 1982.

Behrens, David. In *Newsday* (Long Island). "Tracing Violence Against Gays," November 28, 1982, pp. 6, 17; and "Joining Crusade Against Crime," November 29, 1982, pp. 4–5.

Bell, Alan P. and Martin S. Weinberg. *Homosexualities: A Study of Diversity Among Men and Women.* New York: Simon and Schuster, 1978.

Bell, Arthur. *Kings Don't Mean a Thing: The John Knight Murder Case.* New York: William Morrow, 1978.

Bell, Arthur. In *Village Voice* (New York). "Midnight Ramble Roundup: Chasing the Bat Pack," July 24, 1978, pp. 1, 11; "Gay-Bashing Spree in the Village," January 14, 1980, p. 18; "Death Comes Out," November 26 to December 2, 1980, pp. 1, 11–12; "Shooting at Ghosts: Ronald Crumpley's Lethal Odyssey," July 22–28, 1981, pp. 1, 20, 21; "Black Tie and Blood," October 12, 1982, pp. 1, 11–12, 14.

Bell, Joseph J. "Public Manifestations of Personal Morality: Limitations on the Use of Solicitation Statutes to Control Homosexual Cruising." *Journal of Homosexuality* (1979–1980), 5:97–114.

Berger, Raymond M. "Homosexuality: Gay Men." In Anne Minahon, ed., *Encyclopedia of Social Work.* 18th ed. New York: NASW.

Blumenfeld, Warren J. and Diane Raymond. *Looking at Gay and Lesbian Life.* Boston: Beacon Press, 1988.

Bohn, Ted S. "Homophobic Violence: Implications for Social Work Practice." *Journal of Social Work and Human Sexuality* (1983–84), 2:91–112.

Brewer, Steve. " 'Gay-bashing' Worsens Since AIDS Epidemic." *San Francisco Examiner,* February 2, 1986, pp. B1+.

Brown, Dick. "Johnston Speaks Out for 'My Gay Brothers, Sisters.' " *Des Moines Register,* January 30, 1985, pp. 1M, 2M.

Brown, Howard. *Familiar Faces, Hidden Lives: The Story of Homosexual Men in America Today.* New York: Harcourt Brace Jovanovich, 1976.

Brown, Lightning. "Hope for the Future? Do the Homophobic Campaigns in the Carolinas Reflect National Trends?" *New York Native,* December 1, 1986, pp. 13–15.

Brownworth, Victoria. "Survivor Talks." *Philadelphia Gay News,* July 16–22, 1988, p. 17.

Bull, Chris. "Homophobia Continues After Shooting of Two Ithaca Lesbians." *Gay Community News* (Boston), August 7, 1988.

Butterfield, Fox. "Slaying of Homosexual Man Upsets Confidence of Bangor, Me." *New York Times,* July 29, 1984.

Campus Environment Team, Pennsylvania State University. "Campus Climate and Acts of Intolerance: Report of the Campus Environment Team." University Park, October 1988.

Canadian Civil Liberties Association. *Video Surveillance by Police of Public Washrooms.* Submitted to Solicitor-General. March 1986.

Canellos, Peter. "A City and Its Sins: The Killing of a Gay Man in Bangor." *Boston Phoenix,* November 13, 1984, pp. 1, 6–7, 22–23, 26, 28–31.

Cathcart, Dwight. "Assessing the Legacy of Charlie Howard: The Impact of a Gay Man's Murder." *Bay Windows* (Boston), July 19–25, 1985, p. 1+

Cathcart, Dwight. "The Importance of Truth: Crimes Against Gays." *R.F.D.* (Bakersville, N.C.), Fall 1986, pp. 20–22.

Cauthern, Cynthia R. "900 Black Lesbians Speak." *Off Our Backs* (Washington, D.C.), June 1979, p. 12.

Cavin, Susan. *Lesbian Origins.* San Francisco: Ism Press, 1985.

Cavin, Susan. "Rutgers Sexual Orientation Survey: A Report on the Experiences of Lesbian, Gay, and Bisexual Members of the Rutgers Community; Brunswick, New Jersey." New Brunswick, N.J.: Women's Studies Program, Rutgers University, April 1987.

Chamberlain, Pam. "Homophobia in Schools or What We Don't Know Will Hurt Us." *Radical Teacher* (September 1985), 29:3–6.

Church, Foster. "Probe of Firebomb Stirs Questioning Of Unwanted Sort: Gay Commune Gets Attention." *Oregonian* (Portland), July 22, 1979, pp. 1A, 1B.

Churchill, Wainwright. *Homosexual Behavior Among Males: A Cross-Cultural and Cross-Species Investigation.* Englewood Cliffs, N.J.: Prentice-Hall, 1967; Prism Paperback, 1971.

City of New York, Commission on Human Rights. *Gay and Lesbian Discrimination Documentation Project.* Two-Year Report on Complaints of Sexual Orientation Discrimination, November 1983 to October 1985. Edward I. Koch, mayor; Marcella Maxwell, chairperson; Alberta B. Fuentes, executive director.

City of New York, Commission on Human Rights. "NYC Commission on Human Rights Report on Discrimination Against People with AIDS, November 1983–April 1986." Marcella Maxwell, chairperson; S. Ted Antholes, vice chairperson; Alberta B. Fuentes, executive director.

Coalition for Gay Rights in Ontario. "Discrimination Against Lesbians and Gay Men: The Ontario Human Rights Omission. A Brief to the Members of the Ontario Legislature from the Coalition for Gay Rights in Ontario." Toronto, October 1986.

Commission on Racial, Ethnic, Religious and Minority Violence. Office of the Attorney General, John K. Van de Kamp, State of California. *Attorney General's Commission on Racial, Ethnic, Religious and Minority Violence Final Report, April 1986.* Sacramento, 1986.

Commission on Social Justice, Archdiocese of San Francisco. *Homosexuality and Social Justice: Report of the Task Force on Gay/Lesbian Issues.* San Francisco, 1983.

Community United Against Violence. *Bashing.* David Lamble and R. Hunter Morey, producers. Diana Christensen, executive producer. San Francisco, 1986.

Cone, Tracie. "Murdering the Gay Everyman. Part Two." *Front Page* (North Carolina), December 1984, p. 5. Reprinted from *Winston-Salem Journal.*

Congregation for the Doctrine of Faith. "Letter to the Bishops of the Catholic Church on the Pastoral Care of Homosexual Persons." Adopted in an ordinary session of the Congregation on the Doctrine of the Faith; given at Rome,

October 1, 1986; approved and ordered to be published by Pope John Paul II during an audience granted to Prefect Joseph Cardinal Ratzinger; also, bearing name of Alberto Bovone, Titular Archbishop of Caesarea in Numdia, Secretary. Vatican City, 1986.

Cory, Donald Webster. *The Homosexual in America: A Subjective Approach.* New York: Greenberg, 1951.

Corzine, Jay and Richard Kirby. "Cruising the Truckers: Sexual Encounters in a Highway Rest Area." *Urban Life* (1977), 6:171–192.

Crew, Louis. "Just As I Am: Growing Up Gay in Dixie." *Southern Exposure* [n.d.], 5(1):59–63.

Crompton, Louis. "Gay Genocide: From Leviticus to Hitler." In Louie Crew, ed., *The Gay Academic,* Palm Springs, Calif.: ETC Publications.

Cruikshank, Margaret, ed. *The Lesbian Path.* San Francisco: Grey Fox Press, 1980; revised and enlarged ed., 1985.

Darty, Trudy and Sandee Potter, eds. *Women-Identified Women.* Palo Alto, Calif.: Mayfield, 1984.

D'Augelli, Anthony R. "Gay Men's and Lesbian Women's Experiences of Discrimination, Harassment, Violence, and Indifference at The Pennsylvania State University." University Park, Pa.: Pennsylvania State University, Department of Individual and Family Studies, May 1, 1987.

Delacoste, Frederique and Felice Newman. *Fight Back! Feminist Resistance to Male Violence.* Minneapolis: Cleis Press, 1981.

D'Emilio, John. "Gay Politics, Gay Community: San Francisco's Experience." *Socialist Review* (1981), 55:77–104.

D'Emilio, John. *Sexual Politics, Sexual Communities: The Making of a Homosexual Minority in the United States, 1940–1970.* Chicago: University of Chicago Press, 1983.

Dezutter, Hank and Patrick Fahey. "Knights on Broadway: Gays Fight Back in New Town." *Chicago Sun-Times,* July 21, 1978.

Diamond, Sara. "Still Sane: Interview with Sculptress Persimmon Blackridge." *Fuse: Cultural News Magazine* (Ontario), Fall 1984, pp. 30–35.

Dickerson, Toni, Abigail Norman, Robin Omata, Lydia Dean Pilcher, Afua Kafi-Akua, and Daresha Kyi, producers and directors. *Just Because of Who We Are: Working Tapes.* Edited by Diana Agosta. New York: Heramedia, 1986.

District Attorney's Office (Manhattan), County of New York. Unpublished collection and summaries of ". . . some of the cases involving gay or lesbian victims which have been prosecuted by the Manhattan District Attorney's Office between 1980 and May, 1985." May 1985.

Donahue, Phil. "Queerbashing." *Donahue Transcript No. 04306.* Cincinnati: Multimedia Entertainment, Inc., 1986.

Edwards, George R. *Gay/Lesbian Liberation: A Biblical Perspective.* New York: Pilgrim Press, 1984.

Ellenberg, Lee. "Counseling Service for Gay and Lesbian Victims." Boston: Fenway Community Health Center, February 5, 1986.

Epstein, Robert and Richard Schmeichen, directors and producers. *The Times of*

Harvey Milk. Beverly Hills: Cinecom International Films and Pacific Arts Video, 1986.

Evans, Arthur. *Witchcraft and the Gay Counterculture: A Radical View of Western Civilization and Some of the People It Has Tried to Destroy.* Boston: Fag Rag Books, 1978,

Fahs, Marianne C., associate director, Division of Health Economics, Mount Sinai Medical Center. "Reversed Priorities in the Battle Against AIDS" (Letter). *New York Times,* June 21, 1989, p. A24.

"Federal Policy: AIDS Medical Costs by 1992." *AIDS Policy and Law Newsletter.* Washington, D.C., Buraff Publications, January 6, 1989.

Fierstein, Harvey. *The Torch Song Trilogy.* New York: Gay Presses of New York, 1979.

Finn, Peter and Taylor McNeil. *The Response of the Criminal Justice System to Bias Crime: An Exploratory Review.* Submitted to National Institute of Justice; U.S. Department of Justice. Contract No. OJP-86-002. Cambridge, Mass.: Abt Associates, Inc., October 7, 1987.

FitzGerald, Frances. "The Castro." *New Yorker,* Part I, July 21, 1986, pp. 34–38, 43–44, 46, 51–70; Part II, July 28, 1986, pp. 44, 46–63.

Freiberg, Peter. In *Advocate* (Los Angeles). "Community United Against Violence," October 28, 1986, pp. 10–11, 20; "Sex Education and the Gay Issue: What Are They Teaching About Us in the Schools?" September 1, 1987, pp. 42–43, 45, 47–49; "Helping Gay Street Youth in New York," February 16, 1988, pp. 10–11, 14; "Blaming the Victim: New Life for the 'Gay Panic' Defense," May 24, 1988, pp. 10–13; "A Victim Tells Her Story: Survivor Talks About the Antigay Shooting that Killed Her Lover," January 3, 1989, pp. 18, 20; "Why Johnny Can't Tolerate Gays: Campus Violence Is on the Rise, College Groups Say," March 14, 1989, pp. 8–9; "A Hairstyle to Die From: Skinheads Adopt Your Grade-School Haircut and a Violent, Antigay Doctrine," April 25, 1989, pp. 8–9; "A Light in the Blackboard Jungle: New York Harvey Milk School Finds Its Place," April 25, 1989, pp. 50–52.

Fricke, Aaron. *Reflections of a Rock Lobster: A Story About Growing Up Gay.* Boston: Alyson Publications, 1981.

Gagnon, John H., and William Simon. *Sexual Conduct: The Social Sources of Human Sexuality.* Chicago: Aldine, 1973.

[Gallo, Jon J. et al.]. "The Consenting Adult Homosexual and the Law: An Empirical Study of Enforcement and Administration in Los Angeles." *UCLA Law Review* (1966), 13:644–832.

Gerassi, John. *The Boys of Boise: Furor, Vice and Folly in an American City.* New York: Macmillan, 1966; Collier Books, 1968.

Goldsmith, Larry. "The Boston Project Studies Queerbashing." *Gay Community News* (Boston), May 29, 1983, p. 5.

Goldstein, Richard. "The Hate Report: Gay-bashing Becomes a Federal Case." *Village Voice* (New York), November 24, 1987, p. 13.

Goode, Erich and Richard R. Troiden. *Sexual Deviance and Sexual Deviants.* New York: William Morrow, 1974.

Gordon, Leonore. "What Do We Say When We Hear 'Faggot'?" *Interracial Books for Children Bulletin* (1983), 14(3–4):25–27.

Grahn, Judy. *Another Mother Tongue: Gay Words, Gay Worlds.* Boston: Beacon Press, 1984.

Greater Louisville Human Rights Coalition. "A Survey of Anti-Gay Discrimination in the Greater Louisville Area, 1985." Research Report prepared by L. Gail Bonnell, Sociologist/Research Consultant. Louisville [1985].

Gross, Larry, Steven K. Aurand, and Rita Addessa. *Violence and Discrimination Against Lesbian and Gay People in Philadelphia and the Commonwealth of Pennsylvania: A Study by the Philadelphia Lesbian and Gay Task Force.* Philadelphia, June 1988.

Groth, A. Nicholas and Ann Wolbert Burgess. "Male Rape: Offenders and Victims." *American Journal of Psychiatry* (July 1980), 137:806–810.

Harding, Rick. In *Advocate* (Los Angeles). "Not a Happy Trooper: Forced Out of His Job, A Florida Deputy Becomes an Unwitting Activist," June 20, 1989, pp. 8–9, 11; "Now Hear This: Deaf Gays Discuss the Violence and Ostracism They Face," August 15, 1989, p. 11; "Forget It, Dallas Cops Tell Lesbian Job Seeker," August 29, 1989, pp. 13–14; "Blanketed in Anger: A Patchwork of Protests Upstages the AIDS Quilt," November 7, 1989, pp. 8–9; "Springfield's Shame: A Student's Home Is Torched in a Squabble Over a College Play," December 19, 1989, pp. 8–9.

Harris, Sara. *The Puritan Jungle.* New York: Putnam, 1969.

Harry, Joseph. *Gay Children Grown Up: Gender Culture and Gender Deviance.* New York: Praeger, 1982.

Harry, Joseph. "Derivative Deviance: The Cases of Extortion, Fag-Bashing and the Shakedown of Gay Men." *Criminology* (February 1982), 19:546–563.

Hazlett, William. "Terror in the Streets: Hoods Seeking Kicks Mean Danger to All." *Mattachine Review,* May 1962, pp. 8–11.

Herek, Gregory. "Sexual Orientation and Prejudice at Yale: A Report on the Experience of Lesbian, Gay, and Bisexual Members of the Yale Community." New Haven: Yale University, Department of Psychology, April 3, 1986.

Hinckle, Warren. "The Untold Story: Dan White's San Francisco." *Inquiry,* October 29, 1979, pp. 3–20.

Hinckle, Warren. *Gayslayer! The Story of How Dan White Killed Harvey Milk and George Moscone and Got Away with Murder.* San Francisco: Silver Dollar, 1985.

Hippler, Mike. "Anatomy of a Murder Trial." *Advocate* (Los Angeles), February 17, 1987, pp. 42–49.

Hoffman, Martin. "The Male Prostitute." *Sexual Behavior* (1972), 2:16–21.

Holliday, Bob. "Men Claim Neighbors' Taunting Forced Move." *Daily Pantograph* (Bloomington, Ill.), September 21, 1982, p. 2A.

Howard, Evan Drake. "Extremism on Campus: Symbols of Hate, Symbols of Hope." *Christian Century,* July 15–22, 1987, pp. 625–628.

Huelsman, Ben R. "Southern Mountaineers in City Juvenile Courts." *Federal Probation: A Journal of Correctional Philosophy and Practice* (December 1969), 33:49–54.

Humpreys, Laud. *Out of the Closets: The Sociology of Homosexual Liberation.* Englewood Cliffs, N.J.: Prentice-Hall, Spectrum Book, 1972.

Humphreys, Laud. *Tearoom Trade: Impersonal Sex in Public Places.* Chicago: Aldine, 1970; enlarged ed., 1975.

Identity, Incorporated. *One in Ten: A Profile of Alaska's Lesbian and Gay Community.* Preliminary Report of Findings, prepared by the volunteers of Identity, Inc., and Jay Brause, project director. Anchorage, 1986.

Ireland, Doug. "Rendezvous in the Ramble." *New York,* July 24, 1978, pp. 39–42.

Ireland, Doug. "The New Homophobia: Open Season on Gays." *Nation,* September 15, 1979, pp. 207–210.

Jackson, Ed and Stan Persky, eds., *Flaunting It! A Decade of Gay Journalism from "The Body Politic."* Vancouver, British Columbia: New Star Books, 1982.

Jenning, Steve. In *Oregonian* (Portland). "Rights, Sanity, Lives of Gay People Threatened, Speakers Say," November 16, 1980; "Homosexual Assaults Produce Defensive Countermeasures" and " 'Gay Bashing' Emerges as Vicious Crime of Hard Times," February 8, 1981, pp. B1, B7.

Katz, Jonathan, ed., *Gay American History: Lesbians and Gay Men in the U.S.A.: A Documentary.* New York: Crowell, 1976.

Katz, Jonathan Ned. *Gay/Lesbian Almanac: A New Documentary.* New York: Harper & Row, 1983.

Kauffmann, Stanley. "Harsh Contradictions." *New Republic,* May 12, 1986, pp. 24–25.

Kaufman, Arthur, Peter Divasto, Rebecca Jackson, Dayton Voorhees, and Joan Christy. "Male Rape Victims: Noninstitutionalized Assault." *American Journal of Psychiatry* (February 1980), 137:221–223.

Kelner, Greg and Project Understanding. *Homophobic Assault: A Study of Anti-Gay Violence.* Winnipeg, Manitoba: Gays for Equality, 1983.

Kiel, Frank W. "The Psychiatric Character of the Assailant as Determined by Autopsy Observations of the Victim." *Journal of Forensic Sciences* (1965), 10:263–271.

Kinsey, Alfred C., Wardell B. Pomeroy, and Clyde E. Martin. *Sexual Behavior in the Human Male.* Philadelphia: Saunders, 1948.

Kirschenbaum, Carol. "Instant Activism: A Moment of Truth for Austin's Gays." *Ms.,* October 1985, pp. 80–81.

Klanwatch Project. *Hate Violence and White Supremacy: A Decade Review 1980–1990.* Montgomery, Ala.: Southern Poverty Law Center, December 1989.

Kleinberg, Seymour. *Alienated Affections: Being Gay in America.* New York: St. Martin's Press, 1980.

Kopay, David and Perry Deane Young. *The David Kopay Story: An Extraordinary Self-revelation.* New York: Arbor House, 1977; Priam Books, 1980.

Kramer, Michael. "Fireman's Brawl." *New York,* May 22, 1972, pp. 6–7.

Lederer, Laura, ed. *Take Back the Night: Women on Pornography.* New York: William Morrow, 1980.

Legislative and Social Action Ministry, Lesbian and Gay Interfaith Council of Minnesota. "Data Concerning Violence and Harassment Directed Against Gay Men and Lesbian Women and Their Communities." Minneapolis, February 1983.

Leonard, Arthur S. "Gay and Lesbian Rights Protections in the U.S.: Introduction to Gay and Lesbian Civil Rights." Washington, D.C.: National Gay and Lesbian Task Force [1989].

LeRoy, John. "Crimes Against Homosexuals: Never Pay Blackmail!" *Mattachine Review*, April 1960, pp. 6–7.

Lerro, Marc. "Violent Crime Up in Oak Lawn; Gays Often a Target." *Dallas Voice*, August 1, 1986, pp. 6–7.

Lesbian and Gay History Group of Toronto. "A History of the Relationship Between the Gay Community and the Metropolitan Toronto Police: A Brief Presented to Arnold Bruner for His Study of Relations Between the Homosexual Community and the Police." Toronto, August 18, 1981.

Lesbian Rights Task Force of Maryland NOW. "Maryland Anti-Lesbian/Gay Violence and Discrimination Project: Results of a Project Completed by the Lesbian Rights Task Force of Maryland NOW." Maryland National Organization of Women, March 1988.

Leznoff, Maurice and William A. Westley. "The Homosexual Community." *Social Problems* (1956), 3:257–263.

Licata, Salvatore J. and Robert P. Petersen, eds., *The Gay Past: A Collection of Historical Essays*. New York: Haworth Press, 1986. Published earlier as *Historical Perspectives on Homosexuality*. New York: Stein and Day.

Lipsyte, Robert. "The Closet, a Violent and Subtle Prison." *New York Times*, August 1, 1978.

Lomartire, Paul and Dorothy Smiljanich. "Tampa Gays Fear 'Open Season' " and "How Two Other Cities Work with Gay Residents." *Tampa Tribune*, September 5, 1982.

Lorde, Audre. "Scratching the Surface: Some Notes on Barriers to Women and Loving." *Black Scholar* (1978), 9:31–35.

Lorde, Audre. *A Burst of Light: Essays*. Ithaca, N.Y.: Firebrand Books, 1988.

Lutz, Chris, comp., and Center for Democratic Renewal. *They Don't All Wear Sheets: A Chronology of Racist and Far Right Violence—1980–1986*. Introduction by Leonard Zeskind. New York: National Council of the Churches of Christ in the U.S.A., 1987.

MacNamara, Donal E. J., and Edward Sagarin. *Sex, Crime, and the Law*. New York: Free Press, 1977.

Madell, Robin and Maureen Burke. "Lesbian and Gay Youth Support Needs Survey; Eugene–Springfield, Oregon." Eugene, 1989. (Typewritten).

Maghan, Jess and Edward Sagarin. "Homosexuals as Victimizers and Victims." In Donal E. J. MacNamara and Andrew Karmen, eds. *Deviants: Victims or Victimizers?* pp. 147–162. Beverly Hills, Calif.: Sage Publications, 1983.

Maine Civil Liberties Union; Maine Lesbian/Gay Political Alliance; and University of Southern Maine, Department of Social Welfare. "Discrimination and

Violence Survey of Gay People in Maine." Portland: University of Southern Maine, Department of Social Welfare, 1985.

Mann, William John. "Life After Death: How One Murder Touched a Community." *Advocate* (Los Angeles), March 14, 1989, pp. 26–28, 31–33.

Marotta, Toby. *The Politics of Homosexuality.* Boston: Houghton Mifflin, 1981.

Martin, A. Damien. "Young, Gay—and Afraid." *New York Times,* September 1, 1988, p. A25.

Mattachine Review. " 'Queer Hunting' Among Teenagers." June 1961, pp. 6–16.

McAuliffe, Bill. "Bouza Cites Diligence in Probes of Crimes Against Gays." *Minneapolis Star and Tribune,* November 18, 1986, p. 6D.

McCabe, Charles. "Riverside Drive, 1932." *San Francisco Chronicle,* April 7, 1978.

McDonald, Robin. "Sexual Acts Prompted Action: Homosexuals Say Night Gates at Oak Park Are Harassment. Police Deny Hassling Park-Goers: Authorities Claim 'Numerous' Arrests from Oak Park." *Wichita Eagle-Beacon,* September 3, 1986, pp. 1A, 8A.

McDonough, William. "Anti-Gay Violence and Community Organization." M.A. dissertation, San Francisco State University, 1981.

McHenry, F. A. "A Note on Homosexuality, Crime and the Newspapers." *Journal of Criminal Psychopathology* (April 1941), 2:531–548.

McManus, Kathy, producer, and John Stossel, correspondent. "Homophobia." *ABC News: 20/20,* Transcript of Show No. 615. Produced by Av Westin, hosted by Hugh Downs and Barbara Walters. April 10, 1986.

McNeill, John J. *The Church and the Homosexual.* Kansas City: Sheed Andrews and McMeel, subsidiary of Universal Press Syndicate, 1976.

Merrett, Jim. "Battery May Be Included: What Happens When You Report an Antigay Physical Attack?" *Advocate* (Los Angeles), August 15, 1989, pp. 26–28, 30–31.

Miller, Brian and Laud Humphreys. "Lifestyles and Violence: Homosexual Victims of Assault and Murder." *Qualitative Sociology* (Fall 1980), 3:169–185.

Miller, Merle. "What It Means to Be a Homosexual." *New York Times Magazine,* January 17, 1971, pp. 9–11, 48–49, 57, 60.

Milloy, Courtland. "Closet Life, Phobia and Foul Play." *Washington Post,* April 20, 1983.

Moore, Gene-Gabriel. "North Carolina's War Against Gays." *Christopher Street* (1988), Issue 121, pp. 14–18.

Moraga, Cherrie and Gloria Anzaldua, eds. *The Bridge Called My Back: Writings by Radical Women of Color.* Watertown, Mass.: Persephone Press, 1981.

Morgen, Kenneth B. *The Prevalence of Anti-Gay/Lesbian Victimization in Baltimore: 1988.* Towson, Md.: Chesapeake Psychological Services, 1988.

Morgenthau, Robert M. *Report of the District Attorney, County of New York, 1983–1984.* Office of the District Attorney, County of New York.

National Gay Task Force. *Anti-Gay/Lesbian Victimization: A Study by the*

National Gay Task Force in Cooperation with Gay and Lesbian Organizations in Eight U.S. Cities. New York, June 1984.

Naylor, Gloria. *The Women of Brewster Place.* New York: Viking Press, 1982; Penguin Books, 1983.

New Jersey Lesbian and Gay Coalition. "Discrimination Against Lesbians and Gay Men in New Jersey: 1977–1983: A Study Conducted by the New Jersey Lesbian and Gay Coalition, 1983–1984," [New Brunswick, New Jersey].

New York City Gay and Lesbian Anti-Violence Project. "1987 Statistics" and "Annual Report: January–December 1988." New York [1989].

NGLTF (National Gay and Lesbian Task Force). *Dealing with Violence: A Guide for Gay and Lesbian People.* Tamar Hosansky and Lance Bradley, consultants. Edited by Kevin Berrill. Washington, D.C. [1986].

Niederhoffer, Arthur. *Behind the Shield: The Police in Urban Society.* Garden City, N.Y.: Doubleday, 1967.

Norman, Abigail. "The Problem of Violence." *Catalyst* (1981), 12:83–90.

North Carolinians Against Racist and Religious Violence. "Homophobic Violence in North Carolina: 1983–1984." Durham, 1985.

Office of the Governor, Anthony S. Earl, State of Wisconsin. "Governor's Council on Lesbian and Gay Issues: Violence Survey Final Report." Madison, 1985.

Office of the Mayor, Edward I. Koch, City of New York. *Anti-Gay Violence: Police Training Videotape.* Lee Hudson, liaison to lesbian/gay community. New York, 1989.

Office of the Mayor, Kevin H. White, City of Boston. Executive Summary. *The Boston Project: Toward an Agenda for Gay and Lesbian Citizens.* Brian R. McNaught, liaison to lesbian and gay community. Boston, 1983.

Paul, William, James D. Weinrich, John C. Gonsiorek, and Mary E. Hotvedt, eds. *Homosexuality: Social, Psychological, and Biological Issues.* Beverly Hills, Calif.: Sage Publications, 1982.

Peeples, Edward H., Jr., Walter W. Tunstall, Everett Eberhardt, and the Research Task Force with technical assistance from the Commission on Human Relations, City of Richmond. *A Survey of Perceptions of Civil Opportunity Among Gays and Lesbians in Richmond, Virginia.* Richmond, 1985.

Peeples, Edward, Jr., Walter W. Tunstall, and Everett Eberhardt. "Veil of Hurt." *Southern Exposure,* September–October 1985, pp. 24–27.

Peterson, Robert W. In *Advocate* (Los Angeles). "Los Angeles Police Slapped with Lawsuit: Gay Former Cop Charges Discrimination, Harassment," November 7, 1988, p. 17; "Remembering a Dark Night: San Franciscans Gather on the Tenth Anniversary of Harvey Milk's Murder," January 3, 1989, pp. 14–15; "Texans Blast Antigay Judge: Public Condemnation of Hampton Is Swift and Widespread," February 14, 1989, pp. 10, 12; "Seattle Report: School Is Tough for Young Gays," February 14, 1989, p. 15; "In Harm's Way: Gay Runaways Are in More Danger Than Ever, and Gay Adults Won't Help," April 11, 1989, pp. 8–10; "Alaskan Report: Study Hits Home, Its Authors Say," October 10, 1989, p. 21; "Study Reveals School Days Are As Rotten as You Remember," December 5, 1989, p. 14; "A Shake-up for San

Francisco Cops: Faults Identified; Aftershocks from October Skirmish Continue," December 19, 1989, p. 22.

Philadelphia Lesbian and Gay Task Force Anti-Lesbian and Anti-Gay Discrimination and Violence Hotline Project. "Excerpts from Case Studies, March 1985 through June 1986." Philadelphia, June 1986.

Pincus, Elizabeth. "1979 Peg's Place Assault by Off-Duty S.F. Cops Goes to Trial." *Coming Up!* (San Francisco), June 1985.

Pinson, Luvenia. "The Black Lesbian: Times Past, Times Present." *Womanews* (New York), May 1980, p. 8.

Plews, Philip. "The Evil That Boys Do." *Toronto,* May 1986, pp. 60, 62–63, 86, 88–89, 91–92.

Ponse, Barbara. "Secrecy in the Lesbian World." *Urban Life* (1976), 5:313–338.

Potter, Deborah Anne. "Violence, Self-definition and Social Control: Gay and Lesbian Victimization." M.A. dissertation, Boston College, 1987.

Privacy Project, National Gay and Lesbian Task Force. "National Gay and Lesbian Task Force Privacy Project Fact Sheet." Washington, D.C. [1989].

Project Pulse, Student Affairs Research and Evaluation Office, University of Massachusetts. "Gay/Lesbian Awareness Survey (S85-E)." Amherst, 1985.

Rangel, Jesus. "Rutgers U., in Wake of a Student's Death, to Curb Fraternities." *New York Times* (National Ed.), June 25, 1988, p. 9.

Rechy, John. *The Sexual Outlaw: A Documentary: A Non-Fiction Account, with Commentaries, of Three Days and Nights in the Sexual Underground.* New York: Grove Press, 1977.

Reinhart, Robert Charles. *A History of Shadows.* New York: Avon Books, 1982; Boston: Alyson Publications, 1986.

Reiss, Albert J., Jr. "The Social Integration of Queers and Peers." In Hendrik M. Ruitenbeek, ed., *The Problem of Homosexuality in Modern Society.* New York: Dutton, 1963.

Rich, Adrienne. "Compulsory Heterosexuality and Lesbian Existence." *Signs: Journal of Women in Culture and Society* (1980), 5:631–660.

Richardson, Scott. "Gay Bloomington Homeowner: Harassment Turns Dream into Nightmare." *Daily Pantograph* (Bloomington, Ill.), September 2, 1980, p. 3A.

Right to Privacy Committee. "The Right to Privacy Committee's Brief to the City of Toronto Bruner Study into Relations Between Metropolitan Toronto Police and Toronto's Homosexual Community." Toronto, September 10, 1981.

Rock, Donald. "Entrapment!: To Have Tearoom Sex in the '50s Was to Risk Everything." *Advocate* (Los Angeles), August 1, 1989, pp. 50–53.

Rofes, Eric. "Queer Bashing: The Politics of Violence Against Gay Men." *Gay Community News* (Boston), August 12, 1978, pp. 8–9, 11.

Rosario, Ruben. "Anti-Gay Violence Probed: Homosexuals Join Those Aided by Cop Unit as Attacks Based on Race, Beliefs Increase" and "AIDS Spurs Gay Attacks." *New York Daily News,* February 16, 1986, p. 31.

Rothenberg, David. "Media Watch." *New York Native,* January 1981, p. 7.

Rubin, Gayle. "Thinking Sex: Notes for a Radical Theory of the Politics of Sexuality." In Carole S. Vance, ed., *Pleasure and Danger: Exploring Female Sexuality*, pp. 267–319. Boston: Routledge and Kegan Paul, 1984.

Rupp, Joseph C. "Sudden Death in the Gay World." *Medicine, Science and the Law* (1970), 10:189–191.

Russell, Diana E. H. and Nicole Van de Ven, eds. *Crimes Against Women: Proceedings of the International Tribunal.* Millbrae, Calif.: Les Femmes, 1976.

Russo, Anthony and Laud Humphreys. "Homosexuality and Crime." In Sanford H. Kadish et al., eds., *Encyclopedia of Crime and Justice.* 1st ed. New York: Macmillan, 1983.

Ryan, Noel. "Stavrogin." In Michael Denneny, Charles Ortleb, and Thomas Steele, eds., *First Love/Last Love: New Fiction from "Christopher Street."* New York: G. P. Putnam's Sons, 1985.

Sagarin, Edward and Donal E. J. MacNamara. "The Homosexual as a Crime Victim." *International Journal of Criminology and Penology* (1975), 3:13–25.

San Francisco Board of Supervisors. Committee on Fire, Safety and the Police. "Four-Hour Public Hearing on Queerbashing." October 9, 1980. Transcript of testimony edited for broadcast on KSAN-FM's Gay Life Program and aired October 18, 19, November 8, 9, 16, 1980. Transcript available from Lesbian and Gay Associated Engineers and Scientists, Sunnyvale, Calif.

San Miguel, Christopher L. and Jim Millham. "The Role of Cognitive and Situational Variables in Aggression Toward Homosexuals." *Journal of Homosexuality* (Fall 1976), 2:11–27.

Schur, Edwin M. *Crimes Without Victims: Deviant Behavior and Public Policy; Abortion, Homosexuality, Drug Addiction.* Englewood Cliffs, N.J.: Prentice-Hall, 1965.

Sebesta, Edward H. "On Gaybashing: Its Politics, Methods, and the Gay Challenge Against It; Circa 1978–1982." San Francisco, April 7, 1984.

Sege, Irene. "Northampton's Gays Fight Back: Reports of Harassment Trigger Action." *Boston Globe,* May 22, 1983, pp. 47, 52.

Segrest, Mab. "Gay Baiting: Anatomy of an Election." *Gay Community News* (Boston), February 9, 1985.

Segrest, Mab. "Responding to Bigoted Violence in North Carolina." *North Carolina Forum* (Raleigh, N.C.), 1985.

Sepejak, Diana. "The Willingness of Homosexuals to Report Criminal Victimization to the Police." M.A. dissertation, University of Toronto, 1977.

Shein, Brian. "Gay-Bashing in High Park." *Toronto Life,* April 1986, pp. 37–39, 64–69.

Sheppard, Gerald T. "The Use of Scripture Within the Christian Ethical Debate Concerning Same-Sex Oriented Persons." *USQR: Union Seminary Quarterly Review* (1985), 40:13–35.

Shilts, Randy. *The Mayor of Castro Street: The Life and Times of Harvey Milk.* New York: St. Martin's Press, 1982.

Siegel, Lou. "Violence Against Gays/Police Against Gays: 'Fag Bashing' Is a

Dishonorable Tradition from Which, Alas, L.A. Is Not Exempt." *L.A. Weekly* (Los Angeles), February 26 to March 4, 1982, pp. 8–10.

Sievert, Bill. "The Killing of Mr. Greenjeans." *Mother Jones,* September–October 1977, pp. 39–42, 46–48.

Simon, Roger. In *Chicago Sun Times.* "A Walk on the Wild Side of Gay Life," July 19, 1978; "Playing It Straight in Crimes on Gays," July 20, 1978, p. 4.

Simpson, Ruth. *From the Closet to the Courts: The Lesbian Transition.* New York: Viking Press, 1976; Penguin Books, 1977.

Smith, Arlo. "Dealing with Anti-Gay Violence: 'Homosexual Panic' Defense Is Bigotry in Action." *Bay Area Reporter* (San Francisco), November 3, 1983, pp. 1, 11.

Smith, Barbara, ed. *Home Girls: A Black Feminist Anthology.* New York: Kitchen Table/Women of Color Press, 1983.

Snyder, Ruth. " 'Gay Bashing'—AIDS Fear Cited as Attacks on Male Homosexuals Grow." *Los Angeles Times,* April 10, 1986, Part I, pp. 3, 32.

Stanford, Gregory D. "Violence Rife, Gays Tell Panel." *Milwaukee Journal,* June 3, 1984, pp. 1, 13.

State of New York, Mario M. Cuomo, Governor. *Governor's Task Force on Bias-Related Violence, Final Report.* Douglas H. White, chair. March 1988.

Steinman, Wayne. "Information Collected from Questionnaire 'Answer 16 Questions for Gay/Lesbian Rights.' " Albany: New York State Lesbian/Gay Lobby, January 1985.

Swigert, Victoria Lynn, Ronald A. Farrell, and William C. Yoels. "Sexual Homicide: Social, Psychological, and Legal Aspects." *Archives of Sexual Behavior* (1976), 5:391–401.

Szasz, Thomas. "How Dan White Got Away with Murder and How American Psychiatry Helped Him Do It." *Inquiry,* August 6 and 20, 1979, pp. 17–21.

Teal, Donn. *The Gay Militants.* New York: Stein and Day, 1971.

Thomas, Josh. "Appalachians, Hustling and Fag-Bashing," *Gaybeat* (Cincinnati), August 1986, p. 7.

Thompson, Mark, ed. *Gay Spirit: Myth and Meaning.* New York: St. Martin's Press, 1987.

Trillin, Calvin. "A Few Observations on the Zapping of the Inner Circle." *New Yorker,* July 15, 1972, pp. 64–69.

Turkel, Tux. "Out of Fear Comes a Killing: Homosexual's Harassment Ends with a Tragedy." *Maine Sunday Telegram,* January 19, 1986, pp. A1+.

Unitarian Universalist Association, Office of Lesbian and Gay Concerns. *FYI: What You Should Know About the Charlie Howard Murder.* Boston: Unitarian Universalist Association, 1985.

U.S. Congress. House Subcommittee on Criminal Justice of Committee on the Judiciary. *Anti-Gay Violence,* 99th Cong., 2d sess., 1986.

Vacha, Keith. In Cassie Damewood, ed., *Quiet Fire: Memoirs of Older Gay Men.* Trumansburg, N.Y.: Crossing Press, 1985.

Valverde, Mariana. *Sex, Power, and Pleasure.* Toronto: Women's Press, 1985.

Vasquez, Carmen. *CDBG Quarterly Report: January to March 1984,* April 1984; *Quarterly Report and Analysis of Anti-Gay Violence: January to*

March 1985 (n.d.); *Quarterly Statistical Analysis: January to March 1986,* May 9, 1986. San Francisco: Community United Against Violence, Inc.

Vaughan, Kristi. "Lesbians Uneasy in Northampton." *Hartford Courant,* August 7, 1983, pp. H1–H2.

Veasey, Jack. "Crimes Against Us—Violence Experienced by Gay Men." *Gay News* (Pittsburgh), October 1978, pp. 18–19.

Vermonters for Lesbian and Gay Rights. "Discrimination and Violence Survey of Lesbians and Gay Men in Vermont." Hinesburgh, April 6, 1987.

Vida, Ginny, ed. *Our Right to Love: A Lesbian Resource Book.* Englewood Cliffs, N.J.: Prentice-Hall, 1978.

Violence Project, National Gay and Lesbian Task Force. "Anti-Gay Violence and Victimization in 1985." Washington, D.C., 1985.

Violence Project, National Gay and Lesbian Task Force. "Anti-Gay Violence, Victimization and Defamation in 1986." Washington, D.C., 1987.

Violence Project, National Gay and Lesbian Task Force. "Anti-Gay Violence, Victimization and Defamation in 1987." Washington, D.C., 1988.

Violence Project, National Gay and Lesbian Task Force. "Anti-Gay Violence, Victimization and Defamation in 1988." Washington, D.C., 1989.

Weinberg, Martin S. and Collin J. Williams. *Male Homosexuals: Their Problems and Adaptations.* New York: Oxford University Press, 1974.

Weiss, Andrea and Greta Schiller. *Before Stonewall: The Making of a Gay and Lesbian Community.* Tallahassee, Fla.: Naiad Press, 1988.

Weiss, Mike. *Double Play: The San Francisco City Hall Killings.* Reading, Mass.: Addison-Wesley, 1984.

Weissman, Eric. "Kids Who Attack Gays." *Christopher Street,* August 1978, pp. 9–13.

Wertheimer, David M. "The Rise in AIDS-Related Violence." *The Volunteer, The GMHC Newsletter* (Gay Men's Health Crisis, Inc., New York) (Fall 1986), pp. 1, 6, 9.

West, D[onald] J[ames]. *Homosexuality Re-Examined.* London: Gerald Duckworth; Minneapolis: University of Minnesota Press [1978].

Westley, William A. "Secrecy and the Police." *Social Forces* (1956), 34:254–257.

Westley, William A. "Violence and the Police." *American Journal of Sociology* (1953), 59:34–41.

Westwood, Gordon. *Society and the Homosexual,* New York: Dutton, 1952; 2d ed., 1953.

Wheeler, Steve. "Results of Survey Released by GLRA." *Kansas City Alternate News,* August 9, 1985, p. 42.

White, Allen. "Quinn Statement on Violence Seen as Hollow Gesture: Archibishop Goes to Castro to Condemn Anti-Gay Assaults; Critics Say Opposition to Rights Shows Hypocrisy." *Bay Area Reporter* (San Francisco), August 10, 1989, p. 5.

Wickliffe, Ron. "Queerbashers Meet Resistance in the Streets of San Francisco." *WIN,* August 15, 1981, pp. 15–18.

Williams, Walter L. *The Spirit and the Flesh: Sexual Diversity in American Indian Culture.* Boston: Beacon Press, 1986.

Wilson, Craig. "Gay Bashing: Brutal AIDS Backlash." *USA Today,* March 12, 1987, pp. 1D, 2D.

Wilson, Doric. "The West Street Gang." In *Two Plays by Doric Wilson: "A Perfect Relationship" and "The West Street Gang."* New York: Sea Horse Press, 1979 (1978).

Wilson, Duff. "Gays Threatened by Assault Get Protection Under New Law." *Seattle Post-Intelligencer,* June 12, 1984.

Winfrey, Oprah. "Homophobia." *Oprah Winfrey Show,* Transcript No. 8639. New York: Journal Graphics, Inc., November 13, 1986.

Winters, Marianne. "External and Internal Realities of Anti-Gay/Lesbian Violence." *Open Hands: Journal of Reconciling Congregation Program* (1987), 3(2):10–11.

Yeskel, Felice. *The Consequences of Being Gay: A Report on the Quality of Life for Lesbian, Gay and Bisexual Students at the University of Massachusetts at Amherst.* Amherst: University of Massachusetts, Office of the Vice Chancellor for Student Affairs, June 1985.

Ziner, Karen Lee. "Trouble in Paradise: The Lesbians of Northampton Under Attack." *Boston Phoenix,* June 7, 1983, pp. 1, 6–7, 24.

Index

of, 59-60, 63, 65; characteristics of, 58-62; class background of, 72-73, 78, 80-81, 82, 83, 84-85, 86-87, 88; gender of, 59; groups of, 71-73, 78-82; identifications of, 57-58; interviews with, 71-77, 170-73; language used by, 67-69, 93; lone perpetrators, 82-85; Native Americans as least frequent, 218*n*28; number of per incident and per victim, 62-67; older perpetrators, 83, 88, 112-15, 172-73; pairs of perpetrators, 82-85; police as, 18, 58, 152-62; premeditation *versus* reaction in attacks, 69-77; psychological defenses by, 90; racial identity of, 60-62, 63-65, 66; reaction *versus* premeditation in attacks, 69-77; sources of information on, 56-57

Persian empire, 128

Physical assault, *see* Assaults, physical

Pillory, 15-16

Plaine, William, 14

Pleck, Joseph H., 101

Police: blackmailing by, 279*n*27; characteristics of policemen, 157-58; decoy activity by, 155, 279*n*27; hiring of gay men and lesbians by, 157; as perpetrators of violence, 18, 58, 152-62; response to reported violence, 159-60; selective surveillance by, 156; social status of, 156

Police brutality, 22-23

Police harassment, 12-13

Police raids, 12-13, 18, 21, 115, 137, 152, 162

Politics, lesbians and gay men and, 21-22, 25-29, 115, 185*n*63

Portland, Maine, 72-73

Portland, Oregon, 69

Postbiblical Jewish literature, Leviticus and, 122

Premeditated violence: by groups of perpetrators, 71-73; reactive *versus*, 69-77

Presidential Commission on the Human Immunodeficiency Virus Epidemic, 68

Professional robbers, 18-19

Prostitution, male temple, 121

Psychological defenses, by perpetrators, 90

Punching, as subcategory of general violence, 38-40, 42-46

Racial identity: of perpetrators, 60-62, 63-65, 66; settings of violence and, 49-50, 53; subcategories of violence according to, 40-44; of victims, 36-37, 38, 40, 42-44, 46, 49-51, 52, 55, 195*n*50

Rape: of gay men, 198*n*63; of lesbians, 198*n*63; as subcategory of general violence, 40-46

Reactive violence, premeditated *versus*, 69-77

Reagan administration, 134

Rebellious behaviors of adolescents, 106-7

Recruitment of adolescents by gay men, lack of evidence of, 281*n*29

Reiss, Albert J., 163-65

Responses to violence, by lesbian/gay people, 3, 25-30, 137-140

Richmond, Virginia, 53-54, 158

Robbers, professional, 18-19

Robbery, as motive, 79, 83, 88

Roe v. *Wade,* 135, 136

Roman Empire, 179*n*37

Romans 1:18-32, 121-22

Rutgers University, New Jersey, 108

St. Paul, Minnesota, 25

San Francisco, California, 7, 10, 26, 29, 61-62, 72-73, 80-81, 157, 161-62, 183*n*54

Schur, Edwin M., 170

Scott case, 83, 86-87, 88-90

Sepejak, Diana, 156

Settings of violence: gender and, 49-52; groups of settings, 51-54; individual, 48-51; racial identity and, 49-50, 53; workplace, 53

Sexual psychopath laws, 8

Sexual regulations, in Leviticus, 132-33

Shilts, Randy, 26, 27

Sifra, 122

Simpson, Ruth, 14, 23

Smith, Barbara, 54

Smith/Barr case, 82-83, 84-85

Socialization, gender-role, 106-9, 241*n*36

Social location: of adolescents, 111; of lesbians and gay men, 109-11; of police, 157-58

Social roles, violence and, 95-99

Sociological theory, 2